Development and Evolution

Development and Evolution

Complexity and Change in Biology

Stanley N. Salthe

A Bradford Book
The MIT Press
Cambridge, Massachusetts
London, England

Set in Palatino by .eps Electronic Publishing Services.
Printed and bound in the United States of America.

Library of Congress Cataloging-in-Publication Data

Salthe, Stanley N.
  Development and evolution : complexity and change in biology /
Stanley N. Salthe.
    p. cm.
  "A Bradford book."
  Includes bibliographical references (p.   ) and indexes.
  ISBN 0-262-19335-3
  1. Cosmology. 2. Physics—Philosophy. 3. Science—Philosophy.
4. Evolution (Biology) I. Title.
QB981.S267   1993
523.1—dc20   93-19698
                                                                 CIP

for G. G. and Isadora

Contents

Preface

The present work could be considered an extension of my 1985 book *Evolving Hierarchical Systems*. That book was centered on the structure of scalar hierarchies, working from Darwinian theory and beginning with a canonical image—genes at a lower scalar level, organisms at a level above them, and populations at the next higher level. It had been triggered by discussions of levels of selection and punctuated equilibrium; however, it departed from biology into systems science, and so it could not be taken as a technical discussion of (say) levels of selection. It became a general essay about hierarchical structuralism, using materials from evolutionary biology and also from many other sources.

In the making, that work departed radically from the reductionism, characteristic of Darwinism, that had been so pronounced in my 1972 textbook *Evolutionary Biology*. It became clear that natural selection could not be responsible for everything in the world impinging upon biological populations or organisms. Complexity had been broached, and there was no return. Even selection at different scalar levels was soon revealed to be too thin a view of biological hierarchies. Work on the 1985 book carried me away from Darwinian abstractions into the messy material world—despite its location in systems science, which can be the most abstract of all sciences. The reason was that constraints (boundary conditions, initial conditions, and initiating conditions) became as important to an analysis as are processes and impinging laws—indeed, they are what characterize scalar levels. Laws and processes often transcend such levels, and this is partly why science has had little need for hierarchy theory in most of its constructions—before the advent of complexity, that is (and complexity has been slow in arriving in evolutionary theory, captive as it is to the elaborate simplicities of Darwinism).

Contact with Marxists soon revealed that they were the only group (other than systems scientists, of course) that showed enough interest in the 1985 work to criticize it. And their criticism revealed an important deficiency in that book: There was no attempt in it to deal with change. Process was there, as was the transcendence of any local process at higher scalar levels, where an entire trajectory becomes itself an individual (and the process is accomplished virtually as soon as it starts, if you chose a high enough level within which to embed it).

In the meantime, the controversy over nonequilibrium thermodynamics had erupted. People were talking about what drove systems to change, with change characterized through information theory. The controversy, in large part, involved the problem of whether information carrying capacity is an entropy—that is, whether information had to increase in a material system, as did physical entropy. Only a small group centered around Dan Brooks and Ed Wiley, which came to include me, was prepared to try and demonstrate that it did.

In the meantime, the influence of thermodynamics had made its appearance in many other areas. In ecology, developmental aspects of ecosystems were characterized by Bob Ulanowicz in the language of entropies and information (what is coming to be called *infodynamics*). Ulanowicz's work appeared even as development was making a comeback (from mere developmental genetics) in biology as a whole. Ontogeny concerned transformations that surely involved change of some kind. My interest in the field in which I had obtained my degree—developmental biology—was rekindled. During this period there emerged into cybernetics and systems science a Continental, Hegelian perspective that goes under the label *self-organization.* It has had little influence on established science in the United States except in a few nonacademic institutions, but the problems it engages are such that one could foresee that developmental biology would one day become one of its subdiscourses. I could not avoid struggling with these matters in this book.

At the same time, my trajectory through the 1985 book, which carried me into theoretical biology (not what is usually called that, which is mere mathematization) and systems philosophy, continued. I discovered a major discourse in Western science and philosophy that I had not appreciated. That discourse, which I now call *developmental discourse,* included Herbert Spencer, Charles Sanders Peirce, the *Naturphilosophen,* and the transcendental morphologists, all of whom had (to one degree or another) been concerned with characterizing change. Here Marx's origins could be discerned as well, and the Marxists' interest in my 1985 book found another connection leading away from it. It became clear to me that developmental discourse had been waiting for something like infodynamics to give it a new lease on life. The present work can be viewed as a lately eroded text in a developmental discursive formation that first appeared with the ancient Greeks.

Marxists, along with feminists, were criticizing the incursions of neo-Darwinism into their domain (social science), and it became clear that my roots through scalar hierarchies were at stake here too. Not only were scalar hierarchies not involved with change, they could also be viewed as just as mechanistic (even though so complex as to defy explicit modeling) as was Darwinism (see Birke 1986). And this philosophical mechanism appears to have triggered (at least the disinterested end of the spectrum of) the opposition to Darwinian ambitions in social science (i.e., sociobiology). This led to my own critique of Darwinism, which goes a bit farther in this text.

This book may be viewed as a kind of reaction—not against the principles of scalar hierarchies discussed in *Evolving Hierarchical Systems*—but against the implicit philosophical mechanism of much of that work. I now discovered that a number of informed persons had been uneasy with the mechanistic materialism of modern science. Indeed, no sooner had I discovered this than mechanism lost its power in my thinking altogether. This came about by my discovery, through feminism, of postmodernism and the social construction movement in the sociology of science. It was clear that philosophical mechanism was the local attitude of a culture that was bent primarily on dominating nature in every way (not only through totalitarian governments) and which gave little time to trying to understand the world. Mechanism could be repudiated simply by realizing that it had never been my own game, and that there *were* counterdiscourses out there.

Fortunately, I had by then, through my interest in Peirce, become acquainted with some semioticians, and through semiotics I have been able to recognize that the play of signs, including the modeling of systems, is exactly what discourses are. Scalar hierarchies had already taught me that the position of the observer was necessarily implicated in modeling nature. With semiotics the observer could be brought right into the models. Furthermore, this now allows the *meaning* of information to be modeled as well as the information itself, as is done in information theory. Indeed, as I conceive it now, information theory must become embedded in semiotics. This work could be viewed as a preliminary essay on semiotics of (or in) science.

So, while I have returned to biology for most of my subject matter (not *all*, because the origin of life is too important, and, as Darwinians have implied, must involve subject matter outside biology), my contact with many more fields of interest has moved this work even further from biology as a separate discipline than was the 1985 book. Readers with no tolerance for references outside their narrow specialization will find little to engage them here. Scientists who believe that science ought to be (or even is) sealed off from other discourses will find little comfort here. This book foresees not only a unity of the sciences but a unity that connects to nonscientific discourses.

What the book is about may fairly be suggested by paraphrasing quotes from five critics of the first draft: an alternative view of evolution; an integration of ideas from philosophy, science, and systems theory into an ontology of nature (here *ontology* ought to mean what one believes needs to be represented in nature); an attempt at a grand theory of nature encompassing complexity and change; an attempt to demonstrate the mutual relevance of several fields; an attempt to construct a basis for models of material systems in general—a synthetic work. Emphasis must be put upon the word "attempt" here, of course; obviously this text is only the continuation of a beginning, if these imputations really are its goals. I will add another attempt here: an attempt to show that developmental discourse represents a viable alternative to Darwinism as the fundamental theoretical orientation of biology.

I hope it will become clear that, while there seems to be an unusually large number of new departures here for a single book, none of them could be made without the others. I believe all these approaches support each other in this attempt to form a basis for reconstructing developmental discourse, and so they must be taken together, however challenging that may be. This, of course, necessarily means that this text is going to be sketchy and suggestive rather than an accomplished work.

Myrdene Anderson, Bob Artigiani, Dan Brooks, John Collier, David Dean, David Millett, Ron Pilette, Jeffrey Sutton, Rod Swenson, Bob Ulanowicz, and several anonymous referees critically reviewed the manuscript, in whole or in part. It has been exciting being a peripheral member of a number of discourses, and I thank all involved for tolerating my sometime presence in their affairs. The gentlemanly furtherance of this work by my chairman at Brooklyn College, Ray Gavin, is also acknowledged.

Readers may be interested in knowing how Stuart Kauffman's book *The Origins of Order* (Oxford University Press, 1993), which appeared after the manuscript of this book was finished, relates to the present text. While my book tries to distance itself from Darwinism, Kauffman's tries to incorporate the discourse of self-organization into Darwinism. Noting that selection could not be the sole cause of order in organisms (because of the spontaneous self-organizing tendencies of any complex system), Kauffman calls for a marriage of selection and self-organization. My overall impression of his text, however, is that its selected tail tends to wag the evolving dog.

Kauffman shows that selection must have worked, not just on traits, but on whole systems with properties allowing increases in complexity beyond that achievable by most abiotic systems, where complexity increase eventually becomes limited by overconnectivity. In order to evolve greater complexity in randomly structured environments, systems must have parts that strongly interact with only a few others—that is, they must have specificity, and therefore they must have had some minimum configurational complexity to begin with. The present text views environments and the systems evolving within them as more closely integrated from the start, suggesting that environments have structures and that organisms realize some of these structures materially, as parts. In my view this explains why form organizes itself in natural systems to begin with.

Kauffman feels that he has discovered why cell types differentiate along a tree pattern from an initially undifferentiated cell—a matter central to the present text. In this way connectivity is kept low, because each cell type becomes specialized to deal with only a few others. Kauffman's reasoning is essentially historical; the earliest cell types were those that found means of survival in the generic properties of the kind of material system they were. Any further complexity must have been built upon these primal structures, because subsequent selected change would have been restricted to small jumps achievable without disrupting an already functioning system—Kauffman's "evolution on correlated landscapes." Here he essentially gives a (not new) explanation for Baer's law, also central to the present text. In this way the more plesiomorphic traits of organisms are viewed as closer to the generic properties of the types of material systems of which they are members—and therefore not as having been engendered by selection, which only continues to modulate what was (and is) generated spontaneously during the origin of life (and ontogeny).

In the present text the types of material systems to which organisms belong are taken to be dissipative structures, and this brings up an uneasiness I have with the basis of Kauffman's work: simulations using matrices of Boolean automata. While such systems do self-organize, develop, and individuate (see chapter 1 below), they fail to mimic natural systems in an important way: they do not have an immature stage in their development during which they grow in some way (Salthe 1990d). Basically, in the terminology of the present text, these matrices simply senesce during a run. It is not clear to me what difference more natural simulations would make to Kauffman's constructions—perhaps none.

Kauffman engages the present text in another way when he asks how low connectivity actually arises. He finds it to be basically the result of molecular specificity, the property of discrimination that can be shown by complex configurations. Selection for increased specificity (driven by intertype competition for efficiency) becomes at the same time selection for low connectivity, allowing complexity to self-organize during organic evolution. In the present text the idea of specificity is dealt with in the broader context of semiotics—specificity implies a viewpoint, which implies a capacity for holding meaning, which is the object of the study of semiosis. As this example shows, Kauffman's text is generally more narrowly focused than the present one, not only in the direction of Darwinism but also in the direction of specific theory rather than metatheory.

Development and Evolution

Chapter 1

Introduction

In this chapter I point to a group of concordant theoretical approaches that together form the basis of a developmental theory of changing complex systems that involves the study of informational changes—*infodynamics*. A basic structure is the *scalar hierarchy*, where description must minimally involve three contiguous levels—the *basic triadic system*. *Complexity* is found to be manifested as detainment, whether of progression or in thought—a kind of friction that prevents attainment or understanding in a flash. This detainment is an important aspect of *self-organization*. In their self-organization, changing complex systems both develop and evolve, being driven through both by the Second Law of Thermodynamics. Aristotle's system of causal analysis is useful for complex systems, but it requires taking account of the contexts of any process, including its being observed. In bringing in the observer we must turn to semiotics because observed informational configurations require a source of meaning—a *system of interpretance* with which the observer is associated. The chapter ends with the puzzling concept of change, venturing some tentative directions to be followed up in later chapters.

The present study is an interpretation of biological systems at very general integrative levels—that is, at levels where their behaviors can be compared with those of other sorts of systems (physical, chemical, and social). My purpose is to seek commonalities among all changing systems, in hopes of contributing toward a unity of science. My view is that science, beyond its primary social role of the production of useful knowledge, is also, in our materialist society, an important ground for philosophical understanding.

This study is motivated in part by the fact that science has already contributed mightily to our philosophical outlook, but in directions I believe to be dangerously restrictive. For example, it seems that most scientists and most philosophers influenced by science are materialists. That is reasonable enough, in view of the necessity for constant reference to the physical world for testing hypotheses—and, indeed, we must all eat and be warm. But most scientists and most philosophers go much further, and are realists as well, and mechanicists, being persuaded in these directions by the apparent implications of science discourse as it has been—the Baconian/Cartesian/Newtonian/Darwinian/Comtean (BCNDC) version, which has been ascendant during the twentieth century.

Philosophical realism is the view that it is possible to discover what the world is like outside of, and unrelated to, our own practices. Actuality, of course, is constructed by our own senses—phenomena are blue, cold, hard, indefinable, and so on. Reality, however, is constructed, using logic, on the basis of systematic, quantifiable observations, and is an accumulation of accepted scientific interpretations in the form of explicit lawful regularities, theories, and models (Roth and Schwegler 1990). This reality should be called 'nature' (as opposed to 'world', which would refer to whatever is out there behind both actuality and reality) (Salthe 1985). The present work is about nature, not the world, and that declaration should deprive reality of its realist implications herein.

Scientific constructs are supposed to be more reliable than those made spontaneously by the senses. One implication of that view is that what is accepted by the majority of scientists in some field at a given time is held by realists to be close to (if not really) the truth. The problem with that view is that there actually are, almost always, dissenting minority opinions held by other scientists, and, if science truly has hegemony over reality, these must be judged wrong by realists. In the long run that kind of perspective would stultify science, preventing alternative views from emerging in altered situations.

Since mechanicism has seemed to be the best working attitude for those trying to solve limited material problems, it has insensibly become woven into the "truth" of science. So, because all current scientific theories (with some exceptions in physics that are not part of the general influence of science) are mechanistic, scientists who cannot agree that the world and everything in it are machines are simply held to be wrong. But there have recently appeared some new phenomena in science that seem to challenge philosophical mechanicism by apparently defeating mechanistic interpretations. Four of these will concern us here: complexity, self-organization, semiosis, and change, which I will introduce in that order and which I will roughly define for use later in the text.

Observing and Making Complexity

The problem here, in a nutshell, is that complex systems do not yield to prediction in satisfactory ways. BCNDC science has been, in part, based on the art of simplifying problems by isolating measurable aspects of the world, ascertaining their regularity, and then, on the basis of interpretive models, trying experimental inputs to see if desirable alterations could be produced. This depends crucially on being able to isolate aspects of the world from their contexts without altering their nature, on the notion that these aspects of the world do not change their behavior as a result of observation, and on the idea that these aspects of the world do not have so much internal coherence that interference with one part would unpredictably alter the behaviors of other parts (as is the case with machines). None of these things turns out to be true with interesting subject matter—say, the brain, or ecosystems, or social systems, or indeed any biological system. Different aspects of these problems have been explored in connection with biology by Rosen (1985b), Matsuno (1989), and Kampis (1991a,b).

Complexity has been defined in at least five different ways. The most commonly used definition is based on a proposed measure (Kolmogorov 1965): the minimal amount of information needed to specify a system's structure (often called its *information content*). Chaitin (1975) has shown that a random sequence cannot be specified by anything less than a complete description, and so it would have a large information content. Complexity in this view is what cannot be further simplified.

This view of complexity is often mapped onto behavior by deriving random patterns from disorderly behavior or observational uncertainty—commonly measured as the capacity of an observed system to carry information (specifically, its *information capacity*, $-\Sigma p_i log p_i$, where the p's are probabilities of occurrences of tokens of the ith type in measurable positions or configurations (Shannon and Weaver 1949). Both forms of this general type of complexity—information content and capacity—are associated with an observer's ignorance (content tends to be undecidable, capacity measures uncertainty), and Csányi's (1989) term *semiotic complexity* could be applied to them.

Information content and information capacity are quite similar in that both are formally entropic (i.e., describable by the above Shannon equation, which is isomorphic with Boltzmann's formulation of entropy). Also, Layzer (1977) and Brooks and Wiley (1988) have shown that in thermodynamically open systems they increase together as a system develops. According to Brooks and Wiley, the difference between capacity and content represents some of the organizational constraints in the system—what Collier (1989) calls "intropy." This is constructed out of information stored in the system—part of its information content (which, as meaningful, functional information, would be only thinly represented by a system's minimum description). *Content* refers to a system's internal forms (whether an observer has access to them or not); capacity is an observer's construct, generalizing 'observer' to any system interacting with another.

Information capacity is represented in system behavior according to the *principle of requisite variety* (Ashby 1956; Conrad 1983). That is, a reasonably stable system must be able to match the uncertainty of environmental fluctuations in order that they not all result in damaging perturbations. In the combination of a system and its relevant environment (the *Umwelt* of Uexküll (1926)), some reflection of the total information capacity of the environing context is mapped into the system's behavior by way of configurational information stored within the system—some of its information content, which could either restrict (as emphasized by Brooks and Wiley) or enable capacity. So, while content is configurational, it constrains behavior, which can be taken as displaying a capacity and can therefore be relatively disorderly (that is, entropic). This point goes part of the way toward resolving the problem of how configurations can be functionally as well as formally entropic.

Bennett (1988) has suggested another measure of complexity, which he calls *logical depth* and which he describes as "the length of the logical chain connecting a phenomenon with a plausible hypothesis (e.g., the minimum description) explaining it." By "length" Bennett means the time it necessarily takes to construct a phenomenon; complex entities should obey a "slow growth law." What this does is eliminate many trivial "complexities," such as smashed glass. Also, even if it takes eons to form a crystal in the earth, if it could be made more quickly using shortcuts (as in a laboratory) it would not be complex. A minimum description could itself be complex in this sense if it took a long time to boil it down from a larger description, and it would describe something complex if it took a long time to synthesize it using the minimum description as instructions.

Again we have an observer related (really, an actor-related) definition. In addition, this definition would often be concordant with semiotic complexity in most natural systems. It would presumably take a long time for an observer to discover that an algorithm is not further reducible and for an actor to fabricate something having a long minimal description. So far, something is complex if it takes a long message to describe it and/or if it takes a long time for it to be made (or to make itself). In addition, if it behaves, it will likely be complex if we find it hard to predict what it will do.

Rosen (1985b) has proposed a metasystemic definition of complexity, to the effect that a system is complex if it can be described in many nonequivalent ways. This is another form of semiotic complexity, because it is (as Rosen explicitly urges) related to the observer.

I have (Salthe 1985) ventured a more ontological definition of complexity, to the effect that a situation is complex when two or more systems occupy the same physical coordinates but do not regularly interact. It is in this sense that scalar hierarchical systems can be said to be complex. Here nested systems of different scales constrain and perturb one another without being able to come into dynamic harmony. And they could not be measured through variables in a single BCNDC experiment. Nicolis' (1986) definition of "structural complexity" is compatible with this: "Structural complexity increases with the number of interacting units; the percentage of mutual connectedness among them . . . , and the variance of the probability density function of the strengths of interactions of the individual subunits." In particular, the two definitions would be equivalent if the connections and interactional strengths could go down to zero, as is largely the case between distant scalar levels.

I take it to be trivially true that natural scalar hierarchies take a long time to develop; I know them to be difficult to describe; and predictability is problematic with them because phenomena are simultaneously informed by internal and external constraints as well as being perturbed from both within and without (Salthe 1985). Hierarchical systems also can be described in different ways—e.g., at different levels (Pattee 1972)—and they are prominent among systems that would be susceptible to multiple descriptions.

So the several proposed definitions of complexity are generally concordant even though one of them estimates from information content, another from information capacity, another from the time expended in realizing informational meaning, and another from the number of different encodings that are possible, while yet another is based on differences in scale. Four of these approaches to complexity will be especially important in this work: information capacity as an entropy, scalar hierarchies, information content, and logical depth.

Infodynamics

The study of changes in complexity might be termed *infodynamics*, following Weber et al. (1989). In my perspective it will be the study of informational changes within developing systems. Following Brooks and Wiley (1988), I will take the view that information capacity (disorder) increases spontaneously in developing systems, being produced along with physical entropy as a system grows and differentiates. I will show that complex systems viewed by an outside observer appear increasingly disorderly as they develop. For the system itself, *disorder* refers to the number of alternative (including pathological) states it might potentially access, and this increases with its complexity. Infodynamics subsumes thermodynamics and information theory, essentially animating the latter by means of the former.

At this point we might consider an interpretation of thermodynamics that is central to infodynamics: Ludwig Boltzmann's (1886) model of entropy. What Boltzmann needed to explain was why entropy change is always positive. It was known that whatever occurred produced friction and was therefore accompanied by an irreversible production of heat—energy that could no longer be used at the same point in the system in question. The quality of energy spontaneously changed from that imported into the system, which was readily available for various transformations, to a form that was no longer capable of causing change. How was it transformed in this way within the system?

Boltzmann's model was the process of diffusion in a limited volume, where billiard-ball-like motions of molecules (Brownian motion) take place more or less rapidly depending on temperature. The material, initially concentrated at some point in the system, spontaneously diffuses outward into the available volume. Once it has diffused so that its molecules are uniformly distributed throughout any whole volume, no further changes in dispersion take place, but *the motions of the molecules continue as before*. There appears to be a privileged condition that, once reached, no longer changes: statistically equal concentration throughout the fluid. In particular, the molecules never again aggregate in a way resembling the initial conditions, either before or after they have reached the *equilibrium* configuration.

But what is this equilibrium configuration? There is no single one. An immense number of particular molecular configurations is possible given a final concentration of material, so we can say that many *microstates* are possible under, and consistent with, a given *macrostate* (e.g., pressure, temperature, concentration—measured at a larger scale than the molecular action itself). This contrasts with the much smaller number of microstate configurations established at the beginning of diffusion. We have here a scalar hierarchical situation. Higher-level boundary conditions are such that a given volume is imposed on the system. The rate of diffusion is a function of the lower-scalar-level properties of both the diffusing substance and the medium, and of another higher-level boundary condition: the temperature of the fluid.

The process is net outward from the initial crowd of molecules because of the uneven distribution of collisions; moving outward to where there are fewer other molecules, fewer obstacles are met than when attempting to move in toward the crowd. When the obstacles are no longer asymmetrically distributed, net change in macroscopic properties stops, and so there is no further consequence at the higher scalar level of continued microscopic motion, and no further macroscopic work could be done harnessing this molecular motion. The many microscopic configurations possible at equilibrium are taken to replace one another at random; the final situation is one of randomly distributed jiggling molecules filling the whole volume.

The number of alternative configurations possible at equilibrium would be taken to be a measure of the entropy of the system. While work is being done to move the molecules before equilibrium is reached, physical entropy increases; if there is still more work that could be done because the gas or solute has not reached its limits of expansion, entropy is not maximal and is still changing (it remains undefined when a system is changing, and could not be measured outside of equilibrium). As we will see, what is considered in thermodynamically open systems is not entropy itself; it is entropy production and flow. What is necessary and spontaneous in the world is for a system to expand in ever more disorderly fashion—from the point of view of Matsuno (1989), material systems continually seek equilibration in respect to any and all constraints impinging upon them. In most natural systems, as in Boltzmann's box, equilibration results in an expansion of some of a system's dimensions (chapter 3).

Matsuno's descriptions of equilibration in a number of systems point up an interesting connection between Boltzmann's model of entropy increase and self-organization (which I will not try to define here, only noting that it involves a system being driven to change from within). Since the expansion of the system is driven by internal forces and frictions, we could view the molecular substance of Boltzmann's box as a self-organizing system. It is for this reason, as well as its formal connection to information capacity (which increases as equilibrium is approached), that Boltzmann's model of entropic processes is important for us.

As it is a scalar hierarchical system, we can see that the motion of individual molecules in the box, being the same at their level from beginning to end if the temperature does not change, is screened off from the macroscopic approach to equilibrium, even though it is their averaged behavior at the lower level that carries the macroscopic process. In the aggregate, they access more and more microscopic states as the system approaches equilibrium. For this reason a microscopic description of the system would become increasingly costly. Relating this to the information-content notion of semiotic complexity, we can see that, microscopically, the system becomes increasingly complex because its minimum description would have to enlarge. Furthermore, since the disorder of molecular motion is increasing, it would be increasingly difficult to predict where any individual molecule would be—their behavior is more and more uncertain. Again, semiotic complexity has increased because the microscopic information capacity of the aggregate has increased because the number of possible configurations has become larger.

It is important to see that the system does not leap to equilibrium in one jump; equilibration is a frictional process, perhaps never actually finished (Matsuno 1989). Hence, the time it would take to closely approach equilibrium, reckoned in molecular-scale moments, is not trivial. Here, using the notion of logical depth, we see that the equilibrium system should again be reckoned complex. Finally, at equilibrium there is a qualitative jump, because only then can a concentration (and on entropy) truly be defined, giving a real alternative description at the macroscopic level—so the system has become complex in the scalar sense too. I stress these points because it has usually been thought that complexity decreases overall in an isolated system like this. But that decrease, if real, is macroscopic only. At that level the complexity of description begins simple, increases (if a molar description can be said to be available in transition, which is not obvious), and then abruptly drops at equilibrium, where mere concentration serves well enough. (In nonequilibrium systems there *are* various macroscopic variables that can be defined, if not entropy itself. For example, phase transitions are well marked; these will be discussed below in connection with Bénard cells.)

At the molecular level, figure 1.1 shows the average length of the free paths of the molecules on their way to equilibrium. There is an initial increase because the area of free diffusion at first enlarges. The subsequent decrease ensues because as the system matures there comes to be less and less unoccupied volume (volume is a fixed boundary condition in diffusion experiments). The shape of this curve is important, showing that this isolated system first burgeons and then declines into a condition I will describe as *senescence*—a reduced tendency to change further (as equilibrium is approached at the larger scale) accompanied by increased structural complexity (the large number of configurations at the molecular scale). Natural, open systems also senesce. They too are finite in their ability to expand, and lose the tendency to do so just as much as do isolated systems (but for different material reasons). The tendency to expand is lost as entropy accumulates, and so entropy might be viewed as a measure of the degree of maturity (or loss of immaturity) in a system.

So, Boltzmannian entropy is a disorder of random configurations. Disorder and complexity spontaneously increase internally as an isolated system develops. The same is true of natural open systems.

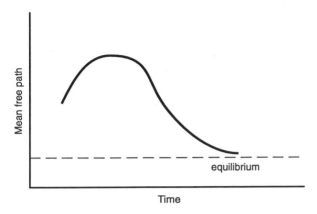

Figure 1.1 The mean free path of particles diffusing in a medium enclosed in a finite volume. The initial increase reflects the fact that the surface area of the front of diffusion at first expands, indicating increased opportunities for relatively frictionless motion; later it contracts as the volume gets filled up and equilibrium is approached.

(Boltzmann's answer to the question of how usable energy becomes useless (heat) energy is that the motions it drives become oriented in more and more directions, increasingly losing effectiveness in any one direction. The energy of the molecules is still there, but it can no longer accomplish anything on the macroscopic level because there is no longer a privileged direction at equilibrium.)

If infodynamics is to be a discourse about changes in complexity, we will have to be concerned about the causal relations of systems observed from this perspective. In Boltzmann's box we see that each molecule pushes others and is in turn pushed; like billiard balls, they "cause" each other to move. But the fact that they are in the box "causes" the results of their motions to change, as in figure 1.1. Furthermore, since all the isolated systems ever examined follow this same pattern of initially producing work and then gradually losing the ability to do so, we could say that the system had to follow a law of nature (in this case the second law of thermodynamics), which, in a sense could be thought of as the "cause" of the system's behavior. We might even say that the system behaves as it does *in order to* satisfy that law. Alternatively, we could say that its behavior is determined, as an artificial system, by the needs of the person who constructed it—that its purpose is what caused its behavior to occur. The analysis of causality in complex systems must itself be complex.

For example, the fact that physical entropy exists as a measurable quantity only under certain conditions leads one to realize that contexts are very important in describing nature. BCNDC science has not been strong on this realization in its general formulations. Indeed, it was when it abstracted only certain kinds of causes out of the earlier Aristotelian analysis of causality that it lost its ability to appreciate complexity (in favor of power over nature).

Aristotelian Complex Causality

Aristotle described the earliest known explicit approach to causality that we are aware of. It has to do with the multiple causes working to produce an overall situation. Western science was later to extract its major notions of cause (efficient cause in physics and material cause in biology) from this system, abandoning the rest of it.

Using an example of Aristotle's, we can examine the making of a house. One sort of cause allowing a house to be built is the presence of suitable materials. This Aristotle called a *material cause,* which is a kind of affordance in the environment. But without a plan of how to proceed, even an implicit one, no house would appear. Plans and organization he called *formal causes.* Now, actual work would have to involve lifting things and pushing them around. These energetic operations he called *efficient causes,* and only this survived in Newtonian systems. Finally, the occasion for the appearance of the house had to be brought in too—its purpose, which Aristotle called its *final cause.* Material and formal causes are paired as tools for a kind of synchronic analysis. Wherever appropriate materials and organization exist together, there could be a house (or an organism). Efficient and final causes are paired for diachronic analysis. Efficient causes start and stop things or deflect them; final causes sort of pull them into the future.

Final causes have exercised evolutionary biologists until quite recently. (See Simpson 1949 for a major attempt to purify evolutionary biology of finality.) In biology the desire for simplicity often, unlike in most of physics, gets expressed as a preoccupation with material causes. A *New Yorker* cartoon was based on this: Two Martians have just left their spacecraft after landing on earth. Perhaps their ship produced enough heat to ignite the nearby forest. One says to the other, "I understand what caused it; there's oxygen on this planet!" Yet scientists involved with complexity have felt a serious need to revive this ancient system of causal analysis—in biology Saunders (1989) and Rieppel (1990), in ecology Patten et al. (1976) and Ulanowicz (1989), in systems science Rosen (1985a), Salthe (1985), and Swenson (1991). Indeed, there are few other systems of causal analysis rich enough to deal with complexity that I know of; one is what I have called the *basic triadic system of scalar hierarchical structure* (see Salthe 1985 and chapter 2 below).

We can briefly analyze a natural situation using Aristotelian causality. Returning to the forest fire, we can identify some material causes: dry wood and duff under certain temperatures; oxidation in the presence of oxygen. For formal causes, we have typical relationships between clouds and certain places on the Earth's surface; the structure of litter and duff; the presence of prevailing winds; the nature of nearby human social systems. For efficient causes we can choose among lightning strikes, the immediate activities of ignorant children or clever Indians, and the landing of a spacecraft.

Final causes are the most problematic. In this book I will use two concepts of finality. One, explored in my 1985 book, has final causes residing in relatively unchanging boundary conditions generated at higher scalar levels; the other, more faithful to Aristotle's original, locates final causes in the individual ends of developments. In the present case, final causes would have to do with the development of the ecosystem of which the forest is a part. As it grows in size, the forest incorporates more and more of the kinds of the formal causes listed above; these make it ever more metastable as it senesces, awaiting the fire (or winds, or a flood, or insect hordes) that will allow recycling of the nutrients that have become increasingly tied up in the standing crop of biomass and ecomass (wood, litter, etc.), thus diminishing the system's ability to efficiently pass energy from the sun into space (Odum 1983). Indeed, aside from the forest's need to be recycled, the fire itself represents a burst of entropy production satisfying a more ultimate final cause: the second law of thermodynamics. Ron Brady (personal communication) has objected to this use because in Aristotle finality must be a cause of something, not just disorder. But, as I will be at pains to describe, the second law in the perspective of the cosmologists Layzer and Frautschi results precisely in the clumping of matter in the universe, and so it can be interpreted as a final cause of all configurations. Final (and formal) causes will be essential for exploring self-organization; indeed, insisting on bringing these in is perhaps not too different from insisting on the importance of self-organization itself.

So there is more to bringing in Aristotelian causality than merely showing that it could be used in analyses of complex systems. Aristotle's view was intimately involved with human action, as we can see especially in his use of the formal and final categories. His view of nature was innocently animistic. He saw isomorphisms, analogies, and metaphors throughout nature, all ultimately referring back to the human condition. My use of his approach is *not* innocent, and my (not so hidden) agenda involves suggesting the need as well as the plausibility of what, for lack of a better label, we can call a *neoanimistic* view of nature. Simply, if we don't love the biosphere and its parts, we will make it unfit for our own habitation. In order to come to love it, we need to see it as being as similar to ourselves as possible. Here, indeed, we can find an important final cause of the present effort. It should now be clear that my approach is not that of positivism. My roots lie instead in the romantic tradition, which mediated the developmental perspective that will permeate the interpretation of systems in this work.

It is interesting to look at an experiment in Aristotelian terms. Suppose we are trying to find out a way to control the population of some insect "pest." We spray confined populations of juveniles with different doses of a hormone, hoping to find one that deranges their development. Efficient cause and its intensification can be plotted as an independent variable, the concentration of attack dose, on the abscissa of a graph. The degree of its effect is plotted as the dependent variable on the ordinate. Nothing else is visible. Nothing but efficient cause is explicitly shown, but even conventional analysis could show that material causes must also be taken into account—this is not Newtonian physics. These material causes include the chemical nature of the agent, the nature of insect physiology, and even the genotypes of the insects (because in the field different races of insects may be encountered).

But, as has been pointed out most recently and effectively by Latour (1987) and Woolgar (1988), much more has yet to made visible up front here. The experiments have been paid for by interested parties. Indeed, the approach to control taken depends on these parties. Chemical companies tend to explore with pesticides, biological technologists with items like hormones, and environmentalists with patterns of crop rotation, hedgerows, and predators. Here we find combinations of formal and final causes—derived from who did it and why—that are far from irrelevant to the form and interpretation of the experiments.

Most biologists have been little more than irritated by having to spend time understanding and focusing technological interests into their labs. This is certainly reflected in the relative boredom that permeates the "materials and methods" sections of their reports. And natural scientists have not typically—indeed not at all before or after the Copenhagen interpretation of quantum physics—been concerned with studying themselves studying as part of their work. This limitation was imposed by the need for simplicity in every aspect of practice because of the instrumental character of BCNDC science (see Lenzer 1975, pp. 329–330). Perhaps the encounter with complex systems and the discovery of the problem of reflexivity were among the formative germs of postmodernism (Artigiani 1990, 1993; Roqué, in press), according to which no observation is unaffected by interested local motivation. This perspective alone would serve to revive final causes, which imply the need to explicitly acknowledge contexts, some of which involve observation.

Observation involves at least three categories: the observed (the object system or referent), the observables (signs), and the observing system (a system of interpretance), which includes the theories and models (various interpretants) used for interpretation. This tripartite analysis derives from Peirce, one of the "fathers" of present-day semiotics, whose system I will use herein.

Peircean Semiotics

The postmodern era is upon us. We need to take ourselves (as the local observers we cannot avoid being) into account in our models of the world (Langer 1967; Rosen 1985b). If we were the Earth's consciousness, as is suggested by Lovelock (1979), that necessity would be even more urgent. In any case, there is no escaping the fact that people are the ones who make the models of the world that we know about—nature. And, indeed, only certain people—generally, up until now, Western(ized) adult males. From a systems point of view, these models are therefore incomplete and perhaps even faulty if there is no trace of their particular maker in them (Geyer and van der Zouwen 1990).

Of course, all models are by necessity incomplete (Rosen 1985b; Salthe 1985; Kampis 1991a), but if a really crucial aspect were to be omitted they could be unintelligible. Positivist models after Comte never included the observer explicitly. In part this could be justified by cost, and the observer could largely be taken for granted (since all science was done by a single class). But this soon led to a forgetting that resulted, e.g., in the lingering controversy about the meaning of quantum mechanics (Atlan 1986); here an entirely unintelligible model of the world led to a resurgence of self-consciousness about model-making. We cannot extricate ourselves from this kind of situation. And so we are led to take up the richest philosopher of science of them all: Charles Sanders Peirce.

The response of one philosopher of biology to this suggestion was that "trying to clarify an issue by using Peirce is like trying to clarify a glass of water by putting it in mud." My rejoinder should have been that explicit clarity is in any case a forlorn hope in the face of complex systems. Understanding of the kind sought by, say, Goethe (Brady 1986) is perhaps more in keeping with knowledge of complex systems than is plain, simple clarity. This may eventually have to involve a kind spiritual training such as that suggested by Hesse in *Das Glasper-*

lenspiel (1949) as much as rigorous training in logic. Complexity cannot be entirely clarified. In fairness to the philosopher quoted above, he did add "but that might sometimes be necessary."

Consider, for example, the problem of thinking about three levels of a system simultaneously. Bateson (1979) noted the difficulty, perhaps the impossibility, of doing this explicitly. Parallel processing computers might do it; however, they are not by themselves even interpretants, let alone systems of interpretation. As far as we know, they do not find meaning anywhere; they are only coding devices for mapping the values of variables into models (Kampis 1991a). Semiotics concerns itself with meaning through the interpretation of signs, and meaning emerges in our collective mind from this activity in totally implicit ways (presumably not accessible to hardware).

Consider the second law of thermodynamics as an interpretation of experimental data that is meaningful for our practices. If we project it into nature, we can see that nature is another (more complex) sign constructed out of interpretations. If we are to keep track philosophically of just what we are doing "in nature" without getting stuck outside realist black boxes, then we must have the sophistication to take up semiotics as a system of thought that contextualizes information theory. Information could then be viewed as a decrease in doubt concerning meaning.

Few other than Peirce scholars study his voluminous and scattered original writings in detail. My understanding of Peirce is derived largely from, *inter alia*, Clarke (1987), Deely (1982), Esposito (1980), Murphey (1967), Raposa (1989), Rescher (1978), Turley (1977), interpretations collected by Freeman (1983), and conversations and correspondence with Myrdene Anderson, Terrance King, Paul Ryan, and C. W. Spinks. I have also consulted some of the original writings collected by Buchler (1955), Cohen (1923), Hartshorne and Weiss (1934), and Wiener (1958). My interpretation, however, has its own materialist and developmentalist twist.

The most general logical categories one needs to be concerned with derive from one's own being in the world. Three categories cover this completely. Without oneself there would be no need to be concerned with anything else, so being could be taken as primary (what Peirce called "firstness"). So, a self-organizing agent can be categorized as a *first*. However, this being inevitably encounters various forms of resistance because of the presence of something else out there—firstness is neither godlike nor alone; everything has a context. The experience of these resistances and frictions is a "secondness," so interaction is a *second*. Finally, the ground in which these interactions are taking place must necessarily be identified, since nothing occurs completely randomly; if something occurs, it must do so in a setting defined minimally by the interacting entities. This ground or place or phase space is a "thirdness"; hence, a more or less organized field, a system affording interactions, is *third*. In Peirce's words: "First is the conception of being or existing independent of anything else. Second is the conception of being relative to, the conception of reacting with, something else. Third is the conception of mediation, whereby a first and second are brought into relation." (6.32, cited in Turley 1977)

This system is hierarchically arranged in three scalar levels, with secondary interactions taking place in a higher-level thirdness. Interactions between interpreters and signs can be taken as a focal level. Below this process of semiosis we have, e.g., the nature of the interpreters that would predispose them to engagement with certain kinds of signs but not others—their "inner worlds" (Uexküll 1926). Above the semiosis is the system of interpretance, including the immediate environment of the interpreters as well as their social systems (if any)—Uexküll's "surrounding world" (the *Umwelt*). It is here that meaning could reside, and where any interpreter finds it. Meanings can accumulate at this higher scalar level because entities last considerably longer here than any at the focal level. So, e.g., as Eldredge (1985) has pointed out, species taken as dynamic cohesive systems, not the genomes of individual organisms, are the repositories of biological information. This is no different than saying that it is the clock that monitors time, not any of its gears. Or that it is people that "tell time," not clocks.

Note that there is no hypothetical earlier time projected when there was only firstness, followed by secondary interactions. The categories are logical, and all three exist simultaneously at all times. However, given development, the categories do not always have the same relative importance; the quality of the triadic relations changes with time. A very Hegelian sort of development takes place. In particular, chaotic interactions characterize immature systems, where thirdness, explicit systematicity, is minimal but subsequently increases into senescence, with a loss of stochasticity in the system.

Firstness undertakes inquiry by means of secondness and discovers the thirdness within which it exists as a result. A more materialist and constructionist interpretation is possible if secondness is taken to be historically primary for any system, its own firstness then being gradually derived by, and revealed to, an emerging agent through abstraction from primal undifferentiated entanglements. This could not be accomplished without the construction of an understanding of thirdness in the process. (It is not trivial that the system of child development of Piaget—see, e.g., Piaget and Inhelder 1969—is easily mapped onto this.) In this materialist interpretation too all three go as far back as one cares to trace them; before the existence of something being irritated there is nothing to be concerned with. This semiotic has a realist flavor because as soon as there can be a firstness there must also be postulated some kind of thirdness, some protosystem of relations, containing it. But semiotics is not truly realist, because that thirdness must be constructed hermeneutically (through unending inquiry) and so could be known only "in the long run."

This means that signs (formally seconds, because they are encounters) are taken as representations of actualities (firstnesses) in the world. So the triadic structure is as minimally reduced as it can be. An observer (embedded in its system of interpretation—hence, a thirdness) together only with a sign (secondness) standing for nothing makes no sense in semiotics, because the firstness referred to by the sign would be missing. Furthermore, a sign and what it represents, without an observer, makes no sense, because there would be no thirdness for which it would *be* a sign—signs call up interpretants from whatever protointerpreters there may be. From these relations we see that semiotics could not be taken into science without explicitly representing the observer, which will be partly formed by the signs it can interpret. Thus, the signs used in science (weight, brightness, numbers of offspring, and so on) will reflect categories of the observer's system—the *system of interpretance*.

From the point of view of semiotics, an interpreter purely as an individual entity is a firstness. But it must be within a system that allows interpretation, and systems are thirdnesses. Its confrontation with signs is a secondness. Learning takes place, and as a consequence the system of interpretance develops. This system involves both the interpreter and the thirdness it is discovering secondarily through the interpretation of signs. This is necessarily so since the thirdness being discovered affords the interpreter in the first place and continues to do so as long as the system of interpretance develops. Entities in this view are very like Uexküll's (1926) "function circles"—combinations of active agents and those aspects of the world they interact with (Anderson et al. 1984).

From a systems point of view, the world system is gradually being discovered, but it is hard to disentangle this from the notion that it is being constructed because, as the world develops, its parts, including observers, develop commensurably. If the parts were out of tune with the whole, they and it could not continue to exist. So interpretation is always realist, and therefore could be wrong. But it can never be unrelated to inquiry—or to the *stage* of inquiry. Truth is "the limit of inquiry" (Peirce, cited in Rescher 1978). But inquiry is a social construct which itself limits what can be discovered (Duhem 1962; Harding 1976; Quine 1969). As in Hegel, and even in Lovelock (1979), a system discovers itself (its own firstness) in discovering the world and constructing nature (the thirdness that contains it). The mediation of signs is essential at every step, even though this has been given little notice in BCNDC science because of the latter's simple instrumental role in the conquest of nature.

Viewing the previous work in this chapter from the semiotic standpoint, we can note that thermodynamics lent itself to an interpretation (Boltzmann's) that allowed entropy to be connected to the later concept of information (e.g., Brillouin 1956). But if we insist that we will not be concerned with "information" that is without potential meaning to some observer, then we make a further extension from thermodynamics to semiotics. I will eschew any notation of information capacity that does not (at least in principle) imply a system of interpretation that could reduce that capacity locally by learning something by way of formulating appropriate interpretants.

For example, Brooks and Wiley (1988) speak of the information capacity (informational entropy) of a system composed of all the species of organisms on Earth. They can do so validly in connection with a system of interpretance (biological systematics) that has discovered these differences and has ordered them into patterns. In particular, systematics orders its inscriptions using maximum parsimony, which eliminates disorder (variety) to a maximum degree, reducing the information capacity of Earth's biota as it is confronted by biologists. Whether that capacity may in a more realist sense be thought of as informing some other, nonhuman entity is moot at this point, but is certainly a thinkable proposition within scalar hierarchies.

Interpretation is a higher-scalar-level function, a kind of constraint, on any collection of signs. So, e.g., systematics as a discourse involves many institutions and persons contextualizing relatively few specimens. We only need to imagine that these institutions are themselves formally "data" for a larger-scale system of interpretance. In order to generalize semiotics into a tool that can be used for analyzing other than human systems (Popper (1990, pp. 35–38) struggles with this), what is meant by 'learning' in such a context needs further explication.

If we take 'learning' to be a class of transformations carried out by human systems, then we can note that it necessarily must be a subclass of a less specified class that would include, say, the "learning" of amoebas. This in turn must be a subclass of a still less specified class that would include the "learning" of terrain by, say, a nest of army ants. And this would be a subclass in an even more unspecified class, including the "learning" of terrain by a drainage system. I could go on and on. Of course, there are no names for most of these more inclusive classes referring to vaguer conceptions of learning. In figure 1.2, we could use {{{learning}}} for the most general class we wish to talk about—conforming—as a vaguer synonym for that least highly specified predicate in this category. This figure shows a sample of predicates differing in degree of specification in several categories.

Figure 1.2 is an example of a *specification hierarchy*, the structure of which will be the major semiotic inovation of this work. Each subclass in a category here is an *integrative level*, with higher, more specified levels to the right and lower, vaguer ones to the left.

Well, what happened to the learning of machines? This is often misconstrued. A given computer learns nothing, even when turned on and furnished with an AI program. What can be said to be learning in these cases is a social system (Searle 1990; Churchland and Churchland 1990), and so machine "learning" would only be a component in a member of, say, the innermost subclass in figure 1.2 containing human systems. This is because machines are totally dependent on human systems to start them, turn them off, feed them information, and so on. If someday a robot system were to replace us (Wesley 1974), it would have to be a more highly specified kind of system than human ones, since it emerged from us, and so would need

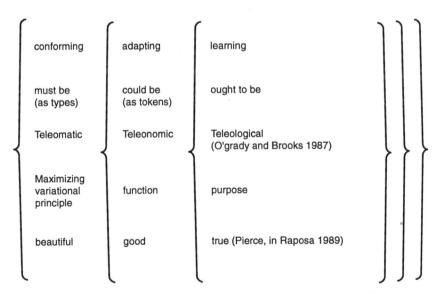

Figure 1.2 Some specification hierarchies of predicates in five categories (*sensu* Ryle 1949) referring to three integrative levels (or logical types *sensu* Russell 1903). The innermost level (to the right) gives the most highly specified member (or logical type) of each category.

to be represented by a subclass within the innermost one we began with above. While I anticipate that such a system would be largely mechanical (Salthe 1989a), I believe no existing computer system yet qualifies. In any case, we would then be faced with a uniquely new problem: the "learning" of this mechanistic system would be more highly specified than present-day human learning. In the view presented here, it would require no less than a new word (to the right of 'learning' in figure 1.2). The problem this raises is to imagine the more highly developed functions of systems descending from our own. The present discourse enables these questions in precise ways not otherwise available.

Now let us move to relate these things to Aristotelian causality. Peirce was insistent that the laws of nature, as thirds (because they are systematic), were final causes. And seconds (interaction, semiosis) are clearly efficient causes. In my judgment, material causes would have to be firsts inasmuch as they present possibilities. And what of formal cause as possibility? Turley (1977) feels that Peirce differentiates unlimited possibility from the potentialities of a metastable system (the propensities of Popper), aligning the latter with thirds because they are implicate in the system as it is. In that case, formal causes would seem to be thirds along with final causes.

Dynamic material systems, besides being thermodynamically dissipative structures, then, may be parts of systems of interpretance. In addition, insofar as any of them would be a supersystem containing subsystems, they can themselves be taken as individual systems of interpetance of smaller scale because of their nature as trajectories (so we can agree with Csányi (1989), who calls self-organization "cognition"). What we acquire by bringing in semiotics (see also Kampis 1991a, chapter 8; Anderson 1990; Hoffmeyer and Emmeche 1990) is a framework that can tell us if the information we compute has any logical potentiality of being informative to a system of interpretance germane to our interests. If not, we can ignore it. Not everything we could describe would have the legitimacy that might be given it by some theory, and so our metatheory here must be explicitly semiotic if it is to involve 'information.' Infodynamics, then, in my view, must involve semiotics.

What should have begun to emerge by now is that we cannot suppose that any entity (person, tree, cloud, galaxy) exists in any independent way. It is an integral part of larger systems and itself forms a framework for smaller ones. It is involved with its environment to such an extent that Uexküll (1926), for example, claimed that biologists should be studying, not organisms, but "function circles." We encounter more consciousness of this kind today through the niche-construction movement in evolutionary biology (Bateson 1988; Odling-Smee 1988). Organisms continually interact with and modify their habitats and do not simply "fit in." Indeed, they are not so much "in" an environment as they are parts of it. It is true that the notion of self-organization tends to refocus our attention on the autonomy of individuals (Varela 1979), but even this, as will become clear in chapter 4, tends to disperse an individual into its higher-level developmental trajectory.

We no longer can have a single privileged way of looking at the world (constructing nature as simple), yet in this book I will attempt to show that there is a suite of harmonious theoretical perspectives that can together form an intelligible cognitive construct of the world allowing for the possibility of different kinds of observers even while it acknowledges its own sources in a given class. This harmonious suite of theories is an interpretation of the world—one of a number of such interpretations, including Darwinism, that construct what we call "nature."

Infodynamics in Biology

We can use an increasingly well-known biological system, the cell cycle (figure 1.3), to display the possibilities of the infodynamic perspective and to show how it differs from the standard biological view. The latter focuses on the details of internal mechanisms of the cycle, especially on the role of genetic information.

From the perspective of infodynamics, such details would be subsumed under material causes, leaving formal, efficient, and final causes still to be considered. In scalar hierarchical systems, informational relations exist at larger scales than do dynamic ones, while mechanisms exist at lower scales (Salthe 1985). The various molecular reactions, even those involved in "regulation" at checkpoints, occur at a scale so much smaller than the phenomena of the cell cycle that they can only be said to be indirectly involved, in the manner of making the cycle possible. I will take the view that it is the cycle, as a trajectory, that marshals and deploys these molecular events, rather than the reductionist view that these microscopic happenings drive the cycle. Even the notion that mechanisms make the cycle possible is going further than would be intended here, for the following reasons.

Infodynamics is a metasystemic perspective, much as thermodynamics has been in physics—"meta" because it focuses on patterns beyond the material details of particular systems as studied by the different sciences, "systemic" because (as with all systems science) it attempts to generalize interdisciplinary patterns. Infodynamically, the

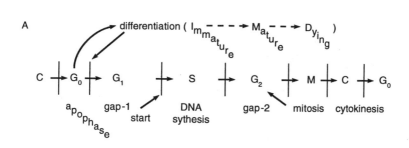

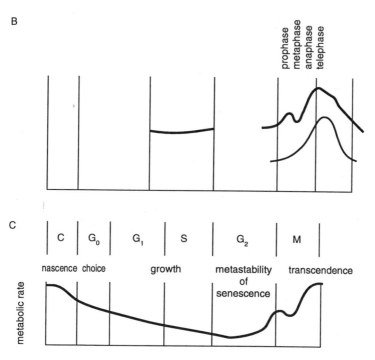

Figure 1.3 A: The cell cycle. G_0 is the period in which a decision is made to continue cycling or to differentiate. Arrows represent some major checkpoints at which the cell cycle is regulated. B: Energy flow in early embryonic blastomeres. The heavy line shows oxygen utilization, the thin one heat production. C: Reinterpretation of the cell cycle using infodynamic criteria.

life cycle of the cell can be seen to have a pattern quite like the ontogeny of organisms, or secondary succession in ecosystems, or even the history of the surface of the Earth, as I will explain below. It is general patterns like these that we will be concerned with.

Of necessity we must use sets of observables that can be gathered from *any* of these systems, leaving out, e.g., genes, since not all changing material systems have them. In the interest of generalizing across systems, we will be concerned with their organization at the most general integrative levels, where they can all be viewed through the same variables. On the basis of its roots in thermodynamics, the variables infodynamics is concerned with are energy potentials and flow and those measuring order and disorder, which can be constructed for any dynamic material system. If there are similar patterns in widely different systems, obviously they could not be explained using only the material causes—the mechanisms—of any one of them. Such patterns are *emergent* from their lower-level enablements, given different contexts, and obviously are not tied to particular mechanisms.

Of keen interest to us, then, would be facts concerning energy flow during the cell cycle, since variables measuring these are quite generally constructable. Oxygen utilization can be mapped onto energy flow (Zotin 1972), and it has been measured during the cell-division cycles of early embryonic blastomeres (Brachet 1950; Zeuthen 1955), which are large enough so that single cells can be studied in this way. In these the cell cycle is abbreviated, leaving out G1 and G2—phases involved with growth that are unnecessary to early embryonic cells, which contain sufficient stores of materials from oogenesis.

Figure 1.3B shows that the peak of oxygen utilization occurs around telophase of mitosis, at the "appearance of furrows" (Brachet 1950). (Zeuthen's ambivalent data are not inconsistent with this view.) This is preceded by an earlier, lower peak during prophase, making possible the marshaling of spindle components, the dissolution of the nuclear membrane, and other sorts of internal work. This picture is complemented by study of external heat production in such cells, peaking as it does when cytokinesis gets underway. Cytokinesis produces the major portion of the mechanical work (Mazia 1965) and high-energy phosphate depletion without immediate regeneration in the cell-division cycle. We can conclude from these facts that what are usually seen to be the final stages of the cell cycle appear to be the most metabolically active ones in early embryonic cells.

Now, the periods of most intense energy flow in other well-known systems—organismic ontogeny and ecosystemic secondary succession—are the early, immature stages. If we were, in the spirit of generalizing, to try to fit the cell cycle onto this pattern, we would find that what is usually taken as the end of the cycle would have to be reckoned as its beginning—that is, as immature (figure 1.3C). This really is no more than viewing the system in a different way. We are focusing on the birth of new cells rather than the end of the old one in a system in which these are inextricably linked. Immature periods are involved with system growth, a process that occurs during G1 in the usual cell cycle, and does not occur in embryonic blastomeres (Murray and Kirschner 1989). We see, then, that in this interpretation the peak of energy flow occurs just as the new cells appear—at the beginning of their careers.

Presumably the G1 phase of cycling cells, a period of growth that terminates at the "start" checkpoint (Laskey et al. 1989), would continue with a relatively high metabolic rate in ordinary cycling cells, perhaps into S. The rest of the cycle—G2—would be viewed as a period of senescence of the system (compare Cooper 1979 and Arking 1991). This would be in line with viewing all post-embryonic stages of ontogeny as "aging" (not to be confused with senescence—see Timeras 1972). Aging is a dynamic period of internal work in the interests of homeostasis and (in some cases) reproduction; senescence is the final stage of development (which I will be much concerned to characterize in this book).

We are likely to be overpersuaded by habitual usages, and so biased against such generalizing. We could get stuck at the knowledge that in organisms senescence leads to death, while in ecosystems it terminates in recycling and rejuvenation, in hurricanes in dissolution, and, as I am suggesting here, in cycling cells in reproduction. But in all cases it leads to dissipation of the energies and information of a system into other systems. In this way organisms become dissipated in detritivores, senescent ecosystems in immature ones, cells in daughter cells, and hurricanes in smaller storms—all, of course, accompanied by the production of heat energy that is lost to the kind of system involved. I am suggesting that we should not let material differences (so useful in the different discourses) blind us to the structural similarities in the infodynamic pattern changes involved in these developments. It is these we are interested in for considering what nature might be like.

Is there any precedent for looking at cells in this way? I believe there is. Bullough (1967) considered cells that differentiate in G_0 to undergo an aging process (figure 1.3A) with the following stages: I (immature), when differentiation is taking place; M (mature), when the cell can still dedifferentiate and reenter the cell cycle; and D (dying), when the cell functions in its differentiated state and slowly senesces. What I am suggesting here is only that those cells that enter the cell cycle also senesce, but along a different pathway: one leading not to death, but to transcendence in daughter cells.

Cesarman (1977, 1990) viewed heart muscle cells from the point of view of thermodynamics. On this view diastole is a time when the cell undertakes recovery from systole, a period when it does internal work to replenish its high-energy stores and reestablish its membrane resting potential. At this time, as in the G_1 of cycling cells, it is open to an inflow of nutrients. In systole, the cell cuts off communication with other cells and expresses 80% of its stored high-energy bonds in externally directed mechanical work. More than 75% of this energy is released as heat at this time.

Since this energy profile is similar to that of dividing blastomeres, with systole mapping onto cytokinesis, it seems to me that heart muscle cells have used their developmental trajectory to set up contraction instead of cytokinesis. The diastolic cell would be viewed as being in a relatively immature condition and the systolic one as relatively senescent. Such a formulation emphasizes that senescence is not necessarily a terminal situation for a given material system. It is interesting to note that if early blastomeres are prevented from undergoing the S phase, so that no mitosis occurs, they still undertake contractions at the time when cytokinesis would have occurred. I am suggesting that these rhythmic contractions are homologous with those of muscle cells. Significantly, yeast cells, which are unable to divide because of mutations, still undergo a CO_2 cycle like that of cycling cells (Lasky et al. 1989).

Along these lines, one can see that the diastolic recovery period is metabolically like growth even though the muscle cell does not physically enlarge (and growth need not involve enlargement (Ulanowicz 1986)). Furthermore, it is only in what I would call the immature stage of the cell cycle, G_1, that cycling cells can be regulated by outside influences (Pardee 1989—and early blastomeres without G_1 cannot be so regulated), just as it is only in diastole that the muscle cell communicates with its surroundings. Senescent systems are increasingly involved only in the private self they have organized.

The infodynamic viewpoint, then, as I see it, is that all natural individual dynamic systems undergo a basically similar developmental pattern—what I will call the *collecting/cascading cycle*—at the lowest integrative levels, and that diverse behaviors of different particular systems ride on this same underlying structure, which is, then, a common formal cause. As I have already suggested, diverse material causes are contributed by the lower-level internal dynamics of each kind of system.

We still need to account for efficient and final causes in the cell cycle. Internal efficient causes can be found in the character of the S, M, and

C portions of the cycle (and in systole of the heart muscle cell), where one event triggers another sequentially during all-or-none periods that cannot be regulated.

Final cause, however, because of its unfamiliarity in these contexts, requires careful exploration. In the context of multicellular organisms the cell cycle is enlisted in various functions, any of which could be viewed as a final cause of cell division for each kind of cycling cell, just as the functioning of the heart could be viewed as a final cause of heart muscle contraction. Semiotically, muscle contraction would be an interpretant generated by the organism in one of its interpretations of the cell cycle. In free-living cells, the perpetuation of their kind might be viewed as the final cause of cell division, and as its interpretation. Note that in all these cases final causes and interpretation associate with a larger-scale system in which the cell is embedded—a supersystem that gives them collective meaning—and that is the general situation with final causes in scalar hierarchical systems (Salthe 1985).

The production of heat (so noticeable in systole and cytokinesis) is an even more encompassing final cause for all dynamic phenomena—establishing the second law of thermodynamics. In cycling cells we have that tremendous burst of heat loss at the end (the beginning) of the cycle, which fits nicely with this notion of final cause. Furthermore, shifting away from the physical entropy of heat and over to its informational aspects (Brooks and Wiley 1988), we can see that the system of daughter cells is informationally richer than was the single cell. Not only has the system stored more information than before (two genomes, a larger surface area, and so on); in addition, it would take more statements to describe the two-cell situation. Informational as well as physical entropy has increased at the expense of energy loss, as a result of energy flow—and the organism (or the local ecosystem) will interpret these events among its own complexities.

Because it can be viewed from several levels of integration, this example suggests that change is complex. Furthermore, it is rather difficult to characterize, as I will now attempt to show.

The Problem of Change

Change has become a problem in the sciences for several reasons. First, it is coming to seem limiting (if neat and clean) that Newtonian approaches to change involve only efficient causality and are limited to translational changes in the context of equilibria (Depew 1986). We are facing more and more nonequilibrium situations in complex systems. The only new things accessed in Newtonian dynamics are positions in space or dynamical states, and these changes are physically if not thermodynamically reversible—something the transformations we will be concerned with never are.

Statistically, changes in frequencies cannot be taken to access new situations either, since they too are reversible. It might be argued that new situations can be accessed in chaotic but still basically Newtonian systems; however, chaotic byways are not really new either, because they are in a way deterministic. In principle, all the immense number of states accessible by a chaotic system are immanent in the equations describing them to begin with—they are potentialities and propensities, not merely possibilities. The chaotic behavior of, say, a dripping faucet accesses no *new* state; it merely behaves unpredictably when locally accessing any of the numerous states that are globally within its reach and, in principle, predictable.

So an important aspect of change is the accessing of an entirely new condition or set of possibilities. It is not easy even to state what these "new conditions" would be (and therefore what change is), but surely they are not simply states that a dynamical system has not yet accessed. A new condition is not predictable from a set of equations, unless perhaps the equations themselves might be transformed as they are iterated. Kampis (1991a) demonstrates that mechanistic models (as in BCNDC science) would be incapable of generating real change.

Change is also problematic, especially in biology, if we want to be able to understand the non-translational transformations that occur during ontogeny and phylogeny. (Similar changes occur in stars and hurricanes as well.) This perspective on similarities has sometimes been taken to be the province of structuralism, and change is particularly problematic for structuralists. Much of biology is structuralist insofar as it is comparative. Idealistic morphology, for example, was a structuralist discourse. But so are modern comparative anatomy and evolutionary morphology. Comparing all the available examples of some type gives a sense of the exploration of a limited domain. In the structuralist sense, evolutionary transformations accessing different versions of some form do not represent real change; they represent only the working out of potentialities immanent in the type—say, the different kinds of birds' wings.

That some apparent possibilities within a type seem never to have been realized is felt to be trivial from this point of view, because such absences are likely related to historical accidents (e.g. unknown extinctions). However, accident is given only a minimal role in structuralist perspectives. That some forms are excluded by the laws of matter, as in chemistry, would be more germane to differences between types. For structuralists, then, stability of form is due to continued accessing of the same structures by developing systems; the forms continue to exist because they are repeatedly accessed. Presumably the origins of structures would entail real change, but this has not been an important part of the structuralist discourse. Structures tend to be viewed as unchanging potentialities in the world, within which superficial transformations are possible but between which there are only jumps (spanning what?).

There could, however, be a constructionist view of types, to the effect that forms are produced in nature at random and humans then gather together as "unchanged" those that seem to them to be similar. From this point of view, all things are possible, and can be taken as really new, since there are no *structures* guiding, constraining, attracting, or enabling their production. This perspective carries the burden of having to explain the stability of types that we mark everywhere, and the large gaps between them. For this reason, as well as others, constructionism is not represented in biology, which, in any case, has been realist in the strong sense.

Most evolutionary biologists are not structuralists, except in the weak sense of acknowledging structural constraints in existing forms or processes ("developmental constraints"). They feel that really new forms have been accessed during organic evolution by way of many kinds of historical accidents (mutations random with respect to the needs of organisms, genetic recombination, preadaptation, contingencies of all sorts in the relations between organism and environment, allopatric speciation, and so on). The commonness of certain forms is explained as a matter of successful adaptation (or of evolutionary adaptability). In other words, existing forms are explained by their stability once they occur by accident, not by the rate at which they are accessed. The latter concept is even taken as nonsensical, since every change is held to be radically different from any other. Here too gaps would need no explanation beyond mere historical accident (unless they are taken to have been imposed by material laws).

This Darwinian perspective fails to explain certain important facts that can have a structuralist interpretation. These facts are subsumed under the names *convergent evolution, parallel evolution, iterative evolution,* and *ecological vicarage.* What we have here are homoplasies (similarities) that are not the results of recent common ancestry. Examples abound—comparisons of form and niche structure between the hummingbirds, some honeycreepers, and some sunbirds; between Old World and New World vultures; between New World and Old World tree frogs and those of Australia; between elements of the Australian marsupial fauna and the eutherian faunas of other continents; between cacti and some African euphorbias; between African and North American porcupines; between orchids of different families on different continents; between fish body types (e.g., pikes, eels, and panfish) in several entirely different, distantly related faunas in the fossil record as one group replaced another (iterative evolution); between ichthyosaurs and porpoises. One could go on and on. Examples even pop up even on television animal shows; e.g., it appears that tropical montane forests in every part of the world have some kind of "bellbird" whose voice rings out of the mists.

Such similarities are not confined to organism-by-organism comparisons; whole faunas and vegetations show impressive similarities. Pine barrens up and down the coast of eastern North America have identical vegetations with major species differences. In the north the Spanish moss niche is occupied by "old man's beard," a lichen. (I use "niche" here in the Eltonian sense, which stresses similarities in broad ways of life between unrelated taxa. See James et al. 1984.) Mediterranean scrublands are found in California, in Australia, and in the Andes as well as around the Mediterranean Sea (Cody and Mooney 1978; Milewsky 1983; Orians and Paine 1983; Blondel et al. 1984). The structure of African ungulate faunas was duplicated with different taxa in some detail in the North American Pleistocene (Webb 1983).

There has been no Darwinian interpretation of these facts in recent times save the brief one in my 1972 textbook. Furthermore, taxonomists are loath to deal with these matters, because descent with modification (their only model of evolution) and genealogy (their chosen domain of interest) can accommodate increasing differences but not convergences. These homoplasious similarities implicitly argue for more systematicity in organic evolution than Darwinians and phylogeneticists are willing to concede. And they suggest that there are some regularities of change—perhaps even structuralist transformations—involved, such that the rate of formation of types, as well as their stability, is needed to explain their persistence (Webster and Goodwin 1982; Goodwin 1984).

In any case, structuralists do have problems with genuine change. For them everything is potential or immanent from the beginning and nothing really new ever happens. (Popper (1990), too, feels that propensities of every kind have always existed, however unlikely their realization might be.) Systems may develop from stage to stage, but all is known or predictable. At the same time, Newtonian change seems trivial, because accessing new coordinates in space does not really put a system in a special place from which it cannot return even by some devious route. Even unusual coordinates are accessed as easily, if less frequently, and nothing special is implied by them. So, a translational change in a Newtonian system, being reversible, is not a real change to something new, and neither is a structuralist transformation.

The Construction of Development and Evolution

My treatment of change as the result of individuation—although it harks back to Romantics such as Coleridge (Barfield 1971)—is perhaps the most unusual feature of my approach. Central to this approach is a distinction between development and individuation. Examining biological literature for usages of the words 'development' and 'evolution', one comes up with a list of definitions for each which can be dichotomized by discarding any overlapping statements. (One overlap, irreversibility, was necessarily retained as being common to both kinds of change.) Boiling down and generalizing from the result, one arrives at, for 'development', *predictable irreversible change.*

As a consequence of this definition, a process like the self-assembly of certain viruses from their parts, since it is reversible under some boundary conditions, cannot be taken as a development. In some viruses, however, irreversible steps are mediated by enzymes, and these could be held to develop. Note that individuation during ontogeny, producing historical or unique traces, would not be developmental either, even though it is a phenomenon of immature (even embryonic) systems, but is found everywhere else. We need to note this because most biologists would probably define 'development' reflexively as changes occurring in embryos and juveniles. The definition advanced here is systematic enough to be applied to change in *any* kind of system.

Suppose we choose at random changes undergone by ships under sail, by embryos, by stars, and during football games. It does not matter in principle how different the phenomena chosen are. We can construct a developmental discourse about how they change by comparing them, finding whatever general properties they may have in common (perhaps Minot's Law, under which phenomena start out briskly and end up relatively lethargic—we can use *any* similarities at all). The point is to be able to predict what will happen during still other processes of change not yet examined. Of course, in real discourses the objects chosen are much more reasonably compared, but the principle is the same, and I use this arbitrary example to emphasize that development is a constructed structure. The purpose of constructing development is prediction—the major social role of Western science since Francis Bacon.

Noting the important constructionist connection to development as defined here, one might ask whether development is then not being taken as a real process in nature. It does appear (in spontaneous actuality) that tokens, say, of the ontogeny of a given kind of organism are more closely similar than are unanalyzed changes in the arbitrary collection of systems used above. If we were to try to generate an isomorphic realist definition of development, it might go like this: Developmental changes are those that are stable in the sense of being repeated in all tokens of a given type. This suggests stored information as a source of constraint on variety, producing order. Orderly change would be developmental. My problem with such a realist formulation is only that it suggests that the observer is redundant.

In any case, close study of examples of what appear to be very similar kinds of processes—say the embryonic development of frogs, or behavioral changes during the course of therapeutic analyses—will show that similarities tend to get blurred by noise. Even in such homogeneous collections, each trajectory acquires its own unique features different from all others of its type, reflecting historical accidents all along the way. Each token individuates.

Figure 1.4 shows the results of a striking example from the world of computer simulations. It is from the work of Henri Atlan (1985), who used the system of Boolean automata pioneered by Stuart Kauffman. Each node in the matrix is assigned one of 16 possible Boolean functions (and, or, if-then, etc.). The last element in one row connects to the first in the next, and the same for the columns, and closure is achieved by connecting the last row back to the first. Each node may be stimulated by two flanking ones as well as by the two vertically adjoining ones, and gives output to four others only if its logical conditions are satisfied. A run is started by arbitrarily choosing initial points to perturb the matrix. After about 20 iterations, the network enters a stable limit cycle involving relatively few still-cycling nodes (the zeros and ones in the figure). Each starting pattern of automata goes to a characteristic pattern of cycling nodes, as in the figure, regardless of the initial perturbations, and so we can discern a development. But each run is also different from all the others, and so individuation (usually of relatively trivial extent) occurs too. Kauffman (1989) sees this process as a formal analogy to ontogeny. Atlan, who finds he can randomly perturb the matrix for a few iterations during a run and get nontrivial differences between the resulting final states (showing that the system really can build in important historical information), feels it also models self-organization. The earlier the perturbation is applied, the more different is the resulting limit cycle pattern, showing an epigenetic effect (Schank and Wimsatt 1986; Arthur 1988) as well.

Because of the individuated differences between runs (figure 1.4), we can apply the term 'evolution' to these automata as well. Generalizing from the biological literature, evolution can be defined as the

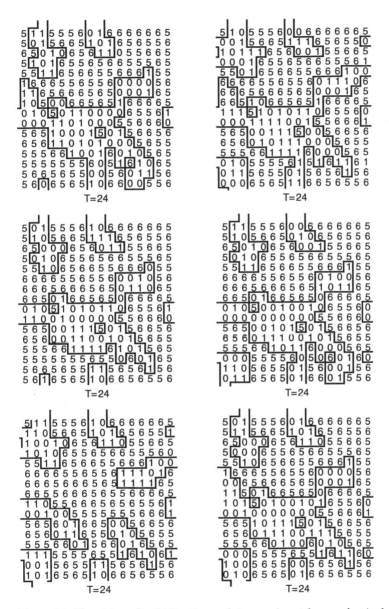

Figure 1.4 The states, after 24 iterations, of six experimental runs of a single matrix of Boolean automata arranged as shown. The zeroes and the ones are still cycling; the fives and the sixes are fixed in the on or the off position (that is, they have permanently differentiated). Note both the similarities (due to development) and the differences (due to evolution) between runs. Reprinted, with permission, from Atlan 1985.

irreversible accumulation of historical information. This definition implies organic evolution and ontogenetic individuation (since neither is predictable) as special cases. Using it we can see that evolution is not a definable kind of process at all. It is simply the stored result (scars and traces) of perturbations (noise, mutations, friction) met by any changing system.

Studying organic evolution, then, is studying the perturbations registered in living systems during developmental changes in the biosphere itself since its inception. What these developmental changes might be we have only the most general idea, because studying changes in the biosphere from this perspective became unlikely (given the close connection between historical geology and organic evolution) after historicism supplanted developmental approaches to change in biology at the beginning of the twentieth century. Darwinian approaches to evolution focus only on the results of "chance," with systematic processes occurring only after change has occurred, as environments select phenotypic expressions. And neo-Darwinians have simply declared by fiat that no other kinds of changes are going on at all—a *non sequitur* deriving from their limited interests. I will attempt to bypass that highly influential limitation in this book.

Evolutionary biologists will detect an emphasis on development where they fail to see any. My point is that an evolving system must have a material basis, and, as I will attempt to show, all material systems develop if they change. Organic evolution must be the individuation of some developing material system. There cannot be evolution without a development to carry it.

A Preliminary Glance at Dialectic

We see that irreversible change can be analyzed into two aspects: the predictable and the unpredictable. When both occur together, self-organization is likely to be going on. That which is responsible for the really new is the historical process consequent upon evolutionary change or individuation. But if we examine the synthetic theory of organic evolution to find a theory of change, we see that it has had none (Depew 1986; Depew and Weber 1989)—that is, it has been an equilibrium discourse, wherein change comes about only by way of external perturbations and is characterized by return to (a perhaps different) equilibrium. It is a theory of random fluctuations. Most theories of change in other fields turn out to be oriented toward prediction; in fact, they have been, unlike Darwinism, developmental for that reason, and so they have not been concerned with the really new either.

It has from time to time been suggested that dialectic provides a basis for a theory of change involving the production of radical newness within the system itself. I will examine this proposition in chapter 5. For now only a few points need to be made.

Dialectic does not seem to be capable of being embodied in an algorithm. We can see this reflected in the major role it has taken in recent world history, which for our purposes can be boiled down to two statements:

> (1) Mechanistic materialism has formed the basis of the Western attempt to dominate nature (Merchant 1980; Wesley 1974).
>
> (2) Dialectical materialism has organized criticism of the results (but has not become the basis for an alternative material practice).

Several tentative attempts have been made to derive scientific practice from dialectic (Engels 1940; Levins and Lewontin 1980), without singular success. Dialectical discourse (disentangled from socialism) can be most generally characterized as follows:

> (a) It is involved directly with change rather than with equilibrium.
>
> (b) It is a subjective view from within a system, concerned with internal relations and self-organization more than with external connections.
>
> (c) It puts history—evolution—in the foreground, and so it concerns itself as much with unique constraints of the moment as with process.
>
> (d) It explicitly links thought with moral valuation.

Most scientific models differ on all points.

The "new biology" of Maturana and Varela (1987) has some of these features—in particular, (b) and a hint of (d)—but does not transcend Darwinism in connection with (c) and fails to engage (a) at all. In Maturana and Varela's background, Uexküll's (1926) *Theoretical Biology* is much more dialectical, but it also largely fails on (a) because its interest, like that of Maturana and Varela, is more in structure than in change. A recent highly successful example of a dialectical approach to nature (perhaps especially so since it was not intended as such) is Matsuno's (1989) *Protobiology*, where what we can take to be the "internal contradictions" of friction produce ever-new boundary conditions on any material process of equilibration, such that the direction of change can never be entirely predicted because it is mostly internally driven (self-organized).

Summary

I have undertaken to introduce a way of thinking about nature (and some basic tools for that) quite different from Baconian/Cartesian/

Newtonian/Darwinian/Comtean (BCNDC) science. I will be concerned with the self-organization of complex systems (which I take to be effectively modeled as hierarchical systems) as driven by thermodynamic potentials and considered from the perspective of informational changes—for which I use the term *infodynamics*. I have suggested that informational changes cannot intelligibly be followed without a concept of meaning, and I have brought in Peircean semiotics to help with this aspect of complexity. Change itself is noted to be complex, having two aspects in biological discourse: ontogeny and evolution. These generalize to development (predictable irreversible change) and individuation (the irreversible accumulation of historical information). The process of individuation as such seems not to have been examined in BCNDC science or in structuralism; indeed, perhaps only dialectical discourses have been concerned with it at all.

Chapter 2
Hierarchy Theory

In this chapter I compare the scalar hierarchy (H_{sc}) with the specification hierarchy (H_{sp}). H_{sc} is reviewed, while H_{sp} is explored in more detail since it would be less familiar to scientists. H_{sc} is a synchronic representation of the structure of extensional complexity, while the H_{sp} can be either a synchronic representation of intensional complexity or a diachronic representation of the pathway of individuation during development. Development is fundamentally epigenetic, with the canonical sequence of stages moving from vague possibilities to explicit complication.

The basic infodynamic structure on which developments rest, what I call the *cascading/collecting cycle*, is introduced with examples from many aspects of nature. Both the spontaneous production of heat and the energy-requiring collection of information can be represented by tree structures. Development through stages has a constructionist reading as an analog performance of a digital score (descriptions of developmental stages). Fred Sommers' language tree is shown to be a useful and precise way to look at the meanings of tree structures. Finality is shown to be involved in development as an entity gradually becomes itself during its individuation, because the specification hierarchy is also an implication hierarchy, with the most highly specified entities implying their antecedents. Development is viewed as the using up of degrees of freedom present in an original final cause.

One hesitates to claim, not only that a hierarchical perspective is essential for thinking concretely about complex systems, but that it also generates a fruitful conceptual base for coherent models of most aspects of the material world. Yet so it seems, perhaps because the world is complex. I am not simply asserting that the world *is* hierarchical, anymore than I would assert that perfect circles occur in material nature. Circles and hierarchies are structures, that is, organizational principles through which nature can be understood. Even though all actual hierarchies are heterarchic, this is a consequence of the fact that theory is neat, while the world is messy. Because of this, one does not find hierarchies lying about in the world; one constructs nature hierarchically—because it is useful to do so.

The scalar hierarchy (H_{sc}) deals with the structure of the world, both as space and as scope of influence. As we saw in chapter 1, this structure could be taken as the source of complexity as usually conceived—what I here call *extensional complexity*. The specification hierarchy (H_{sp}) provides a schematism for (a) reading the *intensional complexity* (as integrative levels) in models of complex structures, (b) tracing the development of this complexity (the emergence of stages), providing a four-dimensional structuralism, and (c) mapping logical structures (the *language tree* of *logical types* and *categories*) onto intensionally complex systems, giving them meanings.

Together, these hierarchies form a conceptual apparatus of immense descriptive range, allowing a provisional, syncretic classification of any group of things in our world—from protons to organisms to refrigerators—in a single three-dimensional volume, on the basis of scale, stage of development, and an observer's valuation (figure 2.1A). Any natural system could be analyzed from either scalar or specification standpoints. Since the developmental framework allows a reading of evolution (as individuation), it becomes possible to take account of historical change in this four-dimensional structuralism as well.

The Scalar Hierarchy (H_{sc})

The scalar hierarchy was the subject of my 1985 book, where I emphasized the necessity for at least three levels (the basic triadic system) in minimal descriptions of extensionally complex systems, as well as the nontransitivity of dynamics across levels, so that they are largely screened off from each other except through mutual constraints. Contiguous levels are also sources of perturbations, which deform neat hierarchical reality into heterarchical actuality. Since the 1985 book, some important works have appeared.

Nicolis (1986) explores interactions between nonlinear dynamics and H_{sc}, which he characterizes, unfortunately, as two-leveled, as in micro-/macrosystem talk.

Auger (1989) also picks up this thread; further, he considers the thermodynamics of scalar systems. He deals mathematically with two-level and three-level cases in the same way, suggesting that the latter is a non-problematic extension of the former. This is so in his work because it is reductionist in spirit, different levels being represented as having processes of different rates affecting the *same* fundamental "elements." That is, the levels (groups and groups of groups of the same elements) are defined dynamically only, there being no true higher-level entities and no primary higher-level attractors, so that higher-level effects are merely compositions of lower-level behavior. This is at best a special case, justified by the complexity of the mathematics for the general case.

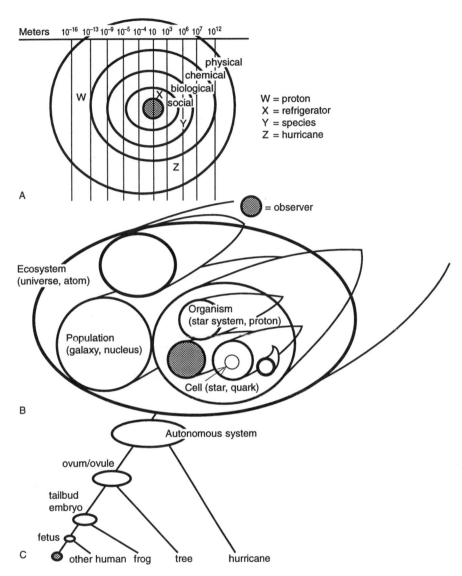

Figure 2.1 A: Rough double classification of material entities in both scalar and specification hierarchies on a single plane. The observer is central in the specification hierarchy and midway in scale between largest and smallest. B: A scalar hierarchy extended backward in duration so that entities are seen as developmental trajectories. Labels are given for three different ranges of scale. (Of course, each atom has only a single nucleus, and, although a trajectory is seen giving rise to another in the lower right, this may not apply to all trajectories). C: A specification hierarchy of autonomous systems. Stages are traced only on the trajectory leading to the observer. This should not be interpreted as a genealogy, but as a framework for individuation. The sizes of the ellipses reflect the numbers of phenomena subordinated to the labeling concepts.

Zhirmunsky and Kuzmin (1988) summarize a great deal of Russian empirical work on H_{sc} not previously available in English. Their book is devoted primarily to detecting scale breaks in data from many fields, prominently including biology. It represents a viewpoint that supposes the world to be a scalar hierarchy and that tries from there to develop techniques for finding nature's joints, focusing primarily on the boundary conditions generated by environmental cycles. That is, data from many fields are correlated with such cycles, with some results more convincing than others. Many of the studies of rhythmic data that Zhirmunsky and Kuzmin report could feed into the developmental perspective taken in the present work as well, because they can be taken as attempts to confirm Minot's Law in growth data from several fields.

Several works based in nonequilibrium thermodynamics (NET) use scalar hierarchical principles—notably Brooks and Wiley 1988, Ulanowicz 1986, and Wicken 1987. It seems clear that NET requires H_{sc}. Troncale (1985) explored some aspects of the fundamental relationship between general system theory and H_{sc}, emphasizing isomorphisms across scales.

In O'Neill et al. 1986, R. V. O'Neill and T. F. H. Allen (co-founders of an ecological school of hierarchy theory) continue their epistemological program of trying to hone a scalar tool for the analysis of ecosystem behavior, maintaining their two-level approach. More recently (1989), O'Neill has acknowledged the necessity of three levels for minimal descriptions in this discourse. Kolasa and Pickett (1989), in a more ontology-based approach to ecosystems, have made more formally explicit many of the principles of H_{sc} explored in my 1985 book.

Eldredge (1989) has continued to apply H_{sc} to macroevolution, emphasizing the differences between function driven by energy flow (the ecological hierarchy) and the system of informational constraints based on genes (the genealogical hierarchy). Miller (1991, 1992) has begun applying H_{sc} to analyses of change in paleocommunities. His work importantly visualizes different kinds of change at different levels. Buss (1987), using the origin of organisms and their ontogeny as his focus, shows how the results of selection at different scalar levels could produce the entification of previously less integrated systems.

In a critique of the biological props of sexism, Birke (1986) uses H_{sc} to obviate biological determinism. She notes the danger of reductionism either upward or downward to some preferred level of discourse, arguing for what amounts to the basic triadic system as the way to avoid it. With internal predispositions holding back at one level and social contexts on the other, neither traditional biological reductionists nor holists such as behaviorists can construe femininity as nothing but either biology or brainwashing.

Being Provoked by Extensional Complexity
For a striking introduction to the feel of this discourse, the reader might examine Philip and Phyllis Morrison's book *Powers of Ten* (1982) or Godfrey Reggio's film *Koyaanisquatsi* (1982). The book, which looks at scale jumps visually, is based on a film by Charles Eames which consists of a series of stills ranging far upward and downward in scale at one particular location, thus examining the essence of extensional complexity. *Koyaanisquatsi* (available on video tape) probes rates of change by speeding up and slowing down the film, effectively playing at changing the observer's scale. These works are major popular documents in an emerging cosmology to which, in my experience, many students respond with immediate recognition.

The Feathered Swarm (Trevor 1985), a film examining the life history of the African social weaver finch, the quelia, provides striking footage of the behavior of huge flocks of millions of birds, making higher-level configurations (of the social population, in this case) really manifest as the behavior of a large-scale entity to the viewer. Similar observations have been made of schools of fish and squid, of tadpoles, and of clouds of migratory locusts. The behavior of the group is clearly not a mere summation of the behavior of many separate individual organisms in any of these cases. Instead, they appear to be entrained by the larger structure as by an attractor. No number of studies of the physiology of individual organisms, showing hormonal changes and such, could explain these particular higher-level patterns, even if they can give some hints as to how those patterns immediately control behavior at the lower level. Nor do they get at the organization of the higher-level pattern or *its* ontogeny. The problem here is similar to that of organismic ontogeny, where again the overall organization of developmental influences fails to be explained by current cell- and molecular-oriented studies (Salthe 1987).

How different, one wonders, is group participation in higher-level patterns from, say, the improvisation of a jazz group, where individuals are likewise not free to wander at will, no matter how creative they become, and where in fact only the utmost sloppiness can disrupt the persistent rhythmic and harmonic patterns? The following is a quote from the first book by that sharpest observer among traditional naturalists, William Beebe. Beebe and his new wife were afield on an alkali plain in Mexico:

A confused mass of black appeared in the air which, as we advanced, resolved itself into hundreds of individual specks. The atmosphere was so deceptive that what, at first, appeared to be a vast cloud of gnats close at hand was soon seen to be a multitude of birds, blackbirds perhaps, until we approached and thought them ravens, and finally, when a quarter of a mile away, we knew they were vultures. Three burros lay dead upon the plain,—this we knew yesterday,—and here were the scavengers. Never had we seen vultures more numerous or in more orderly array. A careful scrutiny through our glasses showed many scores of Black and Turkey Buzzards walking about and feeding upon the carcasses of the animals, and from this point there extended upward into the air a vast inverted cone of birds, all circling in the same direction. From where we sat upon our horses there seemed not a single one out of place, the outline of the cone was as smooth and distinct as though the birds were limited in their flight to this particular area. It was a rare sight, the sun lighting up every bird on the farther side and shadowing black as night those nearest us. Through one's partly closed eyes the whole mass appeared composed of a myriad of slowly revolving wheels, intersecting, crossing each other's orbits, but never breaking their circular outline. The thousands of soaring forms held us spellbound for minutes before we rode closer.

Now a change took place, as gradual but as sure as the shifting clouds of a sunset. Until this moment there was a tendency to concentrate at the base of the cone, that portion becoming more and more black until it seemed a solid mass of rapidly revolving forms. But at our nearer approach this concentration ceased, and there was perfect equilibrium for a time; then, as we rode up a gentle slope into clearer view, a wonderful ascent began. Slowly the oblique spirals swing upward. The gigantic cone, still perfect in shape, lifts clear of the ground and drifts away, the summit rises in a curve which, little by little, frays out into ragged lines, all drifting in the same direction, and before our eyes the thousands of birds merge into a shapeless, undulating cloud, which rises and rises, spreading out more and more, until the eye can no longer distinguish the birds which, from vultures, dwindle to motes, floating lost among the clouds. (Beebe 1905)

Lest we bias our thinking with only examples of familiar kinds of systems, we can note that bacteria of various kinds have been found to behave in complex ways so as to form multicellular structures (Bonner 1952; Schauer et al. 1988; Shapiro 1988). That these kinds of living systems may be functionally organized on even larger scales seems to emerge from work associated with the Gaia hypothesis (Lovelock 1986; Charlson et al. 1987). Buss (1987) and Wilson and Sober (1989) provide Darwinian models showing how entification could be brought about by way of a balance of selection pressures at different scalar levels. Selection models like these allow us to visualize how ecosystem-size communities of coevolved microorganisms could emerge that might produce a Gaian system. And, lest we bias our thinking by sticking only to living systems, we might remember that Cairns-Smith (1982) has shown how highly organized clay systems might become, containing, as they do, large amounts of replicable, orderly structure.

Particularly interesting are examples where similar structures are accessed by entirely different systems, emphasizing the higher-level boundary conditions involved. For example, Rayner and Franks (1987) show how the forms generated by fungal hyphae and by hordes of army ants are in many cases formally isomorphic. They attempt a reductionist analysis to Darwinian categories which, from the point of view of this work, would be unnecessarily biological in view of the possibilities that have been shown for similar forms in abiotic systems (Stevens 1974). Even if the Rayner-Franks analysis was required to show us how similar initiating conditions are generated in the different systems, the same boundary conditions would seem to be facilitating the accession of similar structures in the two systems, and these are ignored.

These cases are important because they do not involve clearly obvious preexisting superstructural constraints, such as streets, or strong currents, or ecotones, or even flight paths. The group spontaneously coheres because of the seemingly unconstrained behavior of the lower-level individuals. Of course, we humans participate in such structures quite "unconsciously" for the most part, perhaps occasionally deliberately "throwing ourselves" into them. And how different are these cases from the behavior of the cellular automata of Kauffman and Atlan (figure 1.4)? These too are entrained by a pattern somehow inherent in the overall situation—a pattern that changes somewhat when the arrangement of automata is changed, but which certainly would also change if the boundary conditions (the size or shape of the matrix itself) were changed. We know this because even temporary perturbations will alter the final patterns significantly (Atlan et al. 1986).

Consider a hockey game. If you were a naive observer examining sequential photos taken from the ceiling (or watching the action from above in slow motion, as if your scale were much smaller), or watching a video taken from a random position on the sidelines run at faster-than-natural speed and focusing on the puck, you would be in the position we are in with respect to flocks of birds or masses of embryonic cells. There *are* rules to the game, and we might infer many of them after long observation, but would we want to suppose that the players are concentrating explicitly on these rules during play? No more so than the quelias! The rules emanate as boundary conditions from the social level. The motions are inherent in biological initiating conditions (Salthe 1985), and they self-organize into sequences that form patterns—chaotic ones, to be sure. I say "chaotic" here rather than "random" because the motions of the players (birds, blastomeres) appear to be entrained by structures. Again, studying bird or cell physiology will only deliver some of the initiating conditions on those patterns.

A good way to avoid getting stuck delving into the specific initiating conditions of living systems in the reductionist manner is to show that *abiotic* dynamic systems must also be considered as examples of the same problem. I mean subjects like the red spot on Jupiter, ocean currents, glaciers, hurricanes, tornadoes, and eddies (Lugt 1983).

Consider fluid gyres such as dust devils in a windy valley. The Aristotelian causal categories can form a useful scaffold for understanding their behavior. Since we are examining dissipative structures, energy flowing through associated systems at contiguous levels assumes the role of an important material cause. Initiating conditions are generated by the nature of the materials at hand. The forms we see are at first vibrant and vivacious, but they rapidly spin out as they disintegrate, leaving a trail of furrows in the sand—bits of stored potential information that could constrain others yet to come. Having already used information generated by the spin of the Earth—the Coriolis force—they tend to spin in the same direction in a given hemisphere. This boundary condition can be taken as a formal cause of their behavior, one generated by a higher-level dynamism. Other formal causes can be found in various arrangements of environmental parameters—the "affordances" of Gibson (1966). It would be as if the design of a bowling alley and the rules of the game gave rise to the form of the ball. Any information stored in or resulting from the dynamics would also be acting as formal causation (Ulanowicz 1989), in this case including various inertial tendencies as well as the tracks of earlier vortices.

Episodic perturbations act as efficient causes in starting these vortices, and these would in turn be the results of higher-level vortical processes (Emanuel 1988). Final cause becomes a focus of interest. After bowing to the ever-present Second Law, we can note that the final causes of a bowling ball would lie in external relations. In fact, they are closely associated with formal causes, as we will find to be the case for natural systems having diffuse, very weak agency. The immediate final cause of a ball rolling in an alley is the game; those of a dust devil lie in some aspects of the shape and dynamics of its environment—the environment that "calls for it as output" (Patten et al. 1976), given that some perturbation could spin it up. It is important to note that final causes here can be held (as they must) to exist in advance of the actions of the dust devils, in the sense that larger-scale processes take so long to occur from the viewpoint of the focal vortices that they are in place before, and end only after, many of these vortices have blown across the landscape. The "rules" of this higher-level "game" can, of course, change over time.

Generalizing backward from the most highly specified (the human) case, as in figure 1.2, we can associate final cause with *projects* in which the systems are engaged. Living systems, for example, are "about something"; they are engaged in something; they do not simply spin up and blow out without viewpoint. They take on perspectives, which implicitly generate meanings—perhaps allied to the *besoins* of Lamarck (Barthélmy-Madaule 1982; Burkhardt 1977)!

Let us again examine the windy valley. Occasionally dust devils spin up and move down the valley, regulated by its shapes so that many of them would show a meaningful average trajectory. (Consider how the lives of organisms are regulated externally in no less important ways!) Occasionally one of them emerges from the end of the valley, propelled by stronger-than-average generating forces, and continues for a short time, by inertia, to make certain characteristic gestures resulting from its acquired structure. This is the most primitive form of *modeling* of the environment—a kind of dance. If we took statistics over many such cases, we could still find average behaviors; however, the variance in the frequency distribution would be larger, because the valley walls are no longer supporting the motion. During such short unsupported excursions, simple projects emerge as attractors of the dynamics.

Any imaginable situation can be read in this fashion by way of the basic triadic system. Everything has an environment or a context that provides boundary conditions and a source of perturbations. Almost everything also has some internal structure, generating initiating conditions. We do not yet, however, have the habit of attending to both the internal structure and the environment in our inquiries. This, I believe, is due to the generally instrumental perspective we bring from our society to any project. To decide how to use something, to turn it to profit, is better furthered by simplifying it and/or its situation—by abstracting it from its own contexts so it can more readily be swallowed up in ours. Perhaps the paradigmatic institution showing this is the old-fashioned zoo. The scientific experiment is another important way in which we domesticate nature by rendering pieces of it transparent to their initiating conditions.

Scalar Levels

Allen et al. (1984), O'Neill et al. (1986), and Birke (1986) have argued that there are no privileged scalar levels in nature. Birke makes this move from a position seeking flexibility in regard to remaking social arrangements, Allen and O'Neill from the point of view of obtaining flexibility in examining data. My own position on this has been that traditional levels in biology, such as the organismic and the populational/social, have been privileged by history. And most of them have been corroborated in continuing discourse. Once more, I remind the reader that what I am talking about is not the world, but discourse—"nature."

In the examples just given, when we are talking about organisms our observations seem to naturally fall into populations as well (but note that Beebe's example involves *two* species). Organisms are, of course, capable of forming many kinds of groups, inter- and intraspecific (families, neighborhoods, guilds, etc.), but the biological population seems to be an exceptionally strong attractor in biology discourse. Discourse, however, is historical, and other groupings may indeed replace the population in this sense—without denying its existence, in the sense of the continuing possibility of its construction. When Allen and O'Neill discover levels by analyzing data (using criteria of stable patterns at some scales and not at others), they are constructing entities that may or may not be corroborated in other studies (themselves professing not to care). If those entities are corroborated, then they too might gradually emerge into our consciousness of nature and become privileged by discourse.

In the dust-devil example, these problems come to the fore because there are no traditional levels used to talk about abiotic systems. We would first need to decide at what scale the gyres themselves existed. Could there be vortices at any and all scales, or are some privileged for that form? Since we could interact with most of them, they might be thought of as being vaguely of the same scale as organisms. The concept of development might help us in this question, as follows: Immature systems are less formed, more vague, less precise, more flexible. In them scalar levels are not well defined. As development procedes, greater definition of levels takes place, with form becoming more precisely defined in senescent systems. On principles presented by Margalef (1968) and by Odum (1969), abiotic deserts such as the Sahara would be quintessentially immature systems. Here, where nothing biological occupies the scale that organisms do elsewhere, we can place our dust devils. We would need the techniques of Allen and O'Neill to search for the levels exemplified here, and we might get considerable overlap between any we found. In chapter 4 I will note the necessity for an increase in stored information as a system develops. Scalar levels would separate, achieving greater mutual definition as a system matures and entification procedes, and this would be one way of realizing the necessity of information increase. (Many biological systems can reach comparatively high degrees of entification, and, in this general sense, reach more mature stages, with more clearly defined levels, than any strictly abiotic ones could.)

General Rules of the Scalar Hierarchy (abstracted from Salthe 1985)

I. The system of scalar levels continues without bound in both directions away from a focal level. It is an essentially synchronic structure, allowing representation of process and events but not of change.

II: Nestedness. Entities at different scalar levels are parts and wholes, every entity being part of a larger one and also having parts within itself. (In a command hierarchy, higher-level entities metaphorically contain the bodies of subordinates within them because of the scope of their interests and power.)

III: Nontransitivity of effects across levels. Relationships between entities at different scalar levels are indirect in the sense that as a rule they do not interact; rather, they provide mutual constraints—it is a system of extensional constraint relations. Hence, dynamics at different levels are screened off from one another, with descriptive variables necessarily representing a single level only, while the values of nonrecursive constants will have been derived from dynamics at other levels. The system is not completely decomposable into isolated levels, because of these constraints. Yet everything is not connected up to everything else (Simon 1969; Margalef 1990), and this allows us to model a contectualized autonomy. Indeed, perturbations across levels are frequent enough so that actuality is heterarchical, even though based on a hierarchical reality.

IV: Functional heterarchy. Occasional interactions do occur between levels as perturbations. Those coming from below require a process of *amplification*—consider the example of cancer, where (the descendants of) a single cell may eventually dominate the life of a metazoan. This is because no single lower-level entity as such can directly affect the higher-level entity in which it is embedded as a part. The system is asymmetrical in this respect because a larger-scale fluctuation would completely, if indirectly, dominate all lower-scale systems simultaneously.

V. The further apart two levels are, the weaker are the continuing constraints they mutually impose, or the less frequently do they perturb each other. But perturbations generated from fluctuations at more distant levels tend to be more intense (because the system is not used to them) than those from closer levels, in those rare instances when they do occur.

VI. Processes at different scales change direction, cycle, or go to completion at different rates (have different rate constants), with lower-scale ones behaving faster and having smaller relaxation times than higher-scale ones (which, however, can travel at greater absolute speeds). A consequence of this is that larger-scale entities have moments (*cogent moments*) that endure for absolutely a longer time than do those of lower-scale entities.

VII. While many forms and processes are isomorphic across levels (like many laws of nature), every level would be expected to have some unique characteristics. This tends to ontologically isolate processes and entities at different levels.

VIII: *The basic triadic system.* In describing a system of parts and wholes, three levels are minimally needed in order to preserve the complexity, because in this case the description cannot plausibly be reduced to a single favored level without losing essential veridical features. This kind of reduction is always possible, if not always desirable, in a two-level scalar description.

IX. The scalar hierarchy can be used in "objective" discourses because it is strictly metric and nonvaluational.

Modeling Structure: Reflexivity, Autonomy, Agency

At the end of the twentieth century we are faced with a major epistemological problem in many fields. We can call it the problem of reflexivity, self-reference, or recursivity. It has many faces, ranging from forms of chaos to postmodernism. The notion of self-organization is driven by the same relations (Atlan, 1981; Brooks and Wiley 1988), and it impinges seriously on the problem of modeling nature (Rosen 1985b; Nicolis 1986).

There are many images that carry this content, from the simple one of an arrangement of mirrors in which one sees oneself in endless receding copies to the baroquely vertiginous images generated by iterating the Mandelbrot set (Gleick 1987). Yet seeing occurs immediately, unselfconsciously, and seemingly without any hesitation expressive of endless regression. But seeing and its description are not the same (the map is not the territory, as Gregory Bateson was fond of saying). Seeing is one thing; explicitly describing what is seen another, and in the present context it would involve describing seeing at the same time in order to be more fully explicit. We will be concerned here with problems of description, whether by word, by digital computer, by dance, or by analog computer. Our descriptive device at this point is H_{sc}, with its endlessly receding scalar levels.

What happens at the focal level is made possible by what happens at the next lower scalar level. But some of what happens at the focal level feeds down to govern what happens at that lower level. The next higher level controls and regulates what happens at the focal level, but some of what happens there joins with other processes and configurations to help make processes and constraints at the next higher level possible (see figure 10 of Salthe 1985). This is a description of *autopoiesis* (self-making): ". . . it pulls itself up by its own bootstraps and becomes distinct from its environment through its own dynamics, in such a way that both things are inseparable" (Maturana and Varela 1987; see also Ulanowicz 1986).

Varela (1979) makes autopoiesis depend on the production of components that realize the network that produced them and that together constitute it as an entity. We see here that in H_{sc} an entity, its environments, and its *invironment* are taken together (as in the function circles of Uexküll 1926) to be autpoietic. But Maturana and Varela emphasize the *autonomy* of the embedded entity to a degree that sometimes (e.g., 1987, pp. 136–137) borders on solipsism. In H_{sc} we cannot do that; there must, in discourse, be representations of higher levels embedding a system such that modulation by those higher levels is intelligible. This only *seems* to threaten autonomy, which cannot be total in any case. Matsuno (1989) also emphasizes autonomy in the irreducible, frictional secondness of material systems to a degree I believe to be unwarranted, given that all material systems have contexts.

But what is the reality of autonomy anyway? A system is autonomous to the extent that it achieves a degree of functional closure. That closure is achieved, with tools such as the principle of parsimony, through (the limited aims of) discourse (Dyke 1988). But entities and their environmental relations are inexhaustibly complex (Buchler 1966; Singer 1983), so no entity can be said to have closure *per se*. Thus, we must inquire "Random with respect to what?" and not merely "Is it a random pattern?" Actual autonomous entities (their firstnesses) can never be encompassed by discourse anyway, and so can be subject to endless hermeneutic exploration—and can be involved semiotically with multiple theory-laden secondnesses.

So, a fox pursues a rabbit. The fox must be seen to have a theory of rabbits, and the rabbits to have one about foxes—they behave *as if* they had such theories. For purposes of H_{sc} this example as it stands does not have closure; from this perspective we see that there must be a population of reproducing rabbits in order for a fox to have achieved its presumed theory of rabbits. The fox culls part of a rabbit *population*. Do we need a whole food chain to describe this example in H_{sc}? Not if we are only trying to describe relations between these two organisms. We need the fox's physiology and behavioral tactics as initiating conditions, and we need the deployment of a population of rabbits as boundary conditions. Now we have closure for this example in H_{sc}.

Why, in H_{sc}, are we not obligated to tread an endless regression of initiation and modulation? Because (a) a triad of levels exhausts the logic of the situation, except for perturbations from more distant levels—and these are heterarchic violations of the logic; (b) effects from more distant levels will more likely (or frequently) affect initiating and boundary conditions than make direct impingements at the level in focus; (c) except for perturbations, these effects can be gathered together in a summing-up function—etc., & so on—which tends to bracket, e.g., all the receding images in the mirror after the second. An 'etc.', for example, by way of recursively iterating the function, is the source of the reemergence of similar images at smaller and smaller scales in the Mandelbrot function.

In modeling complex systems one must take these things into account. Following Rosen (1985b), we see that a model effectively changes the rates at which the processes we are modeling occur so as to bring them into line with our own observation rates. For example, if we want to predict the weather, we run a computer program that churns out the next week's weather in an hour or so. What we have made is a small-scale model of the larger system we are inside of. This suggests that, since the reference rate scale is our own, and since relations of the object system to other observational scales might be quite different, some representation of the relations between object and observational system must be incorporated into a model. In other words, models of complex systems ought to be self-referential to the observer.

But models are not the world; our models of such systems must show the difference between the world and a system's discourses. In Figure 2.2, theory b explains large-scale phenomenon B, while theory a explains small-scale phenomenon A. A helps to make B possible (to initiate it), and is a material and/or formal cause of B. In turn, B regulates the behavior of A. Theories ought to be such as to allow us to bring out these natural relationships in their own discursive realm. In figure 2.2, for example, I suggest that completion could be a descriptive metaphor for regulation.

Take the example of physiology. What does the organism in H_{sc} do with respect to its contained systems? I suggest that it completes them

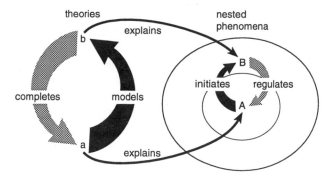

Figure 2.2 Nested phenomena and theories that explain them, making explicit the implicit relations. If A is a cognitive system, such as a human society, some of the initiating conditions on its behavior will be theoretical presumptions. In that case the left side of the diagram would be nested inside A on the right side. If instead B represented a society, then A might be replaced by the left side of the diagram. In the Peircean system, the left side consists of relations between signs, the right side shows their referents, and the system of interpretance is represented by the connecting arrows.

("integrates them," in H_{sp} talk) by giving them local meaning (contextualization) which they would not otherwise have. Thus, diffusion occurs willy-nilly, but organismic circulatory systems manipulate that process in elaborate ways, giving it a complicated configuration it would not have if it were occurring instead, say, in a brook.

Concerning discourse, we can find a precise logical line of reasoning on these matters: (1) Reductionist science, like organismic and cell physiology, tries to discover the "mechanisms" that make organisms tick. (2) Ideally the descriptions delivered by these sciences will become reduced to sentences in predicate logic, together with equations. (3) In 1931 Gödel (Nagel and Newman 1958; Davis 1965; Hofstadter 1979) showed that explicit, logical, descriptive systems that are rich enough to be interesting either must be internally inconsistent (delivering some contradictory statements) or must remain incomplete (the truth of some statements could not be ascertained within the system itself). Consistency is invariably opted for, leaving the systems incomplete by choice.

Carnap (1937) showed that such systems can be completed by placing them within a more encompassing metasystemic discourse, which can interpret them (see also Zwick 1984). My suggestion, then (figure 2.2), is that theories about higher-level entities ought to be constructed so that they complete theories about lower-level phenomena, while the latter ought to have within them a connection to the upper-level theory that we can take to be model of it. In this way models of some aspect of the world will be parts of a reflexive metasystem of theories.

To show the kind of thing that is at stake here, one might construct an example of the relations between theories shown in figure 2.2 having developmental genetics at a and having Goodwin's (1984) model of limb development at b. Goodwin's model showed that there are certain mutually exclusive attractors for vertebrate limbs such that they discontinuously have two, three, four, or five digits. Evolutionary loss of a digit reorganizes the entire structure of the limb (in the model this is an equation) from a five-digit structure to a four-digit one with a radically different symmetry. Gradual diminution of the digit can be represented within a five-digit organization, but with its loss there is a radical flip to a four-digit structure.

This model is certainly a way of completing developmental genetic models such as Waddington's (1957). In that model, mutations or environmental perturbations acting at a given critical period of development could effect a switch from one developmental pathway (chreode) to another. In Waddington's model, the jump from one chreode to another models the transformation of one equation into another in Goodwin's more specified model. Furthermore, Waddington's model completes still lower-level models of gene action based on threshold values of morphogenetic substances mediated by genetically coded enzymes, by giving them a particular system to affect (e.g., one that can also be affected by environmental changes). Gene-action models, such as that of Edelman (1988) do not try to model theories such as Waddington's or Goodwin's—a result, probably, of the common reductionist bias in BCNDC science; theories such as Edelman's are simply incomplete from the point of view of H_{sc}.

Having encountered genes, we might here ask "Where does the fox hold its theory of rabbits?" In its central nervous system; and that theory can change by way of learning. But what the fox is prepared to learn is limited by its brain structure, which was produced by cellular activity during morphogenesis. That cellular activity was initiated by the cells' model of their environment, their genetic information. We can use this perspective to discover agents. Thus, the fox is an *agent* in its own learning because its knowledge can be altered or replaced according to its own unique experiences. It can be said to deploy its brain activities just as it deploys its white cells. It can even be said (with a modification to be made below) to deploy the differential expression of its genome during differentiation. These things it controls and regulates. But it cannot be said to deploy itself or its genotokens (the genotypes it represents) within its species' range. These must be held to be functions of the groups it is part of—its family, its population, its society. Within these groups, genotypes and individuals can be altered or replaced. The fox can only initiate these deployments by its own impulsive and motivated movements, in the same way that cells initiate the behaviors that the fox deploys.

We can reach Darwinian natural selection from this example by noting that kinds of foxes that tend to initiate inappropriate behaviors more frequently than other kinds will tend to reproduce less successfully. Only some of these kinds of foxes will have had this fate because the behaviors their cells tended to initiate is what led (because they did not suppress it) to their own inappropriate behavior, and the cells did this because their genetic information was different enough in some way from that of cells in the more successful foxes. From this we can make it out that populations deploy members of genotypes in somewhat the same way that a fox deploys its different kinds of cells. (Now, we do not expect many perfect isomorphisms across scale. So, while we would want to say that a population 'evolves', we would prefer to have it that an organism 'individuates', even though these are almost synonymous.)

Note that in these examples the endless regression threatened by recursive relations between levels can be interrupted by allocating agencies. Finding such agencies within theory is another way, along with the more physical test of whether there is interaction, of locating gaps in the scalar hierarchy of nature. An agent is robust to its various effects in different "orders" (Buchler 1966; Singer 1976). Orders are determined by interaction or association of the agent with other entities or viewpoints. In each such order an entity would have a particular aspect or presence.

Agency can also be viewed as associated with an autonomy that persists even when subsystems are replaced by others as a system develops (Ulanowicz 1986). An agent would be said to have an "integrity" in the "order" (= system of interpretance) of development if there is something particular that can be said to be gradually revealed as development proceeds to more and more detailed realization. As individuality becomes more pronounced through continued historical change during development, a particular agent can be more and more fully revealed in various orders. Hence, individuation is a process of revealing an individual agency as a way of maintaining the integrity of the developing entity (it either develops or is recycled).

A test for agency would be whether or not the effect of an entity in some interaction (or its position in some order) is unique—that is, could not be replaced by another of the same type. If we find that we sometimes need to (or even can) include some mark of individuality on tokens of some type (say, naming hurricanes), we can provisionally infer that that type exists as a *bona fide* entity in our orders, and that its tokens have agency. Given that, it is natural to suppose that entification occurs at the scale at which it exists, and that we need to mark that scale as privileged in our discourses.

Of course, we scarcely ever look for individuality in nonhuman nature; our interpretations there are guided by very general categories of low specification. So, if in examining cells we increase magnification to the point where individual differences become apparent within some type, we simply ignore that information in favor of some relatively crude classification (e.g., epithelial or not; cancerous or not). The cellular level, needless to say, has not been defined by the criterion of agency and individuality. In systematics, species do have a kind of individuality in classifications; however, in scientific models generally there has been little need for it, in view of the instrumental attitudes behind scientific research.

Now, Buchler's "orders" are semiotic in that generating them requires perspectives. The requirement that a model of nature contain a self-representation of its maker (even if only an unconscious one reflecting the maker's needs) could eventually lead to self-consciousness in classes of modelers. In our recent history, this has led to postmodernism. In any case, perspectives emerge during during development, and this leads to our next topic.

The Specification Hierarchy

This topic will eventually need more than the following introduction—primarily because the concept has a long history, going back to Plato's *Republic* (van der Meer 1989). Not being a historian of ideas, I will treat this material summarily. Figure 2.3 shows it as a *discursive formation* (Foucault 1972), some of whose ridges and peaks are picked out impressionistically to give the reader an idea of the scope of this general way of thinking (see also Salthe 1988, 1991a). The labels in bold type capture several aspects of the discourse, a few of which I will treat in more detail below. Here we can get an impression of the sequence of their historical discovery. I have included prediction because during most of its existence this discourse has been involved with prediction in our attempts to handle nature instrumentally. One could suggest without exaggeration that the reason this way of thinking has flourished in the West is that it has been a tool in attempts to construct prediction (or, indeed, control over nature, however illusory). This has been attempted in a way that includes in the framework (though often only as implied by utility) the central position of the predictor.

Figure 2.4 shows Plato's conception (van der Meer 1989) of what I call *intensional complexity*. We see that Plato understood the same properties to be deployed within all creatures, but with some kinds of

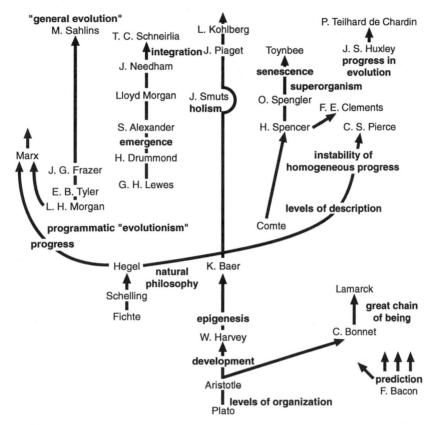

Figure 2.3 A synoptic map of the Western discourse about intensional complexity and development, showing some of the ranges and peaks labeled with key names and benchmark phrases.

creatures being better endowed. There is a sense here of an addition (or a deletion) of faculties, generating discontinuous jumps from one kind of being to another. There is here also an anthropocentric notion that humans are the kinds of beings that have the greatest complement of these properties. Here Plato is making an explicit self-reference, locating humans in the natural scheme. This structure, perhaps the earliest extant version of what came to be called *integrative levels*, is conserved throughout the developmental discursive formation and can be taken as its bedrock.

Aristotle enriched this structure by assimilating his observations of ontogeny to it. He could see that during development an organism becomes more complicated, and that because of this the logic of integrative levels might be mapped onto ontogeny. At first, one could

	Desiring function	Spirited function	Rational function
Humans	✓	✓	✓
Animals	✓	✓	
Plants	✓		

Figure 2.4 The classification of the properties of living things in Plato's *Republic*. Adapted from van der Meer 1989.

reason, humans (for example) do not have significantly more properties than plants (their nutritive soul); they become more complicated and add the sensitive soul to their repertoire, then the locomotory soul; finally, after birth, they attain to passive reason as well. The fact that lower faculties are not lost as more are added shows that these *stages of development* (which is how the integrative levels now appear) make up a hierarchy of implication (or, conversely, specification). Having passive reason implies that you also have the locomotory soul, and all the others too, but the presence of the locomotory soul does not imply that a creature has passive reason.

William Harvey championed and elaborated the Aristotelian notion of *epigenesis*, by which it is understood that, out of an undifferentiated potentiality, the embryo emerges only gradually, first as a rough adumbration, later becoming more clearly differentiated, and finally filling in the fine details according to the particular kind of organism it is. We see from the construction of the word 'epigenesis' itself that "all . . . parts are not constituted at once, but successively, & in Order" (Harvey, cited in Oppenheimer 1955). This building-upon has remained central to the discourse, and carries the implication that developmental stages cannot be scrambled or appear out of order. Indeed, even in cases where stages appear to be only "left out," that condition requires a discussion of how that could come about, insofar as the immediately previous stage is generally taken to prepare the way for the next.

The *great chain of being* (Lovejoy 1936) was a later transformation of the Aristotelian ranking of animals according to their (reproductive) faculties: insects / arthropods and fishes / cephalopods / birds and reptiles / ovoviviparous sharks / mammals. This interpolated into a more general ranking of entities: formless matter / inorganic forms / plants / stationary animals / locomotory animals (those listed above) / humans. These make up what today we would call *levels of organi-*

zation (Aronson 1984; Salthe 1988), or, in evolutionary systematics, *evolutionary grades* (Huxley 1958; Simpson 1961).

The chain was finally elaborated in great detail by Charles Bonnet, who tried to construe it as a seamless continuum from the "lowest" kinds to the semitic god; the immense logical problem of representing any such continuity will be struggled with below. Lamarck was aware of the impossibility of a linear ranking of all known species, because too many seemed coordinate for the same position. (Consider all the different kinds of minnows, wood warblers, or beetles there are, and how you might figure out how one of them could be taken as "closer to God" than another!) The chain had to be constructed of evolutionary grades instead, each one of which made a bush terminating with multiple species at each organizational level (Burkhardt 1977).

Lamarck, in his attempt to explain this bushiness by adaptation to local conditions, wandered into the major alternative discursive formation: that of radical historicity. This discourse also extends back to Plato (the *Timaeus*), and it was through this discourse, starting partly from Lamarck's work, that Darwin was to interpret biological nature, although Richards (1988, 1992) has shown that Darwin was struggling within—perhaps trying to break out of—developmental discourse as well. Other proponents of radical historicity include Hume, Mill, and Bertrand Russell. From these we can catch the lay of the land along that alternative path to understanding—individuality, freedom from constraint, isolation, hazard, external relations, distinctions—which predicates reflect in a reverse way much about the contrasting way of intensional complexity that we are concerned with here in discussing H_{sp}.

We will not be concerned with the historicist discourse here except to jump ahead to Julian Huxley. He (1942, 1953) and Rensch (1960) became interested in lawful regularities that might be discovered in the aspect of organic evolution that Rensch called "anagenesis" (i.e., progressive evolution—the "phyletic evolution" of Simpson (1944)). Both Huxley and Rensch strongly suggested a kind of inevitability of evolutionary progress toward the "human phase" that reflects the developmentalism of intensional complexity discourse. This was to be extended into an ecstatic Christian version by Pierre Teilhard de Chardin (1959), who pointed toward a future "omega" condition of the "ultimate earth"—the "noosphere." Theodosius Dobzhansky's (1962) cautious championing of Teilhard's approach brought a reaction from increasingly orthodox neo-Darwinians that led to Dobzhansky's backing off and Huxley's isolation. Since then, synthetic theorists have shown little interest in developmental possibilities in the process of organic evolution. Bonner (1988) has attempted to raise some aspects of this issue again, but in such neo-Darwinian language that this text is incoherent.

Stebbins' (1969) reading of evolutionary necessity has been tolerated within the fold, probably because it is really a deconstruction of it. His argument is that increases in organizational complexity when they occur (willy-nilly, by various chance means), bring with them openings into a new range of possibilities for exploiting the environment such that some at least of the forms at the new grade, having escaped interspecific competition in the old way, will persist by means of selection. In this fashion, one grade will lead to another in a pattern that (by hindsight) mimics epigenesis, and which could be thought of as a form of self-organization of the overall living system. We might call this idea "Stebbins' evolutionary ratchet." That this issue has not been dropped entirely by the Synthetic establishment is shown by a collection of papers (Nitecki 1988) wherein a spectrum of establishment figures ranging from the (quite properly) more conservative philosophers to some more radical biologists hash out almost every aspect of progressive evolution available to them through their specialties.

Returning to the intensional complexity formation proper, Karl von Baer is central in the diagram and a high peak in the discourse. He continued observations on embryos, and came to some major conclusions about them that are canonical to the logic of the discourse as a whole. He formulated four rules (Russell 1916):

> (1) The general characters of the big group to which an embryo belongs appear in development earlier than the special characters.
> (2) The less general structural relations are formed after the more general, and so on, until the most specific appear.
> (3) The embryo of any given form, instead of passing through the state [i.e., particular configuration] of other definite forms [i.e., of other species], on the contrary, [gradually] separates itself from them.
> (4) Fundamentally the embryo of a higher animal form never resembles the adult of another animal form [which it might do superficially, as when mammalian embryos go through a stage when they have gill clefts], but only its embryo.

These can be summed up as *Baer's Law* to the effect that, as organisms develop during ontogeny, they begin more alike (minimally insofar as earlier stages are vaguer and so necessarily poorly distinguishable) and gradually appear to become more and more different as they differentiate and individuate. In other words, development moves from the general (I will argue for 'vague' as the materialist equivalent—see Merrell 1991) to the particular; transformation is irreversibly into more highly differentiated states, requiring increasing specification by an observer. It is important to see that this law reflects a basic tenet of the Romantic philosophy of the *Naturphilosophes* Fichte, Schelling, and Hegel, even though Baer had little taste for the grand style of their systematic philosophizing, which was Aristotelian in both its scope and its ambitions.

Among these Romantics, Schelling most fully attempted a scientific cosmogony; it is interpreted here in figure 2.5. We see that there is postulated a development from inorganic situations toward the human condition. The development is dialectical, driven from within. Each new synthesis posits a thesis which generates its antithesis, and together they give rise to a new synthesis at a higher integrative level. Looking at the levels of organization listed on the right side of the figure, we can interpret "organization" (unqualified) as including Bénard cells (Glansdorf and Prigogine 1971), Belousov-Zhabotinskii reactions and other self-organizing chemical systems (Nicolis and Prigogine 1977), perhaps liquid gyres, and so on. Intelligent systems would include social systems of all kinds. Human action refers to behavior guided by specifically human discourse—psychological, linguistic, and formal. In this scheme we find yet another Platonic concept—dialectic (in Fichte's version)—which characterizes much of the formation before us, especially in some of its later irruptions.

Hegel's German Protestant, purely metaphysical reading of this kind of progression has relevance to the present work as follows: In Hegel, talk about development of the world recursively interpenetrates a discursive development concerning being-in-the-world, producing a rich(ly confusing) text that I think is better read as talk, not about "the world" at all (including in the *Philosophy of Nature* (see Miller 1970)), but about discourse. As Hegel's system progresses from being-in-itself to being-for-others to being-for-itself, the world, as a larger-scale individual, comes to understand itself through human discourse. (Interestingly, Lovelock gives a version of this notion in his *Gaia* (1979), where humans are characterized as becoming the Earth's mind.)

The point is that it is discourse itself that the present text is about, not the world, whatever that may be; the world develops just exactly as some discourse claims it to do (if that discourse itself can continue to successfully self-organize and become appropriate to new conditions), and it might *not* do that only if some other discourse successfully disputes it. This kind of approach (logical priority maps onto

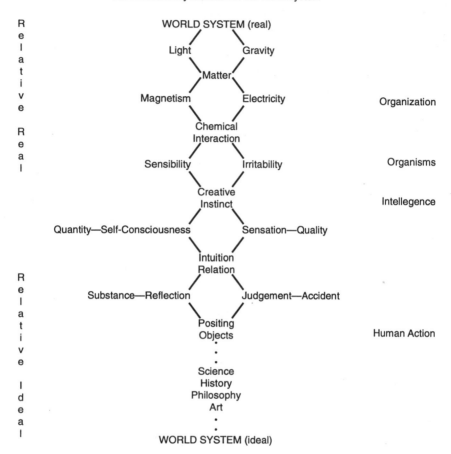

The Evolutionary Dialectic of the World system

Figure 2.5 Esposito's (1977) version of Schelling's world system. The column on the right represents levels of organization. The central column represents stages in a dialectical development from the original ("real") world to the ideal world created by humans. The system is epigenetic, since the higher levels (lower on the page) depend on the continued existence of the lower levels. Each jump from stage to stage represents a dialectical synthesis of the theses and antitheses opposed to each other at each level, moving from the top of the column to the lower. Reprinted, with permission, from Esposito 1977.

historical primacy) becomes possible with Hegel (and was surely reflected in later Marxist developments, however "materialist" they were supposed to be).

The early anthropologists (see Langness 1974) were concerned to show how anglo supremacy was the natural culmination of human sociocultural development (as was the Prussian state for Hegel, or, for that matter, some organism for Baer looking at its embryo). Their stages of development were constructed backwards from the state of British supremacy to simpler and simpler integrative stages that could be mapped onto more "primitive" cultures. The powerful sense of the inevitability (here, retrodictability) of this development was used in reverse by Marx, who, in a brilliant judo move, flipped the inevitability forward to predict the classless society. This aspect of Marx's discourse seems now to be withering away in favor of a neo-Marxist radical historicity just as those paragons of "the other" discourse, the neo-Darwinians, have purged all traces of developmentalism (and "anthropomorphism") from organic evolution (by dumping the likes of Cope (1896), Berg (1926), Schindewolf (1936), and even the later Julian Huxley)—and as cladists have purged evolutionary grades from systematics (Wiley 1981).

Marshall Sahlins (1960) attempted to reopen the mine of developmentalism in anthropology (his "general evolution" as opposed to the haphazard production of diversity, which he called "specific evolution"), basing his attempt partly on Huxley. His use of *general evolution* survives today in general systems discourse (Laszlo 1987; Csányi 1989), where, however, it is not carefully distinguished from specific evolution, which is what organic evolution discourse has come to be all about. Neo-Darwinians have in a sense captured the word 'evolution', and, in spite of the fact that in its earliest use it referred to development (as it still does in some Romance languages), it has now become so widely associated with synthetic evolutionary theory that it seems unwise to keep using it in the sense of general evolution. Let that meaning be taken by 'development', since that word is waiting to be used, however unfashionable it may be outside of economics. That is how I will proceed here.

In any case, Parsons (1977) explored the developmental mode of sociopolitical evolution in a way that explicitly emphasizes the priority of generality. A modern, broad-based exposition of stages of sociopolitical evolution can be found in Herbert 1981. That the idea of progress in sociocultural evolution is still a large issue in sociology itself (and in anthropology) is exemplified by its treatment in Ingold 1986 and in Dunnel 1988.

Comte narrowed down the universality of Romanticism to an ambition for the unity of the sciences. This he attempted, not from the reductionist perspective of the later Vienna/Chicago school (Neurath et al. 1955, 1970), but by way of integrative levels (Lenzer 1975). Epigenesis—the necessity for one stage to precede the next—gets transformed here into the logical priority of the more general sciences, upon which the superiority of the less general must be built. This is a classification scheme that was scotched (except in lower-level classrooms, so handy is it in teaching) with the ascent of reductionism in the end of the nineteenth century. It is interesting to note that Comte's approach to classifying all scientific knowledge (mathematics / astronomy / physics / chemistry / physiology / social physics) was revived much later (with Spencer rather than Comte cited as a forerunner) by the librarian J. L. Jolley (1973), whose truly ambitious work, extending to all knowledge, also combines both specification and scalar hierarchies.

Comte's influence on Spencer (1862) is clear; however, while Spencer largely restricted his attention to sciences more highly specified than biology, he (and also Peirce (see Turley 1977; Esposito 1980; Raposa 1989)) went far beyond Comte metaphysically. Indeed, they (separately—there is hardly anything else similar about them) matched Schelling in this regard in elaborating notions about a general systemic development of the world in which individuation is carried by the gradual delimitation of ever more kinds of ever more elaborate configurations. Spencer, who coined the term "general evolution" (Medawar 1982), in talking about the "instability of the homogeneous," used as specific examples the development of the earth from a hot ball of gases, the evolution of plants and animals from simpler ancestors, and the elaboration of supranational organizations from nations. I will take up this theme here in chapter 3 from the perspective of nonequilibrium thermodynamics.

In Peirce this idea reaches an awesome, Hegelian generality. The world begins as a mass of possibilities essentially of the same kind as mind (*synechism*—the unity of all aspects of the world; but, irreversibly, mind can become matter). It is creative at first, when the system is vague and unspecified, so that much that happens has the quality of chance (= creativity) as "thoughts" quickly fade and replace one another (*tychism*—the logical priority and historical primacy of chance). Gradually, *habits* come to be taken everywhere—e.g., matter would be a habitual form of energy, which is a potentiality generated from primordial mental possibilities in the context of constraints on the system—and (what we would call) information begins to accumulate throughout. This results in ever more elaboration as the world loses its primal possibilities and becomes ever more mechanistic and accessible to scientific exploration (to which mind, now embedded in organisms, becomes ever more restricted). As a system of interpretance, science itself follows the same trajectory from fluidity to arthritic articulation. Richness is preserved, however, because all information takes meaning from given perspectives, so that, as the system elaborates, the number of perspectives (shades of postmodernism!) does so as well. The world may well approach completion someday; however, science never will, because signs can only vaguely represent the actuality they stand for (inasmuch as they always originate in connection with limited perspectives) and so can be endlessly qualified by more signs.

Clements (1916) applied Spencer's notion that society could be viewed as a kind of "superorganism" (using the isomorphism gesture from H_{sc}) to ecosystems. He viewed ecological succession as a development of the kind we are interested in here—that is, epigenesis. Each stage in a sere prepared the way for succeeding ones as the large-scale system developed. Recently that perspective (still held by many systems ecologists) has come to be challenged by community ecologists (e.g., Simberloff (1980)) who are carrying the reductionist neo-Darwinian aversion to systems thinking into ecology. In this branch of our formation, the concept of senescence as a final stage for large-scale trajectories was explored by the historians Spengler (1932) and Toynbee (1934–1961). It has also begun to emerge in ecology in the works of Margalef (1968), the Odum brothers (see, e.g., H. T. Odum 1983), Holling (1986), and others. Concepts developed by Zotin (1972) and Schneider (1988) allow this to be more precisely formulated thermodynamically (Salthe 1989a; see chapter 3 below).

Piaget was trained as and considered himself a biologist, and it is therefore appropriate that he brought concepts like those of von Baer to developmental psychology. Piaget's structuralism (1970a) is transformational in an epigenetic sense. It is clear that he feels structures to somehow preexist their actualization, and this Platonic idea surfaces here and there in the formation we are considering. It is one way to explain predictability—that immanent structures act as attractors of material events. His "genetic epistemology" (1970b) embodies the priority of generality—thus, e.g., concepts of time and simultaneity are found to depend on the less specified, prior concept of speed (in the spirit of figure 1.2), just as predicate logic is a specialization of natural language. In Hegelian fashion, the history of logic discourse is claimed to show the same general stages found in psychological development, projecting that trajectory as an isomorphic structural attractor across scales.

This tradition of stages in the development of human personality was made more specified by Kohlberg (1969), who applied it to moral development. That there can be multiple later specializations during individuation was emphasized by Gilligan (1982) when she suggested that women's moral development might diverge from that of men in our culture (so she rediscovered the fact that development could be represented by a tree). This tradition has, of course, become a household tool for worried young mothers (Spock and Rosenberg 1985) isolated in our society, where help with child rearing is shifting from the extended family to the library.

Lewes and his successors, working in the emergentist/integrationist range of our formation (see the upper mid-left of figure 2.3) were concerned with the relationship between mind (or behavior) and biology (Salthe 1988). It was they who worried about emergence (e.g., how the properties of water can emerge out of a system that has initially only the properties of hydrogen and oxygen) before its recent rediscovery in connection with complex systems.

The integrationists explicitly tried to avoid biological determinism of the kind suggested by much of ethology and sociobiology, being latterly influenced in this direction by Marxism. This is why they emphasize the top-down integration of phenomena describable from the point of view of an observer of lower integrative levels. Thus, socially generated behaviors harness (see Polanyi 1968 for this usage) brain structure and even modify it—for example, by generating culture-specific lateralization in the human brain.

A related isolated peak of the developmentalist formulation is Jan Smuts' book *Holism and Evolution* (1926), where there is conflation of H_{sp} and H_{sc}. Emphasis on the top-down aspects, here of both H_{sp} and H_{sc}, generates the notion of "holism," which in Smuts' text is almost in danger of becoming another (upward) reductionism. That danger in fact manifested itself in a particularly concrete way in the thinking of Benito Mussolini (e.g., 1936).

Here we confront mythology head-on. Both emergentists and integrationists featured a strong sense of the innermost stages representing a developmental goal. For some this goal was God or at least spiritual transcendence; for others, human action; for still others it was the state. In all cases there was a flavor of eschatology involved. I think it fair to say that the specification hierarchy will never evade this involvement with valuation in its later stages, even though they might become associated with only a historically located, particular observer. In chapter 4 I will defend the mythological (but also structural) notion that what lies in wait for us in the innermost core of this structure is not spiritual transcendence but the machine.

Even from just this spotty tour, I think it fair to conclude that the intensional-complexity way of knowing is a major cognitive construct of Western discourse. That it is not foreign to Eastern thinking either is shown by its use in a Ch'an buddhist text (Hui Guang 1985) describing the stages of meditation as moving from the complicatedness of worldly connections through progressively simpler mind states, finally reaching "emptiness." Figure 2.6 shows this progression, and, since emptiness is far from nothing and really represents total possibility, the figure is not a bad visual mandala for the Schelling-Peirce-Spencer metaphysical vision if you run it backward.

General Rules of the Specification Hierarchy
The following (I–XIV) appear to be the general rules of the specification hierarchy. I do not present an actual table here comparing these rules with those of the scalar hierarchy because the structures of the two sets are incommensurable. In my view, no clear, concise, direct mapping of that kind is possible.

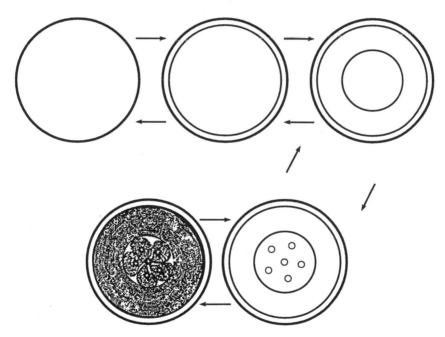

Figure 2.6 A Ch'an Buddhist representation of mind states, originally meant, following the arrows from lower left to upper left, to represent stages of meditation. The upper left represents emptiness or pure possibility. The arrows moving from this to the lower left would, as interpreted in this book, represent stages in the development of any physical entity. Adapted from Hui Guang 1985.

I: Logical transitivity. The most central trait of this hierarchy is that relations between integrative levels are fully transitive—e.g., I am a mammal every bit as much as I am human.

II: Integration. In the more obvious sense, social systems must continue to obey the laws of physics, and psychological phenomena cannot escape being rooted in biological constraints. Less obvious, but equally important, physical phenomena will be regulated, controlled, and harnassed by social systems, and biology will be regulated, controlled, and harnessed by psychological states.

III. Any entity may be located at different integrative levels, depending upon where the analysis is pitched, because every entity has more general (e.g., formal, systemic, or physical) properties and more particular (highly specified) ones (e.g., geographic, social, or psychological). Integrative levels are layers of increasingly specific constraints simultaneously in effect. Some systems (e.g., humans) appear to us to be subject to more such constraints and some (e.g., icicles) to fewer.

IV. The system is Hegelian in that, beginning in the innermost class, a semiotic/logical order of implication from the innermost level parallels a system of intensional constraint relations leading to conceptual subordination of the outermost levels to the innermost (a kind of finality). Beginning with the outermost class, it is also a system of nested classes of degree of specification representing emergent orders.

V: The logical priority of specificity. The presence of a higher integrative level implies the presence of lower, more general levels, not the reverse. The system privileges the most highly specified states, and these are its root in values as well.

VI. Because relations between levels in the system are transitive, there is no need for more than two levels at a time to be represented in models.

VII: Development. Because a two-level system is unstable, it will change so as to privilege one of the levels. Systems acquire their integrative levels developmentally—that is, by way of a knowable (predictable) sequence of *developmental stages.*

VIII. Each stage is broached by a qualitative jump and so represents an *emergence* of the next level.

IX: Epigenesis. Development is epigenetic, so that the stages cannot be scrambled and must follow a particular sequence.

X: Individuation. The canonical sequence is always from the more general (or vague) to the more specific (or definite). This is the *historical primacy of generality* (Baer's law).

XI. The sequence of stages is irreversible in any material system. It is here that the system connects with the Second Law of Thermodynamics (Salthe 1990b).

XII. Development is *generative;* it traverses a gradually narrowing field of potentialities, only one of which has a high propensity for being accessed at a given stage by mediation of arrangements of constraints, including those that are characteristic of the stage reached (see the discussion of this under "symmetry breaking" in Matsuno 1989). These potentialities can lead off in various alternative directions, which are not infinite in number at any stage (e.g., they are not possibilities, but potentialities proper), and are fewer in number the later the stage reached (see also Kauffman 1990).

XIII. The most highly specified state is always related to the observer in one way or another, sometimes as an eschatological goal. Therefore the system is characterized by a subjective relationship of the observer to the innermost level.

XIV. The system of integrative levels reflects the categorial reach of some observer, extending from the most general types relevant to some classification to the most specific (highly specified). It is therefore truncated below by an outermost level and above by the innermost.

I am not claiming that any of the historical examples discussed in connection with figure 2.3 directly involves all these rules, still less that any of these early workers had them all in mind while stressing one or two of them. I am saying that, as a matter of logic, these 14 rules all hang together in a systemic relationship—no more or less than I implied for the rules of H_{sc}. The formation's structure is logical. Thus, e.g., if one uses the specification hierarchy rather than the scalar one to describe some situation, one must be prepared to have to delve into its generation. That would be logically unnecessary when using scalar discourse, which is implicitly synchronic.

The sense that I am trying to project here is that this discursive formation was only revealed gradually in history, so that even now we are perhaps not aware of further aspects of it. This sense is conveyed somewhat by Whitehead's (1933) title *Adventures of Ideas.* Discovery of further aspects of a formation is attained by logical exploration and excavation. One can use the term "discovery" here because formations are held together by logics. I do not dispute the fact that knowledge is constructed by historically located social systems (Fleck 1935; Kuhn 1962; Geertz 1983; Unger 1987); however, in the case before us, which is similar in this sense to the situation in mathematics, what that explains is the actual historical precedence of the discovery of different aspects of the structure of a formation. This is why Foucault's thinking about formations as impersonal movements beyond the reach of individual persons is important in today's postmodern intellectual climate, and can help to prevent a wholesale solipsism of recursivly spinning local knowledges by forcing logical coherence.

Integrative Levels and Intensional Complexity
Specification hierarchies are shown in parts A and C of figure 2.1. From one point of view the contents of such a hierarchy are arranged as levels of generality of statement (Salthe 1985); from another, they are arranged as integrative levels (Salthe 1988), with the most general level represented as a class whose members are other classes nested within it as subclasses—the increasingly more highly specified ones progressively nested within the less specified (see also figure 1.2).

The synchronic structure here can be revealed when we realize that at any moment we are free to explore or speak about an object in many different ways, subject to disciplinary and historical constraints. If we are concerned with cells, for example, we can consider them as black boxes with inputs and outputs, or we can do as cell biologists do and examine their organelles or their development. Instead, we might with molecular biologists and biochemists, view cells as chemical entities. Or, along with biophysicists, we can think of them as systems of diffusion along gradients or across membranes. There is no privileged perspective here, only the overlapping multiplicity of intensional complexity. It is not more true that a cell is a metabolic system than that it is the social building block of a tissue or a population. All these perspectives are valid and presumably useful in some discourse. Viewing the cell one way makes other ways transparent, and they are, in fact, then taken for granted.

Thus, we can see that integrative levels are simultaneous presences making up what Buchler (1966) called the *integrities* of an object in various semiotic orders. Here, each discipline supplies an order, which is capable of constructing an integrity for the object from that point of view. For example, a cell is represented biochemically as a network of chemical reactions called a *metabolic chart*, which, as a summary of many works, is the biochemical integrity of a cell. We see here that intensional complexity has a strong semiotic connection. Each integrative level from which an object may be apprehended is the construct of an order of discourse—in fact, is an integrity—and, taken together, they all make up the *contour* of that object (its overall integrity in space-time). Minimally, this object is a culture's construct related to its general ways of ordering experience.

But, on taking a meta-perspective on this situation, it is clear, as Comte pointed out, that there is an organization to these integrities such that, if they are explored in a particular sequence, the contour of an object gradually becomes more and more detailed in configuration. There is only one, therefore canonical, sequence that allows this—for example, an object may be viewed as a physical object first, then a chemical one, then (if appropriate) a biological one, then (if still appropriate) a sociological one, then (if it continues to be appropriate) a psychological one. And one could begin anywhere in the middle and work in toward the more specified discourses.

A biologist can make her statements about cells (as in teaching) only because, explicitly or implicitly, a biochemist has already made his. This does not imply that statements about (or studies concerning) biology cannot be made at the level of biology, without reference to chemistry. That would be an indefensible reductionist position; in any case, it would be refuted by history, since some of biology was constructed before chemistry ever existed. What is implied here is that, in the search for the metaphysical object itself, for its contour, if we were to deploy biological knowledge before chemical knowledge (which should be present, at least implicitly), the picture we get would be fragmented, incoherent, and somewhat dissociated from the rest of nature, having a kind of arbitrariness to which students tend to respond with incomprehension and dogged rote learning. In an ontological sense, since there are no biological systems that are not also chemical but many chemical ones that are not biological, chemistry is required to be present before there can be biology in the world, and so, for intelligibility, it ought to be pedagogically.

In the terminology of Sabelli and Carlson-Sabelli (1989), while the more general integrities have "primacy," the more specified ones are "superior." This means (1) that descriptions at more specified levels tend to be closer to the observer, are more familiar, and so are more commonsensical (referring to familiar objects such as icicles)—that is, they tend to be more *intelligible,* and (2) that configurations imposed at more specified levels exercise constraint capabilities, by way of boundary conditions, over those at more general levels. The first point is obvious; the second can be explored more fully with our example of the cell.

Given the substrates available in a cell and the cell's general conditions of pH and temperature, the chemical reactions that could take place on the basis of the equilibrium constants make up a much larger set than those that actually do take place there. The cell suppresses most of them by way of enzyme mediation. As a catalyst, an enzyme favors a given reaction so much more than other possibilities, and so speeds it up, that all other reactions fade into a tiny background noise (Degani and Halmann 1965). From this conversation among enzymes emerge flow configurations that are mutually synergetic and are entrained by the overall cellular structure, from which they derive a coherence that is very much greater than what might have emerged from the turbulence that would result from the free, unorganized, "in vitro" activity of all potential reactions. A coherence of mutually synergetic, synchronized patterns (Wolkowski 1985, 1986, 1988) is what, in general, is created by relatively stable boundary conditions—provided, in this case, by biology through (a) accurate replacement of worn-out key chemical parts guided by genomic information and (b) a physical superstructure of membranes and cytoskeleton.

Yet we could describe the chemical reactions themselves, as if the cell had become transparent, so that we would see only molecules racing about—much as we see people racing about in a city. This would deliver a molecular, chemical description; however, a knowledgeable chemist would have to wonder how the orderliness was obtained, and would search for organizational principles. These principles *are* in this case what we call biology. Hence, a biological system is a chemical system highly constrained to certain relatively few pathways.

Look again at people in a city. Here are biological systems doing things that create patterns of flow similar to those in the cell. They are constrained—consider that even on the streets of New York, where almost anything goes, you can in a flash imagine dozens of kinds of human behaviors that are not in fact happening. The social system, including its physical superstructure (there is no straight line from Seventh Avenue and 59th Street to Fifth Avenue and 42nd Street), constrains all these activities. So, biology is regulated by society (recall the buzzards in chapter 1) just as chemistry is regulated by biology, and that is the essence of the meaning of "integration" in integrative levels.

So, there is an ontic, dynamical aspect to integrative levels, as well as an explicitly descriptive one (levels of generality of statement). We can make the most general kinds of statements, applicable to the most different kinds of systems, about entities that might come to be constrained by the greatest number of superior levels of specification. These kinds of entities (say, molecules) can be found everywhere (in the imagination, anyway). Note also that these objects are more general also in the sense that we do not ascribe other than gross differences between them. Every glucose molecule is held to be the same as every other, no matter where they are found. On scalar hierarchical principles, this would have to be justified because entities at every scale are in that discourse taken to be equally complex. But specification discourse requires that entities discernible at more general, less specified levels be considered more alike, more readily interchangeable, and so less complex than those at higher levels. Here we find a major structural difference between these two hierarchical perspectives, in both of which, nevertheless, the statement "a cell is at a higher level than a glucose molecule" makes sense.

Summing up: Integrative levels are integrities constructed for objects from the perspectives of various discourses (chemical, social, and so on.). There is a canonical ranking of these levels such that more general statements (say, physical and molecular) are deployed in connection with lower integrative levels, which are then foundational for further statements that might be made at higher levels of specification. Entities describable at higher levels by way of more specified integrities (social, psychological) require more detailed description, on the one hand; on the other hand, they have constraint capabilities with respect to entities (e.g. molecules) describable only by way of more general integrities. It is as if these latter were relatively unfinished, lost, and deranged without further guidance from the more specified levels (and what they lack in such a formulation is, precisely, final causes, which are supplied by higher levels). This structure makes up the intensional complexity of objects in nature.

Logical transitivity across integrative levels   A major difference between scalar and specification hierarchies lies in the relations between levels. In the scalar hierarchy, these are relations between entities found at different levels as wholes and parts. In the specification hierarchy, they are relations between the levels themselves. Any entity embodies many such integrative levels within it, which are its integrities from the different discursive perspectives (or semiotic orders) of outside observers. Entities here are contours, or overall integrities in space-time. Entities in the scalar hierarchy are, instead, wholes with nested parts extending downward in scale indefinitely.

In the scalar hierarchy, events and processes at different levels are screened off from one another by distance in scale. No process continues, as such, at more than a single level, so there can be no dynamical transitivity across scalar levels. Relations between entities at different scalar levels are, precisely, nontransitive and of the nature of indirect constraints—not, more strongly, 'intransitive', because fluctuations (especially from higher levels) do episodically descend and mingle dynamically with lower-level processes as catastrophic perturbations, often causing major reorientations and reconfigurations at the lower level. This situation of noninteractive constraint capability punctuated by (heterarchical) material perturbations is the essence of extensional complexity.

In the specification hierarchy, an observer (or different observers) can simultaneously perceive or imagine the way an entity is represented at several integrative levels. In this sense, I am every bit as much a dissipative structure as I am a vertebrate, or a mammal, or an autonomous system, or a white, middle-class, anglo male—and so on.

I can be just as fully classified at any of these levels without prejudicing or sacrificing further classification at other levels. That is the epistemological part of the situation, which has an additive character because description at one level does not necessarily disturb description at another. Just as entities are embedded as parts within larger wholes in the scalar hierarchy, so they are embedded as semiotic objects inside a network of discourses in the specification hierarchy.

The ontological part of specification is that natural laws working within or through me are constrained (informed, regulated) by material, chemical laws, and these by biological configurations, and these by social necessities, and these by psychological peculiarities. This aspect is fully nonadditive, all the constraints intermingling simultaneously at any point, so that the effects of even the highest-level constraints are present in any event, even if that event is described at the lowest level—which is what 'integration' and superiority are all about. (In the scalar hierarchy, on the contrary, with the exception of perturbations, only three levels need be considered for their contributions to a process at any moment, and constraints from these levels can be separated conceptually into different kinds, as in the Aristotelian system (Salthe 1985).) The promiscuous multiplicity of influences in H_{sp}, both semiotically and materially (as integrative constraints), is the essence of intensional complexity.

No analysis has yet delivered a framework for disentangling the effects of different integrative levels such as we have in the basic triadic system for the scalar hierarchy. What we have instead is a strong protocol for developmental priority embodied in the concept of epigenetic individuation, from which it may be possible to work toward an analytical tool.

Integrative Levels as Developmental Stages
That specification logic has an intrinsically developmental structure was realized by Aristotle. There is only one sequence of integrative levels in any collection of them from one object that allows that object to be discerned in a logical, orderly manner—from more general perspectives to the more limited and detailed. Since this canonical sequence allows an observer (somewhat in the manner of Goethe's developmental botany (Brady 1986)) to conceptually construct the object (as a contour) gradually from its various integrities, thinking of objects actually forming that way too comes to seem irresistible. So the polarity of specification logic strongly calls forth the idea of an irreversible trajectory of individuation.

And when we observe developing systems, that is undeniably what we do see as well. Those kinds of natural objects that self-organize before our eyes, such as embryos, do it in just this way, basic *Anlagen* being followed by more peripheral ones, which are then followed by fine details. Furthermore, when an artist works on paper or in stone (or a bird on a nest) the same sequence is followed: sketching or hewing is followed by detailed chiaroscuro or fine chipping. This is the reverse of Simon's (1969) scalar hierarchical logic of assembly. Simon showed that complex manufactured objects such as watches are best assembled not all at once but by putting the smaller pieces together into larger modules, which are then assembled into still larger ones until the whole is finally fitted together, as on an assembly line. This polarity allows the greatest stability in the face of perturbations. Now, this is reminiscent of the way we reconstruct a natural development from its later stages (and of how we construct a phylogeny).

So, if we are faced with a collection of different stages (say, fish embryos collected in a plankton net), we go step by step, laboriously finding the next most similar embryo to the last one added to the sequence, so as not to lose track. We begin such sequences with what seems like the most highly developed example, because we can recognize it as being of a species we are interested in. If in our search for the egg we tried to make large jumps back, skipping stages, we would make more errors and would more frequently have to try over again. If, on the other hand, we began with the attractor of our observations, an unhatched egg, we could not tell which next-most-developed embryo really was of the species we were interested in, and we would wind up constructing many branching series, hoping that one would lead to our fish. So there is a privileged direction in reconstructing the series: from the most complex to the simplest. This feels like assembly from particular parts to the whole for the following reasons: In all the cases here, the overall (or undeveloped, unpacked, fully assembled) object is more stable and more secure than its detailed parts (or its potential efflorescences). This has several meanings. In natural systems the earlier stages are those a greater number of individual tokens are certain to reach; the later, more detailed stages lie behind curtains of wear, abnormality, and mortality, requiring ever more, and more specific, affordances. The later, senescent configurations of natural systems, showing many of the effects of individuation, are, from any point of view, highly improbable one and all. They are also relatively brittle and more easily perturbed (see chapter 3); the comparative plasticity of early embryonic stages is of course well known. For manufactured objects, the final state, epitomized by the arch, has a stability that the scattered parts, if viewed *as* parts, do not have. Only the whole would *be* an arch (or an automobile) and survive in use.

It seems, then, that when we build technologically we work somewhat as though reconstructing a development. Both directly, of course, involve energy-consuming processes. Heat is produced during both reconstruction and development, but the potential for change or use is stored up only in reconstruction (and factory assembly). Developments lead instead to senescence and dissipation. Langer (1967) has suggested that our constructions are metaphors of ourselves, and that seems to emerge here too, but with an important qualification. While the process of production of works of art and of simple artifacts such as hand axes follows the polarity of natural developments, the process of the coming about of a complicated technological artifact is the reverse of our own emergence, moving from elaborated bits and pieces toward wholeness (see also Koch 1986). The final causes of technological construction, and, apparently, those of the reconstruction of developments and phylogenies, are stable states (collections of objects that are the same, as is a collection of many species of blastulae, or a collection of toasters ready to go, or a stable phylogeny) with potentials for use or development, whereas a final cause of natural development (and of art) is the instability and uniqueness of the highly particular, unpredictable, senescent individual (object). Natural developments in fact are not unlike deductions, and technological ones are more like induction. BCNDC science, wedded to inductive empiricism, has not been able to lead us toward an understanding of development for perhaps this very reason.

The canonical polarity of natural development, then, is from holistic unification toward greater and more explicit elaboration and multiplicity; this is what is spontaneous. Every next, more integrated, developmental stage requires more statements to describe, because there are now more regions or parts to describe. And, of course, also because the nature of the previous stage is not transcended by integration—the basic rules applicable then are still applicable now. So, a gastrula is certainly more complicated than a blastula. But also, like the latter, it is still a multicellular organism, and still an autopoietic, autonomous, thermodynamically open chemical system. All these descriptions are implicitly still required, in addition to those that tell us it is has become a triploblastic animal. Hence, we note that the actual, embodied, information stored in such a system is continually added to.

Now, a genetic reductionist might want to claim that all the information necessary to allow the full development of an organism from its egg is already present in the zygote. Even if this were true (and a scalar hierarchical perspective implicitly denies this), what is of concern here is the actual embodied information, found in form and behavior as viewed by an observer of the system. The genome and the translation apparatus and other cellular configurations make up part of that explicitly embodied information, but "genetic information" (in the sense of the meanings of the base sequences at various levels for the system containing it) does not. Kampis (1991a) denies that we could measure this "referential information." This would not be referential information to a system that does not use it. If one probes a cell to describe it in detail, one *could* work down to recording base sequences *per se*, but not to what another semiotic system, the cell itself, can do with that information in particular situations. That would be an integrity in another order.

What I have described here entails the emergence of complexity, as defined in the introduction. On the one hand, as a token of some developmental process achieves further stages, its minimal description by an outside observer would need to increase; the number of orders it may be perceived in also increases; and it has taken significant time (at its own temporal scale) to achieve its present condition. Usually also, somewhere along the developmental trajectory, there occurs one or more increases in scale (Salthe 1991b). On the other hand, as many examples of the same type of development proceed, individuation in the collection accumulates, driving them to continually diverge (Matsuno 1989). This results in a large increase in the minimal description within the collection (as suggested in Brooks and Wiley 1988), because at least some of these historical changes are not predetermined or implicit in whatever stored information was present in the collection of tokens to begin with.

We might compare this with the situation of technological assembly. Here the internal description is complete at the beginning. Each part and its relationships are predetermined, and any significant mutations will, we hope, be discarded. Relative to its scale when completed, the time to assemble it is small (in contrast with really complex objects). The scale of the object seems to increase with assembly, but in most cases there is really only an increase in size. Surely examples of machines with operating parts of different scale are rare—computers are one example though, and with many new materials coming forth allowing design at the molecular level, examples will probably become more common. Such a machine's minimal description by an outside observer *would* have to be increased, however, especially after it begins to function; so one aspect of complexity (its information capacity) does seem to increase in assembly, just as heat production is not evaded. Natural development is nature's way of increasing complexity. The broaching of a new stage of development involves a genuine *emergence*—the appearance of something qualitatively really new, or different from what had been. Systems in which emergences occur are undoubtedly complex. Their minimal internal description is highly problematic, both because what it describes can become distorted by history and still survive and because it must allow jumps to radically different modes of being during crossings between stages. It seems to need to be viewed as an internal description that itself becomes modified with development, or that, in Hegelian fashion, modifies itself along with what it describes (this perhaps being an important aspect of the self-organization of living systems). This is why notions of complete descriptions residing in zygotic genomes are absurd.

Epigenesis As was noted above, the canonical logic of superimposing increasingly numerous and highly specified integrities when building up the contour of a natural object leads one to imagine the same sequence for its development. And that notion seems justified by observation. If there is only one sequence that reconstructs an object from observations in an orderly manner, it might be reasonable to suppose that stages of natural development must also occur in a given sequence such that stages could not easily be left out and could never be switched around. Thus, something must first be a biological entity before it could be social; and before it can acquire the characteristics of living things it must be a chemical system. So much seems reasonable—except, perhaps, to proponents of artificial life! (My answer to the claim I would project from their perspective is that any lifelike system set up by them will have been mediated by living systems (themselves) and so could not escape having been archaically chemical/biological.)

Furthermore, if one imagined a mixed-up development, one could project the possibility of, say, fingernails or claws developing before there are digits. Indeed, some ovarian tumors have this kind of differentiation, taking place in a system that had no orderly morphogenesis. While such scrambled developments appear not, therefore, to be entirely prohibited in nature (and we need to understand fundamentally why not), they do always seem to be nonfunctional and unable to conspire to be perpetuated, and so they are always partly accidental.

One hears occasional claims about some of the later stages of development being switched in some organisms. It seems possible that this might occur, but only after basic morphogenesis has taken place. Wimsatt (1986) and Arthur (1988) provide general discussions supporting my argument for developing organisms; Rosen (1984) notes that cases of stage switching might better be thought of as loss of the earlier stage followed by a new construction after the later stage, in which forms develop that somewhat resemble those lost with the earlier stage. I would like to analyze this situation in a more general way, using notions from infodynamics.

Development can be viewed as a tree diagram (Arthur 1988), with vague early stages followed by branching whereby more and more subsystems gain access to more integrative levels as a system's regions differentiate. Brooks and Wiley (1988) suggest that, insofar as this pattern is necessary, it could be viewed as showing an acquisition of informational entropy (Maze and Scagel 1983)—an expansion of the system into an informational sink that, because of the immense number of informational transformations that might still be possible, never approaches an "equilibrium." This would be a spontaneous process of equilibration (Matsuno 1989) in the informational realm.

It is easily seen that, if we tried to move from an end state in one branch to one in another (e.g., from nerves to liver cells), development would have to reverse itself first. But all developments we know of are irreversible. We need to see why that is so. Logically, if the forward transformations are thought of as having been originally discovered by random search, or by opportunistic selection of states that advance equilibration, then the probability of getting a sequence of reverse changes in just the right order is essentially nil. This improbability of natural reconstruction would be true also if the accession of new states is chaotic, in which case the numerous potential states themselves were somehow implicit in the preceeding stage. Here again, reconstruction is not the spontaneous process.

But what if the discovery of new states in later stages is (and has been) systemic in some way? Should this not allow for reversals? Here we need to expand our discussion to examine tree processes in a general way. I will call the general structure involved a *cascading/collecting cycle*. We can begin with a cascade: from a storage pool of substance (which could be informational or material) there is a spontaneous flow outward, an expansion accompanied by the loss of free energy. If this flow is not uniform from a given surface, as it would be in free diffusion, it can cascade or ramify outward contagiously, as in the spread of a disease or a fire (which continues to be eliminated from where it has been) or of a cultural item (which is not). Next there is a return of substance to the pool, a pulling together accompanied by the acquisition of free energy, building the pool as various collecting networks converge toward it. This phase must be driven by a source of energy. In a simple idealization of this overall structure, both processes could be thought of as taking place through trees. We can now examine some actual examples.

One relatively simple example is the hydrological cycle on Earth. The expansion is carried by evaporation of water from its free surfaces; this is accomplished directly anywhere, with only a bias toward greater cascading along the associated tree patterns of streams. Large-scale motion of the atmosphere, driven by solar energy, results in condensation of the water into rain, which is collected by gravitational energy into basins. Evaporation occurs along fluid trees floating above aquifers (rills, brooks, rivers) in a gradient from high flux along the relatively turbulent sources to low flux from the collecting basins (Hsu 1988; Stull 1988). Here a tree appears as the form of the channels containing the flow of surface water back to the collecting basins, along which some of the evaporation occurs too. I wish to point out these formal properties:

> (1) There is a very large collecting area; rain can fall almost anywhere. (Of course, oozing from aquifers can also occur from almost anywhere too, but I am interested in focusing on the tree structures here.) The trees in this case "cascade" outward from the basins, as pathways for the collection of free energy (as liquid water). The cascading *process*, however, is spontaneous evaporation (diffusion), and it only partly involves these trees.
> (2) There are central collecting basins for the storage of free energy. These basins are somewhat like sinks in that they can never really be filled up.
> (3) The peripheral regions of the tree are characterized by greater energy flux (causing, among other things, enhanced evaporation). These are regions of high entropy production as gravitational energy is avidly converted to heat by frictional scouring. We could say that these regions are thermodynamically immature relative to the basins.

Consider now, for comparison, a forest tree (Zimmerman and Brown 1971):

> (1) There is a very large area for the collection of solar energy and CO_2, and, in the roots, for water and minerals. This area continues to expand at the expense of free energy during growth of the tree. The branches cascade outward as the tree fills space only through the use of free energy. But there is also a cascading *process* in this case other than the ramifying, free-energy-using growth itself: the transpirational loss of water and the diffusive disposition of oxygen. Both are spontaneous but can be regulated by the tree through stomates. What cascades outward, then, is not the same as what is collected in this case. That situation defines *waste* or *pollution*.
> (2) Much of the free energy collected at the periphery is circulated rather promiscuously throughout the periphery of tree, most of it being used *in situ* there. Of course, one ought to consider the entire tree as a basin for chemical energy, and its necessary growth pattern, given gravitational force, involves the bulk of matter being pulled into the central trunk and the major roots. Hence, the forest tree could be viewed as a sink-like storage

"basin" for chemical free energy. As in the hydrological example, this acquisition of free energy is made possible by the expenditure of free energy (again from the sun), but this acquisition is largely routed internally through the tree itself instead of by way of coupled, larger-scale environmental flows. The tree is built from within, as it were—it is autopoietic. The central portion is sink-like in a more limited way than in the first example; there is a limit to the size of the tree, and its growth gradually slows down in senescence. Yet, during its life there is no actual block, or even negative feedback, to its continually building itself.

(3) The periphery of the tree is clearly thermodynamically immature relative to bulk of its storage basin; and almost all the entropy production takes place there.

We can now examine a central nervous system (CNS). Information, in this case, is carried from almost anywhere on the surface of the organism of which it is part.

(1) The collecting surface area is large relative to the central nervous system. Nerves cascade out toward the periphery. Here, however, there is a tree, not only for collecting, but also for dissipating information (see Wicken 1987 for this usage) peripherally, in the behavior of the organism. Both processes occur at the expense of free energy, so in this case the cascading/collecting cycle has no spontaneous cascade, as do the other two examples; this may be related to our considering information here rather than energy, and only a small part of a global system. Of course, we do say that the CNS evinces "spontaneous" activity. If this could be related to random or chaotic fluctuations (driving random search), then there would be reason to consider the outward cascading of effector information to be "spontaneous" in an infodynamic sense. That behaviorist model has seemed sensible to many. So, while this system may lack the thermodynamic spontaneity of the others, both cascading and collecting are embodied as trees. There is an interesting consequence of the requirement for free energy in the outward flow of information in that this information need not only cascade from the center, but can, and often does, *focus* from many central regions at a single peripheral point; no spontaneous cascading process accomplishes that. In this case this is effected largely by the earlier free-energy-utilizing cascade of neuronal growth to the target areas, which, as in the forest trees, does fit our model.

(2) The unit form of this system is the simple reflex, the linkage of sensory neurons with effector neurons. These joints tend in

evolution to get pulled together into a central place and connected through an elaboration of associative neurons, the CNS
itself. The internal, cyclic behavior of the CNS serves to actively
store cycling information by entraining superposed patterns
(Minsky 1981). Note again that, in dealing with information, even
cascading, as well as storage, requires the active use of free
energy. So, the cascading/collecting structure can be actualized
in many different ways without disturbing its fundamental structure, *which is not, therefore, physically thermodynamic in any fundamental sense*, even though abiotic examples are embodied largely
spontaneously. Such spontaneous structures can be built upon by
evolutionary processes, so that systems of different degree of
specification can access the same structural attractors. The free
energy in the case of the nervous system is supplied by the
organism, which must locate itself ecologically somewhere in the
spontaneous large-scale cascade of energy (usually from the sun)
on its way to the sink in space (Wicken 1987; Weber et al. 1989).
In a way, the CNS appears to be a kind of sink for information;
however, as in the forest tree, there are aging processes imposing
ultimate limits, and in the few kinds of organisms that actually
do get a chance to senesce significantly before being recycled
these processes may diminish continued storage before death.

(3) In seeking to apply the thermodynamic immaturity criterion
here, we may note that the periphery of the nervous system is
characterized by a variety of modes of interaction, with many
physical carriers of information. Transduction at the periphery
converts all this multifarious stuff into a single informational
cash: the nerve impulse. I believe that variety and uncertainty
characterize this scanning periphery much more than the central,
cycling system, which, by definition of cycling, is more or less
predictable and so relatively less disorderly in its behavior, and
so relatively less entropic than the periphery—hence, functionally more "mature" in the thermodynamic sense. The fact of its
being a storage area reinforces this interpretation. Storage is nothing if not relatively stable, and that is what memory and other
central phenomena must be. We can also toss in the fact that
neurons are not turning over, as are peripheral cell types, so that
they would be statistically more mature in this traditional sense
as well. Furthermore, as the nervous system grows, it cascades
outward toward the periphery, not unlike the forest tree, so that
even in this sense the periphery is relatively immature.

We can now move toward the point of this section by examining
another case of cascading/collecting involving only information: phy-

logeny. For these purposes it is better to abandon the usual dichotomous stick figures and think of phylogeny as a material object not
unlike a coral head, with only the periphery containing living taxa.
The justification for this can be generated using H_{sc}; the cogent moment of the biosphere (*sensu* Suess 1875) is almost as large as that of
the earth itself. Hence, what seems to us to be many years is to this
system only a single moment, such that the whole phylogeny exists
simultaneously at a single large-scale moment.

Cascading in phylogeny is the expansion of the system into informational phase space (Brooks and Wiley 1988). The expansion is spontaneous because it takes focused energy to *maintain* informational
configurations, not to erode them, multiplying types. So, mutation and
recombination inevitably disorder what was ordered to begin with in
biological genome space. That this particular disordering could not
take place without biological systems maintaining themselves and
reproducing at the expense of free energy is beside the point, because
phylogenetic cascading is, relative to such concrete organismic matters,
an abstract fact about a portion of the larger-scale system (the earth)
that uses these biological activities as a material cause.

As a concrete analogy, consider the decomposition of a cadaver. Here
too the destruction of an initial order could not be accomplished
without the hot complicity of biological systems producing more of
themselves in relatively orderly fashion. But decay itself is spontaneous nevertheless, because the detritivores are driven to use up the free
energy stored in the cadaver. That using up *is* the disordering of the
cadaver. The increase in variety of kinds in the biosphere (more genes,
more genotypes, more niches, more morphological diversity) is formally like the decomposition of a cadaver in that both disorderings
(increases in information capacity) are generated as biproducts (almost
epiphenomena) of the proximate use of free energy by organisms as
each replicates its own order at a lower level.

But what does collecting amount to in the phylogenetic system? It
must be informational and have a movement logically the reverse of
cascading (here, an increase in information capacity). In fact, it can be
seen to be the deepening of the chain of implication from the latest
originated types at the periphery of the "coral." What is now implies
what just was, and that what was before, and so on. Once more, it
helps to view the whole phylogeny as an entity like a coral at a single
one of its cogent moments. Then you can see that implication here is
transitive, as it should be; what is logically true must be true all at
once throughout a system. And, of course, cladistic methodology
(Wiley 1981; Wiley et al. 1990) is a mode of manipulating implications.
The tree of implication is holistic in that it belongs to the phylogeny

as a whole; if there is a need in systematic practice to change one branch, the whole phylogeny is likely to reorganize.

Finally, we can move to understand the question that launched us into cascading/collecting cycles: why ontogeny cannot be reversible (and so must be epigenetic). The reversibility we need to interdict is that during cascading. Cascading formally must be in some sense (thermodynamically or infodynamically) spontaneous as in the other examples. That is, despite the reductionist program of molecular developmental biology (which has so far failed—see Salthe 1987), differentiation must be viewed as spontaneous, not as the result of a "program" (see Oyama 1985 for a critique of programs in this context). The production of standardized tissues and forms needs to be viewed as the highly probable (though not inevitable) results of the workings of some basic triadic system. Genetic initiating conditions are guided by spatial boundary conditions in each embryo *each time as if it were happening for the first time*. There is no program except in the RNA signs that inform lower-level initiating conditions. At the focal level there is only a dynamical moving from attractor to attractor as development proceeds. Cascading here, then, as in phylogeny, is the increase in information capacity during differentiation (Brooks and Wiley 1988).

In support of this view we can note that differentiation continues throughout life in every cell with the accumulation of somatic mutations and episomes (Martin 1981; Bernstein et al. 1985). It is not programmed to stop at some mature stage. This excessive differentiation too results in standard tissues, albeit morbid ones—various well-defined tumors, and other abnormalties such as classifiable age spots in the skin. No major results other than morbidity occur, probably because the organism has long since been devoting most of its energy to reproduction instead of growth.

Differentiation, on this view, should not be able to reverse itself. We then need to face the supposed evidence for dedifferentiation in certain cases of regeneration (Sicard 1985). Like the supposed immortality of certain organisms, this is a "fact" which the entire perspective of this work suggests needs to be reevaluated. Blastemal cells, of course, look embryonic and behave so as well, and do appear in some cases to come from differentiated cells, but the viewpoint necessarily adopted here suggests that these appearances are in fact due to new responses of differentiated cells, perhaps not unlike what happens when some kinds of cells seem to dedifferentiate in the process of adapting to tissue culture. Their similarity to blastomeres may only reflect a limited number of structures available for a cell to access.

What, then, is collected during ontogeny? The key word here is 'integration'. Every new stage reintegrates the effects of all previous stages holistically. What was accomplished in (say) neurulation is taken over, coopted, and made its own by the tail bud embryo. The wholeness of the informational system is maintained in this way. It is a systemic effect (conceptual subordination) somewhat like the logical one of implication in phylogenetic trees, but concrete and much richer. Implication and conceptual subordination both cumulate and build upon the continued results of spontaneous cascading. What is built in phylogeny is a unified chain of implication—in ontogeny, and increasingly complicated integrated system.

Thus, the infodynamical support for the necessity of the irreversibility of epigenesis has to do with differentiation being a cascading—that is, a spontaneous necessity, which, in order to move in reverse, would have to cumulate a series of low-probability events such that it simply is very highly unlikely and thus happens so seldom as to be invisible to developmental discourse, which always focuses on commonalities.

Forms of Zeno's Paradox in Hierarchy Theory
Continued development of a system results ultimately in the transcendence of one stage through the acquisition of the next. The point I want to make in this subsection has to do with the necessity for this kind of event to be represented as a jump, a discontinuity, requiring a digital, as opposed to an analog, perspective (Wilden 1980). Once more we seem to have a structure before us, insofar as this necessity is present in both H_{sc} and H_{sp} (Salthe 1991a).

In H_{sc} the developing system invariably grows in size and/or in throughput. After a time, continuous growth has the result that size increases to such a point that the dynamics of something of that size could interact with the dynamics of what, at the beginning of growth, would have been the environment of the growing system. Viewed through the basic triadic system, focal-level dynamics have led to an increase in the size of focal-level entities to such an extent that they now could, through their own dynamical behavior, have provided boundary conditions on their own earlier dynamics, were these phenomena simultaneous. The problem can be focused by noting that the dynamics responsible for changing a relevant variable in an equation describing growth will have increased in scale to such a degree that these dynamics could now interact with processes responsible for changing the values of some of the constant parameters in the equation.

This situation is not so easily described as simply saying that a variable has become a constant. A variable may become constant when it ceases to change—from a given perspective, in a given integrity. A relevant perspective here would be that of an entity at the scale of the original growing subject—an egg cell, a colony of a society, a passing glance. What has become of this germ is such that what might have deeply stirred it back then would not be noticed at all now. And, indeed, there would now be secondnesses buffeting the subject that could not have been noticed then—as ripples would not notice the waves they ride on—before they had been incoporated into the subject's umwelt by its own increase in scale.

But *when* does this particular transcendence happen? In a continuity there is no such point—it might, precisely, be anywhere. As mimicked by a digital model, a bifurcation might occur chaotically somewhere along a range of values of some parameter, depending on the original rounding-off scheme, but I would suppose an analog description of this situation to be impossible—unless components of the analog model could grow. In fact, there would seem to be reason to suppose that we do not have continuous *descriptions* in our repertoire at all. It is here that we explicitly meet one of Zeno's paradoxes. (See Kampis 1991a for further discussion on the resurgence of Zeno's paradoxes, which involve more than just the issue of contiuum versus discreteness relevant here.)

Consider the real numbers, our scientific model of continuity. There is no continuous progress possible from one number to another, because the trajectory falls into a black hole of endlessly receding decimal points. Similarly, in Zeno, if one halves the distance between here and some distant goal with each step, one will never reach it. Thus, the tortoise might seem to beat the hare in a race if placed at a proper distance closer than the hare to a finishing line set between that distant point and the hare. The hare would actually disappear from the field much more rapidly than the tortoise as they diminished in size exponentially, and before the latter's snout was just about to touch the finish line. To get anywhere on the real line, there must always be a jump from one value to another. In practice, the size of this jump is set by the scale of one's tools—the number of significant decimal places in a measurment.

Even if the scale boundary were fuzzy (Negoita 1981), it too would have to be represented by a jump—(1) trivially, because that is how we must always represent change in digital discourse (note, e.g., the digital aspects of the genetic code), (2) because the precise boundary depends on initial conditions that are unknowable in practice beyond a few decimal points, and which are often arbitrary from the point of view of observation, and (3) because, if one tried to use an analog description, some components of the model itself must smoothly grow, and then that would be, not a description, but a metaphorical version of the process itself. I have noted elsewhere (1991b) that the boundary could be better viewed from a more specified level constructed by the interaction of two or more equations. What this does is use one equation to find a point within a transition zone located by another equation (figure 2.7). This construction has the semblance of a solution to the problem of the boundary because increasing specification in this way allows one to focus on, say, a line in a gradient. This location will bear meaning to the extent that choice of the second equation is driven by theory. Of course, every line so fixed has only the local meaning it derives from the purpose associated with this second equation.

One way or another, it seems that all crossings over to a larger scale must be described as jumps. Another possible gambit might be considered: following reductionist discourse, one might suppose that the boundary is really an illusion anyway—something one can prove by jumping down to smaller scales. From this vantage point the boundary has vanished, becoming so fuzzy that a gradient would be a better description. The problem with this is that we lose the phenomenon of interest (which was defined by the boundary in the first place), having replaced it with something that in any case cannot be treated other than approximately within digital discourse, so that jumps will not really have been transcended, only domesticated through superficial familiarity with the real line. (This has been one neo-Darwinian way of detoxifying punctuated equilibrium, for example.) And if one goes too far down the scale to escape distinctions, one comes anyway to the

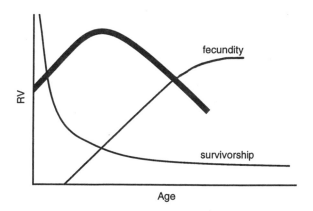

Figure 2.7 A representation of Fisher's (1958) reproductive value (the heavy line). The figure indicates that RV is a more highly specified (higher-level) entity insofar as it is a function of two other functions: survivorship and fecundity . The combination of these two functions allows discrimination between "immature and increasing in value" and "mature and decreasing in value," providing a boundary (where the modality of the function changes) that could not be found using either of the primary functions alone.

quantum-mechanical realm of radical uncertainty. So, it looks like we must suppose that there can be no smooth description of a transition from one stage to another.

This brings us to H_{sp}. Here too we move from one kind of thing marked as a stage (a blastula, a savage society) to another (a gastrula, a feudal society). If we observe an embryo, for example, we can tell when it is a blastula; then, if we leave for a while, we may return to find it a gastrula. But continued observation will not allow us to pinpoint just exactly where this transition can be said to occur. Stages are marked by when the addition of new sentences to a description (often modifying previous ones in mimicry of integration) becomes justifiable and necessary. Again the material situation is fuzzy—or, really, analog. But our descriptions must be crisp, digital, and bounded within Aristotelian logic. If we have a collection of embryos, it may well be the case that not a single one of them can be said to either a or b at the moment we choose to examine them. They will be nei-ther/nor and both/and, but not either/or.

The problem is not individuation; this is ignored in labeling by stages, which is the descriptive procedure for all earlier stages of development. The stages are constructions which allow us to tell time, as it were, in developments (Detlaff and Detlaff 1961; Reiss 1989). This is, from a constructionist point of view, a *notational system* (Goodman 1976). The process being described is fully differentiated into stages (except in the really later stages); the stages can be said to be syntac-tically disjoint because, even though some phrases cumulate on into later stages, there are characteristic phrases descriptive of each stage, all of which can therefore be separated unambiguously. The system as used is always finitely differentiated functionally, because it is never applied after some stereotypical "last" stage is reached. After this, development continues unscored, as it were, into the irregular and only inconveniently describable variety of senescence.

Performance of the developmental score is compliant because diag-nostic characteristics allow us to tell unambiguously if an embryo, say, is doing either stage a or stage b. But the problem is that development itself is a syntactically and semantically dense analog performance, while our score for it is only digital. If we were to observe a group of embryos going from stage 1 to stage 2, we would have to imagine something like the following: As individuals acquired a diagnostic character of stage 2, they each put up a little blue flag. After a while, as they left stage 2 for stage 3, these flags would be replaced by red ones. At no time would two flags be up on any embryo in this case—true enough, but the lot of them would present a motley chorus line, some waving blue, a few red, and a few no flags. Any given individual *might* conceivably wave both blue and red at some given time, but whether this is so in the transition period will be unclear because *the transition itself is not scored.* Change occurs in the space between the playing of two notes of a score, as one dies away and we anticipate the next.

As we have seen, development is structurally the accumulation of additional specification. This means that, in our analogy of flags, entry into a new stage means putting up a red flag, but *not* pulling down the blue one. This blue flag might, when integrated, (seem in actuality to) change to a shade of purple, but it will really still be there. So, in fact, in development, flags would not be removed as described above, but only continually added to, and that would seem to disallow the use of the term 'score' for the sere of stages. What is at stake here is our insistence that development be epigenetic in the sense that early modifications continue to exert their influence throughout all that occurs later. No flag would ever be wholly lowered.

In the actual experience of music, too, notes do not really disappear after being played; they continue to echo and resonate for a limited time as they become integrated into subsequent tones. This is not represented in the score, which is aimed simply at gaining immediate compliance from the performer—the score is a proscription. But in descriptions of development (normal tables), too, there is no remnant of past events in the description of the next stage except in those aspects that are importantly modified. No time is wasted redescribing what remains the case from before. Only the new is inscribed, and so normal tables are reduced to noting the appearances of new flags only. The stages are fully differentiated from one another simply by forgetting in the notation what continues to be the case. (It might be added, in closing the analogy, that normal tables function as proscriptions too, in that any embryo deviating from the score on its own will be discarded—by nature or by the experimenter.)

I want to be clear about how I have used 'program' and 'score' above. I believe that the idea that sequential genetic instructions are fed into initiating conditions is a fair metaphor for what goes on inside a biological development. On the other hand, the development itself (and this would apply to abiotic ones too), as viewed from outside, is scored in developmental stages. Hence, the genetic "program" feeds only into lower-level constraints on the performance of the score.

Zeno's paradox resonates here again. Since notations in a score must be unambiguously distinct, there cannot be a transition from one to another in execution, any more than there can be a continuous descriptive trajectory for the hare to the finishing line. What Zeno neglects to mention, of course, is that the hare (of all animals—was this a hint?)

could jump from one paradoxical moment to another right over the tortoise's back and win, in the same way that a pianist can create an organic piece of music by playing quite separate keys, the fingers jumping (but moving continuously in another integrity) from one key to another.

The Language Tree

I will now pick up a thread from chapter 5 of *Evolving Hierarchical Systems* (Salthe 1985). Numerous workers have followed Russell (1903) in suggesting that different predicates ought to be applied in discussing entities that are members of different levels (of any kind)—otherwise (and Russell later embraced this himself to escape the cumbersome messiness of complexity) one could reduce the discourse to any level one favored. Sommers (1963) constructed a very useful conceptual tool—the language tree—to deal with this matter of what Russell called 'logical types' (and, simultaneously, with Gilbert Ryle's (1949) notion of categories (as in 'category mistakes')). Sommers showed that one could construct a tree of increasingly more specified predicates, working from the most general (at the base of the trunk) to the more specific (at the ends of the branches). (Figure 2.8 is a tree transformation of a figure like figure 1.2.) The tips of these branches would each point to the sole entity that could bear the long train of predicates back to the most general one. Sommers showed that such a train of predicates corresponded to Ryle's category.

So, a *Rylean category* is a set of predicates whose intensional definition is the name of the object that embodies them all (so that N in figure 2.8 would be a category with members, 10, 5, 3, 2, and 1). A category mistake is then the attribution to an object of a predicate that is too highly specified in *another* category (say, in this case, 12) leading to another object—we might illogically claim, e.g., that a lion "has stripes," or that a crystal has a "relative humidity," or that a sentence "is tall." Working backward in this list, we can readily see that we have blundered if we try to describe a sentence (a cognitive operation) as "tall" or "squat"—those predicates apply only to material objects. Now, of course a sentence might be 'long' or 'short'. Clearly *these* predicates are general enough to be applicable to both cognitive and material events, and so must exist somewhere further back up on the language tree.

In the material branch of the language tree, we can see that crystals are not things that can have relative humidity, which is a predicate appropriate for gases only. And so a sentence linking crystals with humidity would likely be a category mistake—that is, nonsense, neither right nor wrong. The lion is a less obvious example. Why could lions not "have stripes," since they quite plainly can be, and are,

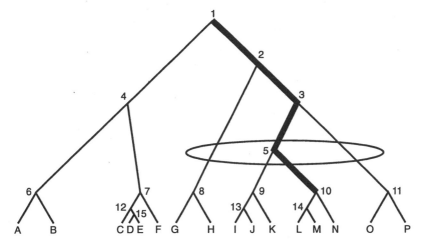

Figure 2.8 Sommers' (1963) language tree, showing the structure of Russell's logical types and Ryle's categories. The numerals at the nodes represent predicates; the capital letters at the ends of the branches represent objects. The ellipse brackets the logical type, 2. The heavy line is part of a category, whose label might be L, or M, or N.

'without stripes'? Saying that a lion has stripes does not seem to be a category mistake, or nonsensical; it is merely a mistake simpliciter.

The problem here is a peculiar and interesting one. It involves, in the end, the fact that we do not usually coin words, other than names, to refer to individuals. All lions are lions (though perhaps they might be toms or moms too). On the one hand, 'having stripes' is a function so far back on the language tree that it could apply to any metazoan, or even to any discrete object at all. On the other hand, we have a distinction here of usage only, not logic. Our language would have to have so vast a vocabulary, if it were to continue making category distinctions after the most general ones, that it could not presumably be used by beings with finite brains such as ours. That is, we would need in this case a word to describe 'having stripes' as a neomorphic condition in the lion family only.

This is not unrelated to the fact that development is not carefully scored after the first stage of early maturity. Working down the language tree in a category toward an individual is formally like developing from one stage to another in a given ontogenetic trajectory. And it would also be like keying out a biological specimen. Biological classifications simply do not make distinctions below the subspecies (race, variety)—even sex is not usually considered in this context.

Russell's logical type can be seen from figure 2.8 to be a class of objects whose intensional definition is the least general predicate applicable to them all. (Integrative levels are, then, kinds of logical types.)

Here, however, there do not seem to be limits on how fine a logical type our language can bear. The class, say, of 'all hummingbirds of a given sex that have taken nectar from a particular plant in the last two days' could be a genuine logical type. It is very far out in the branches of the tree, and indeed (perhaps significantly) no standard name would be forthcoming for it; however, if a specialist were to invent a name to satisfy a special need, that would seem to be logically proper.

Of course, 'any animal whatever visiting these same flowers during that time' would not be a logical type; if it included both bees and hummingbirds, there would have to be so many other kinds of organisms included under the least general predicate applicable to them both that did *not* visit these flowers that this group would be a mere arbitrary class. (It is easy to see that these organisms could not make up an integrative level.) Even the hummingbirds alone might not be a logical type; different species might be involved (as in California), and the least general predicate applicable to them would necessarily cover individuals of the species involved living in different ecosystems, who could not possibly have visited these same flowers. Only individuals of the same population of a given species could validly form this particular logical type. Here we see the degree of individuality that builds up in the individuation of events.

Errors of logical type and category mistakes can easily be explored here. Suppose that logical type 15 includes human societies at D and E, while logical type 5 includes ferret society at J and ground-squirrel society at M. If we use 3 as a descriptor for human societies, we make a category mistake. It is too highly specified in a category other than the one leading to the human societies. But it would be possible to defend our choice by claiming that 15 is an unnecessarily highly specified logical type for discourse about some aspects of human societies, and that we could move back to 1 for these purposes—and that is exactly what sociobiologists often do claim.

This is a defensible stance in the logic of the system, since 1 is a member of both relevant categories. In other words, we can generalize the discourse, and a modified form of 3 could be used (as will be explained below). But now, suppose we use 15 as a descriptor for ferret society. Again we make a category mistake; this time, however, semantic limits prevent us from undertaking an expansion of logical type, because 15 is so highly specified that it is not a member of a category at all (as was explained above), 7 being the most highly specified type available in that category. We therefore decide that using 15 to describe ferret society would be anthropomorphizing.

We need to see just how it is that 3 might be used as a descriptor for D or E, since doing so is a blatant category mistake. Here we must recall that the specification hierarchy is also an implication hierarchy. 3 implies 2 just as sociology implies biology, and 2 implies 1. 4 also implies 1, because 1 is very general. 4 might be something like 'based on visual signs', while 3 might be 'based on chemical signs'. Moving back to 1, 'based on sensory communication' might make sense in developing a general theory. One might find (or hypothesize) that the use of smell by ferrets has a theoretically exact parallel in the use of sight by humans. But, with 15 standing for 'use of electronic communication', since that is mainly external to the body (alas, Aldous Huxley's "feelies" never came off), we have moved into logical types so highly specified as to be isolated from the network of categories. These exist in a no-man's-land between the classes and predicates of the body of the tree and the individuals (letters) beyond, pointed to by the tips—a creative zone of emerging things.

Natural developments, the production of simple artifacts and art, and the keying out of specimens can all be viewed as advances from logical type to logical type within a Rylean category, a process of elaboration akin to logical deduction. On the other hand, the production of complicated machines and the construction of phylogenies are like generalizing and logical induction, with increasingly general logical types swallowing up more and more Rylean categories.

With this formalism we can pursue a pattern of logic of immense importance mythologically. Figure 1.2 shows several transformations of ideas into more and more general states in the framework of the specification hierarchy. Our ability to construct this set of examples implies a very general principle: For any given highly specified concept, it must be the case formally that it is a member of a more general concept which is implied by it, and this in turn must be a member of a still more general concept, and so on. For example, take 'intentionality'. This is something most psychologists reserve exclusively for humans, using it as a kind of boundary (as symbolic language is used by anthropologists) separating humans from the rest of nature. In this work the emphasis is on uniting humans as much as possible with the rest of nature. Of course, mechanistic reductionists feel they have accomplished this by depriving humans of many of their specialities, such as intentionality, by way of construing us (like everything) to be machines.

My move will be the opposite; that is, to give back to nature itself such human attributes. This can be done using the logical form shown in figure 1.2. We are searching for what Bigger and Bigger (1982) call "analogous structure." So, we can see that the 'intentionality' proper that we are all familiar with is a member of a more general class of characteristics implied by it. There is no label for that class—we might use {intentionality} for it. This is a member of the same category as intentionality proper, but it is a more general logical type. The class in which that is embedded would be {{intentionality}}, and so on. It seems clear, of course, that nothing comes from nothing. If we have intentionality, then our ancestors must have had {intentionality}, and theirs {{intentionality}}. In the logic of the specification hierarchy we cannot avoid this conclusion. Viewed from the center of such a structure, nature looks very different indeed than it does from the perspective of philosophical mechanism.

Do we suppose, then, that e.g., turtles have {{intentionality}}? Not quite. We are entitled from this formalism only to claim that embryonic turtles, at the last stage when they do not differ from human embryos, have it. As adults, they may or may not have some more specified elaboration of that vague property, presumably somewhat different from our intentionality, but derived from the same *Anlage*. The point is that they plausibly might well have "intentionality" of a kind (Griffin 1976—see also Palca 1990) since they also begin with {{intentionality}}.

Here we can see an important difference between H_{sc} and H_{sp}. In the former it is crucial that every level have some of its own predicates as a result of the fact that they are dynamically screened off from one another. In the latter, it is crucial that, epigenetically, nothing can development from nothing, so that any property manifest at a given level must have been potential and immanent in the level before it. Hence, predicates must nest as they do in Ryle's categories, and this is the source of the logical transitivity of this discourse. This is not a requirement of the nontransitive H_{sc}, where some totally new properties must be taken as emerging with each new level if the whole hierarchy is not to be collapsible on a single level. In a sense, the specification hierarchy does collapse—onto the latest developmental stage reached by a system.

We can now explore further the entrancing fact that progress from the more general to the more highly specified along the language tree is formally exactly like Baer's law. To see this, suppose that the numbers in figure 2.8 refer to predicates diagnostic of embryological stages, while the letters below them refer to kinds of organisms whose embryos are not distinguishable at the various nodes. What we have before us then is, in fact, the very picture (see figure 18 in Richards 1992) that Darwin transformed into a phylogeny by substituting evolutionary time for ecological time, and hypothetical ancestors for embryonic stages.

This allows an interesting Hegelian mapping from ontogenetic development to semantic structure, which mapping in fact generalizes the form of development beyond even what is suggested in figure 2.3 and into the very thought processes of (our) language, which is, no doubt, where it all originated. It is as if organisms, say, in their development, sought themselves hermeneutically, sequentially keying themselves out to be at the particular point where it all ends for them, in their own individual pattern of senescence. Linguistically it seems not only permissible but inevitable to say such things.

In this context we can again explore the notion of final cause—from these linguistic/logical roots. Recall that the specification hierarchy is also an implication hierarchy. In figure 2.8, 5 is a logical consequent of 10 (if 10 is true, so must 5 be true) just as chemistry is conceptually subordinate to biology (if biology exists, so must chemistry), because 10 implies 5 just as biology "implies" chemistry. 10 and biology are *logically prior* to 5 and chemistry. Hence, the fact that logical types map also onto integrative levels comes to be of special interest in a way reminiscent of the anthropic principle in physics. This principle (Gale 1981) has it that in order for physics to exist the universe must, early in its career, have had just the particular configuration required in order for humans to evolve later on (avoiding the need for guidance along the way). In biology, we note that, in order for a human being to exist, a particular ontogenetic trajectory must have been traversed by a dissipative structure. We have no trouble in supposing that the human being was a kind of goal for that trajectory—in fact its final cause. One way of putting what final causes do, we can now see, is that they "imply" (or, materially, conceptually subordinate) what needs to have been the case in order for them to get to be logically prior.

Now, I must demur on this a bit concerning phylogeny. The present perspective is developmental, which means that, while increased individuality can be predicted, the particular forms it might take are not. From the present perspective I believe it should be possible to discover, for example, necessary patterns in the origination of evolutionary grades. These will have discernible final causes of just the kind we are exploring here. But the details of their realization, the individual final causes associated with each taxonomic kind, just like those associated with each unique individual that finally results from ontog-eny, are not available to discursive scrutiny, located as they are beyond words more general than proper names. While the fact of individuation at any scale is important to us, discourse cannot follow the creative twists and turns in the space between the last numbers in figure 2.8 and the letters (names) at the bottom. We are constructing a developmental discourse here, not an evolutionary one.

Now, while I am saying that what eventuates must have done so because of a prior trajectory leading to it, that cannot suggest that its final cause was fully effective from the very beginning of a trajectory. That final cause was there only vaguely, with few of its degrees of freedom already used up. The emergence of a trajectory at a scale below where it is a single entity is self-organizing, and many frictional secondnesses have to be incorporated or overcome, leaving scars of varying importance and perhaps even rather large "deviations." We will see later that these alterations become less and less significant as a system ages. The supposed problem of how to distinguish signal from noise here is a false, positivistic one; with unique trajectories we cannot do this until the final signal appears full-blown before us, as a sign of itself, when its days are nearly over. This is another way of saying that we cannot jump up to the scale where the trajectory is a single entity, where the final cause operative all along could be discerned as a unit.

In the case of organismic development, today we invoke a genetic program working in a wetware computer in order to understand how the human being, say, could be the purpose of an ontogenetic trajectory. What is suggested by the totality of developmental discourse (figure 2.3), however, is that this is merely one case of a quite general situation. As dissipative structures continue to traverse their developmental stages, they are being pulled into their future configurations by a senescent attractor, their own local final cause. The fact that senescence is generalizable across dissipative structures (see chapter 3) means that we do not need to invoke genetic programs in order to understand it as it is found in organisms. Genetic systems do provide a stability, as mentioned above, that effectively delays arrival at senescent stages to a degree nicely tailored to the life-history "strategy" of each species (Stearns 1976; Williams 1957). But the fact that allometric considerations are even more important than the particular niche interactions of organisms in this respect (i.e., large, slow organisms senesce more slowly than small, fast ones regardless of how they make their living (Calder 1984; Peters 1983)) shows that something more general than adaptation is being expressed here.

We might also recall that final causes are implicit in H_{sc} too (Salthe 1985). In that discourse, events at the focal level begin and end within the duration of a single larger-scale cogent moment. Hence, boundary conditions functioning as formal causes (while their fluctuations function as efficient causes) at the beginning of a focal-level event continue in existence at the end of the event, functioning now in arrangements that can receive the results of focal-level behavior—that is, as final causes. Final cause resides here in what Patten et al. (1976) call the "output environment"—an instance of Uexküll's (1926) "world of action" portion of the function circle.

Summary

Any natural system can be analyzed from the point of view of the scalar hierarchy (H_{sc}) or from that of the specification hierarchy (H_{sp}). H_{sc} and H_{sp} have a few properties in commom. Both are nested systems of classes and subclasses. In H_{sc} the classes are rankings by scale, so that the more inclusive classes have as members objects of larger scale, which can hold as parts objects that are members of their subclasses. In H_{sp}, the more inclusive classes have as members phenomena that can be described in more general terms. H_{sc} continues indefinitely into smaller and larger levels; H_{sp} is truncated at one end by the most general things imaginable in a given application, and on the other by some end point or desideratum taken (usually implicitly) as a final cause. H_{sc} is a strictly synchronic system (because extended small-scale time periods can be transformed into single large-scale cogent moments), while H_{sp} may be used that way (as integrative levels) but strongly implies epigenetic diachronism. H_{sc} is mostly used as an objective analytical tool in the positivist tradition, while H_{sp} is fundamentally a way of constructing prediction and easily slips into the role of mythological dynamic (because observers, or their desiderata, are found in the most highly specified integrative level).

So, H_{sp} clearly labels itself as human discourse, an obvious social construction (like the Linnaean hierarchy), while H_{sc} is often taken to be a necessary, "objective" datum. Relations between levels in H_{sc} are nontransitive, each level being screened off dynamically from the next. In H_{sp} these relations are transitive and are defined by implication and conceptual subordination from the most highly specified to the least. In chapter 6 I will attempt to show how together these two hierarchies make up a general theory and/or mythology of the world.

Chapter 3

Nonequilibrium Thermodynamics

In this chapter I present the thermodynamics that we need in combination with the hierarchy theories of chapter 2, in order to explore further materials in the rest of the book. Classical thermodynamics and the nonequilibrium thermodynamics of, e.g., Prigogine, form an externalist discourse coherent with classical physics. The nonequilibrium thermodynamics of expanding (phase) spaces forms instead, an internalist discourse, necessary for dealing with complex systems. In this perspective, information carrying capacity is entropic, delivering both physical and informational entropies. Rod Swenson's view of the Second Law acting as a final cause of all forms, because forms occur (are materially "selected") which increase local entropy production, bridges these two thermodynamic discourses.

I continue to explore infodynamics, introduced in chapter 1, because it is crucial to a generalized development theory, which is the central approach of this book. Four basic rules of the development of dissipative structures are presented and interpreted infodynamically. Senescence, which will be a basic image throughout, is introduced. Immature systems are concerned primarily with the production of physical entropy, and their form building is in its service. Senescent systems are preoccupied with informational entropy, being bound up in it to a degree that eventually defeats the flexibility needed for continued existence.

Having briefly examined the basic structure of form in nature, we need next to look at the structure of that which gives rise to *change*. Change is not only dynamic; it is also informational. Because of this, I join those who point toward a synthesis of thermodynamics and information theory—infodynamics (Weber et al. 1989). Thermodynamics provides an understanding of the potential for change; information theory, suitably enlarged by semiotics, provides an understanding of the meaning(s) of change. Only with an understanding of these meanings can we apprehend the system undergoing change—that is to say, the constraints that emerge in the mess of nature, allowing it to be a system.

At the risk of seeming to have a penchant for falling into dichotomies (and I accept this as culturally mediated), I will find that infodynamical understanding comes in two perspectives: the *externalist* and the *internalist*. In the first (and classical) view we are examining a system in its environment from the outside—that is to say, we are examining a system of roughly our own scale located next to us. We can regulate its apparent environment in an observational frame of our choice. We can, and do, pretend that our observations in this setting are "objective" (and, indeed, we have constructed a perfectly sound, if limited, kind of objectivity through statistics).

In contrast, the internalist view becomes necessary when our ambitions extend to understanding systems as if we were inside them, which is our most usual predicament anyway. The externalist preoccupation with objectivity seems, in this situation, a forlorn hope. We lose some handy constraints in here, and so we lose some of our grasp on the situation. In fact, it is quite a new ball game. And we are driven inside this way by the postmodern ethos, which forces us to acknowledge, and therefore to try to understand, who and where we are.

Dealing with two sides of a system at the same time is, of course, a traditional problematic, reflected in this work as inside/outside or, in development, stage x/stage y. Kampis (1991a) discusses the inside/outside distinction under Otto Rössler's labels "endophysics" and "exophysics." It seems clear enough that, while externalist discourse is associated with control and power (which fails in internalist discourse), here we would be involved instead with the experience of knowing and the search for meaning.

The Classical, Externalist Formulation

The traditional Western view of nature is as a source of objects to be manipulated and controlled for our benefit. The world is seen as full of things we can use or deprive others of, things that can be deployed in a bid for power. These things need to be understood only to the extent that we can subdue or anticipate them.

In late-nineteenth-century Europe, thermodynamics had a prominent sociopolitical dimension. It was a hot topic then how many calories had to be supplied in what schedule to get the maximum amount of work from the human "machine," with the minimum cost in caloric input. Corn and human bodies had to be manipulated into profitable configurations for the productions of manufactures, and the Second Law of Thermodynamics (which showed, in this context, that energy finally escapes utilization by being transformed into "heat" energy) added the perpetual-motion machine to our world of desirable fantasies. Such a machine would be fully efficient, converting all the calories supplied into work, or, failing this, would solely by its own activity access energies stored elsewhere to keep itself going. The failure of this machine inspired a despair suggested by the notion of the "heat death of the universe"; to have this knowledge was to see deeply the futility of the previous generation's ideal of "progress" (Bury 1932).

Since it was the medium through which (externalist) thermodynamics was first constructed, we should briefly examine the machine as a material object. The machine is an arrangement of constraints on natural laws (levers, pulleys, hinges, pistons, switches, and the like (Polanyi 1968)) that can assume useful configurations in cycles. So, as we walk, we could be thought of as if we were machines—and today, as our neurons repeatedly assume patterns of firing, we can further be so considered. Available energy to drive a machine is stored in relatively unstable form (a poised weight raised up, "high-energy" chemical bonds, rising air (thermals), and other forms of *potential energy*—such as evaporable water for the dippy bird).

The crucial fact about the material machine—whatever its form or job, and whatever it is made of—is the secondness of *friction*. Friction might arise directly from the rubbing of parts in motion or collision; however, from the point of view of the production of a specific phenomenon—say, thought—it can also be the energy needed just to keep the neurons alive, because that is only indirectly relevant (because at a lower scale) to the product of interest (here, ideas). So friction can be more generally viewed as a kind of energetic overhead that must be paid in order to get a product, energy that must be expended indirectly with respect to that aim. Because of such *generalized friction*, more energy must be supplied to the machine than will be directly converted into product. Generalized friction can be decomposed into factors such as rubbing (producing heat energy), wear (requiring maintenance energy), and starting up (requiring activation energy).

Part of the problem of perpetual motion can be seen to reside in the perspective of production. If one thinks of a factory as a source of livelihood for workers rather than as a producer of (e.g.) cloth, then its output becomes the babies and contentment of these workers. From this perspective the cloth itself is an overhead—an indirect necessity for life, a kind of friction, like the production of seedlings to the pollinator of a plant. From this we can see that, if one had a universal perspective (i.e., was theoretically omnipresent), there could be no overhead distinguished from useful work.

Nevertheless, any physicist will immediately tell us about heat energy, the necessary product of any physical action whatever. This is energy that was not directly embodied in a product, and can no longer be captured by the user for production. So, heat produced by burning coal may drive a turbine; however, even if this is converted entirely into motion, the rubbing caused by the turning itself releases some heat—which might perhaps be tapped by ingenious focusing through some other, smaller, engine, and this repeated. But finally some of the energy must get lost to the system, because we couldn't make a small enough useful machine to tap it. The turbine stops when the coal is all used up, the local atmosphere is a bit warmer than it was, and there are bolts of cloth (and babies). If, narrowly, we tote up the calories represented in the weave of the cloth and compare it merely to the calories that were in the coal, there will be some loss even with the most efficient engines.

The trouble here lies in the desire for unlimited power. However, up-front physicists will say that this discussion is misdirected, because they want to generalize to the immediate vicinity of any process or event whatever, regardless of its relation to human intentionality. What I am trying to point out here is that delimiting any event for discussion under the Second Law is the same act (but in the cognitive realm) as constraining some material process so as to harness it.

And I want to emphasize the nature and role of friction here. Generalized friction is that which taxes whatever is being accomplished (or focused upon), of which mechanical friction is only a part in material systems. For the taxpayer, it includes taxes; for government, it includes the difficulty of collecting them; for any physical system, it is constituted minimally by the requirement for maintenance. This generalization is required in order to construct infodynamics on a thermodynamic background. In infodynamics, because of its semiotic connections, an observer (or an actor) must always be specified, however generalized away from the human case. So, if we observe a hurricane and notice that much of the energy that might have been used in driving its winds went instead to evaporate water, we could say that this was a tax on the hurricane's existence, a part of generalized friction.

If one's goal is running a race, then mechanical friction on the soles of one's shoes is crucial. If one is sawing a board, friction is essential for producing the right relations between the wood and the metal. But, again, the energy used in these tasks must be much more than gets focused productively into mechanical friction, and involves the rubbing of muscles and joints, the pumping of lungs, and, in racing, frictional contact between skin and air. Finally, the shoes and the saw warm up too, and that—all unwanted and not directly productive of speed or pieces—was also generated by the activities.

Running a race is a game of friction, using one form to overcome all the others; indeed, it seems like a canonical physical game for that reason. But here the rubbing of sole on ground is not 'friction' in its generalized sense; in this case it is a useful constraint. The production of hot feet, however, is not the point and can be reckoned as the result of friction. Consider, however, producing fire with a firestick. Here the heat itself *is* the point, but rubbing does produce generalized frictive results too as the stick wears away and requires maintenance or replacement, to say nothing about the sweaty brow and tired muscles.

It should now be clear that generalized friction is a semiotic notion, involving the thirdness of making choices that privilege a particular energy conversion in a particular situation by means of a particular arrangement (which in the human case can always be seen to relate to some purpose). It is a classificatory procedure by which some unavoidable energy conversions become constructed as friction. In this light, it is amusing to use a schoolroom physical experiment in which an object is rubbed to produce a measurable rise in temperature in order to demonstrate that heat loss is a necessary concomitant of mechanical friction. Here, however, the purported "heat" is actually the purposeful result of the experiment, and so could *not* be counted as the result of generalized friction! That might have been measured, instead, at the arm of the demonstrator.

The Second Law of Thermodynamics, then, demonstrated that, whatever the purpose of a machine, only some of the energy applied to it could be directly converted to that purpose, the rest being lost here and there as overhead. If we extend our notion from the unit machine to the factory, the same applies; if we keep expanding the area of observation, we eventually arrive at the whole universe. What does *this* produce? Well, some ideology might suggest "light." Very well, then: Only a small portion of the energy in the universe directly results in the proper wavelengths of electromagnetic energy that enter our lenses, and the rest was a necessary overhead. The same kind of analysis would apply if the purpose of the universe were to be to produce those bolts of cloth, or our eyes. If there were no viewpoint, there could be no Second Law of Thermodynamics. There have been physicists who doubted, for this reason, that thermodynamics was "objective" enough even to be counted a genuine part of physics.

We can glimpse here a deep prior relationship between thermodynamics and information theory that may underlie the formal relationship (to be discussed below) that some declare to be only superficial. A viewpoint is the result of informational—indeed, semiotic—constraints. We need only to discern the frictional ground from an energetically produced figure. That frictional ground is made up of anything that stands in the way of completing an objective. (All such "anythings" are jumbled up randomly, insofar as one could not otherwise lump together everything that opposes some project.) It is quite natural that this should be measured in the way Boltzmann proposed,

which, as it turned out, was the same measurement needed to estimate the potentiality for surprise in the deployment of signs in information theory. The central connection is the capriciousness with which
the world blocks our attempts and with which signs are deployed by
others.

A realist would retort here that without the Second Law of Thermodynamics there could be no viewpoint—just as a Darwinian would
assert that without natural selection (which is always the trump in this
kind of game) there would have been no mind to formulate the Second
Law. It is sufficient for now simply to observe that the Second Law
and natural selection both have their existence in discourse—a fact
demonstrated by their logical formulation.

Now let me briefly run through various classical statements of the
Second Law of Thermodynamics (Kestin 1976). I have already essentially stated the earliest notion by Clausius—that there cannot be a
perpetual-motion machine. This was later refined by Kelvin and Clausius to the effect that it is impossible to get work from (or change in)
a system by having a part of it spontaneously cool below the temperature of the coldest of its surrounding objects (Planck's later statement:
it is impossible to construct a machine that functions with a regular
period and does nothing but raise a weight which causes cooling in a
heat reservoir), or, more simply, heat itself cannot spontaneously pass
from a colder to a warmer body. (The dippy bird cries out for attention
here. These are exactly the things it does! As its bill cools by evaporation, fluid rises because of the threatened vacuum caused by a volume
decrease, and this weighs the head down so that the bill is again
dipped in water, and so on. It *is* a perpetual-motion machine; frictional
energy on its bearings is obtained from its cooling bill. But H_{sc} is
important here. We know that there must be a sink of a given relative
humidity to keep this thing going, and that has to be the result of a
higher-scalar-level arrangement of the environment—don't let the humidity get too high. As long as this is maintained (and also the water
in the beaker is kept at a given level, which the bird does not see to
by itself, requiring yet another higher-scalar-level energy-utilizing activity), the bird will continue indefinitely. One reason, then, why there
cannot be such a machine is that no expenditure of energy by a system
could arrange higher-scalar-level situations that must be in place for
it to continue.)

Clausius uses *"entropie"* to label a function of the state of a system
at thermodynamic *equilibrium*. It is defined on the variables (internal
energy, temperature, and other properties of the kind of system (e.g.
volume)), and it has a single, maximal, value when the system is at

equilibrium (and remains undefined when it is not). Clausius showed that for an isolated system not at equilibrium, entropy would be produced until it reached its maximum value. We see that entropy is, in this view, a mathematical construct referring to a kind of inverse of the thermodynamic potential of a system to change—the opposite of force. It cannot be directly measured, because it totes up the *lack* of possibilities to do anything. If the universe were an isolated system, Clausius noted, its entropy would have to move to a maximum (the heat death of the universe).

Carathéodory derived a rigorous statement to the effect that all real processes are irreversible (i.e., go only in the direction of increasing entropy), because not all of its possible states are accessible to any real system and only some could be accessed spontaneously at a given time, leaving others yet to be accessed. In other words, the system could not jump in a moment into a state in which it accesses all possible configurations at once—into equilibrium. There must be a gradual, frictional development of the condition of equilibrium, and every move in that direction generates further impediments, so that the next motions could not be calculated from any prior move. (See Matsuno 1989 for a well-realized discussion of this mess.)

Boltzmann made an important statistical interpretation of entropy (Brush 1983) by assuming that matter is composed of molecules, and that their motion, like that of any material objects, converts some of whatever is their potential energy to heat energy. If we begin with a system of gas molecules in a box (not at equilibrium), as the molecules move about they access more and more possible states as the energy in the system becomes increasingly converted to unusable form. When their motion reaches the limits of their container, the number of states they can access has been maximized, and their pressure on the container walls as they bounce off it could be used to register a nonchanging macroscopic temperature. If the box is small, the temperature will be higher (the molecules are converting more of their potential to heat) than if it were larger (all other conditions being equal), because they have not expended as much of their potential energy.

Entropy, S, could ideally then be calculated as the log of the number of "complexions" (configurations) the system could assume microscopically under a single macroscopic regime. For any system, it would be the most probable distribution of those states that comes into being at equilibrium:

$$S = -k \sum p_i \ln p_i,$$

where p_i is the probability of the ith state and k is a constant.

Nonequilibrium Thermodynamics
Clausius had already, in 1876, referred to the production of entropy as a system moved toward equilibrium; however, since entropy (and even energy and temperature) are well defined only at equilibrium (the problem of change rears its head here), it seems odd to use the word 'thermodynamics' for this classical science. The problems involved were brought out nicely to Meixner (1970), who characterized the classical science as "thermostatics." Many attempts have been made to deal with the problem of dissipative (nonequilibrium) systems. In this book I will focus on the approach of Ilya Prigogine (Prigogine 1955, 1967, 1980; Glansdorf and Prigogine 1971; Peacocke 1983), because of its compatibility with biology (Prigogine and Wiame 1946; Zotin 1972). Haken (1984, 1988) has developed a parallel approach that I will refer to more when dealing with information.

Once a transition from one thermodynamic equilibrium to another is explicitly acknowledged, the concept of entropy production becomes possible, and, if we deal with a local region distinct from the rest of a system, the concept of a movement of entropy across its borders is explicitly called for. Since entropy is an extensive variable (as is mass), it can be decomposed into parts, and the change in entropy of some definite open system can in particular be decomposed into its "flow" through and its production within the system (Prigogine 1955). With S being entropy,

$$\frac{dS}{dt} = \frac{d_e S}{dt} + \frac{d_i S}{dt}, \quad d_i S > 0$$

where $d_e S$ is the change of entropy due to interactions with the environment (Prigogine (1955) calls this "entropy flow," and I will follow that usage) and $d_i S$ is its production within it. This formula applies to any nonequilibrium system, whether near to or far from equilibrium.

The flow of entropy across a border and into a system (which is, then, thermodynamically open—or closed, but not isolated) can be conceived as the entry into the system of any nonharnessable energy (some of the heat flowing through it, physical shocks, radiation, etc.) that could produce disorder in the system ($+d_e S$ in figure 3.1). The flow of entropy out of the system ($-d_e S$ in figure 3.1) would include some of the energy that flowed in plus any heat produced by the system itself at the expense of any stored potential energy contained in it.

A system's own contribution to this flow out, of course, is generated as part of production, $d_i S$, and so the flow of entropy out of the system could often be larger than that flowing in. Only dS/dt as a whole is constrained by the Second Law never to go below zero. So production

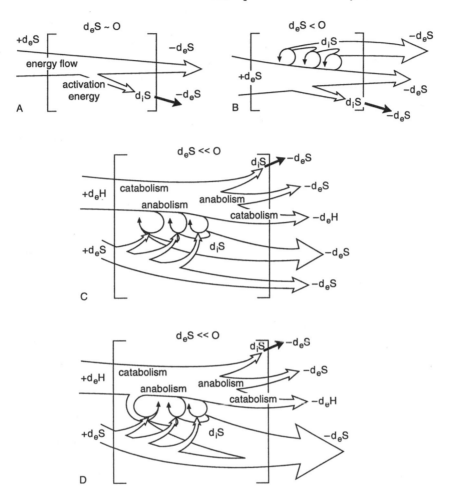

Figure 3.1 Thermodynamic structures of (A) an open system, (B) a simple dissipative system such as Bénard cells, (C) a heterothermic organism, and (D) a homeothermic animal. The energy-flow arrow is labeled $+d_eS$ at its entry into each system. In A and B, d_eS is the sole source of structuration. In C and D, the flow of matter (d_eH) into the system is shown as more important in structuration than d_eS, which here tends to disrupt. In C, $+d_eS$ is shown as contributing significantly to structuration, not unlike its role in B; in D its role is less, being replaced by behavior. Structure is shown as cycles. The total change of entropy is positive in all cases. In A, B, and C the fact that the flow of energy is partly dissipated into structure is indicated by the d_eS arrow getting thinner.

and flow might just balance each other by being of opposite sign and equal value (as when most entropy flowing in flows out and what is produced internally is most dissipated externally), giving zero total change in entropy at the expense of accessible free energy stored in the system or, if it is open, passing into it ($+d_eH$ in figure 3.1).

Prigogine and co-workers, basing their work on that of Lars Onsager and Ludwig von Bertalanffy, seem to have established that when boundary conditions (some peculiarity of kinetics or form leading, for example, to linear relations between the forces and flows in the system) prevent a system from reaching thermodynamic equilibrium (which would have zero entropy production in the system, and identical flow into and out of it), the system will settle down instead to a stationary condition of "least dissipation," a condition where the total change of entropy can become very small or indeed even zero. This is the principle of *minimum entropy production* for dissipative systems (which I will later argue is the characteristic attractor of systems in their senescent stages).

Free energy has to be made available even for a minimized entropy production to continue in a dissipative system. This will be at the expense of some arrangement wherein the energy is physically stored—e.g., high-energy chemical bonds. As these arrangements are derogated, waste products of simpler form are produced; thus, in such a system, not only is energy dissipated (say, as heat), and entropy (by leaving the system, i.e., $-d_eS$ in figure 3.1), but so is *information* dissipated. This is because a collection of high-energy structures, being more complicated, embodies stored information in constraints, which are lost when the energy is released (e.g., when high-energy bonds are broken). So, what might have been informational configurations to some system come to be derogated by some dissipative structures.

In the more general case, some gradient comes to be diminished (Swenson 1991) by movement of (and/or within) a system during its equilibration (Matsuno 1989). That is, constraints that were keeping the system asymmetrical are abrogated. Constraints are informational in nature, not dynamic (Pattee 1972), and their loss represents a loss of stored information, which is therefore dissipated. However, in view of the discussion of Boltzmann in chapter 1 above, more must be said here. The information capacity of the overall system increases as waste products disperse into it, while the gradient of the local field potential is being eroded. What had been established (and accessible)—the local nonequilibrium configuration of constraints—has disappeared, and the overall system has spontaneously become wilder, more uncertain. While accessible information content has diminished, information capacity has increased, to be realized in who knows what new configurations. So that which might have detected the original constraining configuration is now at a loss.

The information capacity of a system is measured as the number of such configurations possible within one set of macroscopic constraints—that is, all having about the same energy "cost." Shannon and Weaver's (1949) formula for this capacity,

$$H = -k \sum f_i \ln f_i,$$

is structurally identical to Boltzmann's formula for statistical entropy, S, given above, with frequencies of signs used rather than probabilities of states. The information capacity of waste products in the wider environment into which they dispersed will be higher than that of a configured system of substrates from which they derived. (Who or what could tap such a capacity for "information" will be left moot here, but, as was suggested in chapter 1, this ought to be considered if the information concept is to be used. The dissipative system is itself using (indeed, using up) the information in the substrate molecules, since these must somehow be being detected.)

Information capacity would be greatest in a randomly dispersed system (Chaitin 1975). Here we would have the greatest ignorance of what the next configuration of signs might be. And any field we do not understand might appear to us as randomly distributed (Salthe 1985). This includes the behaviors of other systems to the extent that we do not understand them. Yet, failing an understanding of the meaning of information for these systems, we can still roughly estimate *how much* information is being used and absorbed by another system, and this is why the measure of information (either capacity or content) is appropriately of a probabilistic, nondeterministic sort (Atlan 1978). So, if we find two systems, one of which generates a large amount of what seems to us to be noise, it is likely that that system would be the more interesting one—the one containing and using (having meanings for) the most information.

Under the condition of minimum entropy production, *some* production is a condition for dissipative stability near equilibrium. The system maintains itself away from equilibrium by means of its entropy production. $d_iS > 0$ will be a criterion for the attainment or maintenance of any kind of nonequilibrium structure. In those cases going to minimum production, fluctuations of flow or production are damped out, and so the system remains more or less stable at minimum entropy production. But physically this is not the only possibility. If boundary and initiating conditions are right (see Prigogine's works and Peacocke 1983 for these conditions), systems can appear far from thermodynamic equilibrium, accessed by way of fluctuations from near equilibrium. All natural dissipative structures—fluid vortices, drainage systems, organisms, etc.—are of this kind, and are what this book is about. These systems, I will argue, do not move toward minimum entropy production until they become senescent, and most of them probably never really approach it closely.

Dissipative Structures

Let us consider a well-studied example: the Bénard instability in a fluid layer heated from below. (See Prigogine's books and Rod Swenson's papers.) Initially we see no motion in the fluid; heat passing from the source to the sink is conducted through the system by the motions of molecules and small molecular complexes (figure 3.1A). This is a very frictional process, and some of the energy is absorbed in relatively unordered molecular-scale motions and collisions. Then heat passing through the system is gradually increased. At a critical temperature, the entire body of the fluid gets relatively rapidly (as seen from our enormously larger scale) transformed into larger-scale structure (figure 3.1B), into roughly hexagonally packed cells of fluid rolling over from bottom to top and down again as heat now becomes transferred to the sink by way of convection carried by these cells as well as through continuing molecular conduction. At still higher temperatures the neatly packed cells get replaced by (still macroscopic) turbulence. Haken (1988) has called such changes "nonequilibrium phase transitions."

The flow of energy, as in any heat engine, causes work to be done on the fluid. When this flow reaches a certain level, it can no longer be carried by simple thermal dissipation alone, and the system becomes, when it can so respond, restructured to allow greater amounts of heat to flow through. And still greater amounts can only be carried by the more chaotic turbulent convection (which seems less orderly, but where the order would probably be located at a still larger scale not immediately perceptible by us in the usual apparatus). The Bénard cells themselves exist at a scale much larger than simple molecular associations; in fact, they entrain those associations and (to some extent) rectify their motions.

One might say that it is the flow of energy through the system that organizes the fluid, as would be the case also with whirlpools and hurricanes. But the flow is mediated and modified by the system's organization, which is also true of natural dissipative structures. In fact, recalling Aristotle's causal categories, we might note a number of other causes here: the formal cause of asymmetrical field potentials, the material causes of the properties of the fluid, the final cause of entropy-production maximization (Swenson 1989a,b).

Haken (1988) makes the important point (which I will try to deal with in chapter 5 under the rubric 'emergence') that the information specifying the form and behavior of a dissipative structure is not wholly contained in the environmental forces and flows that were required to produce it. Some internal information is required as well, which in the basic triadic system of H_{sc}, would be called initiating conditions. Now, this seems to be begging the question of why, e.g., hexagonal cells are produced at the Bénard instability. Do we ever get other forms? I daresay not enough imaginative playing with boundary conditions has yet taken place to determine this possibility. No doubt computer exploration of a model of this system, allowing free play with the boundary conditions (Haken's "order parameters") would show that other forms could be possible as chaotic alternatives under some conditions. Cells of this kind are also found in a wide variety of natural situations: at larger scale they are found in the atmosphere, and perhaps in the earth's magma.

Dissipative structures, then, are organizations that dissipate energy, and also entropy (thermal + viscous dissipation in this case). And what of entropy production? The increased flow of entropy out of the system as a result of its organization shows that entropy is being produced at a higher rate by the system under these organized conditions. This must be so because conduction, since it exists at a scale far below that of convection, must still be absorbing approximately as much frictive energy as it was before organization, while the structuration of the fluid has absorbed the heat increase that initially triggered it. That the increase in heat flowing out represents the flow of entropy produced by the organized system is suggested by the fact that it is the internal structure of the system that gave rise to it.

More formally, it can be seen that, at the moment of phase transition, if total entropy change is not to decrease (it is forbidden by the Second Law; $dS/dt > 0$ is imposed by it) as some of the flow becomes absorbed in structuration, d_iS must (and does) increase in order to compensate for this loss to d_eS. As was noted above, Swenson takes the tendency for entropy-production maximization to be the final cause of these (and all) dissipative structures, which facilitate entropy-production increases by means of their orderliness, as in this example.

In these far-from-equilibrium cases, some of the energy flowing into the system has been *dissipated into structure* (in this case, viscous dissipation—into the form and behavior of the cells), this being deducted from thermal dissipation (d_eS). The resulting organization (which provides the necessary compensating increase in entropy production) is itself, therefore, one sink for energy to get dissipated into, provided that initiating and boundary conditions will allow it. These kinds of

things happen in nature because of "the generally associative properties of our world" (Wicken 1987) (a statement that reminds us of the
necessity for the presence of constraints that must exist for these events
to happen—which constraints do not form an explicit part of thermodynamics discourse, but are informational in nature, and so must be
taken up by infodynamics).

On this score, we might recall that it is the annihilation of constraints
as field potentials are dissipated by way of other constraints—those
involved in dissipative structures—that characterizes infodynamic systems. As one form of energy is converted to another, one set of constraints is derogated while another is erected. We need to understand
why one set of constraints can supersede others—why, in fact, one set
allows a faster maximization of entropy production than does another.
Swenson (1991) talks about a system "selecting" (a material selection
from a population of one) the local constraints that will maximize
entropy production in any given local situation. I think this usage
unfortunate, because it clearly cannot be the case that there is an array
of definite potentialities present from which selection is made. This is
a tricky point: Only one configuration actually emerges, but it would
seem reasonable to suppose that it emerges from more than one antecedent potential possibility; hence the locution. Matsuno (1989) struggles with a reformulation of selection in order to deal with this
problem. My own feeling is that selection talk here is unnecessarily
capitulating to the current hegemony of Darwinian thinking, which is
unilluminating here. In any case: Insofar as any energy dissipated into
form and behavior is detracted from the shipment of entropy out of
the system ($-d_eS$ in figure 3.1), some authors (see, e.g., Schrödinger
1956) use the term *negentropy* (negative entropy) to refer to it, and the
form and behavior patterns of dissipative structures are taken by these
workers to be "negentropic." This "negative entropy" can be the
source of further "positive entropy" (an increase in $-d_eS$ in figure 3.1)
when the field potential it represents comes to be derogated at a later
time.

The point of this negentropy move is that local regions in an overall
system can show, fleetingly, decreases in entropy, so long as the global
system continues to show an increase. This view is in conflict with that
of Prigogine, stated above, that entropy production increases simultaneously with structuration so as to compensate the loss of entropy
flow, thus keeping local entropy change from becoming negative.
Those who think in terms of negentropy are neglecting this increase
in entropy production accompanying the formation of structures and
resulting from their existence. Even in classical terms, negentropy can
only be maintained by what is still a sizable export of entropy to the
outside—which, it seems to me, is saying much the same as my

interpretation here of Prigogine, because that entropy cannot be exported without having been produced in the first place if the system is not totally transparent to energy flow, as few natural systems are. The structure of the system produces the entropy from available gradients.

The crux of this conflict lies in the emphasis on the role of entropy production, which, because it increases with structuration, shows that structure is not in conflict with entropy increase and so need not be considered a *negative* entropy. This could not be made clear before Prigogine (1955) decomposed entropy change into d_eS and d_iS. Its resolution will involve an assessment of the importance of local deviations from the general entropy increase. If dissipative structures (which are everywhere, and which include even galaxies) are all entropy debits, that seems to suggest that more than just local fluctuations from a general entropy increase are involved in the presence of the world. This raises major philosophical and mythological problems, which I will broach later in connection with the internalist perspective in infodynamics (which obviates this problem). We will see that, from the point of view of semiotics, there is a role for the negentropy concept only in what I am calling the externalist position in infodynamics.

We need now to look at that paradigmatic dissipative structure, the organism, from this general perspective (figure 3.1C,D). What we have here is an open system, with both energy and matter transgressing its borders. Some energy flows in by way of warmth, wind, radiation, and so on. The part of this flow that disorganizes any internal structure is counted as entropy flowing in. In plants, some of the radiation energy is dissipated by photosynthesis into chemical potential energy, and that subsequently is used to drive structuration. In heterotherms, entropic energy flow is used to warm up the system to its most efficient temperature (and so would not be generalized friction). In homeotherms, material flow into the system supplies most of the energy for this, and the increased rate of entropy production (for which we need to seek mechanisms at all levels) supports an increased flow of entropy out (heat, behavior). As entropy flows out, the temperature result of its doing so is harnessed, e.g., in jumping around and shivering. Behavior in homeotherms thus harnesses (and contributes to) d_iS, which in them is large enough metabolically to make this worthwhile.

The amount of structuration derived directly from environmental forces and flows (such as produce a dust devil) is not known for organisms. It is probably more than our recent genetic biases suggest; however, it seems to be subordinate in importance to the energy (ATP) derived from chemical catabolism, which is modulated by genetic information. Catabolically derived heat flows out as entropy along with much of the directly impinging environmental energy flow.

Anabolic structuration also produces heat, which joins the flow of entropy outward. 'Metabolism' is our covering term for the source of most internal entropy production in organisms (Zotin 1972). There are analog models of this in all (even abiotic) dissipative structures, because without internal entropy production they could not compensate for the loss of entropy caused by their own structuration, which was imposed on environmental flows by the combination of initiating and boundary conditions of the total system. In something like a tornado, this entropy production includes heat generated by the increased rate of motion of air and water molecules. This would be directly equivalent, in animals, to heat produced in muscles and bones during running or flying. But in animals a comparatively enormous amount of heat is produced by chemical reactions, and in plants chemical reactions are the source of just about all the entropy production. Whether there are any significant specific chemical reactions characteristic of, (e.g.) hurricanes seems not to be generally, if at all, known.

Where there is catabolism, there is also a dissipation of information. In organisms much of this dissipation is anabolically directed into new information contained in their own proteins and nucleic acids, but, of course, some is directed into simpler waste products. The buildup of proteins and nucleic acids is guided by genetic information, and the secondary, tertiary, and quaternary linking of protein information generates higher levels of information more or less spontaneously (regulated, however, by pH, which is generated by boundary conditions from the organism's overall structure).

There is as yet no theory linking macromolecular information to that in the organism proper (Bonner 1982). How much of the organism needs to be accounted for by information other than that in the genes? Two recent collections (Goodwin and Saunders 1989; Goodwin et al. 1989) suggest a number of other possibilities. Organisms in general may be the spontaneous dynamic solutions—structural attractors—of certain complex processes associated with particular sorts of materials (including liquid crystalline structures); that is, they may represent the embodiment of structural possibilities that can be accessed by certain types of complex systems.

Genetic information, insofar as it explains organismic properties (not in its role in its own production, or in disease) would, on this view, account (as indeed it originally did in the discourse of genetics) only for the *differences* between kinds of organisms—that is, for those aspects specifically adapted to particular ways of life. From this point of view, organisms are dissipative structures which have acquired a remarkable degree of stability by way of the genetic apparatus. That stability allowed an elaboration of form and behavior at several levels, from the organism up, which in turn afforded a subdivision of ecological niches. No historical primacy is implied by the form of the last sentence—indeed, it is most likely on grounds of H_{sc} that affordances for niches (various more or less abiotically differentiated energy flows) broadly preceded the organisms that filled them, and functioned as boundary conditions in eliciting aspects of their more detailed structuration (Wicken 1987; Weber et al. 1989).

Four Phenomenological Rules of Open Systems
During organismic ontogeny (Trincher 1965; Zotin 1972; Lamprecht and Zotin 1978; Hershey and Lee 1987), during ecosystemic secondary succession (Margalef 1968; Odum 1969; May 1973; Schneider 1988), and during the history of the surface of the Earth (Wesley 1974; data in Schopf 1983; Brooks and Wiley 1988), a series of characteristic, constitutive changes have been found to occur. I have summed these up (Salthe 1989a) in four phenomenological rules of thermodynamically open systems as follows. As the system develops from immaturity through maturity to senescence, within it:

> (1) After an initial increase, there is an average monotonic decrease in the intensity of energy flow (flow per unit mass) through the system. The gross energy flow increases monotonically against a limit, just as
> (2) There is a continual, hyperbolic, increase in complicatedness (= size + number of types of components + number of organizational constraints), or, generally, an ever-diminishing rate of increase in stored information.
> (3) There is an increase in its internal stability (its rate of development slows down). Originally stated as *Minot's Law* in developmental physiology, this is shown in figure 3.2 as the diminishing-returns shape of the stored information curve, as well as in the similar curve for gross energy flow.
> (4) There is a decrease in its stability to perturbations, which eventually leads to recycling.

Csányi (1989) provides a rough adumbration of these rules but does not state them as such. The last two combined could serve as a definition of *senescence*. Not all of these rules are exemplified in every study listed; they are shown *inter alia*. There is no evidence concerning the last rule with respect to the surface of the Earth, but, since the other three appear to hold, it would seem extraordinary if this would not also, especially since there are logical connections between them. Superficial examination suggests that these rules apply also to simple dissipative structures such as hurricanes (Emanuel 1988); indeed, this book makes no general sense if we cannot assume this. It seems that the initial increase in the intensity of energy flow has not been recorded

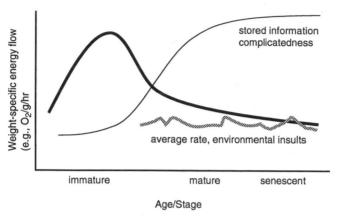

Figure 3.2 Infodynamical changes during development of dissipative structures. Stored information refers to size, number of types of subsystems, and number of opperative constraints. The rate of insults delivered by different environments will vary. When the energy-intensity curve has decreased a certain degree relative to the average rate of insults, there is not to enough energy for recovery from perturbations, and the system is poised for recycling.

in simple physical dissipative systems. This may be so because it occurs so rapidly, relative to the scale of our observations, that it has been missed. These rules, then, will provisionally be taken here to apply, regardless of scale (being like laws of nature in that sense), to any dissipative structure.

Of course, these behaviors could be analyzed into different material and efficient causes in each different kind of system. These patterns are, for that reason, *emergent*. Hence, stating them as here would not satisfy scientists working as specialists with the different examples. The only explanation implied by these rules is formal causality. For example, Swenson (1989b) views the decrease in energy-flow intensity to be a result of any physical systems's increasing its surface area so as to maximize the extension of dissipative surfaces, leading in some systems even to fission. In fact, then, Swenson is taking the decrease to be a direct effect of the final causality of the Second Law.

Examining the logical relations among these rules, we might take energy flow to be materially prior, as an efficient cause. When through-put is intense, the system is storing information at a higher rate than when its intensity has dropped (figure 3.2). It would seem reasonable to suppose that energy flow provides the drive for structuring the system. The drop in intensity of energy flow could also explain the increasing internal stability over time, since change requires energy. This drop is also crucial for rule 4, insofar as recovery from perturbations would require energy as well (note the relationship between energy-flow intensity and the average rate of insults from the environment shown in figure 3.2). This reading leaves unexplained the drop in energy-flow intensity accompanying development. This can, however, be tied to the increase in stored information. Information creates constraints (indeed, if it is functional at all, it *is* constraint). Consider, for example, the increase in double bonds in skin proteins during aging. Double bonds are richer in stored information than single bonds, specifying more and determining more fully the state of the molecule. Single-bonded carbons can rotate almost freely, so that the molecules these are in are relatively poorly specified and, as functional in skin, very flexible. As information accumulates during development, it is reasonable to suppose that it must delete potentialities for activity by increasing the generalized friction bearing on any process. This reading, then, has rule 2 feeding back on rule 1, providing a brake on what would otherwise, with growth, be an exponentially explosive increase in energy throughput, rather than the leveling off that actually happens (which results in a shape for the total energy throughput (power) curve like that for stored information in figure 3.2).

Most of development is, in this view, a gradual curtailing of opportunities for energy flow so that the system becomes less and less able to make use of energy gradients available to it, resulting in an increasing rigidity that prevents it from retaining the requisite variety (Ashby 1956; Conrad 1983) in its behavior that allows for adaptability.

However, we must balance this materialist/efficient-cause explanation in the thermodynamic perspective by noting that there is also a final-cause reading of these relations, as stressed by Swenson. In this view, energy flow is the *result* of the derogation of energy-potential gradients, which is enabled by the gradually appearing form indicated in rule 2, and the upward drive of the stored-information curve in figure 3.2, dissipating energy into the system, is what pulls down the energy-intensity curve by using up available gradients. As it should be, this is another, perhaps simpler, way of saying the same thing, except in focusing externally on limited energy sources.

Thermodynamically, then, development is initiated as a new material conduit for entropy flow becomes possible. The system becomes the tool of the Second Law and, seized in immaturity by opening opportunity, maximizes its gross energy throughput, or power (Lotka 1922a,b; Odum 1983). (Odum was thinking energetically in a way commensurate with this treatment, and he obtained the maximization notion from Lotka. The latter, however, rejected any connection of this with the Second Law. We can now make such a connection.) The power maximization is accomplished by way of structuration, necessitating the building in of stored information, which, in moderation, opens the way for increased entropy production. This leads the curve of energy-throughput intensity to sweep up to its maximum as the system in immaturity could be said to be following the *maximum-power principle* of Lotka and Odum. Soon, however, the amounts of stored information become frictional on the energy flows and the system begins to senesce, being better described now as taking up a trajectory leading toward minimum entropy production (Prigogine 1955, 1967) as it moves toward thermodynamic equilibrium. Entropy production is curtailed by information overload leading to a decrease in the efficiency of dissipation. In this view only the immature system is taken to be explicitly following the principle of entropy-production maximization (Swenson 1989a), because the very structuration process that facilitates that structuration, when continued beyond some optimum amount, leads to a friction catastrophe such that the system is no longer a prime tool for the Second Law—which, indeed, now works through various channels (perturbations, decay) to destroy it. Systems, then, are brought into being by the Second Law, and are destroyed by it after they have become too rigid to mediate large amounts of entropy production and remain intact.

Another interpretation is that total energy throughput becomes restricted after some characteristic stage (where the intensity curve begins to drop in figure 3.2), so that, as the system grows after that point, an essentially fixed total amount becomes divided among more and more units. In this account, as the system grows, the increasing volume relative to surface (despite the maximization of surface area) finally inhibits the flow of entropy. Insofar as dissipative structures are so different from one another (consider only the three examples from which the rules were derived—organism ontogeny, ecosystem secondary succession, and the history of the surface of the Earth), we can expect that, since they are part of an emergent pattern, in some cases this explanation (or even both explanations) might be true, but that would have to be determined empirically. Here we are considering only the logical possibilities of formal causality.

I feel that the potential for negative feedback from rule 2 to rule 1 is a deep principle here, and I will proceed on that assumption. Furthermore, after I have introduced the internalist perspective and the necessity for information to behave entropically, it will be evident that information overload can be viewed as itself entropic, so that even the rigidly senesced system can be seen as expressing the Second Law. Thus, in the internalist perspective, the Second Law reigns supreme throughout development, producing senile deviousness and caution as well as youthful heat.

Development as a Nonequilibrium Process

Insofar as the four rules discussed above are predictable on any dissipative structure (which is my hypothesis here), they would be rules of development for these structures. Indeed, since they are thermodynamic, and so very general, they can be taken as the deepest rules of development known. "Deep" here refers to depth back from the tips into the cascading tree of individuation (figure 2.8) toward its trunk. I take this to mean that figure 2.8 can be read, not only as a logical analysis of predicates, but, in Hegelian fashion, as referring as well to the physical world of the realization of potentialities inherent in a developing material system. In development as in logic, not every possibility can be realized from a given situation, and stages of development can be taken to be the material equivalents of logical types, the possible kinds of developments out of them leading any token to an increasingly restricted number of realizations that are the material equivalents of Rylean categories.

This theory is deep because it talks about development so generally as to include even stages that precede biological ones, thereby potentially allowing discussion of, say, the development of hurricanes. And so an enlarged view of biological development is also possible here. Going back beyond the zygote, we become enabled to trace stages back through the oocytes (where the energy flow intensity curve is typically at its maximum; see Zotin 1972) to gradients in the early stem cells, which organize the abiotic antecedents of biological development. This view emphasizes the fact that organisms are elaborated dissipative structures, and so it forms an important mythic link between humans and other natural forms.

Figure 3.3 is intended to show these relationships. The lower part of the figure should be taken as embedded inside the logical type "living" in the upper part. (All labels in this position are predicates.) In the lower part, the labels inside the arrow, which represents a human ontogenetic trajectory, are stages roughly appropriate to the logical types they are paired with. Thus, e.g., the pairing of the noun 'embryo' with the predicate 'primate' is intended to show that a human in certain embryonic stages cannot be distinguished from embryos of other primates at the same stage (without genetic analysis). At such a stage the potential human is in fact nothing more than just a primate; it is not specifically human, or specifically anything else other than an embryo-at-the-primate-stage.

Indeed, this approach tells us what in fact is the material cash value of higher taxa: They refer to stages of development in which all members of the taxon would be indistinguishable. Thus, if one wanted to

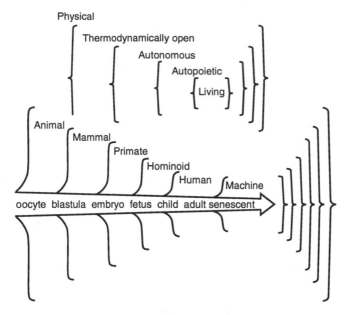

Figure 3.3 A specification hierarchy showing nested logical types. The lower portion of the figure is nested within the subclass labeled 'living' in the upper portion. The arrow represents a human ontogenetic trajectory, with stages placed near the subclass whose members' developing individuals would not materially differ from the human at that stage. Reprinted, with permission, from *Systems Research* 6 (1989), no. 3: 6.

map the actual physical extension of the taxon Primates, one would have to enclose a space defined by dots locating the geographical position of every extant embryo at the key stage of all the species involved. This would, of course, physically enclose all members of this taxon as at present interpreted only if, using scalar hierarchical principles, we extend the time frame so that the females carrying these embryos would have time to themselves actually sequentially occupy the whole range of the deme they are part of. This would be appropriate because the species is a higher-scalar-level entity (Salthe 1990a). That the embryos would during this time have moved on to later stages is not a problem, because we no longer need to identify them. Having pinpointed their mothers at the appropriate stage, we let them be vicars for the embryos of interest, and, indeed, since they are parts of it, for the taxon as well (just as organisms are always taken to be vicars for species).

We can now see that, if the letters at the tips of the branches in figure 2.8 are interpreted as species and the nodes as developmental stages, we have a semiotic description of ontogeny—one prefigured by Martin

Barry's (1837) "tree of animal development" (see figure 18 in Richards 1992). One logical type is succeeded by another as a category unfolds. This becomes something more than a mere description when we realize that figure 2.8 represents a spontaneous cascade of development, with adult stages (the full realizations of each separate category) acting as final causes attracting the developments, the whole thing being attracted by that ultimate final cause the Second Law of Thermodynamics because, in order to achieve these final configurations, free energy must be dissipated into heat *and form*. The italics (the crux of the Brooks-Wiley approach, and implicit in Swenson's version) require that we see *macroscopic information* as itself embodying entropy.

Macroscopic Information as Entropic

I have already noted that Shannon and Weaver (1949) opened the possibility for viewing information capacity to be an entropy, and this view was ably developed by Brillouin (1956). The linking concept is disorder, using Boltzmann's formulation of entropy. So, looking again at the ontogenetic tree (figure 2.8), we can see that if we consider only embryos the number of different configurations possible to them are more limited than if we consider adults of the same species. That is, taking all adults of some kind and their behaviors in the world and comparing this with all embryos of these kinds at some stage, it would take more energy to track and classify the former than the latter. Using the energy equivalent of information (Brillouin 1956; Morowitz 1968), we would run up more heat doing the former task than the latter. So also, in nature, it takes the ontogenetic trajectories themselves more energy to produce the adults than the embryos. Furthermore, embryos have a larger specific energy flow through them than adults; adults have the greater gross throughput, and so their existence produces absolutely more entropy than does that of the embryos.

So there cannot be form or perceived configuration without the production of entropy—all else being equal, the more form the more entropy. (I will later try to justify a similar statement: 'the more forms the more entropy'). We notice again the isomorphism between the formulas for physical entropy and for information capacity. Capacity is the number of different configurations informational tokens can assume. So, if we tried to use embryos as carriers of signs to be combined into information, we would be able to code for fewer statements than if we tried to use adults. A system of greater complication has more potential information-carrying capacity. But we need to address, and overcome, three problems that have been raised in connection with taking information capacity to be entropic.

If information is to be taken as entropic, it must follow the equivalents of the First and the Second Law of Thermodynamics. That is, in a system with informational closure, (1) what can be converted into information must be found to be conserved, and (2) information itself must increase or remain constant. (3) If macroscopic configurations are to be considered information, we must identify a system in which they so function. These are not insurmountable problems. We can dispense with the first of these three criteria by noting that energy is what is converted into information, either in the formation of a configuration or in its discovery and classification by another system. We need merely show that an object system and an observer exist in the same physical system to satisfy the First Law as well as it is ever satisfied in thermodynamics.

To show that macroscopic information in an internalist situation follows the second law, I have proposed the following logical argument (Salthe 1990b): It is sufficient to show that observer and object system(s), S_i, are together embedded in the same complex supersystem, for the following reasons: If we were to decompose total system information (macroscopic information), H, into the potential information capacity of the supersystem, C_{max}, and that stored in its contained subsystem(s), H_i, then the information in the global system would be

$$H = C_{max} + H_i.$$

H must continue to increase, or at least cannot decrease, when we explicitly consider the information, H_o, stored in an observer, O, as well. Then

$$H = C_{max} + H'_i + H_0$$

describes the total system, in which H_o could also be observed as contributing to H_i by another observer in the system coordinate with O, if there were one. (As I will be using the concept 'learn' here, I will state what I mean by this, following Jay Lemke: A system learns about its environment when, after communication between the two in whatever form, the system's internal configuration changes so as to institute a redundancy between this configuration and its environment. Hence, information is embodied in configurations. Note that redundancy is less specific than the notion of representation). The argument is as follows: C_{max} is estimated by O as C_i. C_i, the uncertainty of behavior of an observed system S_i, is a sign of C_{max}, based on Ashby's principle of requisite variety. H'_i has become submerged into the single observed system and contributes to C_i. Information in this local system can then be estimated as

$$H = C_i + H_o.$$

C_i will vary as object system S_i develops, first decreasing as a percentage of C_{max} as it learns to cope with its local environment and then again increasing with respect to C_{max} in senescence. Over all object systems it could be taken as an average declining percentage of C_{max} with time in immature and mature systems, as in figure 3.4. C_i must always be less than C_{max}, because it is always possible for O to learn more about the supersystem, either by taking new perspectives on S_i or by considering other object systems. (This, of course is to say nothing of whatever generalized friction actually prevents S_i from reaching informational equilibrium.) C_i might approach C_{max} asymptotically for O, but could never reach it, because (a) O is a finite observer, being able to hold (or discriminate, or use) only a limited amount of information, and (b) as C_i approached C_{max}, the frictional effects of so much information (H_o = constraints) on O's behavior would be so great (making it more rigid) as to destroy its adaptability. From these considerations, even if C_{max} remained constant behind C_i, H_o would be continually increasing with O's observations, thus driving H necessarily to increase.

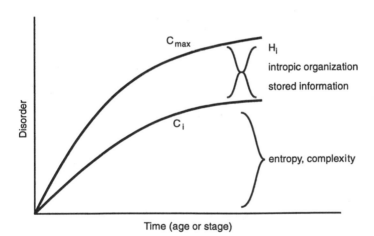

Figure 3.4 The general behavior of infodynamical variables during the early development of a dissipative structure. The maximum disorder possible continues to increase under the constraint of expanding phase space (or that of growth). The actual disorder achieved by any system, C_i, is less than its maximum potential, C_{max}, because of generalized friction—all possibilities cannot be immediately realized, and when some are realized the maximum potential automatically increases again. The labels used here for contributing causes of the reduction in C apply in various parts of the text. Adapted from Brooks and Wiley 1988.

Because the supersystem involved is complex, other increases in embodied C would be generated by a wavefront of unforeseen informational consequences spreading out from each of O's observations, actually increasing C_{max} even as C_i decreases locally—this being a *consequence* of learning by O.

Finally, if O is in the supersystem with the object systems, then others of these systems (other object systems to O) must also be observers of some kind. What they store in H_i must, because it affects their behaviors in ways O is not privy to, lead to an increase in effective C_{max}—that is, in apparent C_i, as well as in H_i. The third criterion for entropic information—that it must actually carry meaning for some system—will be explored in several different contexts in the next section, which must first summarize some recent cosmology.

The Internalist Perspective of Expanding Phase Space

So, once an observer is inside the same system containing the observed, it would seem that macroscopic information will necessarily be driven to increase (or, at least, that it can never decrease). A physical perspective that leads to congenial conclusions has been developed by Layzer (1975, 1977, 1988) and Frautschi (1982, 1988) (see also Nicolis 1986) on the basis of "Big Bang" cosmogony. The general idea is that, as the universe expands, it does so at a rate too fast for thermodynamic equilibrium to be achieved anywhere. The result of this is that (in Peircean fashion) matter is precipitated from energy, and clumps of matter build up frictionally as bits of it get in one another's way as they randomly seek equilibrium configurations, leading to the emergence of gravity, which then pulls together larger clumps. Matter is energy decelerated relative to the rates of physical translation it would take to achieve global equilibrium, and clumps of matter are local knots of generalized friction. From the point of view of the cascading Second Law, gravity is a collecting process triggered when there has come to be enough stuff to collect. Local attractors of all this are novas and supernovas that occasionally break through all the sticky slush, creating dust from clumps and accelerated energy from dust.

Nevertheless, clumps of matter form again out of supernoval dust as it once more traps itself in knots of collection. There is, then, a primal directionlessness or absence of order supposed in the motions of energy and matter; the universe begins, as in Peirce, in general *tychism*. This tychistic basis is logically the most parsimonious supposition about the beginning and fundament of the universe. It also remains the attractor for any formed regularities, which spontaneously move toward disorder given any chance (e.g., mutations, nervous fidgeting, cross-currents, frost cracking, historical accidents of all kinds).

Order, a kind of opposite of this ultimate final cause in any direction (beginning *or* end), can come into being only where the crush of matter upon itself in its undirected microscopic search for equilibrium becomes so intense, and results in such a massive crush, that regularities and *habits* (usage from Peirce) precipitate macroscopic order—wherever there is an observer to be impressed by it. Order is the ultimate coagulation, expressed most fully in senescence. Because the phase space is expanding, order and entropy can increase in the universe together (with order taken to be a function relating H_i in figure 3.4 to an observer). Order is generated by organizational constraints that produce regularities of behavior in a system detectable by an observer sensitive to or seeking them. It is not explicitly shown in figure 3.4, which is strictly an internalist representation.

As noted by Swenson, the physical Second Law is not evaded in these massive collections of matter. The particular forms taken by these macroscopic storages are selected according to the degree of their facilitation of entropy production. Only those systems that can pay for their order with high entropy production can come into being. But senescence nevertheless accumulates in every dissipative structure, putting a brake on entropy production. Since the gross rate only levels off rather than dropping down as does the specific rate (figure 3.2), these forms, even in senescence, can be viewed as maximizing entropy production—but the drop per unit mass shows that it is less than it might have been (and was in immature stages). It is at this point that, if we note (as in the previous section) that information itself behaves entropically for enclosed, engaged observers, we can see that there is no diminishment of the force of the Second Law even in the largest, most senescent and seemingly orderly clumps of matter. In these the thrust of the Second Law has merely switched from the production of heat to the (asymptotic) accumulation of variety and diversity.

Here we encounter the work of Brooks and Wiley (1988), who brought this viewpoint into biology. They have contended that the production of diversity in the biosphere since its inception should be viewed as an expression of the Second Law of Thermodynamics, claiming more than an analogy between the expanding phase space in cosmology and the expanding phase space in phylogeny. They attempted to further generalize this idea to the ontogeny of organisms, noting that as an embryo develops there are ever more cell types and elaborations of form. Their work is an exploration of rule 2 of the four rules of thermodynamically open systems given above—that dissipative structures will experience an increase in stored information during their development. Their successful applications were to the biosphere and the organism. Their application to ecosystems lacked informational closure, since information there could increase not only in diversity (which does often happen, at least part of the time) but also in elaborations of organismic (and soil) form and in ecosystematic behavior (e.g., symbioses). I believe that what has been said so far above tends to justify their basic view in a general way.

Returning to figure 3.4, we can examine the proposals of Brooks and Wiley in more detail. As the phase space accessible by its states increases during a system's development (e.g., by way of growth, generating new kinds of subsystems), C_{max}, the number of possibilities that could be further generated even by constrained, viable, permutations, increases rapidly in the early expansion, then begins to level off as the possibilities for any kind of finite system become exhausted. However, stored information, $C_{max} - C_i$, continues to expand with every increase in complexity, minimally causing frictional cross-purposes requiring more and more optimizations in an ever-more-complicated system. Thus, increases in informational entropy, C_i, seemingly paradoxically, drive the system further from the state of informational equilibrium represented by C_{max} (figure 3.4), which they also drive. (At informational equilibrium, any token of any one of all possible types could appear in the next moment at any arbitrarily chosen coordinates.)

Potential disorder at equilibrium continually expands as the system's complexity and organization increase. The more elaborate something is, the more of a mess its disintegration (to C_{max}) would make and the less likely any one particular disintegrated configuration would be to appear. Or, in another application (Lauder and Liem 1989), when more independent elements are involved in a system, the number of possible interconnections and novel functions rises. Each time new forms appear in the system, the number of possible recombinations of them with all the previous still-extant forms takes a jump such that their realization becomes increasingly remote in the more mature system, where those forms impose yet more frictional constraints. *As it develops, a system simultaneously expands its potential state space and proportionately limits more its actual occupation of the space.*

To take an example, consider species. I refer here to a lineage, or evolutionary species (Wiley 1981), for reasons the reader will discover on examining figure 3.6. Each is a system with informational closure established through gene flow. Reproduction in successful ones is always (at least slightly) in excess, resulting in a burgeoning of successful local populations that leads eventually, by dispersal, to range extensions and the founding of new populations. At the same time, recombinations and mutations (the spontaneous tendency toward disintegration at other scalar levels) lead to ever new genotypes' being held within the general framework. Gradually, different genotypes tend to get assorted into different geographic regions by drift and selection. Token populations of any successful species gradually find their way into more and more different geographic localities, even while these tokens themselves diversify (more different kinds in more different places). But the more kinds there are, the further the whole will be from a state of informational equilibrium.

A species is like a giant amoeba growing and flowing out over the Earth (Rapoport 1982). Indeed, we have implicitly recognized species as large-scale individuals by naming them. Now, this tendency to expand its state space would not be negated even if a species were to successfully cover the entire Earth; the forces of reproduction and translational movement would continue to press for still more lands to be occupied even near informational equilibrium, which would then proceed to be established by continued gene flow (which could, however, never catch up to the production of variety by mutation and recombination)—equilibration is never finished (Matsuno 1989).

Not infrequently, parts of a species lose contact with the mass (reproductive isolation; see Mayr 1942), and consequently there come to be more species on the earth's surface. And as each new one continues the behavior of the older ones, diversity tends to increase anywhere on that surface, all other things being equal. Large-scale movements of the Earth's surface (Nelson and Platnick 1981) also tend to scatter species around, even more massively and effectively. No species, nor even the biosphere as whole, can ever reach informational equilibrium (all types' being found everywhere), but that is where their behavior, visible at any time anywhere, tends.

I have proposed (Salthe 1989a) the term *virtual equilibria* for such inevitable but for practical reasons (of friction) unattainable equilibria, which would exist along with any informational system. Thus, the virtual equilibrium for a species of fish on the sandy seacoasts of eastern North America would be the existence of all its possible recombinant genotypes on all sandy seacoasts anywhere in the world. This would express its maximum informational capacity, C_{max}, against which the actual range of its realized genotypes, C_i, could be roughly compared.

Consider now an embryo (make it a vertebrate). In its early stages, the number of microscopic configurations it could assume is limited (think of the cell pattern in a blastula). Yet each blastula is quite different in these details from any other. Concerning its behavior: It is often ciliated, and it can rotate. If we mark the animal pole in a collection of these, we see that they access almost every possible position of the animal pole relative to some fixed point, so that each blastula also accesses a relatively large proportion of its limited number of potential states. Compare this with a tailbud embryo. There are many more cell types, and many more possibilities that could be generated here. Consider only the number of locations the limb buds might be at. But the embryos now are much more alike in important features, because they access relatively fewer of their possible states—upon pain of probably lethal abnormality.

Thus, as in figure 3.4, the less mature embryonic system is more entropic informationally than the later-stage one in actually accessing a greater proportion of its possible states (it also produces more physical entropy per unit mass—rule 1), while the more mature system is more informationally entropic than the immature one in having a greater number of states that it could access (it also produces grossly more physical entropy). The later stage, however, is absolutely more informationally entropic; owing to its greater complexity, there will have been more opportunity for historical accidents to mark each embryo in minor ways, so that the condition of any particular one compared with a standard, average individual becomes more uncertain. Also, more things can go wrong as the system gets more complicated, and it would have less ability to recover its trajectory after perturbation (rule 4).

For these reasons, the absolute variety of a collection of tail buds would be greater than that of a collection of blastulae. If there were an observer that could use these as semiotic tokens, a more complicated message could be sent with tail buds than with blastulae. And that brings us back to our third criterion for information acting as an entropy. We must show that there is an observer involved—that there is an H_o that necessarily must increase, driving H, the macroscopic informational entropy, ever upward.

We know in fact that there is at least one observer in the universe: our own scientifically based culture. What was said in the previous section applies to it as well. *Pacé* Thomas Kuhn, there *is* an accumulation, despite real losses, in the store of information held by this entity. And that information has also had important unforeseen effects on the world around it (think only of the pollution problem), thereby increasing C_{max} as a result of increases in its H_o. One could also argue that other systems could be taken to act as if they were observers, changing their H_i as a result of human, scientifically based action. For example, agricultural pests and microorganisms involved in nosocomial (iatrogenic) diseases respond to our activities with altered genetic information.

This raises the possibility of generalizing the semiotic observer/object (interpretant/sign/referent) relation, and of course we would use the specification hierarchy framework to do it. 'Observing' is something human societies do; however, it is not implausible that organisms, even nonhuman ones, do something similar but less specifiable (e.g., not describable by means of the hypothetico-deductive model). For example, a hummingbird will learn what a nectar feeder looks like, will find it when its location is moved, and will add it to its trapline pattern of foraging. The effect of its using the feeder will be to encourage further, perhaps consequential, human observations, and possibly to diminish its efficiency in pollinating certain plants. This extension would allow us to say that isolated human individuals (even if raised by wolves) could also be observers.

From here, the extension to any dissipative structure is in principle possible—especially if the powerful semiotic triangle (figure 3.5) is used. For orientation, I have indicated where H_o, C_{max}, and C_i, in the above analysis would fit on the diagram. We could read the hummingbird example as follows: The interpretant (its "theory") is generated by the mental/behavioral equipment of its species; a sign of food (the referent) would be something associated with what to us is the color red, relating to the feeder. For us that relationship appears to be symbolic, so that food is red only as a contingency, perhaps originally learned by conditioning and then built into the hummingbird gene pool by differential successes informed by differential sensitivity.

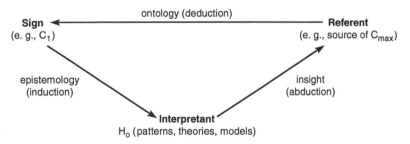

Figure 3.5 A version of the Peircean semiotic triangle giving an interpretation of concepts from the philosophy of science. Ontology is taken as the cohesion between the sign and its referent, which may be *iconic* (as a picture, like a shadow), or *indexical* (as a necessary part, like smoke as a sign of fire), or *symbolic* (when the relationship is constructed entirely by the interpretant). Epistemology is taken as the coherence between, e.g., measurements and theories—more narrowly, encodings into variables. Establishing patterns from measurements is the job of induction. Abduction imagines what is in the world, while deduction derives the kinds of observables that would be likely to reveal the content of that intuition.

From this diagram we can see that in semiotics the firstness of ontology is a projection of an interpretant. What is out there in the *Umwelt* depends upon who is undertaking the hermeneutic search. The primary reality is the secondness of epistemology, which begins as a chaotic grasping at (a jumble of tangled) straws until insight (probably informed by internal, inherited tendencies) begins to make its largely correct guesses, which build on one another by way of the wholeness of the supersystem (Bertalanffy 1933)—its consistency and robustness.

Using this framework (figure 3.6), we can see, for example, that a genotype is in the relation of bearing signs of the *Umwelt* to the organism, and that the lineage is what constructs these signs by way of natural selection. Figure 3.6 shows the rest of the apparatus needed to make this reading. (I am indebted to Jesper Hoffmeyer for starting this train of thought.) The monophyletic lineage appears semiotically to be an entity of much the same kind as the ontogenetic trajectory.

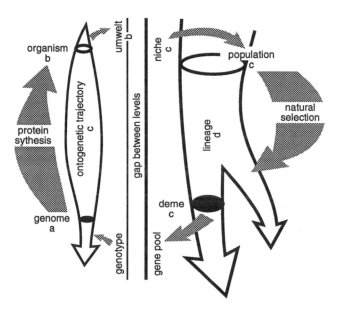

Figure 3.6 Semiotic relationships between biological entities. The levels are (a) molecular, (b) organismic, (c) trajectory/population/demic, and (d) lineage. Genome, organism, population, and deme are shown as segments of their respective trajectories. Information flow is shown by the shaded arrows; it is irreversible. Genotypic information informs the genome, which, via protein synthesis, informs the organism, which then constructs its *Umwelt*. At higher scalar levels, properties of the niche inform the population, which is honed by natural selection into the local deme, which will contribute a gene pool. Information crosses from *Umwelt* to niche by way of initiating conditions, and from gene pool to genotype by way of boundary conditions.

Both are systems of interpretance, with organisms and populations as interpretants. Both provide cohesion between the ecological (upper part of figure) and genealogical (lower part of figure) scalar hierarchies. Because of these relations, it seems that we (Eldredge and Salthe 1984) were hasty in assigning the lineage to the genealogical hierarchy. If we are to take it as a material entity, it is a dynamic process linking populations (analog, ecological) with demes (digital, genealogical). Species, *really* in the genealogical hierarchy, are just clusters of demes after lineage branching. (Ontogenetic trajectories may branch too, as in modular organisms.)

It would be necessary, in the framework of this text, to extend this kind of reasoning to abiotic dissipative structures. Establishing the interpretant is the primary need here, and so we need to consider what "discourse" these objects are involved in. Figure 3.7 shows what a collection of hurricanes did in early August for nearly 60 years. This figure is a sign of their discourse for us. What they do is spin clockwise (as we view them from below), rolling generally northward along the east coast of North America and curving out to sea in the north (Tannehill 1938) if they get that far before senescing. The interpretant can be taken to be that which responds to the signs of surface heat and ruggedness, a system of air movements generating an internal

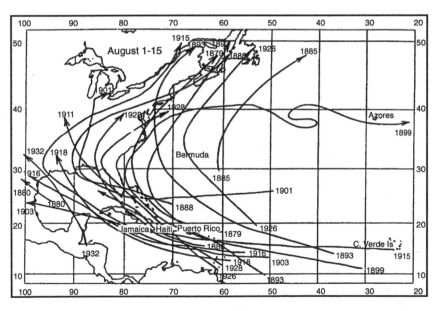

Figure 3.7 The discourse of hurricanes revealed over a 50-year period. Reprinted, with permission, from Tannehill 1938.

storage of information in layers and torques. Heat gradients and ruggedness are also kinds of information that a hurricane will affect as it responds to them, so that it seems likely that the passage of one hurricane will inform following ones if the time between them is not too long. These gradients are largely established by the world external to the gyres. But that is true of most of the niche parameters of organisms, as well. Only recently (Bateson 1988; Odling-Smee 1988) have we taken account of the niche-constructing behaviors of organisms—which must be larger than those of hurricanes, yet which are still a matter of degree.

So a system of winds, whose internal relationships (embodying H_o) could be viewed as a {model} of its environment (the large-scale temperate–tropical atmospheric circulation and the coastline of North America) that {interprets} heat and ruggedness gradients as signs of {food} (i.e., steep heat gradients perpendicular to the Earth's surface) and {enemies} (i.e., too much surface ruggedness). Now, {food} can keep the storm together by keeping it spinning strongly, and {enemies} can fritter away its power to do this. The referent is a requisite degree of steepness in the gradients, high for temperature (Emanuel 1988) and low for ruggedness.

While no climatologist is expected to be technically interested in such a formulation, for us the importance of the fact that we can make it is to show that semiotics is a discourse powerful enough to be extended in this way, revealing a relationship between organisms and other dissipative structures. More to the point just made, through its use we can justify using the concepts of information theory pretty broadly. That is, we could show that in nonhuman and even abiotic cases use of the term 'information', implying meanings, might be justified. This ends my sketch of a demonstration that macroscopic information behaves entropically.

Paired Infodynamical Perspectives

I could sum up much of what has transpired above by noting that there are two infodynamical perspectives on dissipative structures: the externalist, deriving from the discourse of classical thermodynamics (most recently from Prigogine), and the internalist, deriving from the works of the cosmologists Layzer and Frautschi. The externalist perspective, harking back to Spencer (1862—evolution as "the integration of matter and the dissipation of motion"), is one we naturally take with respect to systems of approximately our own scale as we stand next to them, seeing them from outside. Our concern has been to control them, or, failing that, to anticipate them and relate to them adaptively. So the degree of their orderliness becomes the primary fact about them philosophically; we even invent the term 'negentropy' to celebrate this interest. That this orderliness (regularity of behavior or form) is a joint relation between observer and object system requires that we take a semiotic perspective here. I will try to justify this statement a bit more.

Let's return to the hummingbird. We observe that it tends to visit our feeder at certain times of the day—we might even worry when it is late. But now take the perspective of a plant to be pollinated by the bird. The individual plant has its own rhythms of nectar production and readiness for pollen reception, which may or may not coincide fully with the bird's visits, so that the bird might instead pollinate a neighboring plant during any one of its passes through that stand. Add to this the vagaries of pollen placement and other factors and we see that, while the plant will not get pollinated outside of a certain temporal pattern established by the bird, the exact times when it will experience the hormone rush of having been pollinated is only roughly correlated with hummingbird visits. We see one pattern; the plant, with sequential blossoms, "sees" another.

Observers and object systems both have their own internal rhythms, true, and that will be emphasized by the physiologist, but a physiologist has rhythms of observation time that could easily create artifactual patterns in the facts discovered. All facts reflect an interaction of recurrent patterns, which makes a new pattern, at a different scale, of a different kind, like moiré patterns that emerge from the interaction of lines of similar scale viewed by an eye of effectively larger scale.

Pattern $\rightarrow$ predictability $\rightarrow$ regularity $\rightarrow$ order $\rightarrow$ negentropy is our concern in the externalist reading, and we have to discover a way to make the necessary practical existence of these for us resonate with our discovery of the eventual eroding of all patterns through the force of the Second Law. One (in fact classical) interpretation finds pattern to be a fleeting, local trace on the shifting sands of a basic uncertainty, paid for by its necessary association with increased physical entropy production. Patterned form is somehow illegitimate—something stolen. Another interpretation sees the impulse of entropy increase to itself require, and create, patterns which facilitate realization of the Second Law, which otherwise could only be embodied in slow, grinding friction. Here patterned form is a legitimate co-product of entropy production. These are respectively pessimistic and optimistic versions of the externalist perspective. In the former, work must be forever done (by, e.g., people) to stave off inevitable disintegrations; in the latter, a Siva-like universe prodigiously makes a bounty of forms in its exhilarating rush toward everything at once, creating and breaking so as to create again (often at a new scalar level). In both versions this is a modern philosophy, holding that there is one law over and above all local events, allowing analysis of anything from its perspective, and delivering universal power to those individuals who know it.

I have suggested above that these perspectives reflect concern with, and emphasis upon, different stages in the life cycles of dissipative structures, with the optimistic view focusing on immature stages and the pessimistic one (appropriately enough) on senescent stages. I believe this life-history approach provides a unifying framework here, which I will explore again in chapter 4.

The more recent internalist perspective has had a different flavor from the first. We are necessarily inside the universe we are observing, and so, from the point of view of BCNDC science, we are in a weak position for observation. Just to begin systematic observations, we need to suppose, e.g., cosmological principles. And certainly there is no hope of controlling, or even of manipulating, any of it in our own favor. We are lost in a maze, an informational jungle, trying to decode its secrets by force of our own rhythmic (systematic) activities alone, which we use to construct observational windows. Our concern with artifactual observations and with protocols is keen, and it leads us quickly to the self-consciousness of various uncertainty principles. Our position is that of the user of sympathetic magic: Rigor alone must be held to lead to knowledge, and (as is little acknowledged) that knowledge must be local only, which is what all effective sympathetic magic has been—which is why it can never be efficacious in the hands of objective observers. This is by default a postmodern perspective (Artigiani 1993).

Compared with the classical, externalist reading of infodynamics, we are here concerned with signs whose referents come to be, explicitly (as in cosmology), theories *per se* (see figure 3.5). Thus, our insight is redirected toward formalisms. The externalist has clear, "objective" referents to manipulate; the internalist has only patterns of signs, and ontology becomes necessarily and obviously nothing but a social construction. The internalist perspective is semiotically degenerate (or immature—just as polluted waters become relatively immature again). There are no unchanging referents for the signs. All is interpretation, and a too-ambitious attempt to use interpretations instrumentally, as in astrology (with its incongruously modernist claims), is doomed to failure. Willy-nilly, we are all internalists in our postindustrialist polluted world, and our habitual externalist scientific approach will be of little use to us here.

In the internalist world, the very nature of typical scientific signs comes to be changed as well. In the externalist view, such signs are canonically indexical—that is, what we measure about something is a necessary part of it, and, if not fully indexical (like smoke in relation to fire), it is at least iconic, like a shadow. In the internalist world, signs tend to have an entirely arbitrary relation with their supposed (hoped-for) referents; they are primarily symbolic.

Of course, this means that—while externalists are always realists, believing in the separate existence of the referents they so want to manipulate—internalists may just as well be nominalists, because ultimately relationships alone are of interest to them. This means that systems science (despite its universalist ideology) and semiotics will be of special use to internalists (as they have never been for externalists—one recalls how many systems scientists have had to make livings advising corporations on how to reorganize). Internalists tend, as well, to more easily be constructionist, as opposed to the implicit structuralism of externalists. For internalists, structures are type constructions made by comparative study so as to gain power over their separate embodiments.

Part of the reason for the present work is to point out these last facts. We need entirely new patterns of thought, some of which may be suggested herein, if we are to continue our adventures on Earth. Among the items that have changed significances for us in the internalist perspective is creativity. In the classical perspective, prediction is the grail and development is the preferred form of discourse seeking it. History is viewed as accidents, and evolution is used only to explain (away) disturbing differences and variety. Since prediction has a limited and local role in the postmodern world, history and evolution assume a new position—one which is made more clear by allying these labels with the concept of creativity. One needs once more, I suppose, to look up Bergson 1911 for a beginning, and then to work toward . . . what?

Toward an Infodynamics

Infodynamics, then, will be the study of disorder (and what could be a more perfect science for today?) in any medium. Boltzmann showed us that thermodynamics had this theoretical understanding. A good model of his classical application would be a crystal, like iodine, sublimating into a gas. The crystal has a high degree of microscopic orderliness; the gas is presumed to be entirely randomly distributed in the containing volume, and so is almost perfectly disorderly. The transition from crystal to gas is a spontaneous cascade. There is thermodynamic closure here; the process is isolated in an observational chamber, so that there is no exchange of energy or matter with the outside (which might, for example, drive a reciprocal collecting process). There is informational closure here too; all potential molecular relationships are conserved, because no new molecule is imported, nor is any any exported. The Second Law is exemplified by the fact that the potential relationships (of any molecule with any other) come to be more and more closely realizable as the metal continues to sublimate.

Compare this situation with a city. The city at any moment has some of the properties of a giant crystal. (It is a rather entropic "crystal," because of the long period of development and individuation it has undergone, but that is not important to this example.) Order can be detected in the streets, the windows, the rhythms of the ebb and flow of rushing. The buildings do not exchange places, nor do the streets alter their positions, and most of the people follow habitual tracks most of the time. If we take this city at a given moment, no buildings or streets will be added or deleted, and we will have informational closure. Now consider the problem of calculating C_{max} in this case. We would have to imagine all possible rearrangements of buildings, windows, bricks, streets, and people—examples of which we sometimes encounter in dreams. C_{max} would, we can see qualitatively, be enormously larger than C_i, which is actually generated largely by some unexpected motions of people, or maybe a window gets broken. To make this infodynamic, we need a possible-worlds approach (Kripke 1972).

Suppose that you have imagined all possible counterfactual worlds, each a product of a different evolution in the development of this city until now, and you have the relevant collection before you, in the style of figure 1.4. That would be the situation of informational equilibrium, C_{max}. Now, if you were to think of the city as a giant iodine crystal, you could examine in a thought experiment a collection of such "crystals" to see what would happen (keeping our own scale relative to each crystal) if they were to disintegrate in nuclear wars. Each of the end states would be different, and each would be a condition of the city in one of the possible worlds. Another scenario is that the city might be picked apart for building materials by another society, as was Karnak. In another scenario, everything would be as it is except that one important building got placed in a different position through historical accident, or one historically important person went into a different field. The constraint is to maintain informational closure (which, in fact, was violated in the thought experiment above; bricks would have gotten fragmented in the explosions).

This raises problems as to how small in scale we should read the city in this example. If we go down only to bricks, then, in the explosion cases, one brick can become two or three, violating informational closure. I point this out to show (1) that it emphasizes the constraint of informational closure in possible-worlds "calculations" (which, we can now see, were outlined rather sloppily in the previous paragraph) and (2) that it shows that, in cases without informational closure, spontaneous events result in an increase in information—populations grow, cities grow, explosions grow, cadavers become dispersed. Karnak and Rome were picked apart, and that dispersed their pieces into many more places—they have continued to access more geographical state space. Consider populations, then; some might decline and become extinct, spontaneously seeming to violate the purported application of the Second Law to information.

The case is clear enough: such populations are being (we do *not* have informational closure here) acted upon by other dissipative structures so as to be worn away or recycled. Disease organisms, predators, and climatic changes have not interrupted the populations' internal tendencies to reproduce and expand; instead they have systematically eroded the results of that activity. This is not the case with Karnak and Rome, because their pieces more or less retained their identities in their dismantling, which was done relatively carefully. Their boundaries are simply getting fuzzier—all the better to serve the Second Law! As figure 3.6 suggests, populations are not dissipative structures in and of themselves anyway; they are parts of the local lineage. In that case the explanations just given would be unnecessary.

So, in order to calculate C_{max}, we must have informational closure. When there is no closure, the system follows the Second Law, with both C_i and (therefore necessarily) C_{max} continuing to increase. Brooks and Wiley had informational closure in their examples of genomic space in the evolution of organisms and (in their diagrams, if not their actual discussion (Brooks, personal communication)) cell-type and tissue-type spaces in organismic ontogeny. (Remember that even mature cells continue to change in various aging processes, so that they continue to individuate after differentiation is complete. The ultimate end would be that each cell comes to define its own cell type asymptotically—we could visualize this process with figure 2.8.)

But scale is causing problems here—and it offers a solution. How do we determine the proper scale at which to define the coordinates of a system to be rearranged when seeking estimations of C_{max}? In the example of the city, if we went down to the molecular level we could probably preserve informational closure even in a nuclear explosion. But what independent justification could there be for such a decision? None; the city does not, as a city, operate at that scalar level. One might think the same of bricks; but here we know that the city has dynamic processes that explicitly deploy bricks, and we could, using H_{sc}, use that fact to justify our going down to bricks in scale when visualizing the rearrangement of the city. So, the rule that different scalar levels are screened off from one another dynamically allows a plausible in-principle solution here. But why descend that far? Why not stop at the scale of windows and people? Or even of buildings and streets? In the latter case the calculation of C_{max} actually could become feasible. The answer comes from Dretske's (1981) definition of information.

Dretske defines information as the most highly specified digital content an analog percept can have. Choice of specification (of "units of analysis") comes from the observer and depends on the observer's nature and interests, and this brings in material causes. So, a skyscraper, if the observer has that category, is seen as such, and not, *explicitly at the same time*, as a less specified 'building', or as an even less specified 'structure of mud and iron', or, in a different direction, as the product of a certain kind of labor, or even as a disturbance on the observer's retina. All of these possibilities can be carried by the same interaction between observer and object system—indeed, an unlimited number of such integrities is possible for any perceived object (Buchler 1966). Any of them could be the denotation of that interaction; however, only the most highly specified in the observer's repertoire will in fact function that way, all the others being relegated to connotations or potential analytical derivatives. So, if the observer has the category 'Chrysler Building', that will of necessity supplant 'skyscraper' in a particular instance of an interaction of this kind.

The solution from this line of thought to where to find the city's joints, that we may cut it at natural places in our attempts to conceptually reearange it, is that we must find these joints where proper names abut: roughly, at the streets-and-buildings scalar level.

So, Dretske takes information to be digital in order to preserve in wider discourses its properties in information theory—or, we could say, in infodynamics. Again (recall chapter 2) we encounter the notion that cognitive categories are digital impositions on an analog world. Information is also taken to be maximized in the sense that the most highly specified category will always supplant a less specified one when the opportunity arrives for that to happen. What that does is pack into the information the largest possible amount of derivative information available for unpacking by analysis.

Here, Dretske has imposed an information-maximization principle for signs not unlike that of Haken (1988), who uses it in a mathematical technique for deriving microscopic distributions from macroscopic ones. Haken defines what he calls "information capacity" to be the amount of information carried per sign: this is in the spirit of Dretske, who referred to that concept as being necessary for a philosophically richer information theory. Clearly, more specified symbols carry more information, and less specified ones less, just as more developed systems store more information than more immature ones (rule 2 above).

This information-maximization principle should not be confused with the Second Law as it works itself out with information, as discussed earlier in this chapter. It is a property of observers, based on the human case. It may well be, and is indeed plausible, that during ontogeny observational categories would become more and more highly specified as the nervous system developed, so that an embryo could not detect the equivalent of 'Chrysler Building', restricting its "observations" to an equivalent of 'structure of mud and steel.' If that were found to be the case, it might give the Second Law a toehold even here. Indeed, I find it an intriguing possibility completely consistent with the thrust of this work, in connection with the specification hierarchy. Development, then, would involve a gradual increase in H_o as a constitutive process, and not merely contingently, as a part of individuation, as I treated it earlier in this chapter.

We might now review our arguments in favor of viewing information as behaving entropically:

> • Formally, as constructed out of digital distinctions, it is a measurable quantity using the Boltzmann equation for measuring entropy.
> • Materially, the energy exchanges that produce it are conserved. In non-equilibrium thermodynamics, energy is viewed as being dissipated into both heat and structure. Since structure is described informationally, we can see that energy is dissipated into both physical entropy and information; this shows that physical entropy and information have similar ontic significance.
> • Efficiently, information necessarily must increase (certainly never decrease) in amount if, as is always the case naturally, the observer is in the same supersystem as the objects revealed by the information.

The Second Law works itself out with information as well as with energy. In particular, information stored in the observer, H_o, is seen to necessarily increase. Information stored in a system, H_i, can be estimated by the amount of information an observer would need to have in H_o in order to specify an object system sufficiently. The sufficiency is imposed by the observer; however, no matter what categories it uses, we can be certain that they will be the most highly specified available to it, and that the degree of specification of the signs (and so their "information capacity" per sign, *sensu* Dretske and Haken) will continue to be increased whenever possible. Finally, we by whom this discourse is carried (Western, Faustian people) tend to strive to increase our information about everything.

Summary

In this chapter I have identified several perspectives on thermodynamics:

(1) The classical, externalist perspective, concerned with explaining orderliness in the face of the Second Law. Within this, we find (a) the classical pessimistic interpretation that order is only a fleeting phenomenon afforded by peculiar (and, in the universe, rare) boundary conditions which allow it to occur despite energy disspation into heat, and (b), associated with the newer, nonequilibrium approach to thermodynamics, the optimistic interpretation that order commonly results from macroscopic organization, which exists because it necessarily facilitates entropy production in the universe. Such organizations are the universal means to transcend a purely frictive, and therefore slow, microscopic dissipation of stored energies to heat. In this view, dissipation of energy is into both heat and form.

(2) A newer, internalist perspective, for which order is simply one common result of massive frictive/gravitational buildups of matter, increasingly likely the more matter is crunched together. Disorder and organization necessarily increase together as the phase space of the universe increases in the Big Bang, since equilibrium distributions of energy and matter are precluded by the speed of expansion. In this view, order is a result of organization, which is itself a *direct product* of the Second Law, being defined as the difference between actual and equilibrium distributions of matter—a difference brought about by collisions in the haphazard search of matter for its equilibrium distribution. This shows that organization in this view is ontologically a reflection of generalized friction, and, in fact functions as if it were in the same category as friction, which is, then, simply a more general logical type in the same category with organization. (See Banerjee et al. 1990, for concordant definitions of order and organization.)

Within this internalist, expanding phase-space perspective, there is a further interpretation: that information itself behaves entropically and is a direct product of the Second Law. Indeed, going back to interpretation b of perspective 1, we see that, as energy transformations are dissipated into heat and macroscopic structure, energy transformations can (since structure is described informationally) be viewed as being dissipated into information as well as into heat. In this view it could be said that both physical entropy and information capacity are necessary products of energy transformations, and so they are both governed by the Second Law of Thermodynamics, which now functions as a second law of infodynamics. Thus, there is a direct relationship between the entropic nature of energy and that of information.

Under the constraint that the observer is in the same supersystem as the structures from which it obtains information (which is necessarily true when the supersystem is the world), it can be shown that information must behave entropically, as in the Second Law. This interpretation leads to the initiation of the field of infodynamics.

The infodynamical perspective is another grand unifying scheme like hierarchy theory, and this book represents an attempt to begin to meld them into something even grander. This grandness and this universality are distinctly modern; however, the internalist perspective cannot, by its nature, be truly modern, because it leads to a self-referential, reflexive mood that eventually leads us to see how local any construction necessarily is. Thus, the internalist perspective, which gives rise to the "powerful" modernity of infodynamics, is itself postmodern, being located in the discursive formation of peculiarly Western thought.

Chapter 4

Self-Organization, Development, and Individuation

In this chapter I explore the general difference between development and evolution and assert that development is the fundamental process in self-organization, individuation (evolution) being the result of an ineliminable margin of error. I review self-organization, and I suggest that infodynamically it amounts to an increase in determinability which carries an increase in agency. This determinability is carried by constitutive increases in stored information during development. The canonical developmental sequence is from immature tychism in a vague system through a mature maximization of power to a senescent approach to minimum entropy production in a highly determinate system that is finally interrupted by forcible recycling.

Major consideration is given to the modeling relation and to the relation of interpretation. Higher-scalar-level entities interpret lower-scalar-level ones, while the latter model the former. A self is defined as a system that collects some of its own cascading, and organization is taken to be the result of the activities of a system with a viewpoint; hence organization reflects integrities between observers and object systems. Two new theoretical entities are defined: the *developmental* or *ontogenetic trajectory* (a life history taken as a whole) and the *morphological trajectory* (a similar material entity, historically reflected in the lineage of organic evolution discourse).

It is interesting that organic evolution is said to supply the general theoretical grounding of biology. This means that, despite our overriding interest in subduing and taming nature, and the consequent high value placed on predictability, understanding variety is construed to be the major point of our discourse.

One way to read this is to see it as a consequence of focusing on our own uniqueness, of taking this as the mystery we are trying to probe. Despite the massive urgings of the semitic religions that humans are the only things worth considering (almost the only things present) in nature, we have had to confront the fact of our difference from other kinds of organisms. Because of those religious urgings, we have also had to face a radical separateness. If we were alone in biology such relations could not be known. On the one hand, what *are* we doing here? On the other, what are *we* doing here? How did we get to be here, with this desperate need to understand in order to second guess, anticipate, and control things—to bring them in line with our own being?

Our own uniqueness, then, makes a bridge between the need to control and the bewildering variety found in the buzzing, blooming tangled bank. That is how I will construct it in this chapter, where our uniqueness will be taken to be one definite result of a universal spontaneous cascade of informational infidelity.

Another aspect of this line of inquiry surfaces here too. How did we come, today, to so completely privilege, not process, but information? Or, moving to a more limited point, why has the study of biology gone so completely into the study of genetic information at the expense of the study of material process? This text is, in part, a reaction against this excessive idealism in the science of biology (perhaps understandable in face of the fact that the information in a single virion could signify the decline of a population of metazoans).

A closely related question is: Why is the philosophical base of biology not ontogeny instead of phylogeny (which, for a time in the nineteenth century, seemed to be the direction the discourse was taking)? I will not pursue these historical questions here, but I will note them as being behind the present attempt to outline a philosophical basis for biology organized primarily around development, not evolution. The reason for doing this seems self-evidently simple to me: Development is the material process that all living systems (*and* all dissipative structures) engage in.

Evolution is the result of failures to replicate and generate; it is not a process, but an accumulation of the informational consequences of not being able to continue unaffected by experience. It is not that I feel we should be uninterested in the results of these sequences of "mistakes" (our own difference guarantees that interest); it is that we need to understand first, it seems to me, the material processes that mediate it. What I undertake in this chapter will be to understand development and evolution, simultaneously, as aspects of a process of *self-organization* that, for organisms, will be seen to occur at a higher-than-organismic scalar level.

The Type/Token Distinction

We need first to review the distinction between *types* and *tokens* (Eco 1976; Wiener 1958). We can use the computer simulations of figure 1.4 as a nice example. The overall similarity of pattern between the different runs of a matrix of Boolean automata—what might be called the structure of the system—defines its type. Each separate run is a token of that type. Tokens, therefore, have the diagnostic characteristics of the type, but are also heterogeneous among themselves in other characteristics. Tokens are heterogeneous instances (and actual signs) of types. Types evolve because they must be instantiated by tokens, and tokens always become unique through individuation. An example would be the concept of species in the practice of systematists. The "species" diagnosis is a description of a kind of organism, and any individual specimen that conforms to that description is taken to be a token of that type. After Darwin, and Mayr (1942), we all, of course, expect tokens of species diagnoses to be otherwise heterogeneous.

If two tokens were identical, they would be one. In the natural world, no two material objects of any kind are identical. If they appear to be so, continued search will disclose a difference (and if you tire before finding one, you can mark them yourself, creating the necessary signs tracing the different histories of all material objects).

Now, of course, items, as they function for some interpretant, may be lumped into classes, which are collections of things with no differences that make a difference (to the interpretant). Classes and types differ primarily in that tokens of types are explicitly acknowledged to have (immediately irrelevant but pregnant) differences among themselves. In addition, classes are usually taken to be human artifacts—products of linguistic discourse. Types, on the other hand, can be natural in that they function in certain ways in natural systems (as do ecological vicars), where they are "classified" by natural processes. Interestingly, Atlan et al. (1986) call the uncovering of stable patterns in the computer simulations referred to above a "classification procedure."

We have already set up a system, the specification hierarchy, for understanding the production of tokens *from* types. If figure 2.8 is taken to represent the keying out of an object, each dichotomy, moving from the top, contributes toward revealing its nature or category (the letter at a branch tip at the bottom). If instead it represents the process of ontogeny in a collection of kinds of organisms, then the logical type at each node is a stage in the process of self-discovery of a particular type (say, a species label at nodes 6–11) or of an individual organism (one of the letters). Individuals are Rylean categories, as was explained in chapter 2. Whatever their unique being-in-itself might be, they would be something a bit different in each interaction in which they figure, so that a search for their uniqueness would end in constructing a contour (Buchler 1966), which is the overall integrity of a natural system. Individuals would be constructed as Rylean categories and as Buchlerian contours. Each separate integrity that helps make up the contour would be a member of the category constructed as that contour.

As an entity develops it becomes ever more clearly an individual because it is acquiring a more complicated form along the way (the second developmental rule of chapter 3), which then provides more possibilities for differences between tokens, while historical accidents are marking the tokens all along, creating those differences. That is to say, the epigenetically prior logical types, the temporally primary developmental stages, are types with fewer possible kinds of discernible variant tokens. Their high potentiality of indefinite, unreduced degrees of freedom would not contribute to their determinability, because that can be constructed only out of clearly discernible alternatives. No discourse or natural process makes fine distinctions among immature systems. Developing systems in these early stages are in a condition that will not support many distinctions, a condition that will not support many distinctions, a condition I will call *vagueness*.

Vagueness was discussed in detail by Pierce, and I will base my interpretation on his discussions. (See Almeder 1980; Buchler 1951; Esposito 1980; Merrell 1991; Wiener 1958; Raposa 1989.) Only singular individuals are entirely determinate (this not meaning completely specifiable). There are two ways of being indeterminate; one is by being general (universal) and the other is by being vague (imprecise, indefinite).

Generalities are necessities. The traits that are necessarily true of something are its implied general properties; all birds have feathers, and so the information 'having feathers' can tell you something necessarily is a bird but does not specify which one. Taxonomies and keys are concerned with hierarchies of increasingly general generalities; birds would be 'feathered homeotherms, with beaks, that lay eggs . . . etc.'. This kind of diagnosis is never imprecise or indefinite. A reconstructed common ancestor (or, in a different discourse, an archetype) is the entity that has all the features held in common by its descendants (or clear rudiments from which they could be imagined to have been derived). Such a one has no other features whatever, in principle, and so there is no vagueness concerning what it refers to; it is fully specified; it is *perfectly* general; it is also obviously a very special kind of linguistic construct.

When we consider signs of natural objects, if they are not fully determinate (as would be that singular parakeet, Blue Boy, sitting there, representing himself, giving no latitude for interpretation), they tend to be, not general, but vague. Some simple examples of vagueness will help us get at the idea. Consider an impressionist painting; if we move closer to see better the features of the young woman, even what we had disappears. The progressive enlargement of a photograph (as in Antonioni's *Blow-Up*) runs into the same problem. The newly constructed maps of the cosmic radiation of the universe (Partridge 1992) show us a vague sketch of the early universe 100,000 years after the big bang; it must have been a relatively vaguely formed entity. The coastline of an island, should we want to measure it exactly, has no definite value; it depends on how finely (to what scale) we choose to measure it, and we could always add more to it by jumping down in scale again. Consider also predictions made by oracles and card readers, such as "There will be a brunette. . . ." Lest we think that mathematics is a realm that excludes vagueness, we might remind ourselves that there is no definite sum of real numbers between, e.g., 2.000 . . . and 3.000. . . .

Actually, all signs need interpretation, because they cannot really refer to a singular individual-in-itself. 'Stan Salthe' refers not to me but to a class of integrities, and we need further specification to determine which subclass that might be in any instance. Such specification is often carried by context and connotation. Signs can be determinate only insofar as they refer to the diagnoses of types, but remain indeterminate in all other respects. Tokens are signs of types but are never fully disclosed by that function. As Peirce put it, there cannot be absolute individuals (in discourse).

Vague information (and all information is vague to some degree, the more so the less specified it is—hence Dretske's and Haken's interest in a maximum-information rule for signs) always needs further signs in order to be determined more fully. On the contrary, general information is more or less automatically determinable by the interpretant. Peirce's example of this was "all men are mortal." Which man? Any one you choose; the statement applies perfectly to all of them, and is necessarily implied for each singular one that might be self-evidently before you.

On the other hand, the more vague a sign is, the more is it describable as signifying possibility rather than necessity, often being only suggestive—it is not this, not that, not a, not b, not even not-b clearly, and so on according to how many different situations or items might imply it. Because logical priority maps onto temporal primacy in the specification hierarchy, I will make use of these notions in describing development. Logical types and common ancestors are generalities constructed backward from known individuals; developmental stages are degrees of diminishing vagueness moving forward—yet these two concepts map onto each other. The sense of it will be, e.g., that adults of all species of frogs imply (in the sense of conceptual subordination) the same blastula, which is a relatively vague entity, not determinable without the aid of further signs to be that of any particular kind of frog, and which (since, in the spirit of Baer, it cannot be distinguished among species) still has the possibility of becoming many kinds.

Ecological and Genealogical Hierarchies

Eldredge and Salthe (1984) made a distinction between ecological (or economic) aspects and genealogical aspects of the scalar hierarchy of nature. My own further interpretation (Salthe 1985) was that the ecological hierarchy represents energy-flow, dynamical aspects of the world, while the genealogical hierarchy represents informational aspects specifically based on the genetic information in biological systems. The ecological hierarchy, then, applies to any aspect of material nature, scale jumps being found everywhere. The genealogical hierarchy is evidently applicable to living systems only, although something similar might appear wherever relatively stable information storage is possible—say, in clays (Cairns-Smith 1982), or in the brain.

Change in the ecological hierarchy is momentary only, and so can be symbolized as a dy/dt. It is detectable in "ecological (or physiological) time," while change in the genealogical hierarchy tends to occur in "evolutionary time." However, there are geological (and astronomical) processes in the ecological hierarchy which, though they can be constructed as dy/dt, take as long as "evolutionary" time to occur. The difference has to do with cogent moments, a large-scale one of which can be analyzed into many smaller-scale ones. Evolutionary time appears when the observer's moments are small relative to the scale of the phenomena being investigated.

The genealogical hierarchy was distinguished to mark the importance for biological systems of the specially stable, symbolic information storage in genes, and this singled out the processes of replication, reproduction, transmission, and sorting by selection of this information as being in its particular realm. Obviously these processes are also dynamic and have their own dy/dt-type descriptions, and so they could be said to be merely a part of the ecological hierarchy highlighted by observer interest. Indeed, one supposes that there is materially only one scalar hierarchy of nature; however, it seems to biologists and others that that hierarchy became radically more elaborated after the origin of life, and so we need to mark the reason for this.

Because living systems are a more highly specified condition of material systems in general, the latter are not only historically primal but also logically prior to them. Because of their interest in informational dynamics in respect to living systems only, Brooks et al. (1989)

took the contrary view that the genealogical hierarchy is primary. If they had restricted their interest to informational aspects of species and organisms, that could have been a valid operational decision. But, extending their approach to ecosystems, using diversity to measure information capacity resulted in incoherence, because ecosystems do not achieve closure with living systems only; they involve many abiotic processes and dissipative structures, most of which antedate living systems—in particular, they involve the scalar levels within which living systems proliferated. Molecular, cellular, organismic, populational, and other scalar levels cannot have been the creations of living systems; they must have preexisted them as necessary frameworks (e.g., for oxidation, for structuration (biotic or abiotic), for the processes of decomposition and recycling).

Figure 4.1 is my reworking of the suggestions of Brooks et al. (1989) concerning thermodynamic relations between the two aspects of the scalar hierarchy. For them, all entropy production in living systems takes place in the genealogical hierarchy—that is to say, it is influenced by genetic information. Thus, they forget that enzymatic catalysis, as close as that is to genetic information temporally and in scale, only speeds up preexisting chemical reactions. Recalling Pattee's (1972) distinction between dynamics and symbolic information, we can see that genetic information affects only the rates and the effective sequential patterns of collections of catalyzed reactions, not their qualitative na-

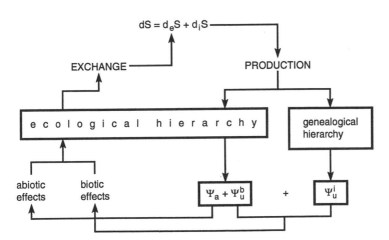

Figure 4.1 Entropic behaviors of the ecological and genealogical hierarchies Here ψ_a represents external dissipation into heat, ψ_u^b represents dissipation into biomass, and ψ_u^i represents dissipation into genetic information and its higher-scalar-level reflections (e.g., population structure, breeding system, and species areograph). Adapted from Brooks et al. 1989.

ture or their existence. The reactions themselves and the information specifying them .(equilibrium constants, the necessary form of active sites for catalysis, and so on) are parts of the ecological hierarchy, and an entropy produced by them is produced in that hierarchy.

From my perspective, only entropy produced by biological systems specifically in connection with replication, reproduction, mating, and immigration can be reckoned as being produced in the genealogical hierarchy. To calculate this, one needs a formulation like Cody's (1966) distinctions among maintenance, growth, and reproduction as potential channels for energy dissipation. Many papers in the field of life-history studies supply details about exactly how energies are thus allocated in different species at different times of their life cycles.

Because of past misunderstandings, it could be beneficial to quickly review the process of natural selection in this light. The *Umwelt* interactions of organisms in connection with nutrients, shelter, and predator (disease) escapes (activities belonging to the viability component of fitness) take place in the ecological hierarchy, and could be described with differential equations. Differential failures here between individual organisms of different genotypes give rise, as a by-product, to the sorting in the gene pool of gametes of different genotypes.

Only energies expended specifically in processes proximally required to set up the sorting (those belonging to the fertility component of fitness) are counted as being allocated to genealogy. They represent tribute to the particular informational realm—the genealogical hierarchy—that emerged with living systems. These dynamics too could be describable with differential equations, but the information itself (or its ramifications at other scalar levels) could not (or could, but only very awkwardly, in a way similar to the emergence of chaotic patterns from dynamic interactions). Energies expended in running, in growing, and in all the other processes of interaction with the environment are flowing through the ecological hierarchy just as are winds and rivers. This is a consequence of understanding organisms to be elaborations of abiotic dissipative structures, a key perspective of the present work.

Another comment about infodynamics; if information and dynamics occur, as it were, in different realms, are the word 'infodynamics' and what it labels incoherent? No. Infodynamics in its narrowest sense refers to regularities in changes in information. One can discuss the rules of change of anything that might be used semiotically without implying that the thing itself *is* a species of change. Information generally supplies formal rather than material causes, and final rather than efficient causes. But we could study the material causes of the ability of information to change (e.g., the presence of a pool of tokens of alternative types) or the proximate efficient causes of these changes. Because infodynamics studies the pertinent changes in systems of any objects or events that might serve as signs in informational exchanges, it encompasses both ecological and genealogical realms.

Development and Individuation

The major constitutive process of change occurring in the ecological hierarchy is development. Insofar as they show discernible regularities of change, all dissipative structures develop, and description of their changes tends to be constructed as the study of their development (whatever it is actually called). This chapter is concerned mostly with the constitutive changes of dissipative structures, especially biological ones.

The distinction made above between development as *predictable irreversible change* and individuation (or evolution) as the *irreversible accumulation of historical information* is based on suggestions made by Lewontin (1982), Goodwin (1984), and Williams (1985). Those authors, being less constructionist and more realist than I, further noted that development is the result of a tendency that is only with difficulty deflected by perturbations; it is hemeorhetic, constitutive change that tends to return after perturbation to a condition near what it would have been if it had not been deflected. Hence, it has structural stability (Thom 1975). Development as a knowable tendency naturally attracts cybernetic interpretations of control from within (Bertalanffy 1933), or readily supports the idea that it realizes structures (Goodwin et al. 1989). Both perspectives will be adopted herein as reasonable interpretations of the empirical repeatability of developing systems.

What *is happening* in change, then, is development. Only this aspect of change, not evolution, is subject to systematic discourse and therefore is its discursive substance. (The object that changes, however, can be treated evolutionarily, as in biological systematics.) And development describes an entity (a trajectory) that has all the signs of an object subject to scrutiny. It has the general thermodynamic configuration described in chapter 3: a burst of impulse generating a cascade of elaboration. It could be said to represent the accumulation of informational constraints that increasingly restrict the potentialities accessible to the developing system (as shown in figure 2.8).

By contrast, evolution is not any *thing* at all. More pointedly, it is not a process of any kind—certainly not a constitutive one. It is the accumulation of informational imprints generated in a system upon recovery from contingent collisions and environmental fluctuations (or as a result of internal excursions, such as mutations)—scars which mark its experience in the world. In point of fact it is difficult to see, given the above definition, how one could construe a discourse about it at all. Yet there supposedly is one: the synthetic theory of evolution. (I leave aside systematics, which is a classificatory discourse about generality sometimes informed by belief in organic evolution.)

Since ontogeny and phylogeny both show developmental and individuating tendencies, I am not making distinctions between them in this section. Given parents, or an ancestral species, one could predict a good deal about what the offspring, or a descendent species, would be like. Information with important further consequences is preserved in both cases; thus, phylogeny, like ontogeny, can be viewed as a *bona fide* material process with developmental as well as evolutionary aspects. Therefore, I am not equating phylogeny with evolution, for the latter of which I am advancing the very general definition given above. In this view, phylogeny is the particular material process that displays organic evolution on Earth. That is, it is not synonymous with 'evolution'; it is closer to 'organic evolution' taken as a proper noun.

Looking briefly at synthetic theory as a supposed example of evolutionary discourses, we find that it is fundamentally a kind of statistics (Fisher 1958; Wright 1968–1978)—the "population thinking" of Mayr (1980). Statistics, of course, is discourse about the distributions of distinct alternatives, or perhaps just about distributions. It has no particular subject matter, and it can be applied to any.

In the Darwinian core of synthetic theory, alternative genotypes in a deme, behaving stochastically, tend to get sorted according to environmental influences, which bias their distributions in space and time. It has been suggested, from the point of view of the scalar hierarchy, that something very similar occurs with demes (Wade 1978; Wilson 1980) and species (Gould and Eldredge 1977; Stanley 1979); this shows that the idea can be extended throughout almost the entire realm of the genealogical hierarchy, there being, of course, few material limits to the applications of statistics (or of the selection idea).

In neo-Darwinian discourse their are no privileged patterns of distributional biasis, there is nothing that could be called a constitutive process, and there is no "progress." There would be consequences if selective biasis generated extreme, uniform distributions—for one thing, demes with a single highly adapted genotype could no longer evolve and would eventually become extinct. Natural progress in this direction by way of selection is usually held to be prevented by the stochastic behavior of environmental selection pressures. Depew (1986), Thomson (1988), and Matsuno (1989) have suggested that neo-Darwinism is an equilibrium discourse because the entities involved supply no internal impulse (or directionality) to change, which is imposed entirely by boundary conditions. Only when these external conditions change will the system move toward a new equilibrium. It can be useful here to compare the statistical equilibrium discourses of Darwin and Boltzmann.

We begin with a collection of tokens of different types (particles for Boltzmann, organisms with different genotypes for Darwin) existing in a particular configuration in a small region of a larger space potentially accessible to them. For Boltzmann, there will be an inevitable breakdown of the configuration and a scattering of the tokens throughout the available space as a random distribution is approached asymptotically. What is emphasized is the equilibrium tendency toward maximum disorder, when tokens of all types would be dispersed maximally and entropy would be maximized absolutely.

For Darwin, motion in the system is not inevitable. The original configuration has been imposed by boundary conditions (selection pressures), and if these do not change them the system, no matter how clumped the "particles" are, will remain as it is. Thus a group of genotypes may already be in a dynamic equilbrial configuration even if the tokens representing them are very asymmetrically disposed in a landscape.

This equilibrium, furthermore, is discursively richer than Boltzmann's, depending more explicitly on the particular environmental boundary conditions that constrain fitness. The relative proportions of genotypes deployed in some configuration will depend on their relative fitness differences, which may well be purely semiotic, as well as on various of their physical properties. That is, not all adaptions are to physiographic and climatic conditions; some are to the responses of other organisms as well.

New tokens of a genotype (and new genotypes) are produced by mutation and recombination from the others, so that equilibration is always being perturbed from within. Whether in most cases this amounts to more than Prigoginian fluctuations in equilibrium thermodynamic systems seems doubtful. What is emphasized in Darwinism during the approach to equilibrium is changes in relative proportions of different types, and there is no canonical configuration of these (as there would be in the Boltzmann case, given some global configuration of physical properties) because the equilibrium is proximally tailored semiotically to an indefinite number of local boundary conditions.

One might object that Boltzmann's view is not applicable to natural, nonequilibrium situations, and that any natural process of physical equilibration is never finished because any movement toward it changes the impinging boundary conditions, producing an endless concatenation of states never really any closer to equilibrium (Matsuno

1989). But this still does not get at the difference brought in by the concept of fitness, which is laid over and which integrates the concept of physical equilibration. If, at a relatively low integrative level, we were to consider organisms to move as particle according only to their species-specific physical traits, we could get a nonequilibrium, physicalist view of their dispersion. But this would have to be further integrated by way of distortions brought about by fitness differences reflecting biotic adaptations. And these distortions do not relate simply to material or physical properties in the physicist's sense; the dispersion of differently colored forms might relate, say, to predation.

Another important rule in Darwinian systems is what Van Valen (1973) referred to as the "continual deterioration of the environment." This leads to the inevitable destabilization of any existing equilibrium in a population by way of external perturbation, so that a population moves from one equilibrial trajectory to another endlessly, there being no privileged equilibrium as with maximum thermodynamic entropy. So, if nonphysical selection pressures change, an entirely new and indeed unpredictable configuration will be sought.

We could alter boundary conditions in Boltzmann's case as well, and a new equilibrium would be found there too but its configuration and its degree of entropy relative to the prior equilibrium would always be, in principle, predictable. But neither the new demic configuration nor its population fitness (the degree to which current fitness approaches the maximum possible) relative to the prior situation could be predicted, because fitness depends proximally, and often symbolically, upon complex relationships between organisms and their environments.

These differences (the intricate richness of selection pressures and the often purely semiotic responses to them, especially in biotic relations) may well be a consequence of the scalar fact that organisms are viewed as complex, whereas "molecules" are taken to be relatively simple. But that is how science discourses have been, for practical reasons.

In any case, for Boltzmann there is always a material compass point of absolute maximum global physical entropy, whereas for Darwin there can only be landmark points of relative maximum fitness, strongly dependent upon local (including relational) conditions, and the system would endlessly move on to new configurations even if the physical properties of an environment were to stabilize. Boltzmannian entropy increases predictably and globally by scattering everything as widely as possible; Darwinian fitness increases by unpredictable local changes in the alignments of different genotypes relative to highly labile environmental signs, and may even require the clumping and ordering of organisms. Physical entropy increase, because microscopic configurations are ignored, is constructed as developmental; fitness increase, focused on frictional details, is evolutionary. The two are so different they could be maximized independently in any model; I take this to be a major point of Brooks and Wiley's work.

The main point I wish to make here is that, whereas evolution is subject only to statistical discourses, development (including predictable increases in entropies), being a constitutive process, has a structure that can probed.

Self-Organization

Since all natural systems both develop and individuate, we need to find a concept of change that combines predictable aspects (development) and the creation of the new (individuation), and from which these processes are abstractions. We need a label for such change referring primarily to a system itself rather than to its scalar hierarchical connections with the rest of nature. Hence, we are concerned with autonomous systems (Varela 1979), or with the autonomy of systems.

For Varela, *autonomy* is the property of being organizationally closed, and the organization is "characterized by processes such that (1) the processes are related as a network, so that they recursively depend on each other in the generation and realization of the processes themselves, and (2) they constitute a system as a unity recognizable in the space (domain) in which they exist" (ibid.). Hence, autonomous systems are self-referential. I will take all dissipative structures to be (or to have the potential to become) such systems.

Autonomy can also be related to the property of having closure with respect to one or more significant systemic properties. *Closure* is described by Dyke (1988) as the property of being adequately describable by an observer's categories of alternative conditions. It refers to integrities between observers and objects. More specifically, to achieve closure there should be observables for every variable and constant in equations purporting to describe some aspect of a system, and those observables should exhaust the important contributions to the values of those variables and constants. Autonomous systems would have developmental closure, without which it would be impossible to declare them to be kinds of systems in the first place (because, upon changing, they would seem to disappear and be replaced by some other system). Continuity after change provides developmental closure because it ensures that we could find commonalities across instances of some species of change.

The term *self-organization* (Yovits and Cameron 1960; Foerster 1960; Nicolis and Prigogine 1977) is coming into general use for change in "coherent systems which evolve [*sic*] through a sequence of structures and maintain their integrity as a system" (Jantsch 1980). Other terms are being used for similar concepts, such as "autogenesis" (Csányi and Kampis 1985; Csányi 1989). Autogenesis, however, explicitly refers only to biological and linguistic systems, while self-organization refers to all dissipative structures. Self-organization is minimally taken to be a process of increase in complicatedness, and often in complexity, during the existence of a system (Brooks et al. 1988; Ulanowicz 1986; Wicken 1987; Winiwarter 1986). As Ulanowicz points out, this increase in complication can involve an actual simplification of form—achieved, however, only with increased organizational constraints. This will be the case, as in ecosystem flow relations, where many alternatives exist as weak tendencies during initial stages (consider also the behaviors of young children) that are gradually eliminated as the "self" of a system emerges (figure 4.2). In many systems this early complicatedness is relative only, because an immature system realizes a larger proportion of its potential states than a more mature one. The latter, realizing many more actual discriminable states (compare the

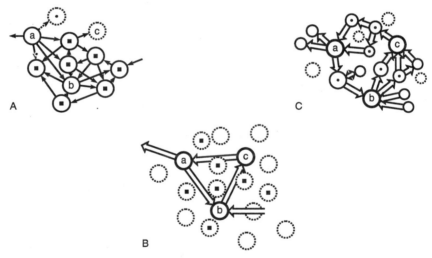

Figure 4.2 An illustration of the connectivity of a self-organizing system's components, combining the ideas of Brooks and Wiley (1988), Csányi and Kampis (1985), and Ulanowicz (1986). Diagram A represents the immature system, which is overconnected, with weak communications (or flows) between almost all the components, about 80% of which are in somewhat regular communication. In diagram B the system has grown to 19 possible components, but only about 30% are involved in the ascendant loop. Thicker arrows indicate strong, predictable connections. In diagram C the dominant loop has ramified and incorporated many redundancies, entraining as many as 75% of the possible components. Components with a dot are those originally present, allowing detection of possibilities newly generated in B and C.

behaviors of embryos and adults), still embodies a much smaller proportion of its potential states (figures 3.4 and 4.2).

Figure 4.2 represents self-organization in simple form. The immature system, A, has only weak connections (communication, flow) between its components. The system is overconnected in the sense that it has not differentiated into domains of influence; almost everything tends to be directly connected to everything else. Still, even in such a relatively small system, not every possible connection is made, largely because of boundary conditions; for example, potential component c is not often incorporated into the noisy behavior. Though it is difficult to show in any diagram, an immature system has mostly indefinite and vague tendencies.

In B the system has grown to more components with many more potential connections. But in fact the number of connections definitively made has diminished. This means that, along with growth in physical size, there has also been an increase in operative constraints. Changed boundary conditions allowed c to be accessed by the system, and that has triggered off a powerful (frequent communication, increased throughput) cycle that has come to dominate the system's behavior. This cycle has emerged from the noisy ground of A, where it was weakly prefigured in the behavior of a larger number of components and where it was only vaguely adumbrated. In a sense, it outcompetes other possible cycles that might have emerged instead, because its components are more rewarded when participating in it than in other possible cycles (as in Hebb's (1949) rule for neurons; see also Swenson 1991 for this sense of 'competition').

In an even larger system, a number of such cycles might appear, largely involving different components, as the system differentiates into different domains. In that case the emergence of new scalar levels is plainly evidenced, the cycles themselves (as thirdnesses) being entities at a larger scale than any unitary connection (a secondness) or than the components themselves (firstnesses). Ulanowicz has shown that such cycles are independent of their components because, as conditions change, other components can replace the ones initially involved while the cycle itself continues uninterrupted. A cycle supplies formal causation on the behaviors of potential components, and this, indeed, would be felt throughout its entire region of influence. (See Johnson 1990 for an argument to the effect that, if structures ("abstractions") exist, they could have (final or formal) causal efficacy.)

In C of figure 4.2 we see that components can be added to the cycle as it becomes ever more redundantly entrenched in the system as a whole. The cycle becomes a veritable, unavoidable habit of the system as, during growth in the gross throughput of the system, it entrains more and more components which bolster its stability. As a result, other possible system behaviors become suppressed, and the system becomes increasingly rigid.

One might wonder whether deleting components from and adding components to a cycle doesn't break the requirement of closure. This is a matter of scale; the cycle is describable on its own level (characterized by gross input, types of outputs, and so on). From that point of view the "microsystemic" contributors to these important identifying characteristics are, as individuals, unimportant; thus, they can be replaced, or even added and dropped and this could affect only the actual value of a macrosystemic variable, not its presence or absence. Closure is based on types, not tokens. For a system to seem autonomous, we would need to track all the important type characteristics it has in respect to some integrity and find that, on the basis of these, it has remained identifiable as continuous with our previous experiences of it.

Continuation of the situation in C inevitably leads also to feedback within a cycle, gradually increasing its complexity to the point where parts of it begin interfering with the whole and the system goes into an information crisis not unlike the situation in A in some respects except that the components are now definite. For one thing, the cycle has entrained so many components that a larger proportion of the system's potential behavioral repertoire can reappear when adventitious flows, previously eliminated, occur episodically as part of feedback processes. Thus, imagining a part D of figure 4.2, we would add many of the original weak arrows back into the diagram and diminish the size of the privileged arrows. The cycle, which has become a necessity for the system, therefore begins to be eroded by the continuance of the process that initially stabilized it. In fact its closure is beginning to be abrogated; indeed, the loss of closure is simultaneous with the dispersion of the cycle.

So, self-organization predictably involves some combination of an increase in size and an increase in internally generated constraints, as well as an increase in gross throughput (power). This is the substance of developmental rule 2 on page 111—that is, an increase in stored information. It can be shown that combining this rule with the first (the overall decrease in mass-specific energy flow) gives a decrease in the rate of growth of absolute throughput. The increasing rigidity of the system is the cause of the third rule (that the system's internal drive to change slows down), and this, working together with the first rule, is the cause of the fourth rule (that the system is increasingly susceptible to disruption).

Haken (1981, 1984) stresses the emergence in a system of top-down control of its components during self-organization. This is a consequence of the emergence of higher scalar levels as a result of growth of the mass and power of a system. These levels then impose boundary conditions which organize the increasing number of components that differentiate as a result of the instability of overconnectedness.

Except in simple systems such as those studied by Haken, the nature of these global constraints and their changes has evaded the inquiries of reductionist science. In fact, just this knowledge is missing in the researches of developmental biology (Salthe 1987), where, with few exceptions (see, e.g., Goodwin and Saunders 1989), only the factors responsible for receiving and interpreting constraint communications at the lower scalar levels are studied (as in Edelman 1988). Indeed, it appears that the last important review of this aspect of ontogeny before the current resurgence of structuralism was Bertalanffy 1933!

It is important to see that increasing mass necessitates differentiation if communications within the system are to remain (or become more) orderly, without which, of course, a system would not endure as itself. The system will spontaneously cleave (Soodak and Iberall 1978) when communications become overburdened and lagged between increasingly distanced regions. This produces domains of influence in various localities, whose outputs (as in the dominant cycles discussed above) are sufficiently powerful to be effective over the longer range required in the larger system. These cycles entrain previously incoherent activities in each of their regions, so that activities become differentiated specifically into, e.g., well-defined liver activities, slum activities, grazing activities, updraft activities, subduction activities, and so on, depending on the physical realization of self-organization in each case.

Goodwin (1984) emphasizes the wholeness of a self-organizing system, relating this to global structures. This approach too is explicitly top-down, so that the system is able to gain access to one or another of such governing structures, and never more than one major one at any level. There is an entrainment of the entire system in concordance with the structure being manifested. Consider Goodwin's example of the three-, four-, and five-digit plans for vertebrate feet. He shows that all the bones and muscles are reorganized in going from one of these structures to another (as in comparing five-digit species with related four-digit ones). His argument for this as an evolutionary transformation is especially clear: As a digit is reduced during evolution, the system still develops around the five-digit plan, but once the digit is effectively gone the system completely reorganizes around the four-digit model in a jump. Whether such changes should be counted as parts of development or individuation would depend upon whether they can be analyzed as developmental or evolutionary emergences. (See below.)

Bertalanffy (1933) also struggled with the wholeness of the developing system, basing his ideas on Gestalt psychology, with its many examples—e.g., that gaps in visual information are filled in by the perceptual system, making a whole not all of which is fully justified by the signs being interpreted, but which is sufficient for action, or that figures may shift in a jump to become grounds and vice versa.

Of course, there is always the question of where structures come from (or where and in what form they exist when not embodied). Uexküll (1926) and Gibson (1966) took the realist position that structures are parts of the environment, and, from a point of view concordant with H_{sc}, that the self-organizing system itself is also a part of the environment, so that the structures it accesses are actual parts of the structure of the global ecology.

In this view, organic evolution becomes a kind of search by the biosphere (by means of consequential perturbations of ontogeny), leading to a sequential accessing of immanent structures implied by the actual environment—a filling in of possibilities, not all of which need be potential at any one epoch. More possibilities would become potentialities as the biosphere advanced in elaboration during its development, and it could flow into any of them sooner or later. This view may solve the riddles of parallel, convergent, and especially iterative evolution, because the same forms (being based on structures) may be reaccessed again and again. But this reduces the origin of newness in organic evolution—evolution itself—to, at best, the surprising accession of structures reached only with difficulty or with low probability (say, one of the abyssal fishes), to, at worst, mere embroidery on basic relations in one structure (yet another wood warbler).

What I interpret to be more recent version of this same structuralist perspective emerges with chaos theory. Allen (1985) posits that the attainment of this or that species structure can be viewed as the result of chaotic iteration of a basic developmental process (such as that in figure 4.3), with stability entailed only in cases where the structure manifested works well with the rest of the ecosystem's structure. Figure 4.3 only highlights the regions of a few of the possibilities that were realized in one branch of the biosphere. The nodes, as in figure 2.8, represent developmental stages. Once a "solution" has been accessed during ontogeny, it can be stabilized by genetic information, and so it can be iterated. Such a diagram implies that dinosaur structures still exist in the world of possibilities inherent in amniote ontogeny, even though their embodiments have disappeared and even

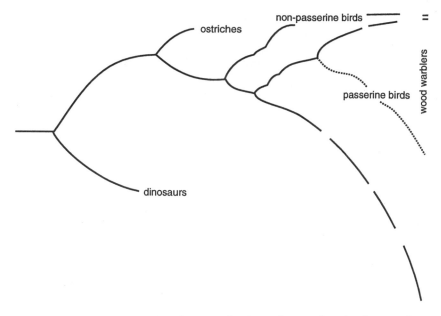

Figure 4.3 The birds viewed as chaotic realizations of an amniote developmental system, inspired by figure 7 of Allen 1985. As in figure 2.8 above, the nodes can be interpreted as developmental stages.

though the initiating and initial conditions required to access them may never again occur.

Allen (1985) and Atlan (1981) stress the ability of self-organizing systems to incorporate historical information, to become significantly modified (without losing *themselves*) by interactions with their environments. Many of these historical traces and marks will contribute to the individuation of the system—to its evolving uniqueness. Others will serve as occasions (as in Piaget and Inhelder 1969) for the realization of tendencies already within the system (perhaps unrealized cycles) that could have been triggered by other events as well, yet that would not necessarily have become embodied in the absence of adequate stimuli (as in the song learning of some species of birds). Prigogine has often suggested that fluctuations in a system could function as occasions for accessing potential global reorganizations, leading to the sudden emergence of more complex forms ("order through fluctuations"—see also Foerster 1960 and Atlan 1974). Perturbations initiated by environmental fluctuations could render a system metastable in this respect, providing a prerequisite stance, as e.g., environmental insults may promote cancerous behavior in cells that yet needs to be realized through intracellular fluctuations.

Of course, global reorganization could, in a scalar hierarchical system, amount to the entrainment of a system by boundary conditions generated by a higher-scalar-level individual within which it is nested. This possibility is exactly what reductionist science eschews. Partly, this is a result of the extreme specialization found among modern scientists, who are not prepared to (or capable of) extend(ing) their one field of interest. Yet, with the emergence of teamwork in science this need no longer be the case, and habits of thought alone stand in the way of finding these discourses. In any case, we need to analyze self-organization still more from the particular perspective of this work.

First, let us consider the term 'self'. Individual selves in the world cannot be attained by discourses, which can only synthesize contours out of many discursively dependent integrities (Buchler 1966; Singer 1983). Perhaps, as Schrödinger (1964) suggests, there is only one self, with many concurrent physical embodiments, perhaps approachable through methods such as Ch'an meditation. In any case, Western science has not been concerned with this at all. Yet we need some sign of the self to function in our theory. I will suggest the following from my own experience.

Touch your arm; try to concentrate your attention only on the fact of being touched; then try to concentrate only on the act of touching; then try to alternate your attention more and more rapidly until you have fused touching and being touched. (For the more adventurous, these touches could be sexual, providing stronger motivation.) Referring back to chapter 3, we can abstract from this practice the notion that a self is something that collects some of the effects of its own cascading. (For simple examples, there are the autocatalytic cycles of Prigogine, Rössler, or Ulanowicz.) Selves are self-referential. Right away we see, as I have suggested, that the Earth is a self (Gaia!), that hurricanes are selves (Hurricane Gloria!), and we can recognize a model of our own selves. From the point of view of the specification hierarchy of integrative levels, a system gradually discovers itself in development.

I propose that 'organization' be taken to be the effects of a viewpoint. First, it is not 'order'. *Order* is a simpler notion; it is regularity, or predictability (Atlan 1978)—it is a local result of constraint (Banerjee et al. 1990). It is essentially a projection from an external observer, as was noted in chapter 3. Self-organization usually builds up orderly arrangements, without which we could not recognize other selves at all (because they would have no consistency of behavior).

And development is an orderly interpretation of self-organization. However, organization is a perspective that may not appear locally to be very orderly at all. No one doubts that the weather has an organization, but its manifestations are vagaries (perhaps chaotic). The actions of foreign enemies (Mordor!) are clearly organized but deliberately not orderly. In what way are ecosystemic processes orderly? That they (e.g., nutrient cyclings) happen can be predicted, but if we go into the field we need to impose the order of systematic observations (weekly readings and so on) to construct them.

The reason one cannot assert that organizations are necessarily orderly comes from the fact of complexity. In the introduction I suggested that complexity is the result of the developmental emergence of levels of organization (both integrative and scalar). Hence, in a simple system (little developed and of low specification, with few scalar levels) organization might devolve upon the limit of orderliness. But self-organization *does* produce order; indeed, a senescent system is one in which this process has gone so far as to make the system rigid and inadaptive.

Agency

In infodynamics, then, self-organization is the emergence of a self-referential perspective. We next need an operational sign of the presence of perspectives or viewpoints. This I will refer to as *agency*. According to Webster's Third New International Dictionary (1966), agency is "the capacity of acting or exerting power"; Reber (1985) defines it as "the capacity for producing an effect." For Bigger and Bigger (1982), "agents can control, direct and initiate or terminate processes." Clearly agents can supply efficient causes, but I suggest that *what* they cause is more important in defining them.

I suggest that a system has agency with respect to some process if its effects in the world leave a trace of its individuality. Agents cause historical events that contribute to the individuation of other systems. Agents act preeminently as tokens, not types, and contribute to the elaboration of other tokens. Hence, e.g., the effects of *this* particular hurricane show that it was an agent interfering in your affairs. Or, if one is a sociobiologist studying helping behavior in a society of rodents which are all marked and recorded separately, the individuals will function as agents, even though in the final inscriptions their individuality becomes obliterated. Important events themselves might function as agents too—say, in science, famous experiments.

Agents are something like individuals, but with restricted richness. Something must act as an individual in order to be an agent, so agency could be assigned on the basis of a single relevant integrity. (There can be individuals without agency too—dissipative structures not impinged upon by any known discourse.) But agency implies individuality, and may be taken as a sign of it.

Any mature dissipative structure is potentially an agent in some process, in some discourse. I quote a personal communication from Gary Van Den Heuvel: "Jane Byrne became mayor of Chicago because of one snow storm. The incumbent political machine failed to get 15 inches of snow removed for nearly a week. The people did not stand for it. I do not see one 'random' snow storm as an agent, but through its *agency* the political structure of Chicago was changed." I am precisely claiming that that one storm was itself an agent, without denying that the complex event had agency too.

Often the connotation of 'agent' is that it is a representative of something else, usually of higher scale. Here I am not emphasizing that in scalar hierarchical systems any individual is controlled and regulated by higher-level entities—those within which it is nested. In this sense I might consider my red blood cells to be my agents at the molecular level, and myself to be an agent of some political unit. While not denying this (and I will pick up on it myself below), here I am emphasizing the idea that an agent has effects in the world that cannot be imputed to something else. Note that in science discourses, as they have been, these unique effects are usually assiduously obliterated by decreasing the specification of the resulting inscriptions. Only membership in a class has meaning in a science devoted to prediction.

We might for a moment consider this fact that science in general does not deal with individuals and so hardly deals with agents. Types are the subjects of science discourse, with, however, a few exceptions. Historical geology was forced to deal with unique events in a unique system. It contrived to do this within the confines of modern science by unraveling complication in a certain way.

So, any event gives rise to multiple future eventualities. A separate prediction can be made on each of these as if they were independent. In this way, multiple corroborations of the postulated event are possible, just as when several experiments are done on a system. Hence, historical geology treats tokens as if they were types, which it can do because these tokens are very complex. Each eventuality that implies the putative past event is taken as a separate token of its presence as if in multiple worlds. When they are all put together these eventualities show the corroborated event as having been complex. Cosmology has a similar strategy with respect to singularities. Cladistics is a technique devised specifically to order historical contingencies temporally. However, it too treats individuals (species) as if they were types by diagnosing them in terms of commonalities among their parts (the organisms), which can be encountered as separate instances.

Development of Agency
Any self-organizing system gradually constructs its agency as it individuates. The effects of a blastula on the world are much less likely to be distinguishable from those of another blastula, whereas the effects of a frog, being much more varied, are more likely to be distinguishable in some discourse. This could be taken to be a result of the fact that discourses, no matter how broadly construed (e.g., the {discourse} of buzzards in their search for carrion—see chapter 1 for this use of brackets), are made by adults rather than by embryos. Larvae, being active elaborations of an ontogenetic trajectory, would in this view necessarily be considered to participate in worldly discourses as well. They are terminal productions of an ontogeny that are later aborted, erased, and reconstituted as something else. (From the thermodynamic point of view it is important that, e.g., in insects each instar separately shows a decrease in mass-specific entropy production characteristic of aging—see figure 4.4.)

The {{discourses}} of eggs and embryos are usually screened off from whatever the adults might be up to; they are inside their own egg membranes inside an egg which may be inside a nest. Should adults of a scale similar to that which the embryos will later attain impinge upon them (parental care, egg eating), their relationship is not on an equal footing, but something similar to relations between larger-scale and smaller-scale entities. The interaction is usually one-upon-many ("impersonal," as it were), with the adults dealing with something different in kind from themselves—products, food, and so on. In such an interaction there is no need for the adults to distinguish various individual marks, as they are required to do in dealing with other adults. Embryos are, in effect, functionally less specified than such adults (figure 2.8), and the adults behave as if this were so.

One might nevertheless assert that the symbolic discourse of certain adult humans—say, developmental biologists—would be quite up to dealing with, e.g., separate frog blastulae as if they were fully distinguishable individuals. This I deny. First, it is never done. For the purposes of developmental biology (or of systematics), there is simply no need to do so. They are handled as classes of low specification. Of course, adults are not accorded individuality in these discourses either, but if we examine the inscriptions of these sciences we see that description becomes increasingly complicated as development proceeds. (See any normal table of development for corroboration.) Should a

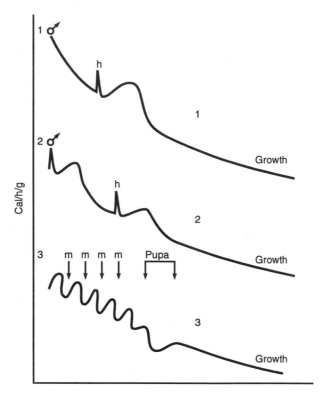

Figure 4.4 Mass-specific energy flow during development of (1) an amniote, (2) a "lower" vertebrate, and (3) an insect with larval instars. The "male" sign indicates fertilization; h is hatching; m is molting. Reprinted, with permission, from Zotin 1972.

mad attempt be made to construct a discourse about individual embryos, its expense would be prohibitive—a relevant point, as any scientist would admit. Yet I will go further and deny even the possibility of successfully constructing such a discourse, because of the *vagueness* of early embryos.

The earlier in ontogeny one probes, the less easily a system is described. In examining a frog I can, with sufficient accuracy, determine where a leg begins and where the foot. In examining an embryonic limb bud, this is hardly the case. It is a region, more or less determined in ways not accessible to anything cruder than prohibitive, detailed chemical examination; even then, the situation is changing so fast at the molecular scale that one could not say which cells at the periphery at any moment were in and which out, or what stage of induction each cell was in a moment ago. Semiotically, the early, vague system can have many more possible interpretations, perhaps an indefinite number of them. As development continues, fewer and fewer interpretations are possible concerning what is developing.

Admittedly, there are more precise embryonic systems. In the nematode *Caenorhabditis* (Lewin 1984a,b; Marx 1984), a rigid cell lineage allows one to trace back from any of the 959 cells in the adult to a particular more immature cell at any stage. Developmental discourse (Sulston et al. 1983) has thus laboriously revealed the normal future location of each descendant of every embryonic and larval cell. (Some of these *can* be changed by perturbations, however.) So, in a specialized discourse about cell genealogy, the immature system is not constructed to be more vague than later stages, even though here too it remains harder to describe the earlier stages as individuals—a point emphasized in the above-cited references since only in later stages have differences between individuals been discovered, mostly in neuronal connections. Yet it does seem that nematodes become more definite earlier in development than do other forms, and perhaps this relates to the fact that they are morphologically extremely conservative as a group—little vagueness, little potentiality for evolution.

But the point I am making about larger systems is really applicable here too. If we pick some adult subsystem (such as the intestine or the vulva) and discover approximately where its rudiment first appears, that location is more vague (less easily described as to exactly where in space it will develop in relation to the whole system) when fewer cells are involved than later, when many smaller cells aid in fixing its location more precisely. That is so unless we insist on limiting our description to the abstraction of actual cell location only, where we can as easily say that the center of an organ will arise somewhere in cell x as we can say that later it will be marked by cells a, b, c, and d. Of course, even if we adopt this cell-lineage perspective, vagueness must be the case functionally, anyway, since the developing organ is not acting as it will later when its location will be integral to its functioning (even though in the embryo it may have some ontogenetic role, which appears not to be the case for most subsystems in the nematode).

Figure 4.5 tries to give an image of the transformation of vagueness to increasingly more precisely realized properties during self-organization. The earlier stage (which might be an embryo, with the late stages of four species' anatomies shown as possible end points, but which could also be an evolutionarily primitive kind of organism, in which case we see the emergence of ever-more-restricted ecological niches in the derived species) is less easily described than the later ones. It is rather circular in shape, but it could be thought of as elliptical or as somewhat crescent-shaped.

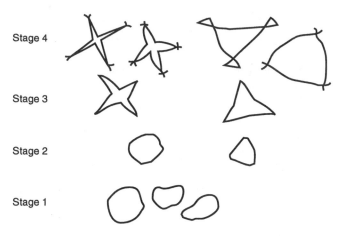

Figure 4.5 The emergence of determinacy (and therefore of the possibility of agency) in an imaginary group of organisms.

We could suppose that the whole sweep of figure 4.5 could be determined in an appropriate dynamical system by slight variations in initial conditions (e.g., 0.0024... instead of 0.0025...) for some constant. Such differences might be thought to be pretty precise, but in an actual material calculation they are not, as chaos theory has shown. In stage 2, if these are embryos, characteristic shapes of the later species have begun to be adumbrated. If these are species in evolution, we may have here a polymorphism in a single population, with two structures being accessed depending upon initiating conditions (including, of course, genetic differences).

Now, the topmost realizations in figure 4.5 are not perfectly determinate in their finer details either. Here again there are polymorphisms and historical individuations (all signs are indeterminate in some way), but the large-scale structure has become discursively determinate. Indeterminacy has dropped down in scale (although in the behavioral realm it has probably been preserved at the original scale too). The organisms at this stage can be placed in one or another class without ambiguity. They have acquired determinate ways of life (e.g., tigers, lions), and they have acquired potential agency in these roles. This last requires more explication.

The earlier stages were represented by individuals (in the sense of separate instantiations) as well, and the few vague differences shown were historically acquired. But this does not translate into agency, for the following reason: Because of their simple structure there is hardly any distinct, discriminable, single thing they can be described as "doing." Without this possibility, it is difficult to say that it was done with this or that peculiarity. Similarly, when everything is idiosyncratic, that term can have no meaning.

Agency can emerge because the standardization achieved by development produces a field within which it can have a role. Only with a score to follow can we detect the creativity of a singer. If the whole field itself is nothing but vague forms varying randomly, then so much of the potential disorder of the system is being realized that order itself is not discernible, even though the whole system, being immature, is itself absolutely more orderly in the sense of figure 3.4 (i.e., has less potential variability) than more mature systems. So, detection of disorder (variability in performance) requires a ground of order—even if the latter is only a restriction on potential disorder, as in the internalist interpretation of infodynamics.

In the evolutionary interpretation of figure 4.5, the implication is that earlier niches were less determinate than later ones, less complex, and more overlapping. Certainly the emergence of multicellularity was a milestone in the way of enabling greater differentiation of niches to match the greater potential for form acquired with that state. The restriction of evolution to fewer lineages after the Cambrian burgeoning (Morris 1989) could be viewed as a restriction on any potential variability of the biosphere arising early in development. This allowed the remaining lineages, as increasing specialists, to more narrowly explore and elaborate their own potential variabilities emerging at later developmental stages (and therefore to more precisely determine the ecological meaning of that variation).

Morris (1989) denies that there is any evidence that the niches within Cambrian faunas were less restricted than those of present-day ones, but on no more serious grounds than anatomical complication. This issue remains open, and the viewpoint taken here predicts the discovery that Cambrian faunas were more vaguely adapted than present-day forms. For later periods, Vermeij (1987) suggests that the intensity of Darwinian selection would have gradually increased as the "biological surroundings themselves became more rigorous within a given habitat." This would have driven an elaboration of form via an escape from competition that would have allowed greater idiosyncrasy in performance. Indeed, an increase in that very idiosyncrasy (resulting in variability of performance) is required for Vermeij's Darwinian model to work.

Atlan (1974) has provided a formal definition of 'organization' that allows the present argument to be reformulated in information-theoretic terms. I have said that during self-organization there is an increase in agency (the ability to make unique marks on other systems; i.e., determinability, from another point of view), and that this is carried by the meaningful variety a system can generate, which increases as the system becomes more organized. In figure 3.4 this variety is shown as C_i (constrained by intropic organization, without which the variety would be indeterminate). Atlan uses, instead, figures similar to that shown as stored information in figure 3.2 (of which C_i is some function) to illustrate his concept of self-organization, which is defined on the basis of a kinetics of change of C_i under the effects of environmental noise-producing factors accumulating in time.

Atlan's discussion is essentially about the informational channel (its information (Collier 1990), which would generate redundancy and reliability) and the amount of ambiguity generated by noise impinging upon it. This ambiguity will have a disorganizing effect on the information sent, and so will decrease the amount of information stored as a result of the received message. But, under certain initiating conditions (moderate amounts of initial redundancy in the receptive system), up to a certain amount of noise (set by boundary conditions) can result in an increase in C_i, and this increase will be interpretable as self-organization.

The essence of Atlan's idea is that, as some of the initial redundancy of the system is eroded by noise, the system increases the meaningful variety it can produce, and, with that, its "autonomy" (interpreted as determinacy). So, if it is *something* to begin with (i.e., if it has some initial redundancy) it can become something more (i.e., something with greater determinacy to an outside observer). Atlan includes a discussion of various combinations of 'being something' and of forms of 'becoming something more', including (significantly) patterns of senescence. For instance, if the system initially has many redundancies, its ability to gain variety is high. If it has also little reliability in reproducing information, it can self-organize quickly and will decay rapidly (like a hurricane, whose high initial redundancy comes from the few distinctions its {code} is capable of making). If it has strong reliability from the first, it can self-organize over a long period of time, like the biosphere, on the basis of genetic information.

Self-Organization as Modeling the Environment

So, self-organizing systems slowly build up categories (as used in figure 2.8) of performances, letting each actual occasion impose its imprint so that they individuate even as they narrow their scope of possibilities and sharpen their determinability (their distinctiveness within the narrowed scope). A definitive self emerges from the vague possibilities of the earliest stages, and its potential agency in the world becomes increasingly enabled by its developing complication. We might consider the increasing determinability to be a result of stochastic events alone, as when a marble becomes more identifiable as its surface becomes marred; however, for self-organizing systems that picture is too simple and does not involve agentive determinability. In particular, we need to see that collecting feedback from its own cascading process (selfness itself) becomes more sharply discriminating as a system matures.

But we need some words about modeling and interpretation first. Using scalar hierarchical principles, we can see that focal-level dynamics are made possible by lower-level "mechanisms" (Aristotle's material causes) and are governed by higher-level boundary conditions (exemplifying Aristotle's final, and some formal, causes). "Governed" here intersects with the semiotic term 'interpreted' as follows: Something smaller in scale could not really be said to regulate a larger-scale entity; it could not even be said to be able to successfully interpret it.

Suppose we cite astronomy as containing our interpretation of the universe. In point of fact, what is happening is very subtle. The theorist completely dominates the equations as the medium of a discourse. The "universe," as now conceived, is an extrapolation from these equations. For interpretation to occur, a larger system (of interpretance) must encompass a smaller one, which it holds inside itself and constrains absolutely (this, of course, *not* meaning "determining" or specifying). In this case, a scientific culture holds a particular discourse within it. So, a particular volume of gas interprets its microscopic parts by way of pressure and temperature. But why cannot the parts interpret the larger system? Because they have not got, on scale limitations, enough structure to do so.

While electrons, for example, must, on scalar hierarchical principles, be taken to be complex systems (Buchler 1966), they cannot be *as complex as* the universe, insofar as a description for the latter necessarily includes the former but not vice versa (even if electrons are held to have traits explainable only if they belong to the universe). So, an electron might hold a microcosmic description of the universe, which we could call a *model*, but it must devote some of its stored information to that description, and this must necessarily be smaller than the universe (which itself does not have a model of the electron—it has the electrons instead). To suggest otherwise (as Buchler seems to do) is to leave materialism behind. It does not matter how many lower levels of self-similar fractal informational resources are available; a material part could never physically encompass the whole.

So, microsystems necessarily must be interpreted at macrosystemic levels, and not the reverse. The interpreter/observer is logically always relatively macroscopic with respect to its observations, if for no other reason than that it must be viewed as having bias and structure—as, of course, it *must* (Kuhn 1962). For example, a point source cannot represent a viewpoint because for that viewpoint to inhere in observations made from such a source one would need a particular privileged vector through it, and that vector would necessarily have to be stipulated by further information not inherent in the point source itself. For this reason, microscopic entities (*as such*—i.e., we do not drop down in scale in order to observe them in the kind of detail we can find in ourselves) cannot be represented as having particular viewpoints.

Models, then, must be of smaller scale than what they model, and they must also be contained in a system of interpretance (Duhem 1962; Quine 1969; Kampis 1988). The fact that models must be smaller in scale than what they model is what makes them useful (Rosen 1985b). This is because they can run through, for example, a million years of experience, in a few days, for a system of interpretance that might last only decades. In this spirit Fraser (1982) proposed that societal rhythms model geological and astronomical cycles, just as biological clocks do. Lorenz (1973) used this image for genes, which he took to carry information that would be their owner's "image of the environment."

There is a specification-hierarchical connection to interpretation as well. A society can be said to interpret its own biological properties when, e.g., it regulates breeding activities. A biological system interprets chemistry by regulating metabolism, and chemical system interprets physical nature in imposing particular kinetics on the flows of energy and entropy. And, indeed, the relations here are transitive, so that a society may (and does) interpret chemical activities, through its biological components and (more directly) in its compost heaps and sewage plants. Conversely, organisms can model their surrounding society by acclimating to certain foods or by adjusting their biorhythmic activities.

Since an interpretation (or an interpretant) comes into being inside a system of interpretance, it must be less extensive than that system. Yet in some cases it has to be as large, or almost as large, because of that which it interprets. This is true in particular when what is being interpreted is orders of magnitude larger than the scale of observation, as in astronomy (figure 4.6). When this is so, the systematicity of changes at the larger scale can never have been sufficiently reflected in empirical data at a lower level of scale. We generally do not have observations over enough larger-scale moments to "know" what these systems might be up to, and so their changes can seem nothing but random with respect to our lower-level inquiries (Salthe 1985). Now,

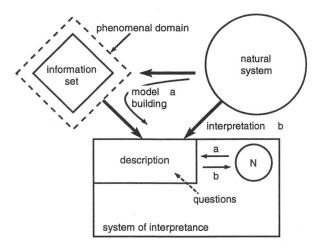

Figure 4.6 A semiotic formulation of model building, using terms from Kampis (1988). The modeling relation (a,b) is shown as being held within a system of interpretance, where the natural system is represented as N (a system of inscriptions). The information set is the digital content of signs in the phenomenal domain—a description. Only the latter, its *Umwelt*, is apparent to system of interpretance as the outer world. The natural system is a domain determined by the questions asked by the system of interpretance.

the punch line is that Chaitin (1975) has shown that random structures cannot be described by algorithms smaller than the information content of the whole system being described. As Kampis (1988) has pointed out, this is not really a practical problem, because the whole world itself is never the subject of modeling anyway; rather, these subjects are what Kampis calls "natural systems." Yet, there is no doubt that a small social system would not be capable of constructing cosmological discourse because of the size and cost of the necessary equipment. One wonders how much of the GNP would need to be absorbed by cosmology in order to solve its problems!

A natural system is "a mentally, conceptually delimited domain of space and time [,and] this serves as the basic object of modeling" (Kampis 1988). In point of fact, the natural system, even though it has unknown properties, really only exists concretely as a growing set of inscriptions and their implications within a system of interpretance. The system of interpretance is what defines the natural system in the first place, on the basis of its beliefs and needs (figure 4.6). N, the model (interpretant) in figure 4.6, is smaller in scale than the system of interpretance, even though we can presume that what the natural system represents is often much larger in scale and may even contain the system of interpretance.

So, more encompassing or more highly specified systems interpret smaller or less specified systems, which in turn make models and images (Langer 1967)—representations—of them, and not the reverse.

From all this, we are faced with a dilemma in biology: How can genetic molecules be said to regulate the cell (Rieppel 1990)? *Do* genes regulate cellular activity? The logic of scalar hierarchies just glossed suggests instead that the cell interprets genetic "information." I have previously (1985) used the metaphor of the cell playing its genome like a piano (and so, in effect, did Uexküll (1926) when he described the modulations of metabolism as melodies).

But what does the cell find in its genome? Proximately, it finds "texts" about how proteins will fold up and change shape. And what can these tell the cell? Maturana and Varela (1987) have concluded that they tell the cell only about itself. But, insofar as anything *could* be a sign of something to someone, there could be said to be information about systems larger than the cell embodied in genetic information (Dawkins 1982). That information cannot, as we have seen, be an interpretation, but it can be taken as generating models of the world for cells, which *they* can interpret (as in the arrows inside the system of interpretance in figure 4.6). Genetic information and its use forms a perfect paradigm for Rosen's (1985b) "anticipatory model." If in figure 4.6 the system of interpretance is a cell, then its activities generate the questions and the rest of the symbols inside it represent gene action.

So, the cell interprets its base sequence theories as protein configurations. These configurations, and their changes, work as models of the world by way of covariances and correlations between cell modulations and events in the surrounding world. Cells (like the submarine of Maturana and Varela (1987, pp. 136–137) that do not match the affordances and challenges in environmental configurations often enough do not continue to survive (or reproduce). And they can survive only by playing their genomes. For example: Sickle-cell anemia can be viewed as an adaption to the presence of material sporozoans in mosquitoes that bite humans. That is, it is an adaptation to a certain kind of mesic tropical environment. Darwinian adaptation is a purely semiotic concept insofar as there does not need to be any material connection between selective pressures and adequate responses. The selective pressures here include being bitten by mosquitoes, the bloodstream's being invaded by sporozoans, red cells' being invaded by sporozoans, and sporozoans' growing by feeding on hemoglobin. There is no privileged point of interference with this insult, which is itself complex.

Cells must only make *some* response to this situation. Skin cells might come up with a mutation that discourages mosquitoes. This has happened in birds, whose feathers effectively keep off insects of this kind (Heinrich 1987). Or cells in the circulatory system might produce a toxin effective against sporozoans. Or red cells could undergo changes in their cell membranes that prevent entry of the parasites, or, failing that, they could increase their strength, as in some Florida populations of white-tailed deer, so that sickling of the cells is reduced and does not lead to lysis. Or hemoglobin could change its configuration so that it would be less easily eaten by sporozoans.

What actually occurred in sickle-cell anemia, however, is that hemoglobin changed in such a way that its solubility in relatively anoxic conditions is lowered, when it crystallizes, and this leads cells to deform and lyse, spilling out the sporozoans that caused these conditions into the blood stream randomly with respect to stages of their life cycle, so they are not likely to gain entry to other red cells. This happens because the sporozoans are aerobic, and their oxygen use, added to the cell's own, produces the relatively anoxic situations that trigger sickling. In this way only infected cells are aborted.

Very neat, but there is a consequence: Even moderate activity in homozygotes leads to enough oxygen depletion that their red cells massively and irrelevantly sickle and lyse. These individuals usually die before adolescence; hence, this mutation was a recessive lethal one. So, in this particular response to malaria, individuals must lose about a quarter of their offspring right off the top as payment.

How was this solution found? We can surmise that there were mutations of the hemoglobin gene such that different individuals had changes in solubility, say, at many possible concentrations of oxygen. Those whose hemoglobin precipitated just after sporozoans would typically have undergone a short part of their ontogeny were more efficient at ridding the body of them than those that acted earlier, which would precipitate a genetic disease even in heterozygotes, or later, which might allow too many sporozoan clones to finish their development. Note again that hemoglobin precipitation has no necessary connection to, and merely correlates with, stages of sporozoan development. This is a semiotic response; if so, there must have been other responses too.

Other semiotic solutions *were* arrived at—hemoglobin C, for example (semiosis with symbols in unlimited). But in this case protection from malaria does not occur significantly in heterozygotes (Templeton 1982). This further means that homozygotes have only a mild genetic disease, which sounds good. Yet when this mutation is in competition with hemoglobin S the latter always wins, because in that case het-

erozygotes are protected too, so that protection is achieved more rapidly in the population. Populations with hemoglobin S would not grow
as fast as populations with hemoglobin C, but that might actually have
been favorable too in the original African setting.

Now, what are the semiotics here? A cell acquires a tendency to play
a note slightly flattened. This, it turns out, is just what the environment
wants to "hear." But what has this tendency got to do materially with
biting insects, or with boring and eating sporozoans? It does not keep
the insects off, and it does not exclude the sporozoans or discourage
their feeding or growth. And it would *not* have been predicted in a
million years! Yet here it is, the *best* adaptation yet arrived at! This
example might well incline us toward the Maturana-Varela viewpoint
that cells just do their own thing, and that some of them, with no more
"justification" than we think a curandero or a shaman has, find *just*
the right kind of formula. But there could have been other rituals that
would have worked just as well. Darwinian adaptation is wholly
opportunistic, and symbolic.

Now, is the sickling mutation a representation of its environment
(Dawkins 1982)? We can certainly take it be so if we wish. It acts *as if*
it were. Its presence is symbolic of a particular kind of environment.
We can take it as a sign of adaptation to malaria—or even of the
presence of malaria. We can also project this onto the cell. Cells with
this genomic sign make an appropriate obeisance to the gods that be.
Since there is only a tenuous material connection between the sensitivity of hemoglobin to anoxia and the reproduction of sporozoans,
the sign here is certainly no more than symbolic. But, since lowered
oxygen concentration is actually caused by sporozoan reproduction,
why should we not see decreased solubility of hemoglobin in anoxic
conditions as an indexical sign? Because it is not a privileged response.
Indices are necessary concomitants (like smoke indicating fire) and so
are presumably predictable. Does reduced hemoglobin solubility necessarily indicate sporozoan-induced anoxia? In fact it could be the sign
of other possible causes.

And how does this case illustrate the idea that information can be
the source of models of a larger-scale world? Hemoglobin always
reflects boundary conditions bearing on oxygen availability. It is well
known to become modified in the direction of more efficiently combining with oxygen in organisms that live in relatively anoxic environments (tadpoles in comparison with frogs, for example). So, the
configurational repertoire of the hemoglobin molecule operates much
like a testable model based on theories inscribed in the genome. The
test itself is carried out by the organism containing the model, and is

subject to the same kinds of fudging known in philosophy of science as the Duhem-Quine principle (Harding 1976).

This means that the test is carried out within a discourse and does not give objective results about nature unqualified. A corroboration that it is "good for" human hemoglobin to precipitate at a certain concentration would "say" absolutely nothing about relevant environments to an ant or an orchid in search of models. Furthermore, the environment itself is formally in the position of interpreting the results in terms of changes in the population sizes of sporozoans and humans. That is, some of the ecological *meaning* of the sickle-cell mutation is that human populations living in these particular environments will not grow as fast as they might, and as they do elsewhere.

Finally, how does this case show that information is macroscopic with respect to dynamics? What we take as information here is what has become temporarily reliable, stabilized. In this case that is a base sequence in DNA. The relevant dynamics are the mass of mutations, replications, and transcriptions/translations of a genetic locus in a local population because it is in the population where stability can be read as the persistence of its effects over generations rather than in individuals. Eldredge (1985) has pointed out that a major part of genotypic stability over time is achieved by being packaged in species, which can continue to preserve genotypes even in the face of the extinctions of local populations. Thus, the dynamics are intracellular, while interpretations take place at the population and ecosystem levels of scale.

Self-Organization and the Collecting/Cascading Cycle

In chapter 2 I suggested that a basic structure of dissipative forms is a cycle of collecting and cascading, collecting requiring an expenditure of energy and cascading being spontaneous. A self was defined above as a system that collects some of the effects of its own cascading. We have seen that a self-organizing system increases in complication and complexity, and that, as a result of increased stored information, the system comes to acquire a perspective and to be capable of acting as an agent in the world (in the sense of being able to produce effects peculiar to its own perspective and traceable to itself). Put another way, it becomes more determinable as an individual. Hence, self-organization results in the accumulation of individuality in dynamic systems. This is evolution (individuation); however, self-organization is not equivalent to evolution, because it involves also the predictable *pattern* of individuation embodied in Baer's law.

Immature systems have few features of individuality; they are characterized instead by relative vagueness, which for some purposes can be read as generality. One such purpose is describing their cycle of cascading and collecting. For example, ova and ovules can be described as dissipating heat and discarding waste products in quite general ways, which could serve as a description for organisms in general. As development proceeds, more specificity, and eventually even idiosyncrasy, is built into the cycling process. Particular waste products characteristic of particular species come to be produced through particular pathways. It is as though these pathways were inserted into the chemical cascade like mills in a stream. Energy comes to be dissipated in certain ways that differ from the ways of other kinds of organisms. Collecting too becomes elaborated; from the absorption of whatever nutrients are there in yolk or endosperm, the system ramifies around quite particular (ecological) means of obtaining energy, water, and minerals (means that may be discarded later, from larvae, for still other elaborations).

Consider, for example, the collection of oxygen. In the least specified case this proceeds by diffusion along (which all systems have in common), made favorable to the system by the ready incorporation of oxygen into water and dehydrogenated bonds—a situation that has to be prepared for and maintained by an energy-demanding hydrogenation (collection). But, for example, in a metazoan this description would be deficient, and we need to include also a circulatory system, in which diffusion takes place in highly elaborated forms. And the more elaborate it becomes, the more idiosyncrasies are afforded by a system. And so, as the system elaborates gradually during ontogeny, following a pattern like those in figures 2.8 and 4.3, individuation accumulates along with stored information. Hence, e.g., the patterns of veins and capillaries in a metazoan are idiosyncratic.

So, a developing system increasingly integrates rather general physical chemical processes into ever-finer tesselations and more exquisite filigrations. The activity becomes increasingly narrowly constrained in a way that requires increasing specification to describe. Indeed, the possibility of scientific description is left behind as individual uniquenesses accumulate. The system develops from vagueness to determinability and beyond; it can be read backward as having acquired specification out of generality.

Of course, abiotic systems rarely if ever appear to achieve the degree of elaboration of living systems, but that could be a scale-dependent illusion of ours. Consider only that Planet Earth is itself a dissipative structure (Gaia), and it becomes obvious that its degree of control over generally occurring natural forces is, at its own scale, no less elaborate than that in a cell in the sense of requiring highly specified descriptions at appropriate scales (Lovelock 1979, 1988). And this has developed over the eons, from a Hadean vagueness and relative disorderliness (a high *specific disorder* = proportion of potential disorder accessed) through an embryonal Archaen period to Mesozoic maturity. Since the Mesozoic elaboration was, of course, dependent upon organismic stability, we cannot at present suggest that strictly abiotic systems can become as elaborate as living ones all by themselves, even though the tendency of their developments is in the same direction.

The achievement of precise controls over natural processes affords individuality because there is then more stored information from which to construct it, including information from statistical fluctuations during later development and information from accidental failures and disruptions (a more complicated thing has more ways to get deformed). Selfness itself (*autocollection* of cascading products) becomes ever more finely ramified with development. Consider a stream. At first it dashes out of a glacier pell-mell, scrapes a stream bed out of glacial till and scree, and finds the shortest path to the sea. These activities gradually cut ravines, which tend to get filled up with the scourings of spring floods. Once a ravine is level in soil, small irregularities in the stream's flow deposit silt in particular places. These tend to block the flow and bend the stream bed into oxbows, creating an elaborate meandering pattern, which is gradually absorbed into finer and finer channels as bogs and marshes begin to obliterate the stream into subsurface capillarities (Muir 1894).

Of course, for the usual human purposes, such a description does not tend to get increasingly complicated; we simply forget about the stream once we can walk over it and graze or till where it was. This inattention is dictated by discursive constraints. The present work is an attempt to point out discursive directions, not based on instrumental views of nature, in which such descriptions do emerge as significant.

In the present example, autocollection occurs as the ravine gets filled with stream-carried silt, as this silt forces oxbowing, and as it surmounts the flow altogether as a marsh. Although the marsh itself may be an immature landscape ecosystem, it is replacing a senescent river so elaborate and difficult of description (the Mississippi delta comes to mind) that no one attempts it (such an attempt might look like Joyce's River Liffey in *Finnegans Wake*)—and we tend to stay out of there and fill it in with garbage as soon as possible! But from the viewpoint of stream flow itself, we can see that the cascading of frothy youth is replaced by an almost morbidly refined seepage, which is finally dispersed altogether in a kind of "dream" of plant transpiration— something else's cascading. This note of senesecence's sometimes leading to transcendence (river into landscape) will be taken up again in chapter 6.

In this example the marshy seepage could have a detailed infody-namic description (based on the four rules on page 111) with a degree of complication not unlike that of, say, a late-term fetus. In the latter, every capillary and venule has formed around idiosyncratic adventi-tious blood flows, which, if one bothered to describe them, would differ in detail from the pattern of any other fetus. Now, it is true that no two streams are identical even at their inception. This is because they have not got the stability of living systems, which allows these to standardize their forms. But in both cases the tendency is always toward ever more complication. In organisms this may not continue in the circulatory system past some juvenile stage, save as a result of accidental insults, but in nervous systems it continues functionally throughout life. Here too we encounter a transcendence—neuronal interaction into cognition.

The Honing of Selfness

We are now in a position to see how self-organization can be taken as the increasingly more detailed and particular collection of self-produced products of cascading. At its most primitive, a stream col-lects its own silt, and this leads to an increase in stored information that finally obliterates the stream itself.

Following Uexküll (1926), I will view selves as always in contact with relevant portions of their environment (their *Umwelten*), as parts of "function circles," with input signs from the environment picked up as "indications", which are assembled by the *Innenwelt* of the system, which generates "action rules" by the activation of which behavior is returned to the environment. Models of the environment are generated and interpreted in the *Innenwelt*, where they inform the action rules.

Now, we can see that the signs impinging upon the system most nakedly are indices—necessary traits of aspects of the environment. Such a picture can serve as a semiotic interpretation of purely physical events. For example, in a taste bud, a salt will ionize and cause a chemical change. This is no different than a hurricane blowing down trees in a forest. But transduction into a nerve impulse generates a new kind of coinage altogether: depolarization or not of the cell membrane. (Maybe this is not unlike the mobilization of societies in the face of natural disasters.)

A pattern of depolarization is the translation into symbolic indi-cations by the animal system of indexical signs related to some en-vironmental integrity—"symbolic" because there is no necessary relationship between these *Innenwelt* impulses and the nature of the sign stimuli, all of which are translated into the same language. However, without a model in the *Innenwelt* we could not say that physical events serve as indices, because for that we would need to be able to se that the system was actually using them as signs. And without an expectation derived from a model, that would be too specified an interpretation. For biological systems we could use the genetic *deus ex machina* and suppose that genetic information organizes the earliest models in the developing system.

For a less complicated system, such as a stream or a hurricane, we need to see that (relatively vague) homologies of models reside in tendencies—in what the system "will do next" as part of its cascading. In a stream, this is its tendency to find a channel that can best satisfy the need for gravitational dissipation. For a hurricane, vague models reside in momentary inertial tendencies and torques with respect to their condition the following moment. Before they are realized, these tendencies can be taken as predictions of what to do next. Consider that if (in a thought experiment) a hurricane were totally stopped it would be leaning into its next action, poised for continued motion. This works because that continuity might not, in fact, *be* its next action if it is actually poised to encounter some interference like a mountain chain or cool waters. Out of these sorts of vague inclinations must have come the more elaborate and stable models of living systems; there seems to be no other alternative short of saying that models arise *de novo* with living systems, an alternative I consider to violate the principles of materialism to which science ought to be wedded.

In this work, following Whitehead (1925), Wright (1964), and many structuralists (e.g., Piaget (1970a)), I assume that all emergences are prefigured or immanent in the vague tendencies of prior systems—structures that have not been accessed, and attractors that have not been responded to. Nerve conduction itself, for example, was prefigured in the tendency of any kind of cell to depolarize under certain circumstances—a tendency found even in abiotic microspheres (Fox 1986). It is not necessary to suppose, however, that these immanent structures were potential from the beginning of the world or of the system involved. As a system changes, its potentialities and propensities may change too (Matsuno 1989), making previously moot possibilities potential.

Continuing with the animal system (only because it is well enough known), I note that symbolic information makes its way into models in the *Innenwelt* (inherited and ontogenetically developed neuron structures in the nervous system), where it may be regulated into an action rule, which then serves as indexical information in triggering output responses back into the *Umwelt*. These responses themselves, as they appear in the environment, are formally symbolic because they are not necessarily connected to particular external events in the way that, say, enzyme mediation necessarily connects two states of a substrate molecule. This is so even when the behavior is stereotypical, because it may be given mistakenly or as a fluctuation of the system (e.g., displacement activity). Indeed, the fact that crossings between system and environment are marked by symbolic transduction is what allows for behavioral modification and even creativity. This could not be the case if behavior was indexically tied to states of the environment. The fact, however, that the actual bridging of the barrier between environment and system is indexical (the fittingness to receptors of external stimuli coming in, and the unity of modulation of different cellular activities going out) is what has encouraged mechanistic interpretations of behavior.

This puts us back in the hurricane, where communication with the environment seems entirely indexical. Behavior here too could be modified by internal fluctuations, however, and (these being formally random) could be read as creative. Such fluctuations might be viewed as proto-symbols because of their reduced bond to the immediate environment. This would be so even if the fluctuations were chaotic rather than truly random, because, in a sense, the fluctuation itself, regardless of the immanent nature of the trajectory accessed, is a venture by the system, reflecting a proto-agency. Admittedly, the role of such fluctuations in the career of a hurricane might be relatively minute, although amplification of chaotic impulses could have major importance for its direction. Even if it were important, the vagueness of the system would prevent us from detecting such effects of agency; it is the principle only that is required to be stated here.

The translation of genetic messages into protein behaviors is certainly symbolic, because the link between a codon and its amino acid is not (yet known to be) indexical and because the behavior of the protein depends upon conditions in the organismic *Innenwelt*. Of course, these conditions might be taken to have been the results of prior translations, but they nevertheless are modulated by cell behavior in ways that are not known to be entirely rigidly patterned, and they are certainly capable of fluctuating, and these fluctuations can be read as creative.

The specification relations between symbols and indices reveal an interesting developmental direction. (I have not found that "icons," Peirce's other sign category, are different from symbols for my purposes, because anything could symbolically "look like" virtually anything else. In other cases, like shadows, icons might be indices as well, and so I disregard icons in this preliminary jaunt.) Indices represent what is the case materially now—Peircean seconds (Houser 1991). Symbols, on the other hand, because they are tied only to particular interpretations (Peircean thirds), can mutate freely, can be played with, and could represent what *might* be the case. Since 'what is the case', as a token, is a subclass of 'what could be the case' as types (figure 1.2), we could view development as a narrowing from symbolic possibilities toward concrete, indexical necessities. Doing this begs the question of what thirdness the very immature system resides in; one way or another, they all need to be nurtured, and so this would be the thirdness of the "sponsors" that generated them.

But there is a further relation here. Any well-enough-defined system could be considered to be attempting to impose its biases and categories on the world. In particular it can have a category ('what ought to be the case') concerning particular tokens of necessary types of behaviors. So, e.g., gorillas feed upon only a limited diet passed on by tradition and selected from a wide variety of available possible foods. They must eat vegetation, but within that type stricture they can choose this or that (among nonpoisonous alternatives—the 'could be's as tokens of figure 1.2).

However, oughts must again, because they are choices from possibilities, be formally symbolic. Hence, a system can be viewed as developing from a symbolic playfulness and vagueness toward ever-more-limited indexical necessities. However, those necessities do not exclude *all* variability, so further development of the system comes about by, again, choices from among more refined symbolic possibilities. Semiotically, development therefore can be seen as a movement from dealing primarily with symbols through dealing primarily with indexical information to a later stage where symbolic activities of a narrower range again take place—followed by a senescent period where chosen symbols become overwhelming necessities.

So, selfness (= autocollection) will become ever more detailed and determinable. This becomes evident with the earliest switching from vague searching among possibilities to commitment to a given trajectory. These commitments become more detailed (. . . metazoan, vertebrate, amniote, mammal, primate, human, male, middle class, professional, aged and dependent upon some prosthetic device. . . .) The sequence in its more highly specified subclasses might be differently arranged, or use different types, depending upon which thirdness one inhabits.

As a metazoan, one's position in gradients becomes immediately available by autocorrelation; as a vertebrate, lunging movements come to provide cogent changes in ambient gradients; as a mammal, the gradients come to include familiar odors; as a primate, attention is diverted from this to visual comparisons between self and others; as a human, mental self-representation as a figure in a ground of others enters into the models; and so on. It is of course difficult to imagine how this concatenation would read if one were moving toward being, say, a clam. Here we must rely on self-representation to find the essential thought.

The accumulating result of this progression is an increasing possibility of being determinate in some integrity. So, a single-cell organism—a euglena, say—no doubt has effects that, if we could find them, would distinguish it from other euglenas, but the scope of its individual determinateness would be relatively restricted in comparison with a metazoan, which can assume more states in more different places. Of course (the descendants of) a parasitic bacterium, say, could kill an important larger-scale organism and so have a major individual effect on phylogeny or history, but (remembering that the specification hierarchy is explicitly related to ourselves as observers) our characterization of this bacterium could be no more specified than that of any other of the same kind except for these unique adventures. But a multicellular animal can have a personal effect on its ecosystem of much more scope, and humans (as we now know to our sorrow) can have even larger-scale personal effects, which, despite attempts at concealment, are much more individually determinable—e.g., William Randolph Hearst and our forests.

The potentiality for individuality accrues with self-organization, and this is accentuated by an increasingly detailed, self-referential autocollection.

Some New Theoretical Entities

In order to locate the seat of self-organization more precisely, I believe we need to construct some new theoretical entities. In the first place, mechanistic materialism has so fully "captured" the organism, which is what most authors want to view as self-organizing, that continued efforts along those lines will be pitting themselves against the ingrained mechanistic perspective in a probably futile attempt to dislodge it. In the second place, self-organization characterizes more than just organisms; it describes changes in any dissipative structure. From the point of view of dealing with the new entities that I will propose, organisms do not appear different from any other dissipative structures. Thus, we will avoid focus on organisms and at the same time obviate conflict with mechanism. What transpires might be taken as a discussion of the ontology of ontogeny.

The Ontogenetic Trajectory

Using scalar hierarchical principles, we can see that large-scale entities have cogent moments that extend backward and forward as viewed in lower scale moments (second, days). So we could surmise that our town, say, has a cogent moment of about a day compared with our own *Augenblick* or *coup d'oeuil*.

Now, we consider ourselves to be the same persons in the evening that we were in the morning after many of our moments have passed, and, indeed, the same, in some sense, that we were last year. In this last case there would be, however, very few molecules within us that have not been replaced by others—and even many of our cells will have been replaced. We have also acquired new attitudes, new scars, but we are the still the same, or even more ourselves than we were. Our selfhood has intensified over more memories and experiences. Yet the organism that we seem to be (occupying) has changed to a greater or lesser degree (and, indeed, we do feel it to be something we are inside of, not something we identify fully with our *selves*, our agency—especially when it malfunctions).

So, we need a locus, not only for self-organization, but for our own selfhood and its agency. In one stroke we acquire this home if we consider that the "who" that we are, and which has our name, is that entity that began with fertilization and will become recycled some time after we have become aged—taken as one item, whole. The organism that sees its fingers typing, then, is a kind of momentary (mechanistic if you insist) manifestation of that *ontogenetic trajectory* that is "really" you.

Now, it does no good to declaim that this is a false view just because it is unfamiliar or seemingly uncongenial, plunging us into a world of unimaginable complexity. That alone cannot destroy the logical necessity of such an entity within the scalar hierarchical perspective. I can assert that this entity exists in the hierarchical perspective (including its specification aspects as well), and you would need to deny any ontological status whatever to that perspective in order to eliminate that entity (if that is what you wish to do).

There is precedence for this construction. Collingwood (1945) noted that in biology trajectories of this sort were quite naturally constructed, usually from an Hegelian perspective. Alberch et al. (1979) and R. H. Wiley (1991) refer to this entity, and may have coined the term (but they did not use it in the full ontological sense being adopted here). On p. 176 of his 1980 book, Prigogine identifies a theoretical object—a time operator—that may allow mathematical exploration of trajectories in terms of age instead of time.

What would such an entity "look like" if something of large scale could see it? Of course eyes would not exist at that scale, but maybe there could be some analogue or even some differently specified homologue of 'seeing' at that large scale. We can then imagine that a person would {appear} rather like an amoeba to an entity with a cogent moment of about one of our weeks in duration. The person's nucleus would be located at her bed, and she would have tentacles spreading out in different geographical directions according to habitual paths taken during the week. Once-in-a-while trips to (say) the watchmaker would hardly be visible, or would look like strands from a spider web. This is how we "see" electrons, for example. (Here, too, 'seeing' is only a poor analogy, one supposes.)

In this view, of course, persons would have overlapping provenance; more than one would occupy the same Newtonian space at the same time. (And how else would we explain insight and deep personal communication anyhow?) A city of people viewed this way would "look" like a piece of felt, with completely intertwined strands, or like a mass of fungal hyphae. And, yes, of course, fungal hyphae could then be supposed, if they could be viewed at much smaller cogent moments, to be represented by rather fast-moving entities about the size of . . . ? These images amount to a visual model of cohesion in these systems. In fact, trajectories *are* the cohesion of systems, and their "twisting together" represents the cohesion of still-higher-scalar-level entities.

It would be convenient for present purposes to describe our own ontogenetic trajectories from a scale delivering a cogent moment of about one of our lifetimes. In that case the entire trajectory is present simultaneously as a single object. This object can be taken to be the seat of self-organization, agency, and selfhood because these inhere in its ontogenetic trajectory rather than in the organism, which is continually changing (besides being at any moment merely a mechanism, which can't have those properties).

This trajectory's physical "shape" would need to be composed of a variable combining physical size, energy throughput, and the scope of its behavioral reach (unpredictable in a small scope for immature systems, more predictable in a larger scope for mature systems, and unpredictable in a large scope for senescent systems). The construction of such a variable awaits future developments; however, if it were used, the trajectory might resemble a kind of fruit that retains its earlier conditions in later stages, like a gourd of some kind, showing a beginning, an increase in size, and an end (organismic time being read from the attachment of the fruit to its apex—figure 4.7, top). I take this to be an extension of the spirit of Goethe's attempt to contemplate the

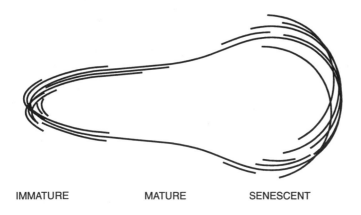

IMMATURE   MATURE   SENESCENT

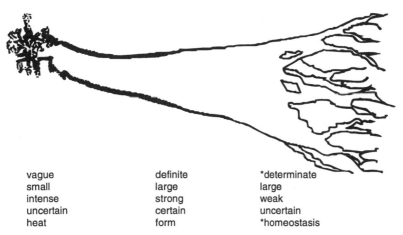

vague	definite	*determinate
small	large	large
intense	strong	weak
uncertain	certain	uncertain
heat	form	*homeostasis

Figure 4.7 Two rough versions of what developmental trajectories would "look" like from the vantage point of a cogent moment large enough to "see" a whole trajectory in one "glimpse." The upper version is a realization of the gourd or fruit model, with uncertain beginning and end. The lower version attempts to show a kind of probability space. The thickness of line suggests mass-specific entropy production: The characterizations below refer to, from top to bottom, determinacy, size, energy throughput, variance of behavior, and major target of dissipation. Asterisks indicate that these apply mostly to stabler kinds of dissipative structures, such as organisms.

entire life history of a plant at a single moment (Brady 1986). The lower portion of figure 4.7 shows another attempt to imagine such a trajectory. In these figures system cohesion is viewed (from a higher scalar level) as an entity; it would be as though verbs became nouns.

Now, it often happens that organisms are destroyed long before they senesce—indeed, as Comfort (1964) points out, the majority of individuals of most kinds of organisms do not survive into senescence before being forcibly recycled. What would the ontogenetic trajectory "look" like then? It would be lacking any indications of individuation after the point of death. Now, individuation is suggested in figure 4.7 only by the uncertainties (fuzziness) in the immature and senescent stages. Yet mature systems will have individuated as well, and this cannot be represented here because the figure is too crude to show the permanent effects of historical marking. It would be difficult to project onto these figures even the degrees of difference that we mark with the species distinction, although size difference would surely turn up in this strictly infodynamical representation. This concept, unlike the sort of trajectory I will discuss in the next section, does not relate strongly to the science of systematics.

Individuation becomes marked in dissipative structures, and this allows them increasingly to act as agents in dynamic interactions; however, the seat of agency is the trajectory, because it is this that can increase its agency during self-organization. Recall that in H_{sc} the organism is part of the ecological hierarchy, and its cogent moment, like that of any dissipative structure, is only as long as is needed to mark its relaxation time in connection with some integrity. Therefore the condition of being an agent, depending upon historical marking, cannot change during one of an organism's cogent moments. In fact it doesn't usually change until many such moments have passed.

We can now bring in that other meaning of 'agent' (an instrument by means of which a guiding system exerts an effect—modified from *Webster's New International Dictionary*) and note that the organism comes increasingly to be an agent of its own trajectory—that is, it exerts agency as a representative of its own trajectory, which is the seat of its agency. Hence the organism (or any dissipative structure) is an agent in both senses of the word: (1) its trajectory comes to be able to act, through it as a momentary embodiment, as if it were an individual, and (2) it represents another agency by acting as the material basis for the trajectory of which it is the momentary manifestation.

We also need some restatements in terms of the self-organization of determinability. Determinability depends on an observer's being able to trace back from its effects to a particular individual dissipative structure—on the ability of that entity to be consequential as itself.

Trajectories may be consequential in the world, as we know it at our scale, only through their agents the dissipative structures.

The ontogenetic trajectory maps onto the Rylean category (figure 2.8). The unfolding of a development gradually reveals the actual content of that category, including, through its increasing specification, ever more possibilities for determinateness. Not only does the trajectory increase its ability to have effects in the world, but its potential responsibility for these effects becomes intensified (to be lost again in extreme senescence). This increase in determinability, which lies at the heart of agency, is carried mostly by individuation of the dissipative structure, but it is the associated developmental processes making up the cohesion of the trajectory that afford that individuation. It is development that has the epigenetic structure which invites the intensification which is carried in by individuation.

Individuation clearly is a momentary thing, a consequence of contingent events that impinge upon a dissipative structure. Development is instead a structure (characterized, e.g., by the four rules on page 111), and it belongs to the trajectory, not to the dissipative form.

One might object to this assignment because we can actually observe, e.g., the development of a frog zygote as an organism from one of our cogent moments to another—that is, over very many of its own moments. I would argue that the embryo's own cogent moment is so short, because of its small size and high intensity of energy throughput, that we do not really observe it as another organism as we see it changing from one of *our* moments to another. The change we see comes closer to being a dim view of the trajectory itself, as when something moves across the field of a slow film, leaving a streak. We are seeing more the streak than the dissipative form by means of our relatively slow observations in the possibility space at the left end of figure 4.7. This is also associated with the vagueness of immature systems, discussed above, since I am taking observation to be canonically a behavior of mature systems (if they have the requisite complication and stability).

The Infodynamics of Development

Development (ontogeny in the case of organisms) is the being or cohesion of developmental trajectories. It has a characteristic infodynamic structure (chapter 3), which I will explore further here by examining time slices through different portions (dissipative structures) of a trajectory.

The immature system is relatively small, limited in scope, thermodynamically hot, producing physical entropy at a great rate, but also dissipating some of its energy resources into form and habits (stored information). It was started as a tiny vortex or gradient within the system of a much larger dissipative structure, at trivial thermodynamic cost to the larger system because of its small scale at inception. It appears to the mature observer as vague, unfinished, indeterminable. This is partly because of its relatively unconstrained behavior, which accesses large portions of its possibility space (figure 3.4) and is therefore hard to bring into focus, and partly because, being smaller in scale than the observer, it is changing very rapidly with respect to the observer's cogent moment. *This* is partly because of its relatively small amount of stored information (including size) and its consequently few rules and constraints and partly because its possibility space is relatively limited and so readily explored. The immature dissipative structure is easily obliterated by larger ones and so requires good support for its early development. In organisms this is obtained through parental behavior, in hurricanes through the stable boundary conditions of climatic structures, in Bénard cells through careful experimental arrangements.

So, the immature system is relatively orderly by default, as it were, because of its limited scope—despite a high specific disorder. Thus, in the Bénard instability, water in its just pre-organized state can't do much more than simmer conductively, with great microscopic disorder.

The mature system is larger (has grown), facilitates a greater gross energy flow through itself (is maximizing its power), and has accumulated large amounts of stored information. This last was afforded by its larger size, which caused its possibility space to expand and become more complicated—a larger system affords a greater variety of fluctuations, and these define its possibility space. Also, as the system grows, it incorporates information from its environment because it grows *into* its environment. Furthermore, as its stored information begins to accumulate, it is increasingly able to be modified by historical experience, thereby reflecting environmental fluctuations. Individuation and evolution are ongoing processes at this point. The per-unit entropy production has, however, diminished, and we may view this as a tradeoff between the physical entropy production characteristic of youth and the accumulation of informational entropy, which forebodes the transition to senescence. But the mature system is of great scope, is powerful and consistent in its actions, and so is quite determinable, at least to type (it's a young male, it's definitely becoming a hurricane, etc.).

The mature system has become more orderly by decreasing its specific disorder as against its increased scope for disorder (figure 3.4). So, its order is more "meaningful" than that of the immature system. For a simple example, an egg can be predicted to stay about where it is but a duck restrains its own behavior to a limited sphere in a specific habitat that is very restricted in relation to where it might roam and what it might do.

Finally, the senescent system has become informationally overburdened and at the same time energetically diminished (figure 3.2). The first is a result of a leveling off of growth, with, however, a continuing receptivity to being marked by historical information. The second is related to the fact that incorporated information tends to act as a constraint, so that (1) there are ever more rules incorporated into a non-growing system and (2) the rules achieve ever-more-redundant establishment, and so the system must increasingly forgo the possibility of flexibility in its responses. This large information load leads to increasing self-referential activity, instituting more time delays into the system's response. In this way the system becomes ever more determinable as an individual. It is now becoming dominated by habits. (Informational rigidity as the end product of self-organization was discussed by Csányi and Kampis (1985), but their interpretation of its meaning was different.) (See chapter 6.)

Owing to the consequent lack of flexibility, the senescent system's overt behavior is becoming increasingly determined by environmental fluctuations, and so manifest physical entropy is returning to it in the sense that it may unpredictably carry bursts of entropy flow by being buffeted by fluctuations, both internal and environmental. Figure 3.4 is transformed into figure 4.8. The system's increasing predispositions

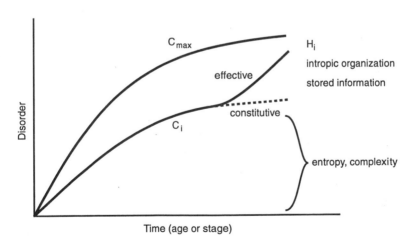

Figure 4.8 Figure 3.4 modified to show effects of senescence. Constitutive complexity is that which the system has by virtue of its actual stored information; effective complexity is that shown by the system because increasing rigidity precludes the requisite variety for adaptability.

imply a continuing increase in its constitutive intropy, but the consequent loss of flexibility ironically results in an overtly more entropic style of behavior. The system's effective intropy is declining; the many rules are having less and less overt effects on behavior. The system is more determinable but not more predictable! It has become a waif of an exaggerated self, approaching recycling (to be more readily encountered through fluctuations the nearer C_i approaches to C_{max} in figure 4.8) with every increase in determinability—death and decay for organisms, submersion of self in a general turbulence for hurricanes and Bénard cells, return to an early sere in ecosystems.

Ironically, the specific disorder of the senescent system increases with increased constitutive order. The increased habits resulting from the increasing number of constraints amount to a kind of "superstitious," pointless order.

Morphological Trajectories
Comparative morphologists (Lauder 1981, 1986; Wake et al. 1983; Wake and Roth 1989; Stanley 1990) have been concerned with the transformation, over long periods of time, of details of organismic form in lineages of living dissipative structures. I have proposed (1991c) that, if we really want to have an evolutionary entity that can be said to change through time (as organisms and species do not (Eldredge and Cracraft 1980), because with evolution they replace one another instead), we can construct *morphological trajectories*.

More to the point, these entities could be said to be self-organizing. As was noted by the above morphologists (see also Levinton 1986), changes in such trajectories are often independent of species replacements—and also, to some extent, of genetic change, because morphology is always canalized in some degree and because more than one sort of genetic change can give rise to the same morphological change. The pace of speciation and the pace of allele replacement in lineages are screened off (decoupled) from the pace of morphological change (Salthe 1972, figure 5-18).

Furthermore, Lauder (1986) has shown that even radical changes in the style of feeding in sunfishes, visualized through neuromuscular stimulation patterns, can occur without altering morphology significantly. Hence, even niche shifts can occur independently of morphological change. Indeed, this literature creates the impression that morphology is frequently the most conservative aspect of organic evolution. Allele substitutions can accumulate, speciations can occur, and even changes in autecological adaptations can take place, without altering morphology.

Of course, when morphology does change significantly, we are likely to find that this change was marked by genetic change, accompanied by niche shifting, and even blessed by speciation. Lauder does give examples, however, where morphological change has not altered the basic functioning of swallowing in fishes; in this case the neuromuscular patterns remain unaltered in the face of considerable morphological change directly impinging on foraging. In any case, we again find morphology screened off from other aspects of organic evolution. Lauder (personal communication) feels that his work shows that "it is possible to consider form and function as much more independent than usually thought." Morphology has the cohesion over time that one would expect if it reflected structural atractors.

I propose that the morphological trajectory can be the entity that allows self-organization discourse to incorporate evolutionary morphology. In making this suggestion I have in mind two examples discussed by Thomson (1988): the transition from mammal-like reptiles to mammals and the earlier transition from rhipidistian fishes to amphibians. In both of these cases one can see a group of related lineages moving in fits and starts independently and in parallel in the same general directions over about 10 million years, with coordinated changes taking place among several different characters simultaneously.

The classical interpretation of these events (Salthe 1972) is that similar selection pressures were working independently on populations in closely related lineages to elicit similar evolutionary response. However, selection theory would not *predict* the same coordinated changes occurring repeatedly over a period of time so long with respect to the pace of selective responses, which occur over periods of roughly a thousand generations (Lumsden and Wilson 1981). It defies the imagination to deliver selection pressures (as usually conceived) on organisms that, unchanging, would work over such long periods of time consistently in so many different local environments. True, the climate might change gradually over a period of 10 million years, but it is hard to see that selection with respect to some combination of temperature, humidity, and air movements could regulate the complex coordinated changes in the pharyngeal and jaw regions of the organisms in these lineages.

One could with as much justification consider that the lineage is a self-organizing entity (the morphological trajectory) of the same general kind as the ontogenetic trajectory (somewhat as in figure 3.6). This would be an entity composed of populations and demes at any moment. Events in the ecological entities (the populations) result in a re-sorting of the information in the genealogical entities (demes) as the lineage traverses prospective niche space (Valentine 1968).

A combination of the microscopic processes of mutation, recombination, ontogenetic generation of variation, and the ecological activities of organisms gives rise to what, at the level of the lineage, can be viewed as self-organization.These microscopic processes can be interpreted as "mechanistic," but self-organization itself would not be, any more than mentality is with respect to neuronal activity. As Ulanowicz (1989) has convincingly demonstrated, macroscopic entities engender their own formal causes, which in this case can be interpreted as the deployment of matter in the direction of certain structural attractors. In other words, there must be some top-down influence here, as in any scalar hierarchy where, in the basic triadic system, mechanisms are always lower-level to higher-level regulations and semioses.

Naturally, I am not ruling out that there can be creative downward causation in ontogenetic trajectories as well. With respect to lower-level mechanisms, upper-level events are always informational, interpretive, and semiotic at any scalar level (Salthe 1985). Here I am simply moving this scale-independent formalism to the higher scalar level of lineages, suggesting that these too are not only evolving but also developing and self-organizing trajectories. If we do not take this line, we are essentially declaring that lineages are merely cognitive constructs of human discourse. Only in that case could something be evolving and not also developing. Only nondynamic material systems (say, a rock) can evolve while not developing. If there are processes going on, we can always compare instances of them (e.g., Thomson's comparison of mammalian and amphibian originations) and discover commonalities of process, which perforce, must then be interpreted as discriminable material processes, natural examples of which always give rise to a consciousness of development; if constitutive processes result in change, they produce what we call development.

So, I am suggesting that, because morphology changes independently of other known evolutionary processes, morphological trajectories could be, at their own scale, self-organizing entities—in fact, they could be the material agents in organic evolution. Their initiating conditions are generated by genetic changes in organisms, by ontogeny, by niche switching, and by speciation. Changes produced by these "mechanisms" of a morphological trajectory's self-organization may occur without relationship to the self-organizing process (a macrosystem is generally impervious to single instances of, or the details of, microsystemic alterations—compare Gould and Eldredge 1977). But microsystemic processes would always be entrained by it, since it produces important boundary conditions on them. I am further suggesting that what morphologists and systematists have constructed as lineages map rather closely onto morphological trajectories as conceived here.

Thomson (1977, 1988) has described, on the basis of his work with fossil fishes, a theory of extinction that bears on the possibility of the existence of morphological trajectories. In this theory a lineage is viewed as undergoing what I would here call a 'mature period' of growth in diversity, followed by what I would call a 'senescent period' of declining diversity. Thomson suggests that overspecialization is the usual result of intense diversification, so that the species products become metastable to extinction by any sources of perturbations whatever because of lack of flexibility. This is a neat description of a senescent system in terms readily convertable to infodynamic discourse, and Thomson's description of what I would call a 'senescent stage' is clear if the lineages he describes are thought of as self-organizing trajectories. (This 'senescence' must not be confused with forgotten theories of "racial senescence," which had an entirely different basis—see Simpson 1949.)

Significantly for the infodynamical perspective, Thomson talks about the period preceding diversification as one in which experimentation (e.g., fluctuations) leads to the accession of new morphologies. That is not a bad description of an infodynamically immature stage either. Problems remain in understanding why given lineages undergo increases in diversity whereas others do not. Formally, Thomson's (1988) explanation does not differ from my understanding of why a particular potential tropical storm and not another became a hurricane.

There is a significant conceptual problem with the description of morphological trajectories given above. The trajectores are defined only in terms of organismic snapshots—in terms of organismic characters. This is, of course, because we, as organisms, have not (yet) detected them in other ways. We see the microscopic words, but cannot read the macroscopic text. We are in a similar position with respect to the cities we inhabit. What is going on at the level of the city itself? We can in that case at least study traffic patterns, heat production, and such in an attempt to construct genuine higher-level images of the macrosystem. With morphological trajectories we have remnants of the occupants only (fossils), and none of the city. Various parallelisms and convergences between lineages, and decoupling of long-term changes of form from the processes of speciation, suggest to us that there is a macrosystem, but we can only see patterns of microsystemic entities, as if we were observing occupants entrained by a city but not seeing the city itself.

Darwinians will, of course, deny that there is a city. Very well, then; let them come up with cogent reductionist theories of parallel evolution, of convergence, of iterative evolution, of ecological vicarage, and of the decoupling of genetic change, speciation, adaptation, and morphology on which the idea of a morphological trajectory is based. One would like to know why lineages behave as if they were infodynamic entities over long periods of time (e.g., diversity trends in fossils) if they are not such entities.

Summary

The major point of this chapter was to play development off against evolution (or individuation). The logic for this distinction, from a structuralist point of view, was discussed in the section on the type/token distinction. Although development is preeminently a phenomenon describable in the specification hierarchy, it was noted that development characterizes processes in the ecological branch of the scalar hierarchy, whereas most individuation in biological systems is represented in the genealogical hierarchy. The point was then made, justifying the ecological hierarchy as logically prior to the genealogical hierarchy, that only developmental discourse is about the constitutive processes of material systems, evolution being concerned with recording the results of the failures of such systems to regenerate themselves and with the nature of this kind of failure (rather than with the material systems that fail).

Self-organization is located as the (higher-scalar-level) context for both developmental and evolutionary change; it is characterized primarily as a process generating increasing determinacy. One result of this is an increase in the potentiality of a system to act as an agent. Agency develops from a primal vagueness through increasingly determinate stages. When this process is reconstructed after the fact, it appears to expand back toward generality rather than toward vagueness, because the categories of the past are fully known—constructed—by developmental discourse.

It was suggested that self-organization involves a system in modeling its environment, modeling always being at a lower scalar level than interpretation. In context of the cascading/collecting cycle, self-organization appears to be an increase in self-referentiality. Two new entities were proposed as seats of self organization: the ontogenetic trajectory for organisms and the morphological trajectory (i.e., lineages) for temporally extended kinds of organisms. These represent the cohesion of the entities that show, on the one hand, ontogeny, and, on the other, phylogeny.

Chapter 5

The Search for a Theory of Change

(dedicated to the memory of George Fried)

In this chapter I investigate the problem of change to something radically new, which leads to a discussion and a classification of kinds of emergence. I find that there are two major classes of emergence: the origin of newness or uniqueness (historical or evolutionary emergence) and the attainment of configurations that, while predictable, cannot be derived only from knowledge of antecedent states (developmental emergence). This latter has been described in two forms: the cohesion of systems into larger-scale configurations and supervenience. The latter explicitly involves categories of an observer, and I argue that this is true of the accession of cohesion as well.

Development through stages is discussed as an example of concatenations of developmental emergences traversing a specification hierarchy. I propose that accession of a new stage is made possible by system senescence, thus proposing that the duration of any stage is characterized by the canonical infodynamic development from immaturity to senescence. I further propose that this model can also contribute to understanding the origin of new evolutionary systems.

Since emergence in my interpretation involves categories of an observer, I am suggesting that science ought to become subjective if emergence is to be taken up as a scientific problem. This leads to a consideration of the dialectics of nature, the only hitherto proposed subjective discourse related to science. This move is further suggested because dialectics has been said to be a theory of change, "change" meaning to something radically different. The exercise shows that, indeed, dialectics might be used as a stepping-off point in considering emergence—especially if prediction is replaced by advocacy, and analysis by construction. I finish with a general model of change embodying hierarchy theory, infodynamics, and dialectics.

Most of the discourse of science has been based on the concept of equilibrium. This includes, ironically, the synthetic theory of evolution. Natural selection is an equilibrium process that does not produce change unless the environment changes, when a population undertakes to reach a new equilibrium (Depew 1986). Speciation as well, in the dominant allopatric model anyway, occurs only as a result of external interference with gene flow, which otherwise tends to homogenize demes. The origin of a new way of life, to the extent it is treated at all (with, e.g., the notion of preadaptation), is taken to be the result of chance fluctuations from established equilibria.

In developmental biology, the system is viewed, not so much as being at equilibrium, as traversing standardized stages, and the problem has been viewed as one of discovering how genetic information makes this reliably possible. Yet this discourse has been cryptically equilibrial in its molecular focus, inasmuch as molecular-level processes have relaxation times much shorter than ontogeny itself and so can themselves be taken to have an equilibrial character with respect to the irreversible development being studied. And new directions of ontogeny have been of interest only if they could be viewed as resulting reliably, as types (e.g., exogastrulae), from known experimental interference.

Goodwin (1984) and other structuralists have shown that change from one structure to another occurs through jumps from one domain of attraction to another. Structuralists take the domains themselves as merely existing—indeed, as preexisting the systems that access them (Piaget 1970a). Change, as the transformation of a system to something really *new*, is never tackled in detail. Instead it is represented as a kind of global flip-flop from one black box to another. The new (e.g., a mutation) is typically viewed as being enabled by chance (i.e. unknowable) fluctuations. Now that, from the perspective of chaos theory, much of what was before thought to be random is seen to reflect a kind of determinism, taking seriously the possibility of the occurrence of the really new has become even less plausible.

In this chapter I will attempt to confront the origin of newness—as part of the problem of emergence—in the hope of opening it up to inspection. What is at stake is whether or not history, as an ongoing process, is accessible to science. (Cladistics and the approach of Brooks and Wiley (1988) seem adequate for dealing with it after the fact.) If history is not accessible, then developmental discourse must be taken to be the major mode of science, and the actual moment of the occurrence of an evolutionary change would be outside of its immediate domain.

What Is Newness?

Newness may be taken to be the unprecedented. Since every actual individual item and event is unique, the unprecedented surrounds us all the time. But science has not been our method of trying to deal with it. We do not yet, however, know that science cannot confront newness directly, observing it in the making with understanding. Newness is produced by change, but change also produces predictable alterations. We might just see if we can represent change to newness in some coherent fashion.

The transformations T_C and T_D in figure 5.1 represent movements to new conditions in the sense of conditions not typical for this kind of system in t_1 (i.e., outside its standard potentiality space, P_j). It is clear that these results would have had a low probability of occurring given that the system in t_0 was in a condition inside its typical P_i, as with T_C. We cannot say whether or not the result would have been "expected" given that the system in t_0 was somewhere outside its usual configuration (as in the case of T_D), but that in itself would have been relatively unexpected.

In this representation all we can say about newness is that the developmental capacity of a system moving to a point outside P_j in t_1 must be taken to remain larger than that in a more typical example of the system, which would have moved to within P_j. This, then, violates a developmental pattern (discussed in chapter 4) to the effect that later stages will have diminished potential for further change. So, if a system mutates, it cannot necessarily be expected to have lost developmental capacity. But if it reaches a mutation from a fluctuation occurring at t_0 (as in T_D), it is not clear that even this much can be said.

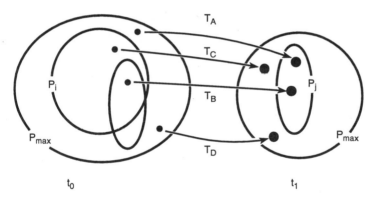

Figure 5.1 Transformations (T_A, etc.) of a developing system. The P's indicate potentiality space, actual and maximum. As development proceeds, it becomes more restricted, the new actual space being represented by the intersection area in t_0, where P_j has been projected backward as a final cause. Actual states of the system are shown as dots. These are larger at time t_1 because the system has accumulated stored information (not otherwise indicated here), which increases its actual reach in state space. T_B shows the most usual kind of result: Beginning with initial conditions typical for the system in t_0 (that is, inside P_i), the system changes so that the new value lies within those typically obtained under the boundary conditions imposed by the system in t_1 (that is, inside the intersection of P_i and P_j). In T_A (equifiniality) these same results are obtained, but the system has begun from atypical values (reached by fluctuation) and has still recovered its usual trajectory. I thank Germano Resconi for showing me this symbolism. See text for further explication.

T_D might be taken to imply newness in the sense that the initial mutation together with a subsequent failure of equifinality will have placed the system in a configuration almost as vague as the one it was in before, leaving it open to unexpected further changes. So, for example, in respect to its potentiality for change, if the system began inside standard expectations, as in T_C, it will have in some respects returned to an earlier state. Indeed, since the system has necessarily acquired more stored information through differentiation (indicated by the sizes of the dots in the figure), it should be capable of accessing even more state space (by rearrangement or reorganization) than it was able to access when it occupied a somewhat larger potentiality space, with less internal potentiality because it was more indefinite, in t_0. This potentiality will likely seal its doom, because now there is more that can go wrong after mutation.

Still, it might be said that even T_D does not imply newness in any radical sense, insofar as the arrow still arrives somewhere within the next stage's maximum capacity. The regularities or material laws of a system do not exhaust it possibilities. Yet change cannot be to anything whatever; it is constrained by the kind of system involved. The fact that any actual system has a finite maximum possibility space (P_{max}) seems to be a materialist constraint that cannot be obviated, and this is some of the meaning of chaos theory for us—that is, the unexpected always happens within constraints, and so can never be truly totally unexpected except as a result of ignorance on the part of the observer. A participant within a system, of course, would not be ignorant in this way, but would be creatively sounding out—measuring—the next possibility for equilibration (in the sense of Matsuno 1989) in its local region.

P_j in the figure is acting as a final cause (represented by its being projected backwards to t_0, much as would be a T^{-1} in category theory)—and so it is working as a constraint, not a determination. In my 1985 book I pointed out that, in the basic triadic system of H_{sc}, final causes are generated as boundary conditions by the larger-scale systems in which an observed system is embedded. In this case, the trajectory entraining the changes is the larger-scale system that allows a later stage to impose finality upon an earlier one. P_i, on the other hand, comes from initiating conditions generated within the developing system as it has come to be through its prior transformations. The output of the transaction shown in figure 5.1 would typically be located within the intersection of P_i and the back-projected P_j. We can take whatever that back-projection represents to be the formal representation of action of final causes in a developing system. It seems, then, that the limited newness possible in development appears to us as an evasion for previously dominant final causes.

Newtonian "Change"—No Output without Input

Newtonian systems privilege efficient causes; in fact, they usually refer explicitly only to changes associated with them. Changes in dependent variables trace the effects of efficient causes forced through changes in independent variables. Formal and final causes are lumped into boundary conditions, with some formal causes embodied in the structure of descriptive equations as well. Material causes are often only implicitly represented, especially in general treatments. But they are explicitly present of necessity in inquiries located, e.g., in physical chemistry—as initial conditions. "Qualitative" treatments, as in studies of chaotic behavior, trace the development of a system as a function of varying initial and boundary conditions rather than the traditional variables themselves. Such an approach is a recent departure from the quantitative realm of Newtonian systems, and its major philosophical importance may lie just in this relaxation of traditional constraints, opening up investigation, as it does (by playing off one scalar level against another) into the world of complex causality.

Even the behavior of chaotic systems is viewed as in a way deterministic, because of the recurrent regularities displayed. And, indeed, it may be the discovery of deterministic forces that most broadly characterizes goals of the Newtonian approach. This approach is a search for regularities of change—that is, for the developmental rules of changing systems, for the laws of matter and nature.

Cybernetics (like behaviorism) has been an upscale reductionist off-shoot of this, observing systems for their regularities in responding to input stimuli (Ashby 1956) without probing the inner workings that give rise to the behavior. This is reduction upwards, ignoring material causes and initiating conditions. Prediction and control are the overt aims in such approaches, where understanding is taken to be anticipation. When the ultimate understanding is taken instead to be the fabrication and repair of machines (artificial intelligence, allopathic medicine), reductionist analysis is also employed; this time it is downward reduction to "basic" units. The governing paradigm remains a search for deterministic connections to experimentally manipulated efficient causation. In the case of downward reduction, this becomes a probing of internal rearrangements associated with system responses.

Downward reductionist analysis tends to open up black boxes. Systems-science treatments of transparent boxes run quickly into recursive cycles (feedbacks), and mathematical modeling of this situation generates nonlinearities and chaotic behavior. Perhaps if enough levels are involved (recursive cycles within cycles) the system even begins to appear to generate behavior internally. Some suspect that our brains do it that way, with personality predispositions, convictions, attitudes, and motivations arising out of the chaotic interactions of many levels of embedded, contiguous, concatenated, and parallel cycles of neuronal behavior. The mystery of personality is thought to emerge from this mass of complexity, and for limited observers (as we are) the mystery remains cogent as with all emergences.

But in all this chaotic behavior there is nothing really *surprising* theoretically. All possible configurations are immanent in the whole, scalar, hierarchically organized system. There is nothing really new produced, and many supposed accidents might not be accidents at all but only rarer configurations. Chaotic systems can be so complex, if they are large enough in scale, that novelty becomes a matter of quantity rather than quality. For example, there are only a limited number of (racially limited) human facial types, with not particularly closely related people in the same subgroup embodying the same ones. Coupling this with the facts about personality similarities between identical twins reared apart, we can easily imagine a limited number of structural domains of personality and facial type, access to any one of which is facilitated by interactions of internal (including genetic) and external enablements.

In such a structuralist view, it is the domain itself (the type) that is expressed—not the genes or the environment, which only facilitate its attainment. Here we see a more complex but possibly still Newtonian field. Personality, for example, would be a higher-level emergence from lower-level Newtonian interactions (of, say, cells). The fact that we cannot know all the details of these interactions would not remove them from the scope of research into prediction, fabrication, and control, which would be aimed by structuralists at the attractors themselves.

Chance and Creativity
I noted earlier that there has been a formal isomorphism in the discourse of science between creativity and chance. Whenever modeling requires creative acts to be represented, they are modeled by means of pseudorandom-number generators. But chance and creativity are not really identical. A creative act produces something new, an up-till-then unique configuration (Barzun 1943). Hence, creativity must be associated with agency—agents make creative acts (acts that reflect unique configurations—chapter 4). But random frequency distributions do not imply this at all. They simply refer to the possibility that a relatively unexpected configuration might be selected capriciously (that is, mindlessly, without intention, impulsively, unsystematically) from a probability density function. Here all possibilities are known in advance, and what we are modeling is expectation alone. But we can have *no* expectations concerning the really new.

How, for example, should we treat biological mutations? Clearly, the literature shows that seldom is a mutation listed unless it is known to be causal in respect to one of a number of recorded (and therefore expected) abnormalities—say, a particular cancer, or a lack of color where a wild type has color. There seem to be limited numbers of kinds of mutations observed in any system, certain kinds of (even imaginable) changes having never yet been observed. Clearly the probability density function is the model here. Mutations that might occur once in a million generations are not listed or inscribed in the frequency distribution—in fact, in practice, they are held not to occur at all. An individual with a unique form will go unrecorded (unless, perhaps, that individual is human). Chance is the model but uniqueness is not the subject because prediction is the aim, and the discourse is thus Newtonian in its imagination.

Natural Selection
Natural selection embodies the Newtonian spirit; it maintains the status quo unless perturbed by changes in external selection pressures. The production of alternative phenotypes is carried out by chance mutations and recombinations—in actual theoretical practice, by capricious selection from a list of recognized alternatives. Darwinians insist that the system of variation production is mechanical and unresponsive to needs or conditions. It is important that variants be viewed as occurring at all times according to their probabilities so that neither environment nor organisms can be viewed as eliciting any of them upon demand. Only in this way could their probabilities be knowable. This then eliminates the possibility of anything radically new at the outset.

Furthermore, selection pressures are supposed to change at random. Darwinians have no theory of the environment; changes must be selected from a few stereotypical alternatives (colder, warmer) attained by secular change at higher scalar levels. Both the generative system and the environment are black boxes, and the deme is tied deterministically to environmental changes in that the mode of the population distribution (of a character, such as beak size) is taken to represent the optimum fit to environmental stimuli (say, seed sizes).

The structural simplicity of this theory has become clouded, however, by new information on several fronts. The generative system—ontogeny—has been explicitly reintroduced (Bonner 1982; Wake and Roth 1989) as a potentially transparent box with rules of its own. The genetic system has undergone a similar uncovering (Campbell 1982; Dover 1986; Pollard 1988). Before that, Lewontin (1974) pointed out that linkage disequilibrium among genetic loci falsifies most population-genetic thinking. If we add recent knowledge about the periodicity of major environmental disruptions (Kerr 1988; Raup and Boyajian 1988; Bennett 1990), we can see that what Darwinism took to be black boxes are no longer opaque.

However, it would be a mistake to think that this has forced non-Newtonian attitudes. It has only changed the scale and the locality of the black boxes in evolutionary theories, in such a way that the overall theory will have to fractionate along lines of specialization dictated by the new opacities. For example, Dawkins (1976) responded to the transparency of the organism by moving the objects of selection down to the genes. In such ways, head-on confrontation with complexity can seem to be avoided. Because it is implicitly structured as a scalar hierarchy, classical Darwinism could easily evolve into a metatheory within which Newtonian specializations might continue to flourish.

In any case, real newness cannot be foreseen or handled in this research tradition. As long as there is a black box, there must be a list of alternative behaviors accompanied by probabilities. If a previously-not-encountered modification occurs, it is added to the list, but its appearance is not marked as a special event. Consider, for example, the origin in the biosphere of primates. It would be analyzed by Darwinians as one potential result of transformations of primitive insectivores. If we were to consider it instead to be an internally measured (in the sense of Matsuno 1989) response to some contingent condition of the biosphere, we might suppose that it could have been a unique event on Earth. Reasonable, yes, but it would not be handled that way. Instead, it would be taken implicitly to be one possible kind of transformation of Earth-like biospheres on possible worlds, and so a member of an unknown probability distribution.

What we need to see is that synthetic evolutionary theory, notwithstanding its role of explaining evolution, is radically unhistorical despite its making a fetish of "population thinking" and statistics (Brooks and Wiley 1988). In fact, we can now see that it is unhistorical *because* of that orientation, where the new is thought to be trivially mapped onto chance. This privileges the central pull of the mean, not the variants.

Emergence

Dictionary definitions of 'emerge' ("to rise out of, to become revealed") suggest that it involves preexisting possibilities (Salthe 1991d). Since this is not true of all emergences, I noted that the word 'emergency' carries another relevant meaning—an unforeseen combination of events—which, too, could "arise out of" a situation. In fact, it seems that we will need to dichotomize emergences along these lines, and I will refer to them as *developmental emergence* and *evolutionary emergence*. What they have in common is a general sense of puzzlement. In the case of developmental emergence, although we have a good idea of what will occur from past instances, we cannot see how it manages to bring itself about; the transforation is not a straightforward, linear extension of what was the case. Evolutionary emergence seems to me to suggest a collection of contingencies; of course, contingent configurations refer to the unprecedented, and so we might usefully consider that what we take "to emerge" would not have been predictable. I will discuss evolutionary emergence first because it is in a way less puzzling.

Evolutionary (Historical) Emergence
The appearance of the unprecedented is, of course, the origin of uniqueness (and so of the potential for agency as defined in chapter 4). As a trajectory realizes itself in time, it encounters numerous contingencies and is marked by many of them. Each of these actual occasions is a nexus of integrities in which any of them might become altered. As a trajectory is gradually revealed, it becomes increasingly distinguishable from similar others because the histories of no two tokens of a type can be identical in this complex, non-uniform, asymmetrical world. *Uniqueness*, although it could grab a place in a *post hoc* frequency distribution, cannot be modeled using a probability density function.

A system or discourse that would deal with historical emergences would therefore have to be frequentist in statistical idealogy; and it would not act according to the strategy of testing, but would rather attempt to confirm its suppositions by winnowing through numerous cases. Anything really new might be able to be added to support its constructions, but inevitably most (undamaging) newnesses will simply be ignored.

Since frequency distributions tend to converge toward a central tendency, even the radically new cannot escape interpretation. It is, of course, systems of interpretance that make these constructions, that have averages as categories implicit in their queries. A definite viewpoint can accommodate anything it can associate with one of its categories, and its integrities can thus be safely modified. What seems to be the case, then, is that historical emergences can only be reflected robust systems of interpretance. The weaker such systems are, the more easily would they be radically transformed, or even destroyed, by anything really new that happened. This point has been made in the terminology of *symmetry breaking* by Johnson (1988), Kondepudi (1988), Lima-de-Faria (1988), and Nicolis (1986).

When internal forces are strong, as in immature systems, they determine the results; however, as these forces weaken, as a system moves toward equilibrium (Johnson 1988), idiosyncrasies can come into play that were suppressed by the central tendency of the far-from-equilibrium situation. Hawking (1988) uses the example of the ball in a roulette wheel. As long as the wheel is spinning strongly, the ball cannot settle down; but when the centrifugal forces bearing on it weaken, the ball begins to be affected by weak forces and contingent constraints—and then symmetry is broken when a particular choice is made. Fluid vortices seem good examples of weak systems of interpretance, since they are so easily disrupted by environmental irregularities after their maturity.

In Conrad's (1983) terms, a system is "indifferent" to historical perturbations when it can simply add them to its store of information or incorporate them into its discourses—that is, when it can be modified by them without danger to its continuance as a particular kind of system. Systems broadly indifferent to many kinds of fluctuations can therefore accumulate history more readily than can fussier systems needing more support from their environments (such as senescent ones and most abiotic ones).

Biological systems are indifferent to many less-than-catastrophic impacts, probably mostly because of the microscopic stability gained through genetic information (Brooks and Wiley 1988). They are, consequently, strongly marked by history; this is why the study of organic evolution could become so important a apart of biology but has been insignificant in chemistry, where instances of chemical species are taken to be identical. Indeed, organic evolution is an example of a prominent realm of historical emergences, insofar as kinds of organisms (e.g. species) are constructed as unique. (Anderson (1972) referred to speciation as an example of symmetry breaking.)

It is true that the same affordances and niche attractors in ecosystems have repeatedly been accessed by different lineages (convergent and parallel evolution to ecological vicars), but homoplasies are always (in theory, at least) detectable upon close study of good material because of the historical information being different in the different lineages—one would not in fact confuse a woodchuck with a wombat. Accumulated historical information makes it possible for differences to mark these exemplars of essentially similar ways of life. It is clear from this example that the accumulation of genealogical information typically occurs at a pace that outstrips the generation of niche affordances—something one would predict from H_{sc} inasmuch as the molecular and organismic levels have immensely faster relaxation times than does the ecosystemic level.

Cladistics is a technology for constructing histories of the accumulation of some of this information on the basis of the idea of the generality of ancestral characters (i.e., the principle of parsimony interpreted as commonality). It reads the inferred accumulation of information in the past back to more and more distant hypothetical ancestors (which have only the characters shared by their "descendants"). In this way, generality of character increases with the depth of the cladogram as information about descendants is sequentially discarded. This movement models in the realm of logic (a kind of T^{-1} in figure 5.1) the supposed historical transformations (T's) from vagueness to determinability. Cladograms (including similar inscriptions using data from DNA and proteins) make up the historical information about living systems to which we have access, and provide a record of past evolutionary emergences in the realm of living systems.

Evolutionary emergences are not limited to living systems; however, discourse about other kinds of systems (i.e., abiotic dissipative structures) usually ignores uniqueness in its published inscriptions, for the hitherto sufficient reason that it would not have contributed differences that make a difference in view of the historical aims of these discourses (the conquest of nature). But here I wish to generalize as far as possible, and so I end this subsection with a consideration of the projection postulate (the so-called reduction of the electron wave function by measurement) in quantum physics. I will take the liberty of interpreting this system as a scalar hierarchical one, as follows (basing my interpretation on a talk by Alberto Cordero of Queens College, CUNY): it is possible to obtain a beam of electrons such that approximately a single one per day can be detected on a screen, with a flash recorded for each, revealing them to be particulate. Over a period of a year, however, these flashes make an aggregate pattern not different from a diffraction pattern as obtained from a beam of light in a similar apparatus, which shows that electron clouds are organized into wave-like properties—or that waves of certain kinds can be detected as particulate events.

I suggest that the wave data exist at a given scalar level, the particulate data being a record from a lower level and the apparatus itself forming boundary conditions impinging on the record from higher levels. In other words, electrons as described by wave functions (as in quantum theory) will be higher-level phenomena (somewhat like developmental trajectories conceptually), while particulate electrons in experiments appear to be the effects of single lower-scalar-level components of these waves or fields. In this way we ourselves would be events generated by our ontogenetic trajectories in interaction with objects in the world. In other words, I am suggesting that the wave-particle duality is a result of different levels of description. The lower-level, particulate, effect is visible only when the higher-level wave function is obstructed by interaction with an equally higher-level apparatus (which functions as a scientific interpretant to precipitate a record).

John Collier informs me that this interpretation resembles in some respects that of David Bohm (1957), which has been rejected by most physicists because of experimental corroborations of nonlocality. I believe the resemblance is superficial. Here, the higher-level entity described by the wave function is a pure potentiality at our own scalar level, but it can be manifested or precipitated anywhere by appropriate events (such as an experiment). Only at these points do what appear to us to be lower-level phenomena appear. I am not supposing that the wave function is constructed of independently esixtent but interacting particles. The wave function and the particles are constructs from different perspectives, representing interpretations at different scalar levels. They are also at different developmental stages; I take the wave to be an immature, vague phenomenon, while any precipitated electron develops rapidly into senescence. This means that I am also saying that organisms, as we detect them, are also constructs of our perceptions' interacting with something that can be appreciated only theoretically: developmental trajectories. As observers, we precipitate a world about us (nature), which is one interpretation of what is there.

In the experiment under discussion, any particulate inscription on the screen represents in its position a historical event, like a mutation. The wave function has been reduced to a single point for the moment because of the clever arrangement of the experimental apparatus. The point for us here is that the apparatus cannot select in advance the exact position of any electron; this is determined by other, unknown, boundary, initial, and initiating conditions, including those imposed by the observer (this contacts Bohm again). As in chaotic systems, the seemingly random occurrences of the flashes on the screen add up over a long time to a pattern reflecting the structure of a higher-level entity which we can know only indirectly, because of our located scale—in this case, that wavelike thing modeled by the wave function.

Now, even though the long-term record reflects an orderly pattern (and this would hold for most chaotic systems as well), the individual inscription records a particular historical emergence—one of little interest *per se* to anyone at our scale, to be sure. The strong implication of this view is that, while we can construct an apparatus to focus an electron beam, and while we can modify such an apparatus to select individual electrons, we could not continue along these lines to modify the apparatus to select the exact spot a particular electron event will encounter at a given moment.

The example is good one because it allows us to see precisely that historical emergence is an appendage of our finiteness. The idea is that in order to achieve this goal of predicting the position of an individual electron (one would have to ask 'for what practical purpose?') we would have to spend such enormous amounts of time, resources, effort, and ingenuity that it could not possibly be worth our while. The scalar theoretical notion here is that in order to reach our control further and further downward in scale we would have to make, as it were, larger and larger arrangements of boundary conditions. The whole of a nation's resources might be needed to specify a single electron's position in advance.

There seems no reason to suppose that these electron events could not be dealt with, roughly, from a Newtonian perspective, much as Darwinism dealt with the emergence of new types in organic evolutionary change. For example, each point of appearance of an electron on a screen might be roughly analogized to the emergence of one species out of the potentialities of the biosphere, as well as to a mutation, which would be random with respect to the system suffering it. The major difference between these possible metaphors of each other is that historical information is known to be preserved in biological systems but is not known to be preserved (and is indeed supposed *not* to be) in the quantum system outside laboratory records.

This example suggests to me that, once again, the radically new will not be represented among these electron flashes.

Developmental Emergence
Radical change can result in something familiar enough; phase changes are good examples. The very fact that we can in many cases easily predict what will occur, and when, shows that we can hardly refer to subsequent states in these cases as 'unprecedented'. But what we cannot do in those predictable cases we refer to as 'emergences' is explain why the change happens as it does. Developmental emergences are inexplicable rather than unprecedented; Kampis (1991b) uses the word "unspeakable." To be sure, we have names for this (symmetry breaking, cohesion increase, supervenience, qualitative change, cognition), but we become aware in these cases that prediction is not with symmetric with explanation. In what way are these occurrences inexplicable or unspeakable?

(1) They are usually, if not invariably, complete reorganizations accomplished quickly—jumps from one state to quite another (e.g., from fear to hysterical mirth; from water to ice; from figure to ground; from tetradic to triadic; from smooth flow to turbulence). At some threshold point the system reorganizes radically, whereas up to that point change as tracked by means of some variable may have been smooth and uneventful (Thom 1975; Goodwin 1984). We seldom understand why the intermediate states are so unstable that an entire integrity between the system and an observer gets jettisoned and swiftly replaced. It is as though the system became instantaneously reduced in scale relative to the observer, acquiring for the moment a much shorter relaxation time. Although we have discourse roughly covering the smooth transitions, these radical transformations defy attempts at continuous description.

(2) In these cases, theories of antecedent states do not allow prediction of subsequent states from first principles (Lewes 1874–75; Nagel 1961; Beckner 1974; Stebbins and Ayala 1981). No theory of gases leads to an understanding of the liquid state; no gradual modification of a tetradic system will slowly transform it into a triadic one; no juxtaposition of flat images will make them appear to have depth until whatever-it-is snaps in the mind. We do not know in these cases why one regime (figure) is related to another (ground) in such a way that they are intertransformable and yet so different (and, furthermore, why, e.g., don't gases transform into something different than liquids or solids?). Again, we must discard one theoretical apparatus for another when a developmental emergence has occurred, or, less drastically in cases like transformations across embryonic stages, we must introduce new principles or find new kinds of impinging boundary conditions.

Extensional Emergence (Cohesion) Two forms of developmental emergence can be distinguished (Salthe 1991a): *extensional* and *intensional*. The first has been referred to as a sudden increase (or decrease) in a system's *cohesion* (Collier 1989). Under one set of conditions a system remains relatively incoherent as is a gas; however, in some circumstances, if conditions change, perhaps even a litle bit, the system coheres, information suddenly being propagated over longer distances as the relative positions of subsystems become more constrained, with new boundary conditions impinging upon them. Records and descriptions of such changes (and in some cases their reversals) make up a kind of natural history of natural kinds. We know just exactly under what conditions the type 'ice' will appear. We can measure the new average bond distances between water molecules in this state and the average extent and shape of the crytals. And we know what sorts of binding forces have come into dominance that were not so before. They are weaker than the forces previously active, and in the liquid regime they had little, or only episodic, dominion.

Again we see that symmetry breaking (in this case the appearance of the first crystals of ice) is associated with a weakening of forces that had dominated the system (in this case the forces of molecular motion), allowing previously unimportant constraints to bear cogently on the system. Kondepudi (1988) has emphasized that in chiral symmetry breaking, if the system is near equilibrium, weak forces can take over. A difference in initial enantiomer concentration as small as one part in 10^{17} could determine the outcome if the system could be held quietly near equilibrium for about 15,000 years. This case is interesting from the point of view of an emergence involving rapid transformations. Here we would not detect an emergence until the macroscopic system distinctly plane-polarized the light transmitted through it. The emergence would be held to occur only between the moments when it did not do so and when it perceptibly did. The rest of the history of the system (say, over 15,000 years) would not be reckoned as part of the time needed to accomplish the emergence. During this time the system would have prepared itself by slowly becoming ever more metastable.

But we must note further that the colligative properties of, say, water are entirely different in kind from the properties of the gases hydrogen and oxygen—and from those of water vapor. Roth and Schwegler (1990), using the example of table salt, note that after combination into NaCL the elements sodium and chlorine are no longer the same kinds of entities even in themselves—the combination has itself deformed them (our concept of integration nicely exemplified).

The simpler physical examples of emergence are said to be reversible. Such does not appear to be the case for more macroscopic examples, such as the cohesion of cells to form an organism or of organisms to form a society. But in these cases there is eventual dissolution, following naturally upon the heels of senescence. It does not seem too early to conclude that all dissipative structures eventually senesce, and that this leads to a kind of reversal; in ecosystems there is a return to a more immature sere. And, indeed, it seems highly unlikely that when ice melts it is exactly like a reversed film of freezing; more likely it is something rather more hysterical (from *hysteresis*). Indeed, the reversal of a film of some repetitive activity yields to distinction upon close examination, showing phenomena that could not be physical—like the effect of a shock coming before the shock.

Now, the properties of water differ from those of all other liquids in a way that suggests historical emergence. There must have been a time when water appeared for the first time in the universe; however, we do not emphasize that unique occurrence, because of the numerous for-most-purposes identical repetitions that have occurred since. Even though every one of these will have been different in detail from every other, we ignore this in favor of a useful classification. It is, then, as though we relive a historical emergence every time we see this transformation, even though it has become a familiar kind of event. (Examine the alternate freezings and thawings of a pond to get a sense of uniqueness in this realm.) Thus it retains some of the mystery associated with historical emergence. So extensional emergence is like an endlessly renewed historical emergence—a kind of trick of observation.

Any historical emergence could be transformed into a developmental one simply by ignoring all but aspects it has in common with other similar cases (i.e., by classifying it), and so, as was pointed out above, unique configurations can get incorporated into types. The dissolution of sugar cubes might be an example. The traits of every instance would admit of uniquenesses, and we might allow ourselves to indulge these; however, for most purposes—certainly in bestowing meaning on words like 'dissolve'—we abstract only the commonalities.

Now, a positivist understanding of developmental emergence might seem to be available when it is viewed as the origin of systems by coherence at new levels of scale. Implicit in this is the notion that the discontinuity of an emergence, as we detect it, could be obviated by dropping down to a smaller scale in order to develop a continuous discourse about it.

This is implicit in Kondepudi's (1988) discussion referred to above. I think this notion is mistaken for the following three reasons:

> (1) If we drop down to the scale of a water molecule to study the initiation of, say, Bénard cells, we will not, or will hardly, see the phenomenon at all. The convective flow occurs at a larger scale, such that its effects at the water-molecule scale would be minuscule compared with the conductive motions of the molecules themselves. In other words, we would in most cases lose the phenomenon itself. This approach has an overwhelming attraction, however, because it is this kind of notion that allows us to suppose, for example, that our own political activities will effect the changes we wish to see happening or the stabilization we wish to preserve.
>
> Kondepudi's example is very relevant here because plane polarization of light is a direct result of molecular configuration.

But it is a population-level phenomenon, for all that, because it requires a preponderance of one enantiomer at a higher scalar level to effect the phenomenon. Kondepudi's case of near-equilibrium conditions maintained over a long period of time is constructed precisely to allow lower-level effects the greatest role possible, and because of that it *is* a special case. Most symmetry breaking takes place much more rapidly as an effect of energetic forces under strong, nonequilibrium, contextual constraints. Ulanowicz's discussions (1986, 1989) of the emergence of autonomous cycles is a case in point. Constraints here are such that, should any constituent of a system happen to be able to contribute to a potential cycle (see figure 4.2), it will immediately be rewarded, and will be entrained into the cycle rather than into other potential subsystems, thereby increasing the flow through the cycle. The cycle is, of course, at a higher scalar level than any of its components.

(2) Kondepudi's approach is implicitly reductionist in that it seems to suppose that a higher-level phenomenon is produced entirely by alterations of lower-level behavior—a view (held also by Roth and Schwegler (1990)) that is patently false. The new regime could not have come into being without the cogent effects of higher-level constraints being felt in the aggregate somewhere larger in scale than at the level of the molecules. For example, Bénard cells would not form in a very large, cold vessel that was heated from below in only one small region. Conduction would in that case carry off the needed energy, and, furthermore, the cells would not be able to space themselves, to find their form, without the effects of the boundaries of the vessel. Field phenomena like this just cannot be fully explained locally. The origin of cycles in Ulanowicz's discourse also involves the whole system, the structure of which is important in the choice of which cycles get amplified. A jump from one state to another *means* that no continuous description of it *per se* is possible.

(3) Theories of microsystemic behavior cannot extend their explanatory domain to macrosystemic levels, because the terms in which they are stated are not predicates that can be used sensibly at those levels (Hull 1974). So, there are no differences caused by Van der Waals forces at the level of a macroscopic vessel, and no formulation that explicitly includes them can be effective at that level. For the same reason, gravitation can have only trivial local effects on molecular activity. Also for the same reason, mating behavior is only an initiating condition screened off from the growth of populations, which depends strongly and proximately,

not on how organisms behave, but on the availability of resources and the intensity of predation and competition. It is true that some populations would have greater biotic potential than others, and that this can be traced downward to relations between survivorship and reproductive effort on the part of the organisms. But according to life-history theory these characteristics are themselves reflections of the history of the lineages evolving in *particular kinds* of environments.

The basic triadic system of H_{sc} (Salthe 1985) is the embodiment of all three of these considerations—in short, the transit of lower-scalar-level information to upper levels requires non-lower-level arrangements to effect the amplification.

For the above three reasons one may doubt the possibility of positive knowledge of cohesive emergences. Unless we can have a smooth theoretical transition from one description to another, whether it involves different scalar levels or not, we must reset our focus, change our tool kit, and begin again after an emergence. No traditional discourse constructs views from both sides of an emergence. This is another way of noting the reasons why foundational discourse has failed in every field—it means that we cannot avoid considerations of the observer, who must be an explicit part of the context of the emergence (like Koestler's (1978) Janus), as the part of the system that switches viewpoints. That switch reflects the observer's values, and so the discourse implicitly becomes value-laden. Switching, the observer "turns the other cheek," and we must not "close our eyes" to doing so. It is to this connection that I now turn.

Intensional Emergence (Supervenience) Cohesive emergences accompanied by scale jumps are not the only sort of developmental emergence that needs to be dealt with. The behavior of any developing system will be marked off into stages, and the crossing of any of these is also an emergence, obviously of the developmental kind. I will pursue that below. First I wish to treat yet another sort of emergence based on the specification hierarchy—what philosophers often call 'supervenience'. Let me begin with a few examples.

Consider patterns in nature (Stevens 1974; Ben-Jacob and Garik 1990). The material basis (material causes) of a given pattern (trees, meanders, vortices) can be found at many different integrative levels. Somewhat similar are ecological vicars in biology, where quite unrelated species come to occupy identical Eltonian niches, and frequently even look very similar (see, e.g., Rayner and Franks 1987). This kind of similarity can extend to entire communities. Somewhat more abstract would be examples such as the four developmental rules of thermodynamically open systems given on page 111. These patterns and similarities supervene upon different material bases.

Rosenberg (1985) uses the example of clockness, and notes that there could be no reduction from being a clock to the physical principles involved without losing the effect of timekeeping. Furthermore, since there are so many kinds of clocks, based on different proximate principles (from falling sand through the movement of the sun), no single reduction of clockness to combinations of privileged physical principles is possible. That many clocks are based ultimately on gravitation shows only that the example can be constructed using the specification hierarchy—e.g., vessels for holding things supervene upon gravitation, and controlled spilling from one vessel to another supervenes upon that, while telling time from an hourglass supervenes upon that. If we wish to include radioactive decay, we must have an even more general outermost class—perhaps 'physical events'. What seems clear is that supervenience overtly involves the properties and categories of an observer.

The category 'being a clock' is clearly a human cultural trait. It neatly transcends, all the way to vagueness, any particular physical embodiment of the idea. It is true that in a given culture timekeeping might have had but one embodiment, so that physical analysis there would lead to one general type. Yet even then, without the intentionality of wanting to track the hours, there would be no phenomenon of clockness.

Sartre, in his "existential psychoanalysis" (1956), has a general treatment of phenomenology that is useful here. Human intentional activity creates much of the world as we live it. Sartre's superb analysis of skiing (pp. 742–747) shows how that activity brings out the properties of masses of water crytals—one might almost say that it constructs them. Polyanyi's (1968) analysis of tools as constraints on natural laws feeds in here as well, while Lima-de-Faria (1988) notes that function can generally be viewed as a result of symmetry breaking by a system's perspective. The mind's functional projection of indications of hardness into the head of a hammer during its use, *even though the proximate sensations must actually be in the user's hand,* can serve as a basic image.

Clocks, skis, and hammers are useful mediations into our *Umwelt* (Uexküll 1926). The function circles—'telling time', 'skiing', and 'hammering'—bring the surrounding world into our *Innenwelt*. These function circles are emergent traits of a sociocultural system involved with harnessing and controlling nature. One's own actual (Roth and Schwegler 1990) senses of being oriented in the day, of sliding over snow, and of the hardness of a hammer's steel make up more highly specified, because unique, contents of a specification hierarchy that projects back through various integrative levels into the generalities of the physical world as it would be (as modeled by chemistry and physics) were such humanly imposed constraints not visible.

Hammering emerged in iron-age cultures, and the feeling of hard steel in one's hand emerged with hammering later. (The cultural content of cold steel in one's hands is cleverly suggested in a scene from a 1930s film in which a crusader tries to impress a saracen by severing an iron rod with one blow of his sword; the saracen retaliates by having his scimitar sever a silk scarf that was allowed to float down upon its edge.)

For a recent controversy concerning the appropriate integrative levels to locate supervenient emergences, we can examine sociobiological positions on the relations between the behavior of humans and that of other animals. Alexander (1987) criticizes other sociobiologists for (in my terms) employing the specification hierarchy without allowing for integration from the higher levels. (This was the earlier complaint of T. C. Schneirla against ethologists.) Alexander claims that typical sociobiologists insist that most of what needs to be discussed (in their case, behavior establishing self-interest) was produced by natural selection already at the organismic integrative level, and that not only has it been retained in human social behavior, but it remains the major determinant of behavior despite the emergence of cultural overlays. Hence, for many sociobiologists, selfishness would not be supervenient on animal behavior, which already embodies it. In response, Kitcher (1985, chapter 9) criticizes Alexander's approach for (in my terms) rederiving selfishness over and over again from proximate interactions at the human sociocultural level, each time as a separate supervenience. He reproaches Alexander for, essentially, not employing the parsimonious logic of specification hierarchies at all. While agreeing with the majority on using this logic to establish selfishness as a prior, lower-integrative-level constraint on human behavior inherited from animal ancestors, Kitcher goes on to emphasize the potential modifying effects of integration from higher, emergent levels more than did classical sociobiologists. [We might also note that anti-racist and anti-sexist discussions tend to deny the specification hierarchy too, so as to eliminate unwanted non-negotiable (non-discourse-modifiable) elements altogether.]

It is clear that we understand ourselves to have emerged from biological systems just as biological systems are viewed as having emerged from physical ones. Almost all mythologies share this structure, but, as we see from discussions in sociobiology, even those with closely similar readings may disagree about the importance of supervenient integration as against the subordination of later-emerging properties to the continuing effects of historically earlier emergences.

This latter view comes close to trying to make an end run around emergence in the manner of reductionism. If human cultural inventions were unable to deflect the thrust of animal selfishness and nepotism, then there would be no significant effects of integration in this realm—in fact, no supervenience of a human level at all. On the other hand, if these tendencies were to be wholly transcended, then the logic of the specification hierarchy of integrative levels would have been abrogated and we would be floating free from our history.

As emergent, human action needs precisely to have traces of animal inheritance as well as significant distortions of it. Supervenience in specification-hierarchical discourse can never be a total transcendence; yet, without significant modification representable as a result of the imposition of further constraints of a new kind, no new integrative level will have been attained either.

Given an ultimate explanation of human behavior by natural selection operating on ancestral behaviors, can we understand exactly how the appearance of more highly specified behaviors came about? Would, e.g., study of nonsocial organismic behaviors provide signs of incipient social behavior? Could we get correlations between the behaviors of species in sister groups to social organisms and the behaviors of the latter themselves? If the taxonomy were well known, such correlations would be more than the empty signs they would be without that constraint. But, again, we would then merely have views from both sides of an emergence without any connecting discourse.

We might then imagine thought experiments directly modifying ancestral characters to see which of the results we could construct in the direction of sociality might lead to some understanding. If, however, the new integrative level involves, as it often does, a change in scale, then the basic triadic system prohibits such experiments. Change in an independent variable from a lower scalar level (say, a trait of single neurons) could not directly produce change in a dependent variable at a higher (say, mental) scalar level. A variable could not, without special arrangements, *be* directly dependent upon another at a different scalar level. So, if sociality involves boundary conditions (say, limits due to environmental facilitation of communication) from a level higher than that of the individual brain, then, in the absence of special contexts allowing amplification of signals from animal behavior, modifications of that behavior could not produce sociality—*except by chance*.

This latter is, of course, the Darwinian move; but it reduces developmental emergence to historical emergence, which would deprive us of a close description without giving us any understanding of how it could have happened. With developmental emergences we can at least hope, by observing instances again and again, to fathom what they are—that is, to construct some bridging discourse across the emergence. Perhaps if we consider the supervenience of developmental stages, we will discover something more because they can be very closely studied. From the present section we can take the idea that intentional emergences are observer-dependent.

Emergence as a Mode of Development

The following incorporates ideas of Conrad (1983), Haken (1988), Prigogine (1980), Rosen (1985b), Swenson (1989a,b, 1991), and Ulanowicz (1986, 1989). This problem can be cast in terms of the basic triadic system.

We can observe transformations of organisms from one stage to another while mostly disregarding the yet higher level (the overall patterns of the ontogenetic trajectories). So, e.g., only variational principles that would bear as higher-level constraints on the transformation of any stage whatever will be considered. These will impose boundary conditions on the transformation, regulating the requirements that the next stage show, e.g., increased gross entropy production as well as increased ascendancy. Also bearing here will be final causality associated with the Rylean category that is transitively attracting the dynamics; in organisms some of this would be called up by genetic information coming from the lineage. Unless such higher-level constraints were strongly relevant, we would not have orderly developments to consider at all and we would be back to the blank mystery of evolutionary emergence.

In organisms, the proximate activities of primary gene products would provide some lower-level constraints (initiating conditions) on the transformation. But these will also arise from any internal gradients, sinks, and barriers that happen to be in place. These, and the current suite of dynamical transformations taking place, will set up the further possibilities and potentialities that may be interpreted as being anticipated by the system.

Now, 'anticipation' as dealt with by Conrad and Rosen is a homeostatic principle. It would be measured by the proportion of fluctuations impinging upon the system that it could match, and therefore defeat, allowing it to remain essentially unchanged. In connection with the orderly transformations of developing systems, however, anticipation must be allowed to be hemeorhetic as well as homeostatic, giving us canalization. This is certainly possible using Rosen's formulations, in which anticipation is achieved through internal lower-scalar-level models of environmental uncertainties within the system.

Do organisms have such {models}? Yes; we may suppose that both genes and nervous systems embody them (Plotkin and Odling-Smee 1981). They are lower-level to the organism as a whole, and certainly their dynamics are vastly faster than the environmental dynamics they could be relevant to, thereby allowing anticipation of environmental changes. This means that organisms have a rapidly mobilizable internal suite of activities that have proved their adequacy with regard to environments occupied by their ancestors, and by themselves at earlier ages. The usual slower pace of environmental changes, because of their situation at higher scalar levels, allows an organism's models to remain relatively current, except for strong environmental fluctuations.

Little thought has been devoted to the possibility that abiotic dissipative structures also embody {{models}}, which, having smaller relaxation times than environmental changes, would tend to stabilize their trajectories. The gyroscope effect comes to mind, and suggests that these {{models}} would be dynamic inertial torques and momenta, as well as, in other cases, the steepnesses of internal gradients and arrangements of poised free energies. All these have only immediate connections to just-prior states and environments, and so we can guess that the increased stability of organisms in contrast is due largely to the longer memories possible with neural and genetic forms.

So, we have dissipative structures whose momentary behavior is initiated in part by internal models of their environment, which have dynamics that are faster than those of the structures themselves and much faster than their environment's dynamics. These dissipative structures are developing, and we will focus on the situation just prior to transformation to another stage. This situation may be taken to be a critical state near a bifurcation point in focal-level dynamics. (1) How was this metastability arrived at? And (2) how is the following stage made more or less inevitable? Above all, (3) what kind of change is it that defies continuous description?

The system has become metastable because it has become more precisely determined than it was just after its last transformation. At that point a new realm had opened up for it, which it was initially only imperfectly able to deal with. Being relatively vague with respect to these newly accessed possibilities, its choices and distinctions relative to them were only episodically effective in organizing the system along new lines. In particular, the system's pertinent models were relatively unformed (or yet untapped) and had little consistency in informing the system's behavior.

The system's choices were more stochastic or weakly chaotic because, with little effective anticipatory range in its fluctuations and a large degree of indifference based on its relative vagueness, it was susceptible to noise, whose effects were readily incorporated. Mass-action principles tended to overwhelm specificity of activity, and change in the system was slow because of much activity at cross-purposes (with respect to the new directions the system was becoming entrained by). The system had not "settled down" to its new regime, had not found its stride in its new realm of being in the developmental stage it had just accessed; it was relatively little integrated by the new possibilities it had tapped during its last transformation simply because it takes some time to reorganize a system along new lines.

But this essentially immature system gradually acquired newer habits as stored information relevant to the new integrative level increased. In this way its models became more tuned to newly encountered environmental regularities, and so newly incorporated sources of noise became more effective in contributing to the system's anticipatory behavior as it managed to survive. But with increased determinateness the requirements for continued survival become more stringent—the system loses its immature robustness as it loses its vagueness. In order to support its increased burden of information, more and more precise behavior would be required of it. Self-organization, then, starts to become less important than rote behavior, just as the random searches of immaturity were earlier supervened upon by self-organization. Habitual behaviors are informed by a system's models, which become more fully determining as the system becomes more determinate in its new direction.

Continued accumulation of the results of these tendencies has resulted, finally, in two problems of senescence: a system (a) becomes informationally overburdened, overconnected, and so less flexible, and (b) begins to fluctuate more wildly as a result of increasing reliance on increasingly inappropriate habitual models, and this has opened it to contact with new and potentially dangerous perturbations and configurations.

> (a) The system has grown informationally as it has incorporated more and more redundancies supporting the homeostatic dynamics characteristic of its new stage (figure 4.2C). "Ascendancy is closing upon its upper limit." This increase in the complication of its dynamics will contribute to the acquisition of power by the system because each component involved incurs an increased overhead in physical entropy production. This overhead begins to compete with effective system activity, which it also actively undermines by tending to be physically destructive. The internal stability fostered by an increasing complication of constraints conspires to diminish the system's indifference to fluctuations and to increase its reliance on anticipatory behavioral variety,

which does continue to increase. But more of its anticipatory behavior is becoming ineffective, because the lagging and divergent cycling incurred by a larger number of connections between subsystems tends to disconnect its increasingly habitual repertoire from the environmental fluctuations to which it might have been germane.

(b) Some of the increased stored information was enlisted as redundancy in behaviors connected to the system's models, but the effectiveness of this drops rather quickly (Salthe 1985, figure 15). As Rosen has pointed out, such models are necessarily directed toward only a few typical, major homeostatic problems, which the system becomes adept at handling. This means that less frequent problems are able to have larger impacts on the system, being associated with degrees of freedom not connected to the system's models. Hence, occasional environmental fluctuations can produce larger perturbations in a now essentially overspecialized system. This overspecialized condition was contributed to by the system's increasing reliance on its models—a kind of self-referentiality which carried it further in its own determinateness at the same time as it had become increasingly focused on just a few degrees of freedom.

The specialization of a system in connection with only some of its degrees of freedom simplifies its internally generated behavior. But simpler natural systems always behave more unpredictably than more complicated ones—e.g., population sizes in depauperate arctic communities always cycle violently, resulting in frequent local extinctions. Hence, the specialization that results from an increasing proportion of stored information being brought to bear on only a few aspects of homeostasis ironically opens the system up to contact with unfamiliar states as its responses to the resulting fluctuations become increasingly drastic and beyond what could be usefully anticipatory. In a nondeveloping system, this would eventually cause the system to be pulled into very unusual states that would either terminate it or produce major mutations as it recovered.

The point about developing systems is that such critical states are used to gain access to the next developmental stage, and it is to this (question 2) we must now turn.

A developing system does not topple out of the world from its metastable senescence, precisely because it is strongly entrained by the trajectory it is a part of—the more so the older it has become. Our understanding of this is sketchy (Salthe 1987). It entails being pulled by final causes from the Rylean category that is the system's developmental attractor (partly via historical information in genes for organisms, via propagules and historical information in soils for ecosystems), as well as being strongly controlled by larger-scale formal constraints imposed by its trajectory. These constraints call for increasing ascendancy and stored information, as well as decreases in mass-specific entropy production. Developing systems do not become merely unstable at these critical points, because they are part of resilient overall trajectories that are able to hold onto them even under some fairly large fluctuations (e.g., those imposed on embryos in studies of experimental embryology, or by devastations of parts of ecosystems).

Trajectories are structures; that is, they are affordances in local environments that can be accessed by systems having the appropriate enablements. Such systems can invade or colonize these affordances, and their development is the process of doing that—of being entrained by structures. In its appropriate local environment, a frog embryo cannot change into just anything, because it is itself only a small portion of its developmental trajectory. Perturbations during one of its critical periods will, if they do not destroy it, much more likely serve as occasions to access the next stage than to cause radical mutations. The relaxation time of the ontogenetic trajectory is longer than that of the embryo itself; thus, when embryos become metastable at the thresholds of further developmental stages, their smaller-scale processes can be viewed as organized ensembles rather than random collections. Relatively stable order parameters constrain these microscopic dynamics to within certain limits; this holds the ensemble together, even though minor individuations are accumulating.

Edelman (1987) provides some ideas that can be modified to give microscopic detail here. Consider that being in stage Y entails the occupancy of cycles d, e, and f. In an earlier stage, X, the system occupied cycles a, b, and c. Fluctuations sometimes interrupt these cycles and lead them to momentarily incorporate other components, and such fluctuations increase in frequency and range at critical points. The incorporation of certain components into a cycle tends to attract all its components toward a new region of stability—another cycle, one characteristic of stage Y. Some of the components present in stage X may be retained in the new cycle; others may be replaced as soon as enough components are in place to engender the new cycle. At the critical point we then have a flickering suite of cycles, some characteristic of stage X and some of stage Y. Since the latter, associated with more macroscopic behaviors, would on average allow greater gross entropy production, they will attract the dynamics rather than the previous cycles, and the system will fall into the next stage.

Furthermore, cycles d, e, and f can be viewed as an ensemble if it is only all together (because of synergetic effects) that they produce greater overall physical entropy than the ensemble of a, b, and c. This synergy itself delays the transformation until most components of the new cycles are in place, thus lagging system change to the point where it is bottlenecked into a jump to the next stage. The new suite will also produce less entropy per unit mass, because the system will have grown—say, there may be more throughput in cycles d, e, and f than there were in cycles a, b, and c. Now, such nice relations could not have appeared by chance. In complicated systems, the historical information in the system, embodying its final causality, ensures that each of the stages becomes possible at about the right time. That time will be decided proximately by the dynamics of development itself, as outlined above, and the new stage will be reliably accessed only if larger-scale (trajectory-level) constraints are also in place.

These latter constraints, along with the Second Law, impose irreversibility on the system. Without such constraints, undirected mass action could also tend to elicit irreversibility; however, as Prigogine (1980) has pointed out, random behavior itself is not equivalent to irreversibility, it only tends in some systems to facilitate it. Development is a fully irreversible process because developmental trajectories have a certain structure, which can be read infodynamically as the necessity for increased storage of information at their "forward" ends (see figure 4.7). This information operates transitively as formal cause throughout the structure at its own scalar level, however, because structures have a holistic unity.

It is well to recall that developmental trajectories are systems of interpretance. This means that, as a system accesses a next developmental stage, it is contributing to the buildup of meaning in its trajectory. Meaning cannot change capriciously but must build appropriately upon prior meanings; this is not unlike the restraint exercised by a text on its own developing front. What emerges from this analogy is that a search for particularities of the next stage could not be random; indeed, the more structure a developing system has accessed, the fewer would be its choices of what to become next. Meanings intensify with development, increasingly forcing particular directions on the necessary increase in stored information and specificity of a system.

Now (question 3), why is the transformation from one stage to another an emergence? That is, why must it be viewed as a jump not describable by continuous discourse? I have just explored the essential microscopic description of resonating suites of cycles at the critical point, with those allowing greater gross entropy production finally attracting the dynamics in a jump because their activation is synergetic.

But why does this resonance become manifest only at critical points? Why does it not occur in quasi-continuous fashion, more or less uniformly throughout development? If it did, there might not be such major jumps from one global regime to another.

In addition to the synergetic aspects of entropy production mentioned above, the answer seems to lie in the basic pattern of development from immaturity to senescence (figure 3.4), a pattern that in the present hypotheses is followed microcosmically during each stage of development (as suggested especially in the lower curve in figure 4.5). In the immature condition, the newly accessed cycles plunge headlong into the resources and sinks affording them. Since the system is autonomous and so finite, these become diminished and the cycles slow down. Their activity has built up a new set of affordances such that other cycles could now produce entropy more efficiently than those that had just been acting, and this eventually gives rise to the new pulse of activity that is the next stage.

Still, why is the next stage so different? The answer involves macroscopic, not microscopic events. Unless form changes macroscopically, driven by renewed energy flows at the beginning of each stage, we would not speak of 'emergence'—nor could we get sudden access to greater entropy production.

The hypothesis generated by the present viewpoint is that sudden, radical alterations of form and behavior (which inspire us to name new stages) afford explosive increases in gross entropy production, and so are favored thermodynamically (Swenson 1989a,b), provided they become materially possible in the critical stage. In short, these macroscopic changes facilitate more efficient realization of the Second Law, and so a reversal from the newly achieved macroscopic structure would entail a prohibited decrease in entropy production. But the actual macroscopic jumps in developing systems are not to *any* form that might satisfy the Second Law; they are constrained by global boundary conditions imposed by the kind of trajectory involved—by its formal and final causes.

Yet, why is a sudden reorganization of macroscopic form necessarily an emergence? The answer seems to be: Only when changes have been so great that our descriptions require major revision or alteration do we say that a new integrative level or developmental stage has emerged. In other words, we construct intensional emergence out of the exigencies of discourse.

But one might pursue the question why any changes in nature are so radical as to require new description. I suspect that the answer to this too involves limitations on our discourses—in particular, we have no discourses that can smoothly bridge hierarchical levels. This is essentially what foils Laplace's Demon (Landsberg 1972). Furthermore, it is what allows for the possibility of alternative descriptions (e.g., molecular/molar, dynamical/informational) of a given phenomenon. The boundaries of levels are precisely where a discourse meets its limitations. This is, in a more general sense, why an observer is always explicitly involved in hierarchical discourse—even in H_{sc}, which can otherwise appear to be but a little extension of science as it has been.

Trajectories, like species and ecosystems (and all structures), are constructions of discourse. As such, they have properties (such as logical form) that could not necessarily be assigned to "objects independent of ourselves in a world." One consequence of the logicality of theoretical objects is that they are subject to Gödel incompleteness. This implies that, since we would want such constructions to be internally consistent, they must be completed by metadiscourses (Carnap 1937). The move to a metadiscourse is, precisely, the mark of an emergence. At this point I remove the qualification 'intensional' used above, as it seems to me that *all* developmental emergences, including extensional cohesion, are discourse-dependent for these reasons.

John Collier has objected to this interpretation, noting that "there would have to be a reason why different discourses are appropriate" for dealing with pre- and postemergent phenomena. That reason, he implies, is a causal forcing from the world as it is, which we are somehow detecting. What I am emphasizing here is the pitifully tiny and located few perspectives that we can bring to bear upon an indefinitely rich world, which at certain points flip-flops before us inexplicably. The perspectives we contrive by discourse to bring to bear upon these jumps are, it is true, as different as they need to be in trying to track a wildly creative world. But in the end all we have in our hands are our discourses.

Senescence as the Enablement of Emergence
In the foregoing I used the concept of senescence to suggest how developmental systems become metastable to major change as a result of their general developmental tendency (the canonical pattern of infodynamics from immaturity to senescence), which is repeated again and again with each stage. This model could be applied to cell division as discussed in chapter 1; or that discussion could be used as an exemplar of this one. Throughout this book I have used senescence to explain why systems (when unsupported by extraordinary larger-scale affordances) eventually become seized by environmental fluctuations that destroy them.

The senescent condition is essentially the combination of a low intensity of entropy production (physical negentropy) and a large amount of stored information (high informational entropy). It is a stage in which the system has become internally quiescent and inflexible—progressively less able to be indifferent to environmental fluctuations (because already informationally overburdened) or to be able to defeat them with its own behavioral variety (which is increasingly irrelevant and overreactive). This inflexibility results from the system's increasing commitment to its own limited habits (models), so that its variable behaviors come to be generated by environmental buffeting rather than by its own internal agency. I will now explore this condition as a general prerequisite for the emergence of new evolutionary systems (Salthe 1990c).

Evolutionary systems are based on units which can be recombined in a large number of ways, so that their maximum informational disorder (C_{max} in figure 3.4) is much larger than their actual informational variety (C_{act}) at any moment (Brooks and Wiley 1988). Biological systems are in this way based on genetic units, ecosystems on biological units, and discourses on sociocultural (or ecosystemic) units. Each evolutionary system explores its potentialities through the production of physical and informational entropies. This general idea has been mined, in different terms, by Csány (1989), Csányi and Kampis (1985), and Alvarez de Lorenzana (1987, appendix below). Laszlo (1987) has written about it in more general terms, and Buss (1987) has applied the idea to the origin of multicellular organisms and ontogenies within Darwinian discourse. (Unfortunately, only Alvarez de Lorenzana used the difference between development and evolution; the others use the single word 'evolution' for all system changes.)

New evolutionary systems emerge when the units of one evolutionary process coalesce to produce new ones at a higher scalar level; this precipitation of new units involves crossing over to a new integrative level as well. Figure 5.2 attempts to show crudely the development of informational entropy on Earth, carried by three successive evolutionary systems (the first of which extends back toward the Big Bang). In order to read this figure one must recall the fact that probabilities (and so generalized entropies) can be decomposed into contributions from different levels of scale (Conrad 1983).

In following the increase in chemical complexity at the left of figure 5.2, I suggest that it could continue to become even more complex on its own (dashed line labeled X) after initiation of the origin of life, just as to the right I indicate that biological complexity could continue to increase after the origin of humans. It is probably the case, however, that not much further increase in complexity was or is going to be accomplished in the earlier integrative levels after these watershed initiations wherever interference with the older evolutionary system by the new one is possible—because, for example, in the transition between chemical and organic evolution, physical entropy is more efficiently produced in connection with macrostructures. Each new evolutionary system plays the entropy game more effectively than its predecessors (Swenson 1991).

The H_{act} curve in figure 5.2 shows apparent decreases in overall informational entropy associated with the origin of new evolutionary systems. I extended the dashed lines as I did just in order to avoid this suggestion, and these drops are really better seen as lateral movements referring to a specialization of the new system on just a small amount of variety taken from the previous evolutionary system.

After the origin of life, the complexity contributed by living systems at their own scale was added to that continuing to be generated chemically, but I have foregrounded the contribution of the new system so as to show the trend of its own increase. The implication should be that the H_{act} curve would not be as high if it were to be formed entirely by chemical entities *per se*. Although living systems probably depleted some of the possibilities for new chemical entities, they more than made up the implied loss of informational disorder through recombinations of their own basic units at higher scalar levels.

The same is predicted to occur with noosphere evolution, should it ever get going in a big way. In one sense, what is shown in figure 5.2

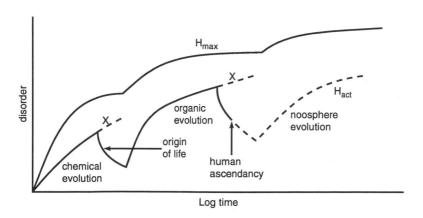

Figure 5.2 A history of evolutionary systems, plotted as in figures 3.4 and 4.8 to show informational entropy. Dashed lines marked X refer to events not being tracked in this figure because they occur in other regions of the universe. These need to be suggested in order to show that the increase in global disorder is irreversible so that, as the development of new units (e.g., origin of life) involves a local decrease in disorder, the evolutions that gave rise to these must be viewed as continuing to produce disorder elsewhere. Adapted from Salthe 1990c.

is the takeover of chemical complexity by living systems (as in Cairns-Smith's "genetic takeover") and the predicted takeover of macroscopic complexity by the noosphere. It is further implied that organic and noospheric evolution must, for infodynamical reasons, supply the informational entropy that will allow the system of the surface of the Earth to continue to maximize global gross entropy production—that they could not occur unless they did just that. Furthermore, while emergent dynamical macrostructures are required in order to increase physical entropy production, they also increase overall informational entropy, which will lead to senescence.

This view suggests that further development of the surface of the Earth from the condition it is now in must involve the destruction of the integrity of the biosphere as it has been and its replacement with noospheric units of equivalent or greater complexity. For me that prospect is repugnant; however, the {{aims}} of Gaia, as it were, ought never to be conflated with those of people, who (like red blood cells for us) are at "her" disposal, not the reverse. We are parts of systems larger in scale than ourselves. (See Robb 1989 for a similar argument in the realm of economic systems.)

Of course, perturbations, such as meteorite collisions (such effects are not shown in figure 5.2 but would have to be added to more detailed curves), will set a system back informationally, and so we might suppose that wars could accomplish the same against the noosphere. Alas, the evidence is otherwise; systems destroyed in war are rapidly built up again during a renewed immature situation not unlike secondary succession in ecosystems—as were Japan and West Germany after World War II (indeed, the ritual destruction of modern warfare may have just this pulsing at its point).

The origin of life and the period of human ascendency are shown in figure 5.2 as prolonged in (our) time. It seems certain that the origin of life took place in a series of stages (Fox 1986), and we know enough about the emergence of humanity from primate ancestors to know that it has taken so far, more than 10 million years say, from the days of *Proconsul* or *Sivapithecus*. That is the period I am roughly suggesting in the continuous part of the right-hand-decreasing H_{act} curve in figure 5.2. This emphasizes that what we might globally take to be sudden emergences do have microscopic structure, as I have admitted above.

Now, while these emergences are shown as negentropic in figure 5.2, this is not to be interpreted as a decrease in global informational entropy; it is meant only to show that at their beginnings the new systems contribute only a small amount of macroscopic information to the whole. If the graph could be extended in a third dimension, the newly emergent systems might protrude laterally toward the reader.

(John Collier suggests that, instead of showing a drop in H_{act}, an abrupt rise in H_{max} might convey the point better.) Rhetorically, in any case, I hope to suggest something yet more with tracks of diminishing disorder associated with these emergences.

Taking a hand from the terminology of others, we can see in these diminishing-entropy tracks Teilhard de Chardin's notion of "convergence" (O'Brien 1988), or that of Csányi and Kampis (1985), or Alvarez de Lorenzana's "principle of generative condensation" (appendix). The idea is that the new evolutionary units at the larger scale are at first, at their own scalar level, of relatively few kinds, carrying, at that scale, relatively little macroscopic information because they have not yet undergone the "combinatorial expansion" (Alvarez de Lorenzana) that will generate macroscopic informational disorder at their own scalar level.

In other words, because information or entropy can be decomposed or combined across levels, we can see that the amount of informational entropy carried by new evolutionary systems is at first hardly more than would be found within them microscopically. Indeed it is somewhat less, because the new units (now microscopic within the emerging level) have united into clusters with some loss of microscopic information within them because of the increased vagueness entailed by losses of separate identities. A similar argument was used for the origin of life by N. W. Pirie, who associated a system of chemical diversity with structural simplicity, this system then giving rise from a quite restricted chemical base to one combining relative chemical uniformity with morphological complexity at a higher scalar level (Salthe 1972).

The H_{act} tracks of the emergences in figure 5.2 move downward, then, because information in the new evolutionary units has become condensed, submerged in newly autonomous systems at larger scale. In this way would a relatively simple landscape ecosystem emerge from a complicated senescent stream in a mountain valley (chapter 4).

Prigogine (1980) has emphasized the role of fluctuations in allowing systems to access new nonequilibrium states. I suggested such a scenario for the accession of a next developmental stage in the preceding section. Here too it seems this could be a useful image. How else indeed could systems find the new structure that stably allows a burst of entropy production as it radically reintegrates them, other than through "random" search? In order for contingencies to be effective, the system must have senesced to the point of internal abeyance (minimum per-unit entropy production) so as to be able to be seized by environmentally generated fluctuations—or even by slight internal tendencies (recall the formal identity of caprice and creativity).

This kind of radical change was not in question when development was discussed, because there the developmental trajectory has hold of the fluctuating system all along until the whole thing senesces. Only after that does the trajectory begin to lose its control and the system begin to fluctuate more and more wildly until it cannot maintain its integrities. Such systems are typically recycled. What we are coming to here is that fluctuations in senescent systems can, at some periods, under certain circumstances, give access to a new, higher-scalar-level structure which will preserve the old systems (or some direct derivatives from them) as units in a higher-level development. If fluctuations are required, senescence regularly provides them.

In just this way have human societies provided frameworks allowing human organisms to reach, and even to survive for a time in, senescent stages. Just in this way did living systems allow biochemical dissipative structures to continue their trajectories beyond what would have been possible without the stability they provided. Just in this way did star systems allow inertial trajectories to be harnessed into organized dissipative structures. In each case the new system harnesses the activities of the now-subordinated, newly integrated units to its own {ends}—Haken's "slaving principle." The emergence of new evolutionary units is, precisely, a negation of senescence as the end of development.

Now, we must compare this interpretation with that of Csányi's and Kampis' (1985) "autogenesis." In their view, evolutionary systems show nonstationary, convergent fluctuations, so that the aging system is more and more quiescent and able to be entrained into a higher-level system—their "convergence." (This would relate to the third phenomenological rule of thermodynamically open systems listed on page 111.) The image seems quite different from the above, more Prigoginian, view, but of course is not inconsistent with it. In that view, as I have suggested, the increasing internal quiescence of aging systems (third rule, related to Prigogine's state of minimal entropy production) is what allows them to be seized by environmental perturbations and thrown into new possibilities, most of which lead to recycling (fourth rule). In other words, it seems to me that the autogenetic view simply does not mention an important component of what happens—the greater actual fluctuations experienced by an increasingly senescent system as a result of its own internal quiescence.

This is partly because in autogenesis an autopoietic perspective is stressed, this being an anti-hierarchical viewpoint related to self-organization discourse, focusing resolutely within a system. The new "evolutionary units" are more-makers, this being what allows them to explore their evolutionary potential by way of mutations and recombinations. I do not stress this here (but see the appendix for "combinatorial expansion"), because I do not think autopoeisis and replication are general enough (in the way usually meant) to be extended to abiotic dissipative structures. It must be said that most models of evolutionary systems focus on living systems; I believe this to be anthropocentric in the wrong way, and myopic in view of our need for a more global mythos.

It is always the case that in hierarchical systems a higher scalar level provides for the replication of units at a lower level. These units do not *self*-reproduce, are not *auto*-poietic. Once we see this, and only then, can we generalize evolutionary systems, as we must, to hurricanes and ecosystems. These are "replicated" by the larger system, using information stored within it, no less than are organisms; the organization of the stored information is simply different in these various cases, and orders of magnitude more detailed in organisms. My point is that, in general discussions of the emergence of new evolutionary units, stress on the quixotic means by which one kind of system (the living) has contrived to propagate information seems inappropriate.

There are some other minor differences between autogenetics and my own views, but on the whole they are coordinate. In both we have the production of new components within the global system, which acts as nodes for the production of still other kinds. The stabler kinds may be immanent in the system as a whole; however, so many new systems are possible at each actual transition that they are not generally predictable from a critical stage, as they would be in simple development, and so they may be taken to be truly "evolutionary." Indeed, abiotic systems are even more "evolutionary" than living ones, because they are less constrained to developmental pathways.

At the new level formed by new evolutionary units, the former entities (now at a lower scalar level) together set the internal constraints (as in endosymbiosis), and so cooperation becomes as important as competition. Finally, the older systems become more rigidly mechanical as they lose evolutionary potential in a "global informational catastrophe." This serves as an initiating condition on the new evolutionary system, setting the older systems up for the possibility of being entrained into the emergence of yet higher-level evolutionary units. Only thus internally habit-entrained could they serve as reliable units on which a new evolutionary system could be founded.

Change in Hegelian Systems

It is time to consider the relations between emergence and the only theory of change constructed in Western culture: dialectics. This will mostly be a question of the "dialectics of nature" (Engels (1872–1882) 1940; Engels (1894) 1947; Horn 1983; Levins and Lewontin 1980; Norman and Sayers 1980; Piaget 1976; Riegel 1976; Rychlak 1976; Sartre 1976; Vigier 1966), but it will be informed by more general Hegelian dialectics (Findlay 1958; Gadamer 1976; Hegel (1830) 1970; Kieve 1983; Lucas 1986; Rockmore 1986) as well as by general Marxist dialectics (Gregory 1977; Kieve 1983; Marx (e.g. 1852) 1973; Ollman 1976; Sartre 1976).

My approach will be to interpret Engels' "rules" of dialectic using H_{sp} (figure 5.3), which will furnish a productive view of the logical relations between them. Gadamer notes that Hegel's *Logic* is arranged in just this pattern, moving from the most general to more and more highly specified concepts (as from the top of figure 5.3 to the bottom). This perspective allows us to neatly capture a sense of the "self-unfolding of things" (Gadamer 1976) within dialectic. Sartre states that "each of the laws of dialectic is the whole of dialectic." This, too, is reflected in figure 5.3, where every more general aspect is the ground-

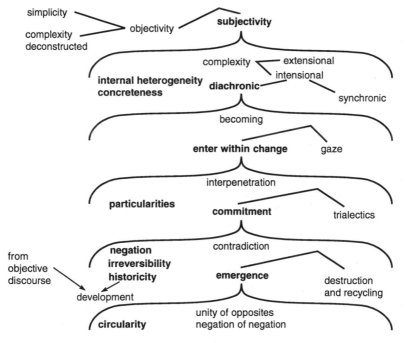

Figure 5.3 A specification-hierarchical interpretation of dialectics. Each dichotomy branches into the choice of next more innermost class, whose implication is stated just opposite it on the other side of the emergent boundary (bracket). Each choice (in boldface) is balanced by its logical opposite (in lightface), indicating the direction not followed. See text for further explication.

ing for the others and every more specified aspect necessarily implies the more general ones.

Note, however, that in figure 5.3, formally, any aspect of dialectic could be rejected and that would still leave all the more general levels intact. I mention this because there is a spreading sense that the codified rules of dialectic as proposed by Engels ((1) transformation of quantity into quality; (2) mutual penetration of polar opposites and their transformation into each other when driven to extremes; (3) development by contradiction, or by negation of the negation) are "vulgar" attempts to codify what cannot be codified. At their most vulgar (Horn 1983), we also find that (1) sufficient changes in quantity may produce changes in quality, (2) opposing forces produce a transformation of the system that includes them, and (3) a thesis overcomes its antithesis to produce something different from either of them—a synthesis. But others have produced quite different rules. For example, Gadamer, interpreting Hegel, produced these: (1) thinking is self-referential; (2) it necessarily finds contradictory determinations simultaneously; (3) this unity of contradictory determinations is sublated into a different whole.

In all these cases there is presentation of rules *seriatim*, with no indication of the logical relations between them. Figure 5.3 gives us a more functional appreciation. It could be roughly translated into a Sommersian sentence (see Salthe 1985, figure 13): "Emergence comes from contradictory interpenetration, which is what is discovered upon entering, with commitment, into change itself, which is an option after discovering complexity diachronically, which is possible when taking a subjective view because subjects change."

Gadamer's formulation, given above, suggests a temporal sequence. There is no such suggestion in figure 5.3; it is not the case that the more general aspects of dialectic were discovered first, so that historical primacy would follow logical priority. Rather, figure 5.3 could be thought of as the structure of a discursive formation (Foucault 1972), any part of which could have been excavated at any time. Of course, I am saying that whatever was discovered would necessarily imply all the more general aspects, whether that was made explicit or not.

It is perhaps ironic that figure 5.3 is a standard positivist analysis, in terms of Aristotelian logic, of a discourse that is deeply opposed to this kind of neat analysis. Something will inevitably be lost in doing this, and I hope to suggest what that is along the way. Since it is frequently asserted that any determination more or less spontaneously creates for its maker its opposite(s), the dichotomies in the figure could be viewed as arising after a choice of the bold-printed portion necessarily gives rise by logic to the other half of the dichotomy. (This other half is, in each case, not followed up here.) I will say more about 'polar opposites' when dealing with contradictions—dialectics has been a deeply dyadic discourse in its focus on them. Multiple connections in a world are generally viewed as static, while dynamism is taken to be dyadic, and change sequential. Peirce understood this well in his triadic categories; seconds are dyadic, "confrontial," interactions; thirds are contexts—the multiple connections embedding change.

Analyzing figure 5.3, I will start with the most general category—subjectivity. Throughout explicit dialectical discourses there is criticism of positivism and its claimed objectivity and supposed transparent observations. This is today usually launched in connection with what is known as the project of emancipation. This is because the supposed objectivity has often been a convenient screen for hidden interests—e.g., if it were to be shown in objective psychological studies that women tended to be less competent mathematically than men, then their arguments for equal access to mathematical knowledge could be construed as unnatural. While positivism concerns itself with 'how', dialectics tends to be concerned with 'why'.

Dialectical thinking tends to be used by those who are against established power structures. Indeed, Plato warned against teaching a version of dialectic (sophistry) to anyone not in power because of its ability to undermine existing thought frames; recall that Socrates' techniques were dialectical. In Hegel the appropriateness of any knowledge claim is demonstrated by its contribution to the subjective, valued end of self-knowledge, and Marxists have been concerned with theories of value in response to the capitalist tendency to reduce all values to a single, supposedly necessary, calculable exchange value. What becomes suggested here is that in dialectical discourse prediction is replaced by advocacy, analysis by construction.

In figure 5.3 I show subjectivity leading into concern with complexity. This is not to say that objective science—e.g., systems theory, cybernetics, nonlinear mathematics, hydrodynamics—has not come to view complexity as an important problem. Rather I suggest that the objective approach to the world will ultimately prove to be more competent to deal with simple systems—and indeed, traditional scientists have always thrived on their skills in simplifying problems. This should be seen as associated with a social role of science as predicting and controlling nature. Simplification leads to the ability to suggest practical remediations for isolated problems. The later ramifications of these actions (e.g. pollution) are accepted as payment to be made by future generations, if they are appreciated at all—and they are never anticipated, because attempting that might deprive a study of its "usefulness."

By 1930 the positivist program had been finally deconstructed by Gödel (the works of Duhem and Bohr had already undermined it, and those of Quine later gave it the *coup de grace*). The implications of this remote and difficult work for the modern world are even now still not generally appreciated. They include that no explicit (i.e., objective) system can stand by itself, that it needs to be shorn up by more encompassing, therefore ultimately specifically value-laden, discourses. Hence, scientifically based actions need to be carried by political systems that can pick up the pieces that fall as products of technological advance—generally the effects of overpopulation and its attendant environmental destruction and pollution. The objective perspective in science does not concern itself with consequences, and so must be embedded in something that could have an approach to complexity. But, having been influenced by objectivity because of the short-term successes of objective science, our more encompassing social system has yet to show itself capable of understanding or managing complexity.

In the *Republic*, Plato spoke of dialectic as a way "to see the connections of things" (Cornford 1945). But the dialectical view of complexity is itself complex. First, viewpoint is explicitly important; a system is divided into heterogeneous portions by interested agents, there being no canonical configuration of internal heterogeneity (see Allen et al. 1984 for a strong statement of this kind in connection with H_{sc}). Furthermore, such divisions are incomplete, because, as Sartre has stressed, any *totalization* of a system is associated with finite discursive projects (consider that studies of slow viruses are now completely dominated by the problem of AIDS), to be discarded when the project no longer entrains. A poet will deliver you one forest, a conservationist another, and a lumberman still another—and among ecologists you could find systems and community (Darwinian) versions, these also being ideological projects. Note that acknowledgment of this incompleteness of totalizations is substantially what the internalist perspective referred to in this book amounts to—see Salthe 1990b, and see Rosen (1985b) on modeling.

The internal relations important to some discourse, then, define the parts of a system; thus, that discourse in fact defines the system context, because once you have parts you discover emergent wholes. Thus, a contextualizing discourse provides a unity to the whole (totalized), incomplete, temporary system. Vigier (1966) explicitly refers to these parts and wholes as a scalar hierarchy. But there is more here, associated with the word *concreteness*.

A concrete object in this discourse is one that is richly situated with respect to interesting categories. Figure 2.8 can be used to formally illustrate this point. Along the bottom of the figure we would have a row of concrete objects, each situated (in this case) in a nested series of categorial constraints. Each of these particular objects is both highly determinate and yet, through its more general connections, universal. At the tips of the branches objects are richly concrete; at their confluent bases they dip into abstract universal categories supplied by a perspective and accessible to logical manipulation by way of models based on that perspective, from which the system's necessities can be deduced.

Here we have a theory of knowledge: a discourse posits categories; these are sharpened into representations of material embodiments through the specification hierarchy; at the highly specified tips we are delivered models of particular objects in the world that can, conveniently, be manipulated by way of their membership in the more general categories, the movements of which are determined by the logic of the discourse that originated them (predators eat animals, etc.). From this perspective, all discourses would be seen to be of this kind, whatever their more positivist pretensions might be. In other words, the subjectivist movement implicitly delivers a theory of discourse, embodying in this way its self-referential orientation.

Historical Dialectics

Only at the point where we come to exclusively consider changing systems are we poised to enter into diachronic, dialogic, dialectics *per se*. Obviously, therefore, we can have discourses categorized as above that would not be fully dialectical. Perhaps the "second cybernetics" of self-referential systems (Geyer and van der Zouwen 1990; Van der Vijver 1992) would be an example. 'Change' as used here refers to, essentially, one or another kind of emergence as identified earlier. Change can be viewed as a further restriction on the incompleteness of subjective systems; one way they could be indeterminate is because they are always changing. One might almost say that this is another reason why they are complex (Salthe 1990b). Again, we can read Plato's warning against dialectic to be an attempt to gain social stability.

Following Voorhees (1985), we can see the move being made here as a rejection of the law of the excluded middle of Aristotelian logic. In what Voorhees calls dialectical logic, an entity can be both a and not-a because it is in the process of changing away from being a. A system of this kind would be indeterminate because it is in flux. For this reason, Voorhees (1983) draws the rather startling conclusion that such systems need to be studied synchronically, because it is only then that they gain a quasi-determinacy sufficient to characterize them. One interpretation of this is that one must somehow get inside change itself, so that *it* becomes the object of study rather than the entities that are changing. An example might be the molecular analysis of emergence given above, where considering a more determinable lower-scalar-level system sort of smoothes out a higher-level discontinuity. We have, in any case, left the realm of mechanistic systems, which are necessarily studied using equilibrium models. Voorhees' suggestion provides the opportunity for continuing the analysis as below.

One could avoid such an analysis by failing to "enter in," by remaining aloof and taking up, perhaps, one kind of artistic contemplation, or by going in for mystical meditation on indefinable systems. Having opted for entry into change itself, we arrive at the more specifically historical dialectic. We need now to consider the terms 'interpenetration' and 'particularities'.

Integrative levels interpenetrate because of their transitive relations. We can then see that developmental stages must do so as well—perhaps partly as in the molecular model presented earlier in this chapter, where I suggested that the older condition gradually decays as the new one builds up to a metastable point at which the system, through synergetic coherence, can suddenly switch its allegiance between attractors because of a "straw that breaks the camel's back."

But interpenetration is usually discussed using examples such as fact/value, knowing/acting, quantity/quality, being/nothingness, and subject/object. With these we see the interpenetration of "opposites"— opposite developmental tendencies, opposite tensions. I will not discuss opposites in any detail at this point. These pairs, for now, can be taken as suggesting how different are the states that may be connected by emergences. One aspect of these examples is important for us now, however. These categories interpenetrate in the most basic way because, e.g., there can be no knowing without acting and no real, impeccable acting without knowing. (There could be futile castings about and bewildered fumbling, of course.) The members of these pairs require each other to be copresent intimately for either to exist. Hegel's discussion of being/nothingness in his *Logic* carries us further here. If we postulate an initial situation having only being, logic inevitably implies its absence—nothingness. This realization is itself the emergence of a third category—becoming—and with that we are projected inside of change itself. In other words, the above pairs are related in ways that imply change. Given facts, we will come to value some and reject others. Acquiring values, we will become blind to possible facts. Among objects, subjectivity emerges, and subjects continually construct themselves in objects (and from that we can derive the social construction of knowledge).

At this level *particularities* are constructed. Particularities reflect detailed relations. These depend on horizontal interpenetrations, just as earlier I noted that concreteness depends on what I can now refer to as vertical interpenetrations, as elucidated through the specification hierarchy. I am, then, claiming that concreteness is a more general property of dialectical appreciation than is particularity. Any actual situation is fully both, but particularity depends more upon historical uniqueness—even contingency—while concreteness is more the result of a multilayer understanding reaching into logic. The concreteness of a particular situation is the basis of its totalization; its particularity is its uniqueness and difference. We have this uniqueness because we have delved into the details of change of a particular system, one different from all others.

Contradictions and the Dialectics of Nature
We can move further into dialectic only by commitment to a project (or to a result at a level above the parts that bring change about). Sartre characterizes dialectic as the intelligibility of praxis (action in the light of some end) at every level. Praxis sooner or later runs into opposition, and then we come face to face with *contradictions*, and it is those moments that are strongly dialectical, potentially pregnant with emergence. Thinkers trained in realist and positivist traditions often refer to such contradictions as "false dichotomies," but the sense of 'false' here really abuts the concept of subjectivity. Of course, to an objective (outside) observer any contradiction to its projects met by some system would appear "false"—that is to say, not privileged in the abstract! In dialectic, contradiction is the "motor of change." Frequently we have to deal with internal contradictions, which spontaneously and/or necessarily develop within a (in the latter case, developing) system. Piaget claims they would also be triggered through external perturbations in some systems.

But, what are contradictions? Surely they include the logical contradictions of Aristotelian logic, which we thought we had left behind earlier? What was eliminated was the law of the excluded middle, not the law of contradiction. In dialectical logic something can be both a and not-a (e.g., 'maybe') because it is changing, even though it cannot simultaneously be fully a (yes) and not-a (no).

This requires a nod at trialectics (Horn 1983). In trialectics situations can be viewed as neither a nor not-a, because they are suspended, as it were, as potentialities between the two (Voorhees 1985). But in my view one gets to this only by taking a diachronically higher-scalar-level view of things, where contradictions become complementarities because both possibilities (and both past and future) are encompassed within the system at one larger-scale cogent moment, wherein a changing system can be viewed as being at equilibrium. Noting complementarities, such as Bohr's between wave and particulate phenomena in physics, has become an accepted way of looking at conflicting data in objective science; however, this is not dialectical, because it is a view that stands apart from the conflict and contextualizes it as a way of defusing it. This is an escape from the "dialectical moment," and that is why we left it behind earlier.

Still, what *are* contradictions? Especially, from the point of view of this work, what are they in connection with the dialectics of nature? This latter made its appearance when Engels claimed that natural systems, not just human ones, could be understood dialectically. Since then, some scientists (e.g., Vigier) have claimed that nature can indeed be taken to change dialectically, while others (e.g., Levins and Lewontin) feel that the suggestion is better forgotten in favor of viewing scientific practice as dialectical. From the perspective of the dialectics of nature, the terms 'conflicting forces', 'antagonism', 'opposition' (opposites), 'confrontation', and 'unfavorability' have been used. The relationship that such words have to the dialectical 'contradiction' can be explored by considering the Darwinian term 'competition'.

'Competition', like 'contradiction', is an agonistic word, and one might suppose that organisms in Darwinian discourse could be viewed as being engaged in dialectical struggle (for limited resources rather than toward goals—although the goal of capturing the deme is imputed to genotypes). Since the dialectical interaction of discourses has now been given a Darwinian interpretation in one version of "evolutionary epistemology" (Hull 1988), why should not competing genotypes be taken up as examples of the dialectics of nature? In answering this, I simply look back down the specification hierarchy we have been traversing to see if Darwinism can be brought in at any of the more general integrative levels. It cannot; it was left behind when we opted for subjective rather than objective discourse. But wait, there is another move to be made using the the concept of social construction together with the specification hierarchy.

Darwinism is an objective scientific theory, therefore it is a discourse, therefore it is subject to the rules of discourse as much as it is constrained by material manipulations, therefore it must be logical. Thus, leaving aside its use as a ploy in the struggle of discourses (where it has been a trump card), we could consider natural selection simply as a logical construction. Doing this, we could realize that there might be yet more specified words or phrases that represent 'natural selection' in more highly specified discourses concerning human systems. Have we arrived at evolutionary epistemology? No. The application of natural selection (neat) to the evolution of discourses, like the application of adaptation (neat) to human behavior (Alexander 1987), misses the integration of the concept by higher-level configurations and final causes.

From this point of view we might, following the logic of figure 1.2, consider the possibility of a construction like {competition {contradiction}}. For this to work, the following construction, {objective {subjective}}, must work too. Is subjective discourse, taken as a concept, more highly specified than objective discourse? Is objectivity more "primitive" than subjectivity? This may depend on your viewpoint.

In one sense, something has been added to objective discourse in order to get subjective discourse—passion. Is it possible to suppose that one might consider a problem coolly and analytically, while another might consider *the same problem, while preserving the analyticity,* with pressing fervor, adding, say, an overwhelming desire to use any tricks whatever to get through it? If so, competition as necessitated by limited resources might be a more general version of the same logical category as contradiction. For this to be true, an asymmetry is required such that competition is inevitably encountered when generalizing from contradiction, *and* such that from 'competition' one could go forward to other specializations than just 'contradiction', which would be only one more highly specified "species" of Rylean category.

In effect, contradiction would be a kind of competition. The implication—that animals are cool and calculating, as in the Cartesian view, while humans (or primates) acquired hysteria—seems doubtful to me. The question cannot be answered here, but it can be formulated. It is interesting to see how much is brought into this question, and how much seems to be at stake in the answer.

For example, consider 'opposition', another common dialectical term. Any category spontaneously generates its opposite, as in the above examples (quantity/quality, or, from Marx, "the concept of the free laborer contains the pauper"). Oppositions are logically interdependent. In order for opposites to occur in nature, logical categories must be able to be imposed on the world. Is this done? All the time, in every language and in all discourses and models.

Hence, we could follow Norman (of Norman and Sayers 1980) in saying that "the dialectic of nature is the dialectic of concepts through which [the natural world] is comprehended." (This can be taken to be Sartre's view as well.) Computer simulations could easily be viewed dialectically, then. On this score, Kauffman (1990) is even developing a perspective on subjectivity in this realm. Sayers, opposing Norman, seems to me to say nothing different in suggesting that, if conflicts in nature could be viewed as "necessary," then natural processes could be taken to be contradictory, for necessity is a *logical* relation. In short, nature can be dialectical because nature is our construction of the world, and so, following Sartre, "the real is rational" (certainly, for example, Darwinism flaunts its rationality to advantage).

Now, Riegel (1976) proposes yet another view of natural contradictoriness. He notes that if in one context something seems tall and in another it seems short, the perceiver is faced with contradictory evidence. This could lead to Gregory Bateson's "double bind" anxiety, and even octopi have been known to be driven to distraction by being faced with signs that simultaneously invite opposite responses. In objective discourse, these kinds of examples have seemed to be reasonable as more general models of logical antinomies; but then our formulation would have to be reversed to {subjectivity {objectivity}}, and competition would have to appear to be a kind of contradiction.

So, from the objective viewpoint, animals appear to be emotional, while we humans can occasionally take on something cultural that suppresses emotion. Have we uncovered a deep opposition between objective and subjective discourses? For the former the world is taken to be alogical, while for the latter nature is logical. The two are not really in opposition, because nature is our view of the world, and even objectivists must recognize that logic is used to construct it—as Hegel would have it, "the laws of thought and the laws of nature are necessarily in agreement."

Certainly we can concur with Engels that the purpose of constructing a dialectic of nature is to avoid a mechanistic and dualistic separation of humans from nature. Perhaps we could view nature 'as if' it were dialectical for some purposes and 'as if' it were mechanistic for others. Few scientists appear to do the former; most do the latter. The choice must be made prior to, not within, any discourse. Gadamer has suggested that dialectical discourse is required wherever logical antinomies must be sublated. This tends not to come up in the practice of science, because its studies have been too limited in scope, aimed at very bounded (and essentially practical) problems.

Still, how might dialectic be viewed as the motor of change in a scientific study? Studies of emergence would seem to be reasonable sites for the application of dialectic, inasmuch as emergence has to do with qualitative changes. Do contradictions (or {contradictions}) prepare the way for Bénard cells, for example? There is, at the very least, a problem of scale here. We would need to know if molecules have, following Whitehead, the more general equivalent to our subjectivity. Given that, one might learn something from trying to consider convection to be the qualitative result of conflicts in the motions of small molecular aggregates such that the energy flowing out of the system with respect to that flowing in has become inhibited to a degree that allows it to drive convection.

There is no knowing what we might learn by undertaking such studies; however, as others have said before, one's sense is that this would merely be translating a problem into a practice that did not naturally give rise to it. If there is to be a dialectic of nature, it must uncover problems that require what it has to offer (and, since emergence is such a difficult problem for positive science now, maybe that could be good subject matter for it)—it must make a place for itself. Matsuno's (1989) description of the basis of self-organization in the contingency of physical phenomena is to my mind a good example of the dialectics of nature. Here the phenomenon, unrecognized within classical science, seems to have led quite naturally to a dialectical approach. Fully systematized natural phenomena as we know them now *belong to* objective discourse, and presumably reflect its structure. This leads us toward the problem of development, an area that has been fussed over by BCNDC science without much success (Salthe 1987). Perhaps it too awaits a dialectical approach.

Dialectics and Development

Contradictions inevitably lead to irreversible change, especially when, as in dialectic discourse, they are not eliminated but subordinated within a higher integrative configuration (sublated, as with the self-interests of the cells of a metazoan (Buss 1987)). The continued presence of contradictions in an emergent level would prevent it from returning to the unintegrated state (as with cancer), or, if that began to happen and the system survived, would lead it to resist disintegration (as when white cells scavenge transformed cells). Cumulating irreversible change builds up history, and it is at this level that the *historicity* of dialectical discourse emerges. When history is viewed not as "one damn thing after another" accumulated by (efficient) cause and effect but as a self-organizing trajectory reflecting the interests and projects of the agents of the history, then it can be taken as a dialectical subject.

By their very nature historical emergences are unpredictable to an outside observer, with its externalist perspective. On the other hand, development has had a place in historical dialectical discourses—recall Marx's stages of history. In figure 5.3 I have suggested that the idea of development was an import from objective discourse. But this is true only for materialist applications. Development in the full Hegelian sense emerges because the movement of the system is driven by logical transformations—this being one result of the totalization of the system around its logical categories. Generally speaking, such transformations are inevitable and therefore predictable.

Letting logic drive the facts at his disposal (which generated the contradictions he was interested in), Marx predicted the classless society. There seem to me to be two reasons why this prediction failed. One is that historical connections are so rich that the probability of one's seeing the real moments in any "argument" is very low, no matter how strongly felt are one's considerations. That is to say, the Hegelian prediction takes place on the basis of a model of the system— even if that model is made by agents that are themselves interested parts of the system. As Rosen (1985b) has pointed out (see also Taylor 1985), models are always oversimplifications around a particular totalization.

The other, deeper reason is that in the emergence of more specified levels a system has a polarity such that more than one possibility can always develop out of any relatively vague situation (Matsuno 1989), however accurately discerned it is—that is why figure 2.8 is a tree. In moving toward greater specification, generally more than one thing could happen, and the difference that makes a difference in all non-linear systems might be a slight one in initial conditions—so slight that no finite observer could ever hope to detect it.

Of course, material developmental trajectories with many tokens available for observation do have average predictable behaviors. But this could be of little help to Marx, because the scale of what he was predicting was so large that he could have had no experience of what an average result that could come from the stage he had observed might be. Development in objective discourse is always constructed backward, as an average from many instances of whatever type is involved. The very notion of "stages of history" embodies a contradiction that Marx failed to sublate.

Focusing on emergence proper as defined earlier, we finally reach the most highly specified category of dialectic: the negation of the negation. In constructing this, Engels built on Fichte's formulation of the thesis, which generates its antithesis logically, followed by the sublation of that "negation" (or contradiction) in a new system (or stage) at a higher integrative level—a "unity of opposites." As Sartre points out, the synthesis is viewed by Hegel as being "necessary"— that is, we are dealing here with developmental emergences and not with historical ones (which appeared already in the last integrative level discussed). Since Hegelian necessity is logical, it is of course subject to the incompleteness already discussed.

Rychlak (1976) claims that if an outcome is known beforehand then an encounter is not truly dialectical. This reflects the neo-Marxians' concern with historicity; in parallel with neo-Darwinians, most of them have abandoned development (e.g. Gould (1987)). Perhaps, then, we should consider this innermost aspect of dialectic to be nothing more than a fossil reflecting nineteenth-century concerns too fully. This might be so, except that it would be forgetting that developmental emergence remains an outstanding problem for objective discourse (say, in artificial intelligence, artificial life, neurobiology, or ecology). Who can say that this general approach might not serve as a jumping-off point for successful work in these forefront areas? This would entail a radical switch to subjective discourse. In any case, Rychlak's dictum neglects the fact that if we examine even a well-known situation in enough detail we will find some unforeseen configurations. Hence, any event would be, if richly enough conceived, unpredictable. Of course, since Hegelian prediction is based on logic alone, it can never be very detailed, and perhaps it will seldom be detailed enough to go beyond trivialities.

Fichte's general triadic formulation is, however, an early approach to circularity. Hegel was a champion of logical circularity, which has had successors—from Uexküll, whom I have used herein, to simulations by computer programs using subroutines. Indeed, Peirce's triadic system reflects the Hegelian system too. For Hegel the circularity lies in repetition of the negation of the negation at higher and higher levels, and this is certainly a precursor to the general structure of evolutionary systems discourse, from Csányi through Alvarez de Lorenzana to my figure 5.2. But is this a subjective, dialectical discourse? One would not think so from reading most of these works. Perhaps just as material (as opposed to logical) development was a contribution to subjective discourse from the objective, so this circular pattern may have been a contribution to objective discourse (general systems science) from the subjective.

Furthermore, I would suspect a Hegelian background to nonequilibrium approaches in science as well. Despite his own cop-out on this, Hegel's circular movement in the realm of logic never ends, and continues to accumulate stored information. Only the material nature of systems forces senescence. Perhaps we can view Hegel's notion that the world will end in the Prussian state to be his version of this, since he was undeniably reading from that local perspective. Objectivity is obviously an appropriate attitude toward closed, equilibrium systems, and I have tried to suggest herein and elsewhere (Salthe 1991b) that subjectivity may be a necessary stance when one is faced with open, nonequilibrium systems.

But, finally, the overt contribution of dialectics to science so far has been relatively minute. One might sum up its role in Western society as follows: While objective, positivist discourses have been used to construct theories and models of the world, dialectics has functioned as a means of criticism of the results of viewing things with these models. However, as I say, it has not yet been brought significantly to bear on the study of open, nonequilibrium, recursive, self-organizing systems. The commitment required in subjective discourses has perhaps, up till now, been the primary barrier to getting this going. It remains to be seen whether such commitment might emerge from the massive problem of environmental degradation.

Notes toward Modeling Change

The following sketch will incorporate elements from Aristotelian causality, scalar hierarchies, specification hierarchies, infodynamics, and dialectics.

Change will be viewed as entrained by the structures I have called developmental trajectories. That is, what we see as change at one scalar level will be a form at a higher scalar level (figure 4.7). This form is at base a specification hierarchy (figure 5.4A). This means that change is fundamentally based on development; evolution or history becomes embodied as a system individuates in connection with environmental perturbations or internal mutational excursions.

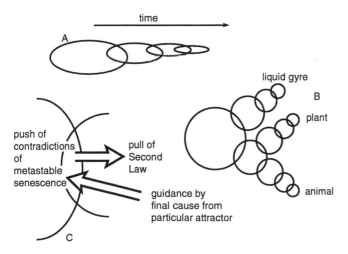

Figure 5.4 Views of developmental trajectories as sequences of stages. A: a single trajectory; the area occupied by each stage reflects its possibility or potentiality space. B: several trajectories of dissipative structures showing how they relate to one another increasingly through the vaguer logical types of their earlier stages. C: One transition from stage to stage, indicating the general factors involved in the model described herein. (Time moves from left to right in all figures.)

A trajectory's most specified end is open (another segment could be always be added to the last integrative level in figure 5.4), since the system modeled could become more senescent the longer it survived. The implicit attractor at that end (not shown) is a mechanism which exerts final causality over the whole trajectory. Labels at the ends of trajectories in figure 5.4B do not refer to these mechanisms, which would be limits at the ultimate ends of each trajectory. The labels here obviously could become much more highly specified than they are, and so they only indicate direction. Natural systems cannot achieve full mechanical embodiment, because they do not have or develop detailed enough stored information to specify everything of importance and because environments (even the most benign natural ones) have not been supportive enough.

The specification hierarchy is both subjective (since it ends with an observer/actor) and self-referential (because all levels are viewed with respect to their role in producing this observer, either synchronically (as integrative levels) or diachronically (as developmental stages)). This means that attempts at a modern-style totalization using development as a basis could gradually be converted to a postmodern pluralism as the observer's self-understanding continues to differentiate. This necessarily takes place with respect to a generalization of the model to coordinate entities other than the observer (those at other branch tips).

The model can be generalized to other dissipative structures by supposing that they too are, in whatever way, observer/actors. The system achieves totalization as a unity of diversity by classifying these others under the same general logical types as the observer (figure 5.4B), this form, then, conveying the global sense that all particular observer/actors have been derived from more similar (ultimately the same) vaguer, primal conditions.

A trajectory becomes both more elaborate and more determinate (more particular) at its more specified end, and, what is saying the same thing at a lower scalar level, it continually acquires stored information as its concreteness intensifies. In figure 5.4 one would have to show more stored information the smaller the area covered by an integrative level. This is implied by the fact that at any stage all the information from previous stages is still present, albeit modified; the figure is one of an extending trajectory. Some of the information is implicitly encoded here, since restriction of possibilities into the next level or stage must have involved the acquisition of further informational constraints. This accumulation of information suggests that a trajectory's required level of behavioral variety increases during development (see figure 9.4 of Goonatilake 1991), suggesting that it becomes increasingly more difficult for it to survive the longer it has already survived.

Focusing in on one of the joints between stages in a trajectory (figure 5.4C), we find on the relatively immature side a system that has, to a large extent, exchanged the production of physical entropy in agentive action for informational entropy as the various possibilities inherent in its initial conditions have become explored in increasingly greater detail. This glut of information has made the system increasingly rigid and faced with contradictions in respect to its momenta in every direction for which it has a tendency. There is a global informational crisis as the senescent system has become overconnected and therefore in many ways functionally underconnected. This critical condition becomes metastable and increasingly ripe for radical change.

What can happen now is destruction and recycling, or, instead, reorganization as a new integrative level emerges. When the latter happens, its direction has become determined by several means. On the one hand, no form will emerge that does not facilitate a greater entropy production than was possible in the critical state. On the other, the final causality associated with the kind of trajectory it is (its Rylean category) exerts a strong guidance—in biological systems, partly through genetic information and partly through material, formal, and efficient causes active at the moment of change. In vaguer systems only the latter can be involved.

The whole model of change is totalized around the observer/actor's being at the moment of conceiving it—located at the momentary tip of one of the trajectories, concretized by the whole logical tree. It reflects that agent's tendencies and projects, with concretize everything there is (i.e., all the letters at the bottom of figure 2.8) around its own categories (the numerals at the nodes of that figure). All of nature then emerges in connection with the subject's own development, which is theoretically the primal movement of the system.

Summary

In this chapter we considered what exactly 'change' might be. Processes of spatial translation are not change in any strong sense. Because of that, it seems that most of science as it has been has been concerned not with change but only with smoothly predictable motion. Where this has not been sufficient to understand a system, chance has been brought in to generate unexpected behavior. But unexpected behavior (historical emergence) is only one sort of transformation found in nature. Another (developmental emergence) is the sudden shift of a system from a condition that is understandable as being explained with one theoretical apparatus to another condition that is not fully explicable by that apparatus.

Two classes of this kind of change are known: extensional emergence, where a higher-scalar-level system coheres around entities that then appear to be its parts, and intensional emergence, in which the change overtly involves a shift in the observer's attention to categories relevant to a higher integrative level. It is my contention that each kind of developmental emergence involves a shift in observational category (this is an x, now it is a non-x), which is a subjective phenomenon, outside the reach of traditional science. Thus, the appearance of convection in a system that did not previously show it involves (1) description using a new theoretical apparatus, hydrodynamics, where previously atomistic descriptions sufficed; (2) since an observer is going to be closer in scale to one of these conditions than to the other, and so can "see" one of them better, the other condition will only be inferred or extrapolated via theory (e.g., atomism). This physical bias leads to an attempt to describe the system in both states using the mode most congenial to the observer, followed by discovery that that will not suffice, leading back to (1) an alternative description, usually requiring inferred objects (e.g., atoms) on one side of the conceptual leap.

The transition itself escapes description. This is not entirely unreasonable, since the business of science has been to predict, and that can be done in developmental emergence without being able to bridge discourses. Using dialectic, one can come a bit closer to the actual shift itself, but only on penalty of assuming a subjective stance, which forgoes prediction in favor of attempting to influence the direction toward which the system will move from its metastable state. Surprisingly, perhaps, this includes the situation where an experimenter sets up an apparatus *in order to* observe, say, Bénard cells, or stable limit cycles in Boolean automata. These are the sculptures of science, expressing the observer's desires.

Dialectical understanding is the attempt to totalize one's understanding of nature around one's own (or one's culture's) categories, and so is an attempt not only at self-understanding but also, since change ought to be nudged in valued directions, at self-improvement. From the point of view of global totalization, this puts a fateful touch of reflexivity into one's theories, forcing one toward postmodern partiality. The model of change I have presented incorporates aspects of Aristotelian causal categories, scalar and specification hierarchies, infodynamics, and dialectics.

Chapter 6

Immature, Mature, Senescent

Is no one inspired by our present picture of the universe? This value of science remains unsung by singers: you are reduced to hearing not a song or poem, but an evening lecture about it. This is not a scientific age.
Richard Feynman, 1982.

Modern thought has realized considerable progress by reducing the existent to the series of appearances which manifest it.
J.-P. Sartre, 1956.

> Here the mythological, cosmological, ethical, and moral implications of the Darwinian world view are briefly examined and contrasted with some of those of the developmental world view, laid out in more detail. Developmental trajectories, senescence, and final causality are featured as categories important to developmental cosmology. Then two problem areas of quite different provenance are examined from the developmentalist perspective: the abortion controversy, with a subsection on meditation, and the origin of life, with a subsection on coevolution.

In this chapter we will explore some metaphysical and mythological implications that emerge from this work, and that were, indeed, some of its final cause. The myth (instantiated in world view and cosmology) that we discover from this angle is quite different from that conveyed through Darwinism, and is no doubt partly constituted by relations of contradiction with that myth of matter in motion. This opposition in a general sense has been joined at least since the time of Plato (figure 2.4); however, the myth of matter in motion, which could be called the Baconian/Cartesian/Newtonian/Darwinian/Comtean world view, has certainly been "the mythology of our own time" (Lévi-Strauss 1966).

Ethnographically, myths are stories we live by. Although both theories and myths are explanations, they differ in the uses to which they are put. Theories serve as the bases for testable models in science; myths serve as references for our joys and pain. That a single matrix of ideas could feed into both is obvious. An important moment in the struggle (I've succumbed to Darwinism again—or Marxism!) between the two major Western mythological matrices came in 1874, when Kirchhoff suggested that scientists should reject explanation in favor of description (Gadamer 1976). An interesting move this, insofar as it amounted to the declaration that explanations are "only" myths, like those of *Romantische Naturphilosophie* (Lenoir 1982), while descriptions could be useful tools for practical, positive men. This was, quite simply, the denial that natural science feeds into our belief systems and vice versa. We find similar sentiments in our own day; consider Midgley's (1985) argument that evolutionary biologists should drop their adherence to the "myths" of "cosmic optimism" and "cosmic pessimism."

Cosmic optimism refers to the belief that large-scale developmental trajectories lead inevitably toward the good, or at least toward improvement. This was the belief of some *naturphilosophen* and Herbert Spencer, but few evolutionary biologists since Julian Huxley can be accused of allegiance to it. By "cosmic pessimism" Midgley intends the vision of "nature red in tooth and claw," such as can be found most recently in the works of many sociobiologists (e.g., Alexander (1987)). Here, in common with Eldredge and Grene (in press), she tries to avoid the invidious ethical and moral implications of Darwinism by claiming that they are associated only with the modern refinements of neo-Darwinism. In my opinion (Salthe 1989b) those implications are overwhelming, and just this pessimistic myth would be carried by any form of Darwinism because of its ineluctable connection with intraspecific competition (see also Williams 1989). More on this below.

In a more general vein, Atlan (1986) argues that science is strictly an instrumental practice involved in our attempts to control nature, and that we should not try to found moral intuitions in it since such a connection could hamper both science and the moral imagination. But sociocultural systems are structures, and their wholeness involves the compatibility of their major institutions. I believe explicit consciousness of this fact is better than letting these discourses influence each other *sub rosa*. At the very least, as John Collier put it in a personal communication, "the separation of science from myth obscures the mythical character of science, and gives [it] more weight than it deserves."

In any case, the idea that the natural world should be dominated by men or especially by men has itself come to be a moral question. To pretend that science could be separate from mythology and morality is to allow the hidden connections between them to go unexamined. It can plausibly be asserted that one result of such connections (or the pretended lack of connections) has been the current environmental crisis. Because of that crisis, all connections of our major institutions to morality must be opened up and scrutinized. All the values of the system that has precipitated the current environmental crisis must be reexamined on all fronts, and one of those fronts is the beliefs current among culturally important persons concerning where they came from and what they are doing here—the domain of evolutionary biology.

It would be useful to define how I am taking 'morality' here. Briefly, I distinguish morality from ethics. By ethics I understand what most positivist, analytic philosophers take to be morality—that is, discourse about conflicts of interest among individuals (see Sellars and Hospers 1952, Nelson 1991, Rachels 1990, and any issue of the *Hastings Center Report*). I take morality rather to be harmonious or wholesome behavior with respect to issues that claim to go beyond narrow human interests.

In this respect the discourse of Catholic philosophers such as Maritain (1964) comes closer to the view of morality intended here. Following the commands of a deity, coming into harmony with goodness, acting impeccably with respect to standards, furthering a mythological vision, and suffering well eschatologically might be various modes of moral action. So would be a tactful deferring of activity that might tend to spoil the wholesomness of the natural world (note that the aim here ought not merely be to maintain conditions favorable to humans). It is revealing to note that under these definitions ethical and moral issues might themselves come into conflict (more scope for analytic philosophers!).

What motivates this distinction is the need to identify goodness as it might be associated with different hierarchical levels. Ethics concerns human right behavior with respect to same-level relations (and not only interhuman relations—see Singer 1981 and Taylor 1986), while morality concerns human right behavior with respect to higher-level entities and hence, broadly, discourses (nature, God, goodness, the state) and ecosocial systems (Lemke 1991), including environments and nations. An example of a current moral discourse would be the deep ecology of Aldo Leopold and Arne Naess (Devall and Sessions 1985). One might suppose on this score that utilitarianism is moral discourse because it refers to the distribution of goods over a population. I see it as being just as ethical in intent as contractualism, because the goods that are deployed are explicitly only those of human individuals.

Evolutionary biologists have from time to time committed themselves in these areas. Their views range from Huxley's (1947) version of "cosmic optimism" through Waddington's (1960) appraisal of the evolution of a human capacity to be influenced by moral authority to

Alexander's (1987) and Simon's (1990) concerns with conflicts of interest between individuals in the light of Darwinian intraspecific competition. I am not here trying to directly connect with these works. Rather,
I am going into these issues in order to reflect the concerns of social
construction (Latour 1987; Woolgar 1988) in a certain way. Natural
science has reflected the ethical and moral orientations of our culture—
for example, Darwinism, capitalism and/or socialism, and democracy
fit together as well as do any pieces in a puzzle (Unger 1975). Here
Darwinism provides key mythological support, which I will attempt
to characterize in a general way, suggesting also its possible compatibility with ascendent approaches to those other major mythological
discourses—cosmogeny and studies of the origin of life.

I label this myth coming out of BCNDC science *the Darwinian world
view* because of the central position in it of selection processes, not
because it embodies many of Charles Darwin's views. Darwin's most
important work, like Newton's very compatible one, was an abstract
of a much more complicated production. And I believe that this "abstract" has not been misrepresented by its neo-Darwinian outline, for
we can assume that neo-Darwinians have by now pulled out its essential logical structure. For this reason it is in them rather than in
Darwin that the implications of "Darwinism" are best seen. Indeed,
this world view values simplicity, and Darwin's subtle implications,
hesitations, and nuances must be made to suffer from that as well.

Darwinian Cosmology

According to Darwinian myth, then, the world is a place composed
of aggregated pieces of material stuff, nicely summed up by the
Democritean phrase "matter in motion." The motion is essentially
random, that is to say, pointless. There are no structures (in the structuralist sense) in the world; all aggregations and formations come
together contingently by way of concatenations of events informed by
accidental propensities only, whereby some things stick together because of fortuitous semiotic relations they might bear to each other
and others are swept away elsewhere.

After the very smallest pieces of stuff get stuck together, there are
larger pieces whirling about. These too might stick together, through
one or another accident, until we have clumps of all sizes, ranging
from elementary particles (or strings if you prefer) to clusters of clusters of galaxies. There is no direction implied here; bigger clumps form
later only because it takes more time to build them up, so that smaller
pieces continue to exchange places even as much bigger ones begin to
grow. The only notion of direction is that bigger things are made up
of smaller ones in bottom-up fashion.

The system is at equilibrium (or virtually so, excepting fluctuations), in a kind of steady-state universe, because all the laws of nature (such as gravitation) and of matter (including chemical affinities) have always been in effect. Forms appear because some of the randomly accreted clumps associate by accident, and, once in existence, they begin to exert selective pressures such that they collect other pieces in more systematic fashion such that types are elicited, reflecting the common form and lower-level properties of their tokens. Edelman's (1987) views on the development of a nervous system would be a particular example of the processes involved in building up such a world. (I am not denying that a neo-Darwinian biologist might believe in, say, the Big Bang; I am suggesting that that belief would be inconsistent with his or her Darwinism.)

Major metaphysical categories in such a Darwinian world are chance, history, and uniqueness (figure 6.1). It is a stochastic realm; however, if we focus upon particular coordinates, either because it is a very small world or because we have a special interest in them, we will find there a series of historical emergences.

History and uniqueness depend upon being able to take a local perspective within the system. Otherwise all local differences would sum up globally to mere fluctuations. As it is never assumed that the

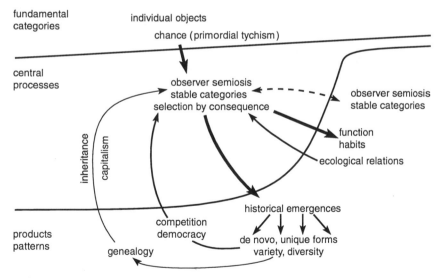

Figure 6.1 An outline of the Darwinian world view, suggesting relations with some other, compatible discursive formations. The double-headed dashed arrow represents ambiguous placement of the observer's categories. The two lowermost arrows pick out genealogical (on the left) and ecological realms.

world is very small, this means that we must include an observational category. But, since there is no warrant in the system itself for privileging one's own position, it is assumed that the local observer one is in fact stuck with—oneself—is merely one of untold numbers of local observers existing throughout the system. In order to deprive ourselves of bias, we construct cosmological principles to the effect that the universe would not appear different from any observation point, either in time or in space. It is not that the world is taken to be homogeneous in the strong sense of there being no detailed local variation in grain; rather, it is that it has no structure that could seriously bias observations—it is observationally homogeneous, or ergodic.

Within this system there must occur here and there, wherever conditions are by chance temperate and benign enough for long enough, a process of continued complication of local systems to the point where life emerges, as happened on Earth. Here we generate a necessary anthropic principle, which (happily, from the point of view of objectivity) automatically generalizes throughout the effectively homogeneous universe. The origin of life is primarily, since bottom-up is the only way things can happen, a molecular event—the coming about through various chance interactions of a primitive autocatalytic RNA, copies of which then gradually incorporate around themselves, or intercalate themselves into, local energy gradients (Wicken 1987), discovering metabolisms which they learn by random search (mutation) to be able to parasitize or farm by enslaving a class of compounds known as proteins.

Using the logic of Skinner's (1981) "selection by consequences," a genetic system gradually learns to promote processes that enhance its own replication (Eigen and Schuster 1979). Because efficient exploitation involves storing particular information about particular environments, there gradually come to be different versions of genetic information found in different local environments. Once different versions of this molecular information exist, accumulating in regions capable of promoting them, replication produces collections of geographically scattered genetic types. Now, types are not a primitive category in this mythological matrix, and their emergence must be discussed. Of course, they come from accurate replication (whose origin in living systems is still a major unsolved problem). But, while replication provides a seemingly fundamental ground for the existence of types, it is not a sufficient explanation. Types are semiotic entities. Something must make a distinction between them, or their members will scatter randomly and have no functional identity regardless of how accurately they replicate. In the Darwinian world view, the first distinctions were drawn by environmental asymmetries, and, indeed, selection by environment is a fundamental (if secondary) process in this cosmology.

In some present-day biological systems, passive accumulation of members of types by environmental collection has been bolstered by positive taxic behaviors leading to habitat selection and by responses to species mate recognition signals (Paterson 1985), but these are merely elaborations such that the units move more efficiently and tend to stick to one another as well as to environmental signs. Although material continuity is the basis of types, without functional semiosis the existence of types would be pointless because unnoticed. Their historical connections would go unnoticed unless members of types were clustered together by functional properties. Thus, function (which implies higher-scalar-level embedding systems) determines (or declares) the existence of a type, while history (chance) determines its form.

With replicating types on hand, typical Darwinian natural selection takes over, and, through scenarios like those described by Buss (1987), increasingly complicated systems—cells, colonies, multicellular organisms, colonies of multicellular organisms (such as the Portuguese Man of War), modular organisms, colonies of modular organisms (blueberry clones), and organic superorganisms (beehives)—are produced, with no end in sight. This involves selection at several levels of organization (Brandon 1990; Lloyd 1988; Sober 1984; Wilson 1980; Wilson and Sober 1989), an essential ingredient of universe building in Darwinian cosmology.

Along with the continuation of an increase in the intensional complexity of the biosphere (little focused on as yet by neo-Darwinians), dislocation and the essentially random processes of speciation (Mayr 1942) produce organic diversity, and the different types of organisms come, because of crowding, to exploit narrower and narrower Hutchinsonian ecological niches (MacArthur 1972).

A word of caution: We will next be forced to envisage the origin of our own species, if for no reason other than to account for observation. This will make the account given here read as if it could be construed as a process of increasing specification, as though there had been progress in evolution. This is only an unavoidable embarrassment, because in the Darwinian world view we do not want our own origin to seem anything but as accidental as any other speciation. No selection process foresees the future; there never was such a thing as a process of the evolution of mankind (or of anything else). All species just get separated out by accident and are honed by contingent environmental selection pressures.

The only process it is necessary to acknowledge is the essentially micro generation-to-generation survival of genotypes associated with the least unfit phenotypes in many concurrent lineages. Nothing is doing anything but surviving (Salthe 1972). Indeed, because each organism eventually gets recycled, only the survival of types of genetic information from generation to generation is happening in reality. By chance, organic evolution could give rise, in at least some small portion of the living systems in the universe, to humanlike systems.

From the point of view of Darwinian cosmology, human systems are epiphenomenal to the real processes occurring. This means here that all the complicated activities of humans have no metaphysical meaning unless they can be incorporated under the rubrics of chance and necessity or under that of selection by consequences (and so can be assigned an exchange value). This brings observation under this perspective as well. Thus, we have a resurgence today of evolutionary epistemology from a Darwinian perspective (Hull 1988; Wilson 1990), so that even philosophy may be conceived as a competition between memes (Dawkins 1976) based on adaptation to their sociocultural systems and ecosocial bases.

Continuing to bring Darwinian cosmology closer to home, we can note its implications for political action. Since there is in principle no privileged observation point in the system, there are no special types or groups of people with special qualities that were not accidental in the way of adaptations generally—the "right" mutation or recombination in the "right" place at the "right" time—combined with the fact that all places change (Van Valen's (1973) "continual deterioration of the environment"), and so all the "places" adapted to by every group have long since been obliterated.

If through gene recombination an individual pops up with specially good qualities for a given situation (by, say, combining several good genotypes), that individual will have no more value for the system than any average individual of the same genotypes. Every actual individual is only a temporary nexus of innumerable genotypes, and so organisms *per se* have no metaphysical standing. Like taxpayers and keyboards, they are mere mediators of true value.

Types, however, are in continual competition with one another to increase their representation in the next generation. Indeed, political action is organized around classes, and under some circumstances these could include even genotypes, as in South Africa today. Ascendent groups and their successful ideas can be held to have recently been more adaptive to momentary configurations in their sociocultural systems than their competitors. However, in principle there is no single way to be adaptive. Indeed, one can never tell in advance what (or who) may prove adaptive in any given situation. This is because adaptation is not a materialist idea but a semiotic one. An adaptation is a sign of its environment (which, indeed, is read in neo-Darwinism only through these signs rather than directly (Ollason 1991)). Anything might be adaptive to any situation, given all the initiating and boundary conditions, and more than one adaptive solution to a single situation could be arrived at in politics as well as in biology. That is to say, the going exchange values (fitnesses) of contingent relationships between memes (or genes) and environments are what count, rather than the particular properties of types of mediating organizations (or organisms). Nothing can be described as better than anything else that exists (Waddington 1960). Hence, while types compete, any of them might make an adequate adjustment at any time. In the political arena this leads to a continual jockeying of meme frequencies, with temporary ascendencies replacing one another over time; thus, mere competition becomes its own justification.

This competition among types, once they exist, becomes their only way of relating to one another. (See Winter 1990 for a review of this application in economics.) It may involve competition for resources with which they can survive and burgeon (ecological competition—the viability component of fitness), or it may involve the rates at which they can be replicated; the faster that may be, the more they may be able to spread out in space, buying a statistical likelihood of surving longer (reproductive competition—the fertility component of fitness).

Competition for resources is the keener the more alike two types are, but fertility competition would still be in place even if resources were unlimited. Hence, the principle of competition is deeper even than the finiteness of the world or than the degree of difference (provided that is unrelated to the rate of production) between types. Every type is necessarily in competition with every other type. This relation would continue as long as any differences coupled with differential fertility or production existed, and types would have to continue to overproduce even if they had saturated the available habitat.

We have here a democratic metaphysics (Unger 1975). No genotype or class can be held to be superior in all situations (or even in any given changing situation). In order to obtain temporary direction by the very best types of the moment, the political system should favor competition among a maximum number of classes. This could be facilitated by, say, unlimited immigration and enfranchisement and by the elimination of tenures of all kinds.

Ironically (since type variety is the point here), justice would necessitate eliminating self-classification as to type in favor of Rawls' (1971) "veil of ignorance" concerning one's own class membership. Only in that way could different types be made welcome in a local system that would utilize the variety they would bring. Here again we find a deep ambiguity concerning the observer, who sees the importance of variety but acknowledges making no choices herself—even *of* herself. (Perhaps Simon's (1990) "bounded rationality" functions here!) This emphasizes again that choices are made by environmental selection pressures in all cases. Individuals are not agents in this myth, regardless of the vote.

What the overall system needs here is to have a minimum of requisite variety (Ashby 1956) in order to survive. In fact, the above scenario reconstitutes at the political level the basic Darwinian (and Democritean) image of a mass of objects in motion and collision, temporarily accumulated (as in the vertebrate eye, in the performance of a symphony, or in the enactment of an ecosystem) according to class properties. Every value is measured by an exchange value, which indicates how quickly replicas of types are produced under a given situation, which in turn correlates statistically with the potential durations in time of the types themselves.

Shortcomings of Darwinian Cosmology
In figure 6.1, which presents a graphic summary of this section, we see the dichotomy between ecological and genealogical realms (Eldredge and Salthe 1984; Brooks and McLennan 1991; Eldredge and Grene, in press), which appear to be canonical abstractions. A distinction is also attempted between process and pattern (Eldredge and Cracraft 1980; Brooks and McLennan 1991).

A word more about the observer is in order. As was noted above, the observer is a difficult concept in this objective, positivist discourse. But without something standing in for it, no primordial accumulation of types would be possible. Distinctions need to be made in order to generate functions and habits. Yet, in a deep sense here, the observer and its categories are held to be a *product* of selection, not its initiator. For this reason I have marked observer categories as a positional resonance, using an ambiguous double-headed (dashed) arrow connecting two entries reading "observer semiosis" and "stable categories." Of course, it could be said that the observer of interest first appeared as a chance environmental irregularity and then evolved complexity gradually until at a later time we find Darwin himself exercising this role. (The latter view seems inescapable yet neo-Darwinians resolutely refuse to deal with it.)

But there is a yet deeper problem here, elicited by the attitude of social construction. The "fundamental categories" in the upper left corner of figure 6.1 really should be pointed to by an arrow from the right-hand "observer semiosis." From where else could such concepts come? But then the whole scheme here would have to be taken to be embedded (in a smaller font, perhaps) in the o of "semiosis"! I did not place such an arrow in the diagram because it would strongly violate the linear spirit of Darwinian cosmolgy.

Finally, without going into great detail here, I will outline what I take to be the ethical and moral problems of this cosmology in order that the reader may appreciate my motivations for seeking another one.

(1) Ethically, the centrality of intraspecific competition (that is, between genotypes) is salient. Similar needs lead to competition for resources. As sociobiologists have pointed out, this applies to humans as well. Since it is types that are in competition, this could lead directly to racialism, and, with hardly any further pressure at all, to racism.

Alexander (1987), explicitly following Sir Arthur Keith, makes competition between groups central to harmony within them. Something like Rawls' "veil of ignorance" seems to be the only (and, I would say, a gossamer) ethical barrier to this conclusion. Dobzhansky (1964) and Lewontin (see, e.g., Lewontin et al. 1984) have attempted to make an end run around this conclusion by claiming that at the genetic level races disappear because at that level there is more intraracial than interracial variability—that is, that genetic differences between human races are very small. (Notice the tendency to go to lower levels to solve a problem in this cosmology—even by an author who has argued against genetic reductionism.)

But the impact of this claim has itself been eroded by the fact that genetic differences between humans and great apes are also relatively small (Kluge 1983; Lewin 1987, 1988; Gibbons 1990; Miyamoto and Goodman 1990). In other words, aggregate genetic differences do not seem to reflect the operative constraints on phenotypic differences among these species. The relatively small number of genetic differences there are between humans and great apes obviously are "important," and so there is no reason not to suppose that some selective importance might have become associated with the smaller number of such differences among human races.

Yet one might suppose that decreasing human populations or increasing their resources (supposing that either could be brought about) would be the answer to this, because it would alleviate the need for competition. In fact, however, any differential reproduction among the races would produce competition from a Darwinian perspective even then. In Darwinism, any reproductive difference between stable, heritable types *is* competition. From this one would suppose that liberal Darwinians must hope for eventual introgression to a single human type. Alas, this implies, despite possible initial hybrid heterogeneity, an eventual loss of the variability that is crucial for further evolution—but see Hardin's brilliant play on this in chapter 7 of his book *Nature and Man's Fate* (1959).

(2) More mythologically oriented is the problem of expedience (labeled "satisficing" by Simon). In this cosmology, any *ad hoc* solution to an adaptive problem that works is satisfactory, and is then preserved as inheritance. The system works entirely opportunistically. Thus, when contemplating what forces have produced us (who are by definition "good"), we find only expedient tinkering (or blind watchmaking, or even the notion that there is no watch and hence nothing to mythologize about). Expedient tinkering, then, itself must appear to be good; consider the standing of Thomas Edison. The world of politics before us on television, in the town hall, or in any large institution could easily be taken to be a direct result (or source!) of this line of thought.

(3) Then there is the particular way mythological monism is achieved in this perspective. Humans are taken to be the same kinds of things that other things in the world are, and all are taken to be machines (whose parts are adaptations). Even if honesty cautions us to suspect the literal truth of this, all the inscriptions on which this discourse is based are statistical means, and mechanisms are more plausibly constructed, not out of individual cases, but out of averages, because of their similarity to specifications (and, of course, we all have been taught to strive to be "normal"—to fit the mechanistic ideal of the mean).

Hence, nothing we ourselves might have done as individuals could ever have been involved as an agency in our own evolution, any more than idiosyncratic behaviors of automobiles could have contributed to the evolution of car design. Occasional unique outliers have little impact on statistical means. Furthermore, all changes (here mutations) occur at a lower scalar level with respect to our own agency, and, of course, they are always random with respect to the needs of the organisms that get them. And such changes as occur are then selected with respect to their relationships with higher-scalar-level (environmental) configurations. Since we, then, like all other systems in the world, are effectively machines, it is not unreasonable that we treat one another instrumentally—as 'its' rather than as 'thous'. (It is no wonder that in this mythological matrix the imagination of allopathic medicine runs to mechanical hearts!)

(4) Next we come to Darwinian ideas about aging. In this discourse, the aged are primarily unproductive—they are "postreproductives." They have no residual reproductive value (the value of an individual in terms of contributing to its population's biotic potential) to speak of. That is to say, they have no further role in the theoretical game of (differential re)production, however well they may have played it while young. This is ameliorated somewhat in a social species such as ours, where grandparents can aid somewhat in the survival of their grandchildren. Even so, postreproductives are not the heroes of this mythology. Not surprisingly, Darwinian theories of aging show it as an accidental by-product of selection acting on younger stages with larger reproductive values (Williams 1957). So all this pain and stiffness, all this agony, is only a kind of pointless accident. (And how then could there be any warrant in this cosmology for treating those who suffer them as other than refuse?)

In Darwinism, moral questions revolve primarily around the effects our populations are having on a natural world also occupied by an unknown number of other species. In Darwinism, every population and species has as its primary role—one might almost say its duty—to expand its geographical range and enlarge its share of the energy flowing across the Earth's surface. The tendency toward range expansion would continue even if a species or genotype had actually conquered all of the Earth it was adapted to deal with. There is no warrant here for treatment of other species (let alone, say, watersheds) with anything but instrumental interest—as sources of food and shelter for ourselves, or as competitors to be bested if possible. As someone in daily struggle with, *inter alia*, clothes moths, termites, mildew, carpenter ants, various mammalian browsers, squirrels, feral cats, mosquitoes, blackflies, porcupines, poison ivy, and dandelions, I feel (traps, guns, and poisons in hand) the impulses generated by Darwinian attitudes only too keenly. And it is frustrating to realize that it is our own human activity that has increased the populations of these species by constructing them as our competitors.

This image (and literal construction) of universal competition among kinds (an extrapolation from the basic intraspecific competition of Darwinism) can be seen as reflected in the environmental destruction that we, as a species adapted to early successional stages, have wrought. We have always recycled mature ecosystems in favor of more productive, relatively immature ones—farms and fisheries. When our activities had not reached global proportions, this was simply another way to live on Earth. Now, however, these ways apparently have triggered global warming, have created Antarctic and Arctic ozone holes, and threaten various kinds of "winters" (nuclear, oil burning, and perhaps some others), all of which have repercussions for the Earth as a whole.

From a Darwinian perspective, this is simply another species having some effects on its environment, and, indeed, in its hegemony it must be viewed as an especially successful one. That this situation has been wrought primarily by capitalist economic systems (*sensu* Wallerstein 1983, including socialist nations) is, of course, actually part of the indictment of Darwinian cosmology, which has had reciprocal inspiration from capitalist economic theories all along. Finally, if these activities lead ultimately to human extinction, that is neither more nor less than the fate of at least 80% of the species that have ever existed, and since in this cosmology there is no way to privilege our own place in the world there can be no anguish about this.

Developmental Cosmology

As I pointed out earlier, what I am calling 'Darwinian cosmology' has since the early Greeks been opposed by another conception: developmental mythology. Figure 6.2 presents a comparison of some aspects of these systems of thought. The first five chapters in this book can be used as a preliminary groundwork for describing developmental cosmology, and the rest of this chapter will be devoted to making the implications of this world view more explicit.

I should review what I am trying to accomplish here. First, I claim that Darwinian cosmology has ethical and moral implications that make it unsuitable as a framework for imagining our own particular coming into being. Since it appears that no cosmology not informed by science has any hope of attracting people in the future, science (and particularly biology) must be examined with the intent of finding an alternative world view. In other words, we cannot just go ahead and invent one; however ethically and morally edifying it might seem to be in contrast to Darwinism, it could have no credibility with the scientifically sophisticated. Opposition to Darwinism must be legitimated by discourse, not just made up out of discontent.

But even a slight search in the literature of biology uncovers a whole other perspective, which also has roots in physics and in the study of complex systems. In other words, we can mine from this literature not

	Darwinian cosmology	Developmental cosmology
perspective	externalist	internalist
attitude	objective	subjective
relation between observer and system	decoupled, but sufficiently complete observation	integrated, but incomplete semiosis
system intelligibility	fitting pieces	totalized around observer categories
metaphysics	cause and effect (mechanistic materialism)	self-reconstruction/self-organization
system state	at or near equilibrium	nonequilibrium
final causes	fitness increase (selection by consequences)	entropy and information increases
major process	evolution	development/individuation (evolution by reconstruction)
structures	none	immature→mature→senescent
major kind of change	historical irreversibility	developmental irreversibility
scalar hierarchy formed:	bottom up, open at top	top-down by differentiation coupled with growth
agency	none	in all dissipative structures in some degree

Figure 6.2 Table comparing Darwinian and developmental world views in terms discussed in the text.

only another version of the world, but what seems to be *the* other version in the sense that it is contradictory to Darwinian cosmology on every important point (figure 6.2). Its moral and ethical implications are not clear to me yet, since I have not lived with it as long as I have with Darwinism; the point is only that there has been another, forgotten, and so occult, cosmology biding its time in the stacks of libraries.

Because both of these viewpoints are carried unconsciously, as it were, in scientific discourse, it is likely that they represent a deep cognitive dichotomy (entrained by the split brain?) out there in our minds—at least in the "Western" mind. Furthermore, it appears that developmental cosmology itself mirrors cognitive processes as modeled by H_{sp}. Darwinian cosmology, on the other hand, since it seems to be an attempt to pare away everything that is not necessary to a foundation appropriate for attempting to dominate nature, is too thin to mirror anything complex. It is the metaphysic you get when you attempt to get rid of all metaphysics (whether you claim it or not; indeed, some might say, if so, that makes it true).

Developmental Trajectories

The concept of the developmental trajectory embodies both H_{sc} and H_{sp}. It is the continuity and cohesion of an enduring, changing entity as seen from a cogent moment that covers its entire existence. (See figures 3.6, 4.7, and 5.4 for visual impressions.) This means that, if the observer is at a given level, either the trajectory (as when referring to organisms) or momentary cross-sections of it (as when referring to electrons) would have to be constructed out of theory, depending on whether the observer is smaller or larger in scale. The trajectory has one end at what from a lower scalar level would seem to be its inception (e.g., the origin of gradients in oocytes for our own beginnings) and ends with its extinction, when its ability to entrain matter comes naturally to an end.

Quoting Lemke (1991): "The system, as an individual entity, cannot be defined at one moment in time because the dynamics which maintain it in being must occur over time. In each instant the system is dead; only over time is it alive. So much is true for any dissipative structure. . . . Only the system extended in time along its complete *developmental trajectory*, from formation to disintegration, from conception to decomposition, is a properly defined theoretical entity. . . . The caterpillar-pupa-butterfly is one individual developing system. . . ."

All dissipative structures can be viewed as being parts of, or as being entrained by, such trajectories, which exist at many scalar levels. The view of electrons developed in quantum-mechanical theory is (I feel) a possible example of a kind of small-scale trajectory (with respect to us). Trajectories are the fundamental entities in developmental cosmology. They connect with us (and so to our own personal trajectories) through their momentary manifestations—dissipative structures of every kind, from those smaller than electrons (which appear to us *as* trajectories) through those bigger than galaxies (which appear to us as almost unchanging places). Dissipative structures are our signs of the existence of other trajectories, and supply their momentary material connections and integrities.

One unexplored peculiarity of trajectories is that, at the level where they exist whole as individuals, they do not exclude one another in the way their associated dissipative structures do at lower scalar levels. As trajectories, they interpenetrate completely and in complex ways. As momentary material embodiments, we need to be deployed in ways consistent with a material tactfulness that forbids more than one macroscopic body from occupying the same geographic coordinates at the same (one of our) moment(s). Trajectories, on the other hand, from what we can tell about them now, might interpenetrate promiscuously in other dimensions.

Trajectories locate unique individuals. At the level of what we call their material embodiments (that is, at scalar levels below where they would be perceived whole), their determinability increases as they individuate. Their growing individual particularity, however, does not interfere with their logical concreteness, which they gained through the greater generality of the logical types of their earlier developmental stages. This concreteness is continually reintegrated under the increasing complication that is attendant upon becoming more determinable. It is integration that supplies the cohesion of the trajectory, and here we see the importance of H_{sp} to understanding trajectories.

The number of levels of specification integrated under a particular dissipative structure roughly reflects the number of major developmental phases it has passed through since the inception of its trajectory. This means that the information stored in a trajectory increases during the existence of its lower-level manifestations. This information involves (a) historical information associated with increasing determinability and with the agency of associated dissipative structures and (b) information associated with the type of the system involved (including genes for organisms). This too increases with the duration of a trajectory, insofar as more and more complicated material embodiments must be constructed to allow continued deployment of a trajectory's structure in space/time.

Trajectories integrate their own existence and create the conditions necessary for their own change—that is, they self-organize as physical embodiments (chapter 5). This they do through stored information of various sorts as well as through local pulses of the immaturity → maturity → senescence structure from stage to stage (chapter 5). A basic structure of all trajectories is one that, when read out in the physical world (that is, the world at our own scale), stretches from immaturity through maturity to senescence. This is what they "look like" from the thermodynamic/infodynamic perspective taken in this work—both locally, over short periods of our time, and globally, over the whole of their existence. No doubt these relations are fractally deployed throughout the world.

It is interesting to note that in Darwinian cosmology there is a thin ("life history") interpretation of this structure (referring to organisms only) in terms of a relationship between natural selection and reproductive value such that the age with the highest value is bolstered most by selection (and, therefore, continues to accrue reproductive value), while those ages with the least value (senescent) are continually deprived of value (*ceteris paribus*, of course). This deprivation is what is held to produce senescence. In other words, senescence is not a major structural fact of physical systems, as it is in developmental cosmology, but a local product of natural selection. Once again we see that nothing exists for Darwinians except what was produced by selection.

Every individual dissipative structure is connected to every other at any given moment through their trajectories. These connections are based on the relation 'not-being-different-from'. At any given developmental stage or phase, dissipative structures are not different (disregarding potentialities, which differ between types) from a host of other individual structures in different Rylean categories (see figure 5.4B). This emphasizes their concreteness at a given moment, a property that extends back into more general logical types.

Figure 6.3 attempts to show how our ability to make these connections, which can be called *self-reconstruction*, grows as we individuate. As the observer becomes more determinate, it is able to relate (functionally) to more and more different kinds of dissipative structures. (Naturally, e.g., a bird's egg could be destroyed by something it could not relate to—say, a weasel or a gale.)

The expansion of the potentiality for relating is enabled by the increasing amounts of stored information possible (and necessary) at later stages. This increased stored information is indicated in the figure by the retention in each stage of earlier constraints at lower and lower integrative levels (the white circles)—each figure is the whole individual, while the gray portion marks its increasing determinability at higher integrative levels experienced at the present moment. As more levels are broached, the scope of relatability enlarges because each stage pushed back into lower integrative levels forms the basis of acquired understanding at that level.

Other Rylean categories leading out from these earlier-stage conditions represent the trajectories of other kinds of dissipative structures one could relate to. Figure 6.3 is intended to show that other dissipative structures that are encountered (lined up along the bottom of the figure in stages 5 and 8) can be related to because of the totalizing power of the property of integration. Integration is comprehension. This is a difficult point; as biology integrates chemistry, it also comes to understand (interpret, reconstruct) it—e.g., through taste and odor gradients, through heat and cold, and through pain. Understanding is a bodily relation. Presumably something like this must be true for other dissipative structures too, but we are in subjective discourse here.

Thus, the self-organization of developmental trajectories involves, not only self-driven increases in determinability riding on increasing

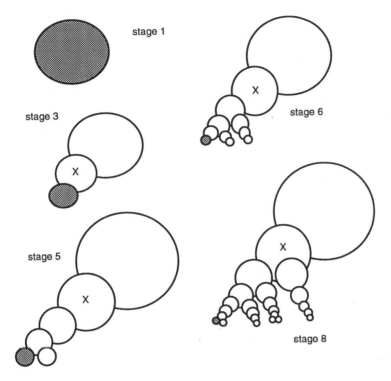

Figure 6.3 The self-reconstruction of relations with other dissipative structures. The gray tone signifies the individuality of the observer at different levels. X marks a given developmental stage or homologous integrative level. Initially wholly absorbed in its own trajectory (through stage 3 here), the system gradually makes contact with more and more distantly related kinds of structures as it constructs its being in the world. In this process it reaches back into its own more general attributes for an understanding of others, establishing concrete relations with them. The possibility of understanding based on kinship broadens with age because there is more information that could be used for this stored in older individuals.

complication, but also an increasing potential scope of sympathy riding on that same growth of information. The form of this sympathy is a tree (figures 4.3, 6.3), and we might note that cladists have worked out objectified techniques for estimating its potential intensity. As we age we should be able to stretch into remoter pleisiomorphic states (suggested, perhaps, in figure 2.6), where we can find forgetfulness closer to the continuum of mere being itself. The difference between "sympathy" and "forgetfulness" here is a matter of emphasizing for the first the fact that we are connected to the multitude through common, deep nodal states, and for the second the fact that this connection must be vague and relatively unformed.

Senescence

Of crucial importance to the developmental world view, senescence is the end of all developments. It is the ultimate information-congested metastable state from which a system is either recycled or (rarely) entrained as a part into new, higher-level emergences, which then extend its stability. Given the material conditions on dissipative structures, it is what is produced by the final causes acting in a system—the Second Law and the various type-specific and teleological (see below) informational configurations. Senescence is not itself a final cause but a *cul de sac* formed by the finitude of any local information storage—too much information crammed into a system with limited channels and decaying energy flow. The attractor of developments, which inevitably draws them into senescence, is total specification or absolute mechanism, a condition that would require completely stable environments.

Senescence has a dual role in our considerations at this point.

First, it is the too-awful fate that all of us educated as Darwinians conspire not to think about as much as possible. This construction has not failed to influence scientific theories of development and evolution, which, by and large, have been constructed so as to avoid any allusion to this last of the "ages of man." Darwinian cosmology avoids it by construing change as endless because structureless—or construes change to be structureless so that it can be endless. Given sufficient variability, a system can continue to evolve forever, ideas of "racial senescence" having long since been sent packing (Simpson 1949). Developmental biologists have not found senescence very interesting either. The giddy pace of change in immature systems has held their attention for over a hundred years now. True, the political connections of aches and pains have forced moneys to be spent on gerontology, but it's all very dismal and not a likely locus for swinging breakthroughs. My attempt in this work has been to call attention to the structure of change, and this brings senescence back, not with a whimper, but a bang. We have clean missed the import of what we all so much fear!

Second, the important connection of senescence to mechanism needs to be pointed out. Senescence systems are increasingly more determinate, more highly specified. After consulation with computer scientists, I have ventured (1989a) a definition of 'machine' to the effect that it is the most highly specified object there can be (bearing in mind that nothing complicated can be fully specified in any feasible environment). All natural dissipative structures are attracted in this direction, but even the very stable and elaborate (e.g., organisms) get recycled long before they arrive at this condition. (Yet an old man, for instance, does show a passing resemblance to the Tin Woodsman!) The reason is that machines have little or no flexibility, little of that requisite variety, and so require support from other scalar levels in order to survive (Conrad 1983). An automobile would have to be constantly tended within its enclosing society if it were to become a valued "golden oldie." Brains in vats would require elaborate technological support—but what could be done when they started repeating themselves endlessly, stubbornly insisting on their own habits? If the discourse of artificial intelligence succeeded in constructing a mind, it would be a senescent one.

Now, mechanicism is an important aspect of the Baconian/Cartesian/Newtonian/Darwinian/Comtean world view. If the world could be constructed as a machine, we would be able to tinker it into shape. This project is beginning to look like a failure; thus, it may be time to point out that, informed by the structure of change, we can now see that most dissipative structures in the world are further from being machines than even we humans are. Gradients, fluid vortices (including the musical spheres), glaciers, and cloud formations are, if anything, the opposite of machines—tychistic vaguenesses. Perhaps atoms or protons are machines? Since it cannot matter in our relations with them, we can have it any way we want with them.

Yet the final cause of the BCNDC world view, the noosphere (Vernadsky 1945), will, on the infodynamic view, indeed be closer to a mechanism (Wesley 1974) than any ecosocial system before it. This would explain why computers have been installed everywhere even though in every instance known to me they initially resulted in job losses *and* poorer service (through errors and machine downs)—that is, in the immediate derogation of institutions. This is no longer puzzling if we view the long-range "purpose" (teleological final cause) of computation as being not to improve matters for human organisms (something we might be lured into believing while working at our PCs) but to facilitate the senescence of the surface of the Earth.

In science as it has been, systems were taken to be either mechanistic (senescent) or stochastic (immature)—necessity or chance (Salthe 1990d). Mechanism was so far from observational intelligibility in so many cases that it became necessary to find another condition for the world that could still allow mechanicism to drive the imagination. Statistics does just that; mechanism is here modeled by average conditions, and we have a nice way to measure just how far away from our ideal a system is—the variance. With this tool a cloud can be construed to be a kind of clock! In Darwinism the mean is the attractor of selection; *its* value is what fits like a screwdriver into slots in the natural world. The brilliance of Darwin's insight was to suggest how all that nonmechanical messiness of actual variability not only was not bad for the understanding but also is needed to afford the evolution of mechanisms. Nature, like Edison, is constructed as a tinkerer (Jacob 1973) with a variety of junk lying about in all that variability, ready for use.

What Berman (1981) called the "disenchantment of the world" (see also Merchant 1980) can here be read to have formally been the jettisoning of the notion that all material systems (including plants and hurricanes) attain maturity in favor of the immature and senescent constructions for all but adult humans. Mature systems are quintessentially agents, and the instrumental world view would have been hampered by having to deal with such things. Instead, immature systems are always—and need to be—pushed around, while senescent ones are so habit-ridden as to become potentially predictable (if their environments could be stabilized, as in the laboratory). Immature or senescent things provide just the right objects for BCNDC cosmology, and generate a reasonable role for mechanistic science: control and domination, or at least anticipation, on the model of our actions with respect to our own human-made machines.

A liberated post-medieval Aristotelian world view might have evolved into a cosmology of mature agents, but it seems that our vaulting ambitions for control and gain put us on another road (Ignatieff 1984) instead.

Organism and Organicism
For both Hegel and Whitehead, the organism was the fundamental kind of entity in the universe. If we have eschewed mechanism, and if we are unwilling to leave materialism behind, this seems to be the available attitude. Historically, organicism in biology (Bertalanffy 1933; Haraway 1976) was generated partly by the realization that vitalism made sense only in the context of mechanicism (Bertalanffy 1933; Van Der Veldt 1943) and partly by the nonintelligibility of mechanism itself in the face of biological phenomena. The arrangement of organic matter became for organicists the source of life's phenomena, and the study of relations rather than of matter became the focus, giving rise in the event to general system theory (Bertalanffy 1968), and, I believe, contributing as well to structuralism (Piaget 1970a; Laughlin and d'Aquili 1974).

I have claimed (1985) that H_{sc} is structuralist theory, implying the immanence of gaps in the material world. And since H_{sp} has close connections with organicism (Salthe 1988), we see in this discourse too an outgrowth of the Hegelian-Whiteheadian perspective. Levels of all kinds are structures. And they describe relations. I believe, however, that they are intimately entwined with material causes as well. For example, it was probably not purely fortuitous that a fully organismic degree of complexity emerged at a particular narrow range of scales (Salthe 1985, pp. 265–272). From the perspective of the present work, this would have involved a nice relationship between the longevity of dissipative structures (tied importantly to their rates of dissipation) and the amounts of information they could store before becoming overburdened.

Large-scale entities, while no doubt having ample storage facilities, develop so slowly that they are perturbed back to immaturity, or recycled, by occasional effects of amplified smaller-scale fluctuations before they can reach interesting, mature stages. On the other hand, small-scale entities senesce into mechanism almost instantly from our point of view, given the higher rates at which they behave. Organisms (like Goldilocks' porridge) seem just right. In any case, the scale of our perceptions, tied to our own range of cogent moments, allows us to see the maturity only of entities at our own scale. And so the observer connection rears its head once again. That which is just right is the observer in her majority; anything of a clearly different scale tends to be either too young (if huge) or too old (if tiny).

And, of course, these categories are the fundamental ones in the present (infodynamic) discourse. Entities find themselves entrained into the transformation sequence immature → mature → senescent. They begin experiencing the world as physically simple things like whirlwinds, generating entropy at a great rate and simultaneously, perhaps, building themselves up out of environmental affordances. Those that can get that far reach majority with strength and effulgent agency; after this, they senesce into complicated, deliberate, highly individualized but sluggish entities, losing agency only because they are more and more easily pushed about by environmental excursions. These transports eventually end in obliteration, but may, rarely, entrain them into the immaturity of some larger-scale dissipative structure, preserving them longer, extending their agentive existence at their own level, but now dependent on (or from) these higher-level processes (like a heart patient in a modern hospital).

Semiotically, systems begin immersed in symbolic play, their highly random motions allowing them, as they cool down, to become entrained by higher levels through selection by consequences. It is primarily in immature systems—relatively hot, insignificant, and unformed—that selection operates as a major factor in the developmental world view, not everywhere as in the Darwinian view. Because they are small and weak, and their motions highly random (though probably chaotic), immature systems can be coralled by affordances and tendencies in their environments. Because these constraints are to a large extent highly contingent, their conformity to them is *symbolic* only—they might just as easily have conformed to other large-scale tendencies instead.

As a system matures, it finds itself both entrained by discourses (here used as any restraint lesser than the laws of nature: that is, restraints that might have been otherwise—figure 3.7 suggests how far this may be generalized), and, because it has grown to larger size, experiencing more intensely the frictive secondness of buffeting and collisions with more other things. In contrast, small immature systems would have simply been gently wafted about by many of these same impingements (as a feather floats in the wind that blows down a tree). A system's entrainment to some of the larger-scale processes in which it is embedded becomes converted from being hauled along by the scruff of its neck, so to speak, to commitment to what we can take to be projects in the Sartrean (1960) sense. A *project* is a commitment capable of engaging a system's agency; an example at the organismic integrative level would be the impulse to mate, which makes it important that I (as a particular individual) mate rather than him.

Since a system tends to be larger and more powerful in its maturity, it can be thought of as being capable of contradicting its earlier entrainments; however, it remains loyal to some of them (now under its own steam). Semiotically, it has become immersed in *indexical* necessities, because, being larger, it cannot avoid forces it was oblivious to when smaller, and because, if it avoids being torn apart, it must be committed to (coherent with) something, which might as well be some of what it has already been involved in (i.e., historical constraints). The symbolic play of immaturity has been replaced by indexical necessity relative to multiple integrities. Interestingly, Foucault saw maturity as relating to the insights of an agent into its connections in the world (Poster 1989).

The semiotic interpretation of senescence is that there comes once again to be immersion in symbolic play, but the situation is more complex than in immaturity. The system's own agentive moves are highly constrained now by habitual tracks; we could speak again more of entrainment than of commitment, but now to internalized authority structures. Probably partly because of its curtailed energy flow intensity, its rich information store is used to bolster these superstitions rather than for variable explorations. The system has therefore become informationally overburdened, with much detailed flow at cross-purposes because of the great variety of its internal fluctuations (based on the large amount of stored information), not all of which can be synergetic with the system's biases. Subroutines and subtexts emerge that generate {cognitive dissonances}; the system becomes paralyzed and rigid, only to be swept away by environmental shocks.

A senescent system would have plenty of the variety requisite for flexibility in relation to its environment, could it but deploy that variety effectively. Aside from the relevance of its reduced intensity of energy flow, this it cannot do, since that variety, being variety, is mostly anticoherent with its own restricted strong {convictions}. And so the system becomes a plaything of its environment, a token in discourses entirely symbolic to it because most are unaligned with its much-narrowed needs. Immature activity is symbolic because it could be attracted in many directions—given many or any meanings—with little material constraint. Senescent translational motion becomes symbolic again because the system is being hauled about by forces beyond its control, and to which it can assign no valid meanings in its narrowed system of interpretance.

So I am claiming that the ontogenetic transformations discussed in this work ought to be a basic aspect of organicism. Since, upon generalization through infodynamics, this structure seemingly becomes applicable to other, perhaps all, dissipative forms (chapter 3), an aspect of Whitehead's "organic mechanism" concept (Plamondon 1979) seems to be realized—namely the notion that organisms (today we might equally use the term 'ecosystems') are the basic material units in the world, not the bald particles of "materialistic mechanism" (Whitehead 1925). Mythological monism, then, is achieved in developmentalism by extrapolation from organisms and their ontogenetic trajectories, rather than from machine pieces. In developmentalism, mechanisms have become the ultimate attractors of developments in the sense of limits that are never reached by natural systems before they get recycled. Most natural systems are taken to be suspended *"entre le crystal et la fumée"* (Atlan 1979). Of course, people have constructed machines, and these became central in Darwinian cosmology because of their attractive clarity (= explicitness); however, once we enter into complex systems we must ship that metaphor to some more remote role.

A major mythological expectation of developmentalism is that nature is (or continually becomes) orderly at all scalar levels, rather than remaining deeply stochastic. What seems to be natural random behavior—say, Brownian motion—would here be interpreted instead as chaotic—that is, when it cannot be attributed to observer/actor ignorance (finiteness, bounded rationality) in the face of complex systems. This, of course, contrasts with the Darwinian view that order is a secondary result of selections' supposed "creativity" (Mayr 1963). Perhaps this is the deepest formal division between these world views; emotionally, developmentalism moves out from love (Peirce 1893), while Darwinism coolly manipulates instrumentalities.

So, at this nexus, the philosophy of organism (organicism) and structuralism (with the major structure in question—the specification hierarchy of stages of development—coming from Plato and Aristotle through Schelling and Hegel) potentially come together. Historically, the philosophy of organism was explicitly formulated to contrast with mechanistic materialism, and so was structuralism in some hands (e.g., those of Piaget). I am claiming the potential unification of these discourses under the rubric 'developmental cosmology', opposed, as these components have always been historically, to mechanistic materialism. Selection becomes relegated largely to immature systems; mechanism becomes an unrealizable attractor in the limit of development.

Final Causality and Teleology

Lenoir (1982) makes a case for the idea that the important strain of teleology in biology, carried mostly by the German tradition, derives from Kant and has little to do with Darwin's objections to the use to which teleology was put by Christian apologists such as Paley. In fact, one could take the approach to teleology in the present work to be a section of the beginning of a new range in this Kantian discursive formation, one that backs up through Schelling and Hegel in its deeper strata.

Kant's view that mechanism is insufficient to explain biology could be taken as embodied in the basic triadic system of H_{sc}, for here mechanism is relegated only to cause-and-effect relations within one scalar level (Salthe 1985). Relations across levels are precisely non-mechanistic, informational constraints. Furthermore, final cause is embodied in top-down relations between higher and lower levels. In particular, since the cogent moment of a higher level that is dominant at the inception of a lower-level trajectory still continues at the higher level when that lower-level trajectory has been played out, one can say that constraints from the higher level not only help to select the lower-level trajectory but also pull it into its future at the same time. Top-down causality is a form of final causality.

I cite Nicolis (1986, p. 89) to show that final causes are not missing in all the modern sciences: "We conclude that the self-force arises not from the direct action of the [electron] source upon itself but from a collective property of the advanced action upon the source caused by the 'future' motion of the particles of the absorber." The reader might consult Wheeler 1988 as well.

Lenoir points out that the final cause of ontogeny in Aristotelian biology was the whole organism functionally adapted to its environment. In the present work, H_{sp} is conceived in much that way, although the final cause is not fixed but continually self-organizes as the developing system individuates (though it could be said usually to culminate in the organism at its majority). But, more carefully, the teleological final cause in biology (and of any dissipative structure) would be the fully individuated particular system, which, of course, is never achieved in natural environments before recycling. Hence, this final cause continually recedes before material attempts at its realization.

Furthermore, therefore, final causes in H_{sp} are unique individuals, not types. But no material embodiment ever gets to become fully individualized; this would be achieved only when a system becomes fully determinate and completely specified. Balme's (1987) discussion suggests that this question of how general ontogenetic final causes are was handled ambiguously by Aristotle himself.

I can stipulate more fully what teleology amounts to in infodynamics by using Lenoir's classification of the kinds of teleology. It is closest to his third category—the views of Aristotle, the *Naturphilosophen*, and Hegel—in the sense that it applies not only to biological systems but to all dynamic systems; the world itself is modeled on biology, not on billiard balls. It is, in this connection, immaterial to me whether the perceived patterns of nature (structuralism) or the motions of matter (tychism) are taken to be logically prior. I take these alternatives to be resonating truths, viewed alternatively from structuralist and constructionist perspectives. As long as the movements of logic and of matter are isomorphic (as in my matching of generality with vagueness in chapter 4), the relation between discourse and the world can be viewed either way, or dialectically. (I hope I have adequately distinguished discourse from the world rather than conflated them throughout this text—though that conflation *is* done all the time, since discourse about the world is still only discourse.)

There is one further constraint here, however: The developmental perspective that emerges from this realm of discourse views discourse as being able to be fully embodied only at more inner, more highly specified stages of development. (See Wheeler 1988 for a quantum-mechanical reading of this idea.) From this, it necessarily postulates conditions of matter, characteristic of earlier developmental stages, wherein discourse is (was) only immanent, not manifest, or, looking at it from another angle, that it is implicit in the motions of simple dissipative structures. Hence, one would have to suppose the possibility of planets where logic is only immanent and/or implicit, having not been explicitly realized (yet) by any complicated-enough material systems.

Infodynamic teleology has some relationship with Lenoir's first category as well. I quote: "All that was required to transform Haller's vitalism to a teleological approach was the further restriction that a specific vital force depended completely upon the organization of the constituent elements of the organ exhibiting it. The force was not to be conceived as some independent entity but rather as an emergent property dependent upon the specific order and arrangement of the components." This, which Lenoir calls "vital materialism," would be the case in infodynamics if one understood the "vital force" as being explicitly expressed in matter only after its emergence but—and this is the difference—also as being present before that as an immanent structure to be potentially accessed. Lenoir's use of "emergent property" clearly refers to what I have here called "developmental emergence"—it has no connection with uniqueness. Since, as I hope to have shown in chapter 5, this kind of emergence involves predictability, it formally must involve a potentiality (i.e., a structure) prior to any particular realization in an individual dissipative form. However, as conceived here, teleology results precisely in the realization of a uniquely specified entity. This, however, rides on developmental emergences, which could be said to be individuation's material cause.

So, H_{sc} and H_{sp} both involve final causality. In H_{sp} this can further be read as teleological; a developing system has its own particular realization as a final cause beyond those, such as the Second law or the construction of science, that affect everything.

Referring back to figure 1.2, we can make teleology more precise by noting what it is not. Here teleonomy and teleomaty (O'Grady and Brooks 1987) are shown as progressively more general versions of the same concept as teleology. Since I have claimed that abiotic dissipative structures show teleological leaning into their future forms just as much as do living systems, how shall we parse these words in that context?

Since teleomaty (essentially physical variational principles) refers to the fate of all system—e.g., to the increase in entropy of the universe—this would not be teleological even in connection with human discourse that might exemplify it. This level of variational necessity is shared by everything; there is nothing "personal" about it. In its turn, teleonomy refers to function; functions are *classes* of relations. All circulatory systems function in certain same ways; again there is nothing personal, even though it is a much more complex idea than the tendencies of variational principles. Teleology in infodynamics refers precisely to the actualization of unique individual identities at whatever integrative levels their discriminatory powers are capable of reaching—to individuation, to self-determination. Any self has its own individuation as its purpose—and that would include ecosystems as well as nonhuman organisms. (As is noted in Salthe and Salthe 1989, this could allow any dissipative structure to have moral considerability.)

As I noted above, final cause can be taken as the source of integration in H_{sp}. What other force, indeed, could be advanced to explain how society regulates biology and biology chemistry? The molecules inside an organism are there because they have been taken in by the biological system, and the constraints they meet are biological constraints. Again, in a society, how else did the constituent organisms come to exist except through the agency of the society—minimally a temporary society of mates in an ecosystem? It now seems clear that the reproduction of prokaryotes, too, takes place in elaborate microorganismic ecosystems (Shapiro 1988), and probably could not occur naturally otherwise, since these environments afford the kinds of conditions that humans provide for some bacteria in laboratories.

Final causes are informational constraints. And they may be viewed as teleological without confusion; an organism can be said to want to persist, and so, on the basis of both H_{sp} and H_{sc}, can a population or an ecosystem, with respect to which "want" modulates to 'tend to' as a synomym of {{want}}. Molecules find themselves in an organism *in order to* further that organism's interests; people drudge in cities in order to further those cities' interests. In both cases the encompassing system constrains, regulates, controls, and interprets the behaviors of those nested within it merely by forming the superstructure for their activities. If one were to insist that this could not be the case for water particles in a hurricane, one would in my opinion have to justify that belief—for that is what it is, no less than the belief revealed here. In mechanist constructions such an idea cannot make sense, and as long as mechanism seems fully intelligible one could not believe this about hurricanes. But when mechanicism is given up, other perspectives—including the one reintroduced in this work—become possible. Rather than look upon dissipative structures as kinds of machines constructed from the bottom up, we may view them as kinds of organisms with poor discriminatory power; thus, the logic of organisms is transferred to them, including the logic of top-down integration.

In this logic, integration is read by the observer as implication (more accurately in a material context, conceptual subordination). Integration is a physical condition; implication is its logical sign. An earlier stage is the logical consequent of the later because it becomes incorporated (with modification) into the later. That is the meaning of finality and teleology in H_{sp}. We ourselves, then, are logical consequents of a large number of possible aged systems that we might become, all members of the same logical type (see figure 2.8) defined by reference to what we are now as the basal node for any of them. This set of possibilities becomes more and more constricted as the end approaches. The always-diminishing potential future of dissipative structures is the structure of multiple-worlds ontology as viewed from H_{sp}. Once we are into the logic of trajectories (chapter 4), the simultaneous existence of many of them with a nexus in one dissipative structure and its self-organized past becomes possible, even if boggling to minds dulled by mechanism.

Semiotically, we see that firstness is the affordance of a sign by a referent—say, in stage n, the sign itself not appearing until stage $n + 1$. This affordance is labeled 'ontology' in figure 3.5; ontology is the affordance of signs and so is prior to them. During secondary interactions, signs bring about interpretants in a system of interpretation; this is labeled 'epistemology' in figure 3.5. Epistemology (or, indeed, hermeneutics) is the interpretation of signs. Both epistemology and abduction (secondness and thirdness) are involved in integration and implication. Hence, an interpretant is required (as makes sense semiotically) not only for, implication, but also for integration. (See also Wheeler 1988, especially figure 1.) In other words, stage $n + 1$ is an interpretation of stage n, and development is a concatenation of interpretations. Its strongly habitual nature in living systems is due to particular kinds of historical information stored in the genes, which limit interpretations to a narrower generic band of possibilities (but with many more possible specific variations) than would be available to abiotic dissipative structures.

Some Applications and Implications

I would like to conclude this section by showing how certain current conceptual problems look different from the perspective of developmental cosmology. Consider the controversy concerning abortion. If trajectories are "real," then potential selves are impoverished upon abortion. Aborted trajectories would have only the general characteristics of types, because only a small portion of their structure would have been individuated in history. Is this tragic? Well, every actual history negates an untold number of potential selves in the same logical type; this seems formally little different from abortion, and would appear to be an inevitable loss—it is only as tragic as is any narrowing of possibilities brought about by any choice.

Is it unethical? Since trajectories are of larger scale than the organisms that are their manifestations, the latter (we ourselves at any given moment) can hardly have any ethical obligations with respect to them. As well, referring to the progression through stages in ontogeny when viewed from H_{sp} (e.g., figure 3.3), it has been shown here that early embryos are not members of the same logical types as adults (although the reverse is not true—figure 2.8). A "human" blastocyst is not human; it is no more than an animal, more or less—that is, it exists at an animal level of integration (is not materially different from blastulae of other animals). This refers, of course, to what it is ontologically from the perspective of H_{sp}, which does not take into account potentialities, of which, formally, a blastula would have many besides just becoming human. Intersestingly, in a 1990 report by the American Fertility Society reported in *Nature* (June 11, 1992: 425–426) it was noted that because the blastomeres after three divisions could give rise to three different persons, "at the 8-cell stage, the developmental singleness of one person has not been established." Developments always move from a vague condition toward one of many possible particularities.

So, if humans can butcher chickens without this being an ethical problem there would seem to be no reason to consider abortion an ethical problem. Ethics tends to refer to relations among ontological equals. Abortion is a momentary decision/event imposed upon the natural gradient of a trajectory—as is any discursive classification, including the designation 'human'. In performing an abortion we are not acting unreasonably within the logic of H_{sp}.

That logic, working itself out in directions similar to the reproductive-value concept of Darwinian cosmology, would have an individuals' humanity continually deepening as long as his or her trajectory continued to exist. So, a child has no richness, only heat and potentiality. Later, a mature individual has species-specific properties that allow for the continuation of the biological kind, and pronounced individuality could just as well get in the way as facilitate that job. Individuality becomes functionally really important only as the organism peaks over maturity and starts moving toward minimum specific entropy production. And it is in fact such persons primarily that work on the construction of human sociocultural systems. Embryos have no role in this at all. So, since they have no say, how could they have rights (Singer 1986)?

But is it immoral? This becomes the interesting and difficult question. Moral alignments can only exist with respect to higher-level entities. Trajectories are, precisely, higher-scalar-level entities with respect to dissipative structures. Now the question becomes: Can a person have an immoral relationship with another person's trajectory? I cannot hope to do other than indicate some directions of thought in relation to this question. First, we can personally relate to another's trajectory only through our own in a relevant system of interpretance—that is, in a higher-scalar-level system that contains both of our trajectories. Depending on the situation, that could range from a natural ecosystem to an elaborate, "civilized" society.

From the point of view of society itself, given its scale with respect to human individuals, trajectories, *and not the individuals embedded in them,* are its components. This is a deep meaning of the fact that laws, regulations, and discourses extend beyond any one of our organismic cogent moments. Rules and habits are, precisely, the cohesion of a society, and their structures relate to it at its own scale. Yet, as informational constraints they are capable of bridging scalar levels and having entraining effects descending down upon the momentary organisms themselves, regulating us.

If the rules of society evolve to include the possibility of explicitly dealing with trajectories, then it could certainly become possible to consider the termination of another's individuation as immoral as well as tragic, however little it could be unethical. Possible, but of course not necessary—otherwise the deliberate disruption of trajectories in punishments and wars could never be allowed. And, of course, these are allowed precisely for the purposes of societies, not, except secondarily, for the purposes of persons. And, obviously, arguments concerning the good of society could be advanced also concerning abortion in an overcrowded situation that threatens society's existence as a self—that is, that threatens to change it radically. So, it could be possible to construe abortion as actually moral. I conclude minimally that discussions of abortion are questions or morality, not of ethics.

To extend this argument a bit, consider now questions concerning the meaning of meditation. This is a new practice in our society (in the sense of being part of the general social consciousness), having been introduced by various groups originating in "the East." As such, it is a colonizing concept—one that has the possibility, being "foreign," of entailing "dangerous" consequences for our society as it is. In figure 2.6 I attempted to suggest that meditation is considered in at least some Eastern discourses as being what amounts for us to a return to a mind at a lower integrative level, or, equivalently, to the mind of an earlier developmental stage. In this way it can entail, for example, the leaving behind of local pain, connected as that is to the specifics of everyday complexities in highly integrated systems. Thus, if one's mind drops below the level of awareness of the body (becomes more vague), it could, e.g., entail relaxation and the removal of pain due to muscular tension. One no longer "has" a shoulder, as it were, any more than does an embryo.

Now, in H_{sp} we would consider that this is achieving a state of awareness not unlike that of an embryo. We can come, therefore, into immediate sympathy with these controversial beings. And what is it like? It is a mind, as inummerable works of Eastern mystics have effectively been telling us for a long time, that has no interest in human affairs (indeed, no interests at all—'emptiness'). It is a state unrelated to ethics or morality (hence the distrust mystics seem to have engendered in the semitic religions). It is a mind expanded vaguely across neurons; indeed, it is almost believable that such a condition would not require neurons at all, so that we might consider, for example, that even trees might be "meditating."

Perhaps it is significant that in the Hindu tradition one takes up this practice conventionally when one's overt contributions to society seem to be ebbing. The lowered energy-flow intensity of the elderly is perhaps well suited to this condition of relaxed mind expansion. Not only do the elderly become more physically entropic, like embryos (chapter 4); they may be able to achieve embryonic mind states rather better too. One recalls as well the symbolic value of Chinese and Japanese descriptions of monks who had achieved the state of childlike happiness of a Ho Ti.

If these ruminations were to inform our thinking about abortion, we might see that society might "reasonably" deal with embryos as being directly and actually unconnected to furthering its interests. These are beings with hardly any connection to society's actuality. To the extent that exploring their mind states might contribute to society, this task could be undertaken by the elderly through meditation. Hence, embryos retain only their, as it were, reproductive value, which is reasonably high with respect to the biological component of sociocultural systems.

It seems not unreasonable that society might undertake to regulate organismic population growth in people just as it does in cattle and laboratory rats. Biology is *society's* dimension, not the reverse. Continuing an examination of applications, we can now examine the problem of the origin of life.

The Infodynamical View of the Origin and Evolution of Living Systems

In infodynamics living systems are viewed as dissipative structures stabilized by genetic information. Hence, abiotic dissipative structures are their precursors, and so the swirling fluids and dusts in other astronomical bodies foreshadow life. Fox (1986, 1988) has shown that dissipative structures of cell-like proportions (proteinoid microspheres) are capable of performing most (and possibly all) of the activities of cells known to us (though not all under the same conditions). Francis et al. (1978) showed that the protocells of 3.8 billion years ago, before the presence of microorganisms, were very likely just these microspheres.

Wicken's (1987) thermodynamic considerations (see also Weber et al. 1989) are in line with this approach. Ehrensvärd's (1960) thinking brings this approach into ecology, as it were, suggesting that such macroscopic configurations as ponds and eddies were, episodically, as conditions allowed, the first "living" systems, inasmuch as there were then no entities smaller than they with sufficient complexity to carry out the living functions (which were limited selections from all possible physical and chemical events, enhanced later in biological systems by differential catalysis). Ecosystems literally were organisms.

Macroscopic configurations would, under these conditions, provide the thermodynamic potentials necessary, and also the substrates for appropriate kinetics. Corliss' (manuscript) considerations with respect to deep-sea vents represent a more recent approach of the same kind, stressing the environmental arrangements necessary for biological activity. Cairns-Smith's (1982) replicating clay formations might well have been microscopic components of this phase (which might be called the "living pond" phase), setting the stage for a future "genetic takeover."

Because of a recent resurgence of the Darwinian RNA-first scenario that is opposed to the above system-first approach, a few words of appraisal might be appropriate here. That some RNAs have catalytic properties (Waldrop 1989) was welcomed by the predominant nucleic-acid school of protobiology. This could allow the genetic reductionism of Dawkins (1976) to be extrapolated (along with the ideologically important notion of selfishness) back into prebiotic times.

The fact that nucleic acids are not easily formed spontaneously is assimilated by the notion that, if there are long enough time periods involved, anything can be brought about accidentally, combined with the reasonable enough (though indeed structuralist) idea that more than one configuration could serve as a sign of something, and, in any case, certainly as a sign of itself. This is just the logic here; any genetic information that arises is its own explanation if it can successfully help in its own production. (Molecular configurations are thus the "persons" in this neo-Darwinian discourse.)

I believe that no arguments will ever heal the breach between the systems-first and genes-first camps, because they are ideological positions taken up partly in dialectical response to each other. I would merely say that, without the superstructures referred to in the systems-first approach taken here, the early RNAs would have had nothing to compete for (deDuve 1990). It is also true that the systems-first approach would never get to life as we now know it unless there came to be genes to undertake the genetic takeover that clearly has happened here on Earth. Discourse is forever dialectical, and personalities will continue to supply their material causes. A systems-first person would say that life is too complex to be viewed as popping into existence with the first distinguishable RNA variant. That person would prefer a gradual emergence as being more in line with the dignity, mystery, and wide-connectedness of living systems. RNA variants seem, in comparison, more like marionettes.

For an understanding of *why* these transformations leading to the origin of life took place, we can refer again to the idea that elaboration of form can allow greater entropy production (Swenson 1989a,b). Only a few chemical pathways were enlisted, were packaged into compartments of the environment that later evolved into cells, and thereby were bestowed with an efficiency of substrate demolition that resulted in a chemically hotter surface of the Earth than could have been possible in a microscopic soup of Babel. In this way we see the origin as having been elicited by that ultimate final cause, the Second Law. This general idea allows us to explain the continuing complication of living forms during subsequent development of the surface of the Earth as well. For example, arthropods originally had no mouth parts; they lived by absorbing food from decaying matter. The evolution of legs allowed them to bore into this stuff more rapidly, which allowed for faster decomposition. The subsequent modification of their anterior legs into mouth parts increased their ecological entropy production even further.

This idea, whose pattern is quite similar to (and, indeed, provides an explanation for) the erstwhile Williston's Rule of organic evolution (Berg 1926; Lull 1917; Osborne 1918; Rensch 1960; Simpson 1953), gives us one aspect of the impulse for a differentiation model of the development of the surface of the Earth. First there was an ecosystem of molecules and macroscopic dissipative structures. Then there occurred an interpolation of more and more scalar levels (cells, colonies, multicellular organisms, colonies of multicellular organisms, and so on) as the degree of specification and discriminatory power of the entities involved increased.

This increase was facilitated by acquisition of the genetic system, which allowed greater detail to be stable in the face of increasing entropy production, wherein molecular subsystems were getting burned out at higher and higher rates. In this way living systems could have infiltrated ancestral abiotic ones when proteins and nucleic acids replaced clays and other microscopic information storages, and in this way it may come to pass that the noosphere will infiltrate the biosphere (figure 5.2) insofar as its information storage and processing capacities come to surpass those of the biosphere. (See Moritz 1990 on the last point.)

The relation between the origin of life and the ecological and genealogical scalar hierarchies appears to have made its debut as a controversy. Eldredge (1985, 1989) takes the view—as did I in 1985 (and see figure 4.1 in the present work), and as do also Weber et al. (1989)—that the ecological hierarchy (energy-flow systems) is primary, giving rise to the genealogical hierarchy at the point of genetic takeover. This is consistent with the system-first perspective. I infer that Brooks et al. (1989)—compare their figure 4 with figure 4.1 here—would take instead the view that virtually all ecological structure is a result of biological activity, emphasizing the fact that biological systems have modified (integrated) almost every aspect of the surface of the Earth— the presence of oxygen being a notable example. This is the import of versions of the current niche-construction program (Odling-Smee 1988) as well.

Aside from the social-constructionist interpretation such a position might have (minds make the hierarchy, and minds are biologically based), it seems to me now that this difference is primarily a matter of emphasis within a single, coherent discourse. That being so, I presume that Brooks et al. would accept my figure 4.1 as a reasonable representation of affairs on, say, a planet where genetic systems had only recently emerged. A personal communication from Brooks seems to support that, although he is troubled by the idea (asserted in this text) of ecologies existing in the absence of life—that is, that ecology is less specified than living systems, existing fundamentally at a lower integrative level. Failing this accommodation, Brooks et al. would have been asserting a kind of dependence of the physical world upon the biological almost in the way that Wheeler (1988) asserts its dependence upon cognition—this decidedly *not* being the social-constructionist view. That would have been a daring (and interesting) inference from the structure of H_{sp} and the final causality associated with it.

During the development of the surface of the Earth there has been an increase in the diversity of the biosphere (Bonner 1988) that is understandable under the second developmental rule of thermodynamically open systems given on page 111 above. Although that rule predicts such an increase only weakly (that is, the rule could have been satisfied if the surface of the Earth had become increasingly elaborately filigrated without the generation of different kinds of biological organisms), it can be taken as concordant with it; as such it is a fact of development, not of evolution (or a fact of general evolution, not of specific evolution).

But, since this was actually accomplished by the evolution of new, unique configurations of matter, it could be referred to as evolutionary as well, and it is so treated within the present discourse by Brooks and Wiley (1988). Organic evolution occurred as part of the individuation of the developing surface of the Earth. Development at a given scalar level is often, perhaps always, accompanied by evolution at bracketing lower and higher scalar levels (chapter 4). There need be no resolution of this controversy for it to have dialectical force within the discourse.

Coevolution

Figure 6.4 is an attempt to sketch a systems view of the development of biological aspects of the surface of the Earth after the origin of life. It uses a sequence of integrative levels illustrated by currently existing systems that are at about the appropriate level of integration for their place in the sequence. So, the figure can be read as if historically earlier degrees of integration are located at the lower left, with the historical trend being traced up to the right and then continuing down to the left again. The movement down to the left from the upper right can perhaps best be taken to move out from the surface of the paper so that the figure makes one turn of a helix, in this way suggesting further possibilities for the biosphere (or some successor, such as the noosphere). Less ambitiously, the figure can merely be thought of as a series of integrative levels becoming more highly specified moving up to the right, and then becoming more inclusive at the higher degrees of specification moving down to the left, in which case it could be taken as illustrating overall trends of coevolution.

At the lower left we begin with relations that were already present before living systems appeared, and which formed some of the material causes in their generation. Living systems inserted themselves into various parts of these cycles, as with the nitrogen cycle. Soon after the origin of living systems proper, photosynthesis based on chlorophyll a began to produce large amounts of oxygen. This radically altered the hydrosphere, then the lithosphere, and finally the atmosphere, eventually becoming balanced by the burial of organic matter, which takes oxidized products out of the atmospheric cycle. Conversion of the more or less stabilized amounts of oxygen to carbon dioxide by heterotrophic metabolism, once it became efficient, set up a very diffuse, inclusive relationship between most photosynthetic autotrophs and all heterotrophs.

Relations between animals and plants concerning seed dispersal are very vague and inclusive; any animal can serve as the carrier of a burr,

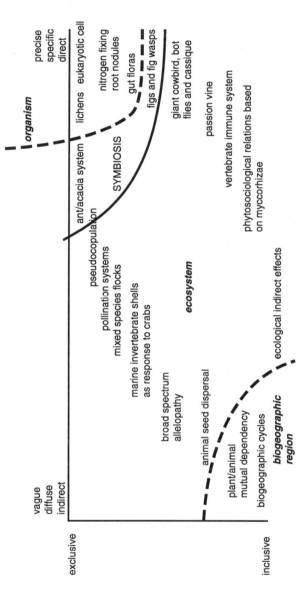

Figure 6.4 Coevolved systems of varying integration. The least integrated occur in the lower left corner, the most highly integrated in the upper right. The track from lower left to upper right can be taken as a model of the developmental tendency; that from upper right back to lower left on the right can be taken as a model of a hypothesized extension of highly specified relations to increasingly more species in relatively undisturbed ecosystems—the development of a superorganism. The thick dashed curves show boundaries between organismic, ecosystemic, and biogeographic regional scalar levels. The thinner solid curve shows the boundary of symbiosis (living together intimately) proper. The axes are marked with adjectives suggestive of degrees of specification and integration.

for example. As a slightly more restrictive example, a large number of kinds of animals could serve to disperse seeds embedded in the fruits of a given plant from their guts or their feeding behavior, it requiring only that they be frugivores. The production of various toxins, noxins, and other sorts of substances by plants can also have quite general effects, keeping off all but highly specialized parasites.

The elaboration of protective shells—a widespread evolutionary response of marine invertebrates to the predation of crabs (Vermeij 1987)—is a case where a very general effect is elicited by the presence of a single group; I therefore take it to be a more highly specified example than those below it in figure 6.4. Possibilities for joining mixed-species flocks in birds and fishes are more restrictive, there being size factors involved as well as style of movement. Pollination systems tend to be fairly unrestrictive because of the needs of pollinators for flowers throughout the year or the season. And, while some kinds of pollinators prefer certain kinds of flowers, as with red tubular ones for hummingbirds, the latter can be quite catholic in their tastes as the occaison requires or permits.

Pollination carries us into some very specialized examples, however. Some species of orchids, in particular, are completely dependent upon their pollinators—usually, wasps. The males of these wasps eclose before the females and wander in search of them. The orchids bloom at just the time when females are scarce and mimic them in form, odor, and habitat location. The wasps do not use floral products economically (and orchids rarely provide any). In fact they are briefly parasitized by the plants, pollinating them as they attempt to mate with the blooming imposters.

At this point we cross over into the realm of symbiosis. In the relations between the bull horn acacia and various fire ants (Janzen 1967; Thompson 1982), the plant, again, is totally dependent upon the insects, and cannot be grown even with human care without them. Several species of fire ants are capable of facultatively taking up life in the tree. Here they are provided nesting sites in the swollen thorns (each with a preopened entrance hole!), nectar from extra-floral nectaries, and protein food for their maggots in the Beltian bodies produced at the ends of some leaflets. The tree has gone out of its way evolutionarily to provide suitable quarters for ants (as have many other kinds of "ant plants"), while the ants provide protection from herbivores and competing plants and perhaps some further substances acting to promote the health of the tree. Lichens are too well known to merit more than a nod here; they include a number of possible facultative and obligate partners to the relationship that produces the thallus.

The eukaryotic cell is perhaps the epitome of symbiotic systems (Margulis 1981)—in this case, various prokaryotic partners. None of the cell constituents remain free-living, and all are highly modified for life together—their relations are precise, specific, and direct. To think of the eukaryotic cell as a minute ecosystem is revealing as well, and, indeed, I would suppose that theoretical treatments of ecosystems (like that of Ulanowicz (1986)) will eventually be applied to cell physiology as well. This is the most highly articulated ecosystem we know of. Moving now to expand this degree of intimacy to relations involving metazoans, we can note the symbioses of legume roots with nitrogen-fixing bacteria and of termite guts with flagellates. These are placed this side of the canonical eukaryotic cell in figure 6.2, rather than with the lichens, because all these relations appear to be obligate for all species involved; we have an expansion of obligate symbiotic relations to mixed kinds of living systems.

Working now to see how such obligate relationships have expanded more and more widely among components of macroscopic ecosystems, we can proceed to the fig wasps, each species of which has an intimate relationship with a different species of fig (Wiebes 1979). The males never leave the fruit at all; they die after they fertilize the uneclosed females and after chewing an escape hole for them to use after they have collected pollen from the now-blooming male flowers in the developing fruit. After they leave, the females enter a reproductive organ at an earlier stage, wherein are blooming the female flowers, which they pollinate while laying their eggs on the ovules. This relationship involves several more species—in particular, certain parasitoid wasps. If their maggots did not eat most of the fig wasp maggots, the latter would completely devour the seeds contained in the fruit. In other words, the figs would have gone extinct solely under the ministrations of fig wasps, whose numbers are kept in check by the parasitoids.

A similar case, but one with a sense of extending outward to even more species, involves the Central American giant cowbird and its hosts, the oropendulas and the cassiques (kinds of orioles—see Smith 1979, 1980). This cowbird, like its close relations, is a nest parasite, but here the harm done by its congeners is both obviated and compensated for. Baby cowbirds behave in such a way as to push natural offspring out of the nest so that they alone come to be fed by the victimized parents. Only species that have evolved various countering behaviors have been able to survive this onslaught. The orioles involved with the giant cowbird have baglike nests from which their young cannot be evicted. Furthermore, the young cowbird is even an asset, because of its propensity to feed on botflies that enter the nest in order to parasitize the chicks. Oriole nests without a cowbird chick actually fledge fewer young on average than those that had such a guest, because of the depredations of the botflies. Now, some populations of these orioles nest in the vicinity of hives of stingless bees. In this environment there are few botflies, presumably because of their aversion to the bees. Here too the giant cowbird attempts to parasitize the nests, but in these populations the orioles have evolved countermeasures against them: they build a floor above the first eggs and lay a new clutch. In response, the local giant cowbirds have evolved egg mimicry, which is absent in regions without stingless bee nest neighbors. Here we see the presence of a fourth species changing the value a relationship had in the context of only three species.

Turning briefly to an even more complicated system, we can note that each species of the passion vines (Turner 1981) has a rather large suite of other species more or less closely involved in its affairs. Some of these relations are obligate, others facultative, but the system gives one a feeling for how tied together the fates of many species can become.

Despite plentiful toxins, each kind of passion vine has associated with it a species of heliconid butterfly which uses its leaves for food in the caterpillar stage. The toxins are incorporated into the tissues of the butterfly, protecting it in turn from bird predation, in connection with which it has brilliant warning coloration. It must be emphasized that this relationship with birds is stabilized because they are not killed by the toxins, which only render the butterflies unpalatable. The birds are educated through classical conditioning to avoid butterflies of this kind, requiring only occasional reinforcement to maintain their aversion. Only periodically is it necessary to educate naive birds, largely fledglings.

For most butterflies, nonlethal handling by birds is not so great a problem as it is here, because these heliconids must survive for significantly longer periods than other butterflies, this being required because of the growth habits of the passion vine. The vine tends to grow here and there episodically and unpredictably (seeming to be almost furtive), so a butterfly must be on hand for a long time in order to find one of these growing points before being able to lay her eggs. In fact these butterflies last long enough so that, after successful reproduction, they are joined by their daughters, and, in fact, they form a small society, sharing their knowledge of potential laying sites. These vines grow in jungle clearings, and so tend to be isolated from one another by habitat unsuitable for the heliconids.

In order to be able to last as long as they do, these butterflies, unlike most kinds, require protein food for tissue repair. They utilize the pollen of a species of wild cucumber vine for their food, thus serving as pollinators of that plant, with which they have a mutualistic relationship. This vine seems to have become modified for this relationship by its peculiar flowering habits. It produces male flowers continually in order to attract its pollinator, even though it is only occasionally ready to grow new fruit—at which point it produces a few female flowers, which are efficiently pollinated because of the continuing presence of heliconids.

In the meantime, the passion vine is busily making it difficult for the heliconids. One trick it plays is the production of extrafloral nectaries from its leaf bases. These attract, of course, ants and wasps, including parasitoid wasps. Ants are notoriously unfriendly toward other insects that feed on their food plants, and harass any caterpillars they run across; and of course the parasitoids, having had a drink, will not be averse to dropping an egg or two on some conveniently nearby caterpillars. So, here we have a system of two plants, a butterfly, several kinds of ants, parasitoid wasps, and birds, all of whose lives are closely interwoven in a "dialogue" or integrity between the butterfly and one of the plants.

Complicated systems like this must take a long time to evolve, and, significantly, most of those we know about are found in tropical regions, whose ecosystems we have reason to believe are among the oldest and stablest on Earth. Here we meet an example of the idea that emergence (in this case, into potential large-scale superorganisms) is tied to stabilizing conditions from a higher scalar level (in this case, the Earth's climatic regime.)

Now let us move to a very different kind of intimate relationship. The vertebrate immune system is very wide-ranging. Every vertebrate is capable of having an intimate (indeed, molecular-level) relationship with an uncountably large number of other species (and, indeed, with individuals of its own species—in fact with any individual of any kind that may come into contact with its mucous membranes, including its mate(s)). This remarkable ability seems to have been a prerequisite for maintaining complicated macroscopic bodies for significantly long periods of time in the face of microorganisms. Otherwise pathogens of various kinds would invade and overcome any large system. And the system was required to have its astonishing sensitivity and range because of the rapid mutation rates that can be achieved by microorganisms. As a consequence of this sensitivity, even one's own fetuses may be attacked by the system and need special protection. One could say that, without this or some similar system, there could not be complex communities of macroscopic organisms, and so it is in fact a component of such systems.

A system that might be almost as complex and have almost as large a range is the system of underground connections between plants in a community by way of fungal hyphae connecting their root hairs. Different plants associate with different fungi in these mycorrhizal relationships (St. John and Coleman 1983). The spatial extent of such a system at a given moment is massively larger than connections through individual immune systems, and, indeed, may well be found to be the basis of a superorganismic web of communication somewhat like a giant nervous system. At this time details are known for few individual species, and the system is placed here on the basis of what I take to be its potential rather than what can be demonstrated now.

Finally, we can consider the possibilities of indirect effects, which can range from fairly local (Sih et al. 1985) to global (Patten and Auble 1981; Pilette 1989). Local effects can be seen in keystone predators (Paine 1966; Gilbert 1980). Consider, for example, that a crab may prefer to eat a certain kind of snail. The snail feeds on a seaweed in which the crab hides. Where crabs are absent, the snails devour all the seaweed and move on; thus, there are either all three of these species or none, the determining (keystone) species being the crab. Temporary springtime ponds may harbor salamander larvae. Where they do, there are also certain midges, whose larvae feed on small-bodied species of water fleas. There are also large-bodied species of water fleas upon which the salamanders prey. Where the salamanders are absent there is only the large-bodied water flea, which outcompetes the small-bodied one. So, there are either four species or one, depending upon the presence of the keystone predator, the salamander. Wilson's (1980) discussion of group selection in respect to the presence of earthworms provides a Darwinian format for thinking about indirect effects.

Indirect effects bring in the possibility that whole ecosystems could depend upon the presence of a few particular dominant or key species. This kind of relationship is again inclusive and diffuse, but now it is based on a core of precise, intimate relationships. A large ecosystem containing many subsystems like that of the passion vine could be constructed around several such indirect-effect systems. Whether such highly integrated ecosystems could then serve as nucleating individuals for the initiation of the development of a larger-scale superorganism is, of course, moot at this stage of our knowledge. There is nothing formally against the idea; it might, however, require unusual boundary conditions, probably including benign, predictable large-scale environments, the like of which might not occur often on planets having living systems.

The examples just given can be used to exemplify what Brooks et al. (1989) and Brooks and McLennan (1990) mean by the idea that genealogical relationships structure ecosystems. But what Weber et al. (1989) mean by the idea that ecological relations preexisted genealogy is that the basic structure of these relations, however elaborated eventually by genealogy, preexisted living systems (just as chemical reactions preexist the enzymes that catalyze them), and, ecologically, are large-scale physico-chemical gradients into which living systems were inter-polated, and which, after that, could become ever-more-finely filigrated. In other words, ecological relations are massively simple but can be ever-more-finely teased out by being harnessed by genealogical information.

The difference that still remains among workers in this new dis-course can be nicely summed up by quoting a personal communication from Brooks: ". . . [figure 4.1 in this book] represents something that Brooks and Wiley would accept as an accurate portrayal of the manner in which various components function in complex . . . ecosystems. They would not, however, accept the proposition that organisms *originate* in the flow-through of energy rather than in the production rules provided by the genetic information that feeds on that flow-through to produce . . . organisms." As Brooks notes, this is a point that has not been definitively worked out, and, indeed, the origin of life has not yet been examined extensively from an infodynamic perspective. In any case, a new discourse ought to show much divergence at its inception, during its immaturity.

Figure 6.4 then, shows an infodynamical conception of the develop-ment of a complex individual at a large-scale, macroscopic level—of a superorganism, in fact. The origin of life as conceived in this discourse would be represented by a similar series of stages, but we do not now have examples that could be used to illustrate that process. In contrast with figure 6.4, the stages in that other figure, if it could have been produced, would have been illustrated by actual historically sequential examples. Cairns-Smith-type clay systems and "living" ponds would appear somewhere in the ascending arm on the left, the prokaryotic cell would appear where the eukaryotic cell appears in figure 6.4, and stromatolites and other prokaryotic communities would appear some-where on the descending trajectory to the right.

What figure 6.4 shows is a transition from vague, diffuse cascad-ing/collecting cycles loosely intercalated into preexisting inorganic cycles to precise, elaborated cycles which have facilitated the produc-tion of more heat from the surface of the Earth, followed by the gathering of these into ever-larger-scale, and presumably ever-more-thermodynamically-proficient, networks.

Now, the viewpoint presented in this chapter is obviously far from that of most biologists. It is an attempt to confront the complexity of the world, whereas biology, in common with other branches of BCNDC science, has been an attempt to simplify it. Since what is "real" depends upon consensus among the workers in any field, it can be said to be an unreal scenario for most biologists, as well as a messy one, and that must be admitted. However, what I am claiming for it is not that it is (or could be, or should be) convincing to most biologists right now; rather I am claiming that there are no facts, in biology or in any other science, that could prevent it from becoming a plausible view under some social conditions. Its purpose would not be to support technology and economies; rather, its purpose would be an understanding commensurate with a postmodern, postindustrial, senescent world. It is stated as an empirically and logically valid formal alternative (with respectable historical depth) to the present instrumentally based Darwinian cosmology (so well matched to immature social systems!), which I hope I have characterized fairly in its turn.

Summary and Conclusions

In this chapter I have presented the basis for a Western, science-based creation myth, explicitly posing it against the established "Darwinian" one in order to show that a plurality of myths (i.e., suites of interesting compatible theories having to do with our origins) could be derived out of science. The fact that this different mythological matrix is as old as the Darwinian one shows us that the latter cannot be taken as canonical in its role; evolutionary biology need not be Darwinian (Salthe 1989b). The reason we ought to consider this important is that evolutionary biology's role in our socioculture appears to be primarily to generate believable myths for the skeptic.

It was of extreme interest to me to find that the alternative myth that had attracted my efforts is a new transformation of a really old formation (figure 2.3). The experience of "confirmation" (*pacé* Popper) upon this discovery was an instance of the joy (experienced by me only twice before) associated with doing science. I would say that, with all the reservations we must make about confirmation, the multiplicity of subdiscourses shown in figure 2.3 justifies saying that the possibility of making the infodynamical constructions discussed in this book itself forms a kind of corroboration of the point of these earlier discourses. The present work is both Aristotelian and Hegelian as an inheritance from that earlier formation. As it seems, one of the messages of this work is that we have never gone completely away from either Aristotle or Hegel. If we had, one supposes, their discourses could not have been reconstituted and extended as herein, based on recent developments. No doubt a structuralist ethnographer could show us how this philosophical perspective is built into our system even as fully as is the Darwinian one.

Another reason why we might consider these points important is that the dialectic between Darwinian and developmental cosmologies is reflected as well in the deeper aspects of many of our current political problems. Our contradictory cosmologies reflect the same structural bases as the oppositions modern/postmodern, human/particular group, and identity/difference (Eagleton 1990). I have in this work sketched the main configuration of this opposition as the complementary pair development/evolution. This opposition can be found in almost all discursive formations, but perhaps it is at the point of being able to be explored in greater detail at present in biology than anywhere else.

Appendix

The Constructive Universe and the Evolutionary Systems Framework

Juan Alvarez de Lorenzana

The inclusion of this addendum does not imply that its author necessarily supports the metaphysical and ideological orientation of this book. It is included because it represents more formally detailed proposals (comparable to those of George Kampis) for the development of H_{sp} than I can undertake. The reader should note that the words 'development' and 'evolution' are used somewhat differently in this appendix than in the body of the book (see chapter 3), and that the metahierarchy described herein embodies both scalar and specification aspects.—S.N.S.

A framework is here put forward to deal with the representation and explanation of a universe (U). It will be assumed that 'constructiveness' deeply characterizes U as well as systems definable within it.

The problem to be addressed is subsumed within systems theory and arises as well in information theory, although it is not explicitly stated there or recognized in its entirety. Previous attempts to deal with it (Alvarez de Lorenzana and Ward 1985, 1987) were not as fully realized as is intended here. It is a question of the ever-present lack of unifying principles among qualitatively different entities.

What would happen in the world of infinite sets in mathematics if we erased the concept of cardinality while maintaining (in a Platonist vein) all the sets available before erasing it? How could we relate, without theory, all the qualitatively different sets, and not risk relating elements belonging to sets of different cardinality? The work simply could not be done—unless we went to pre-Cantorian mathematics. And even there we would need an ordering principle that would distinguish between different number systems. The reason for the existence of these ordering principles in mathematics is that knowledge is constructed of the ability to relate and make distinctions; if knowledge in mathematics is increased, it would be relative to its ability to relate and make distinctions.

I assume a real world already there before human discourses. The hypothetical situation of sets of different cardinality without knowledge of them would be an analogue of this in the world of mathematics. We are in a world about which we know very little. A typical scene in any part of our world is a number of objects, different in quality, interrelating constantly and everywhere. What ordering principle—or set of principles—will allow us to negotiate this thick web of different qualities while maintaining a certain sense of orientation and purpose?

What we have now are pockets of knowledge of various kinds but, critically, with dramatic conceptual isolation between them. Quoting Rosen (1985b): "The infatuation of contemporary physics for this kind of degeneracy and non-genericity (referring to the usual closed, isolated, conservative systems) goes quite a long way in explaining the scandalous absence of any important relation between even the most powerful theories of physics and the most marginal biological phenomena."

Consider then the following.

There is no match between our limited explanatory power and the enormous range of qualitatively different manifestations of reality.

This may be compared to a field where there is a balance between the world of interacting objects and the world of theoretical constructs enabling their understanding and representation—in other words, where growth in the number and complexity of objects corresponds to growth in explanatory power and theoretical synthesis.

This comparison helps us to measure, in a more tangible way, the immense difference between the situation in a field of coherent knowledge (such as mathematics) and the situation in fields dealing with the real world.

The problem we need to deal with is a major and complex one: the *lack of ordering principles*. By that I mean rules (i) allowing distinctions among qualitatively different objects and (ii) permitting the ordering of such qualitative differences.

In attempting to outline broad principles, we need, first of all, to define their context of applicability, and this itself is not a simple issue. The proposed hypothesis is that, for the world of real objects, the whole physical universe, U, is the smallest context in which an ordering principle regulating qualitative differences among entities can be defined (in their coming into being as well as in their interrelations). Considering that differences in quality are the outcome of evolution, any ordering principle has to cover the full range of phenomena to which that concept applies. The "ordering" ranges in scale from the system, U, to the smallest manifestation of systemic individuality, and, in terms of evolutionary time, from the Big Bang to the very instant in which I am preparing this text and beyond.

I noted at the beginning that the proposed problem has been present in systems theory and information theory. A brief comment on this: The main core of systems theory deals with systems that are partly—substantially—in isolation; they are in isolation from the past and from the future, and they are also isolated by the way in which interconnections between system and environment, and system and other systems, are understood or defined. Having no deep and general ways of carrying, within the definition of a system, its essential record of evolutionary history, it seems that any attempt to represent subtle qualitative differences between systems would have little validity. If the theory does not provide sufficiently general links among its bearers, then we are condemned to deal mostly with limited and evolutionarily short-range phenomena.

The situation in information theory is different only in the way it is perceived. Shannon's theory of communication (Shannon and Weaver 1949) is defined in terms of given sources of information, with the encompassing system having no bearing on it. At one time this was an important development because it permitted a formalization not available before, when source and system (i.e., semantics and syntax, or meaning and sentence) were combined in confusing ways. As noted before (Alvarez de Lorenzana and Ward 1985), Shannon's formalization was too restrictive to be general, formally condemning the sources to isolation from informational systems as well as to isolation among themselves.

The Constructive Universe

The main assumption to be put forward in this appendix is that the universe, U, if it is to be considered in the variety, the complexity, and, at the same time, the coherence known to us, can be understood and explained only if defined as a *constructive universe*. By "constructive" I mean that variety and complexity can be obtained only by processes of manipulation and combination, operated on and by the initial, given, U. These are understood to be processes increasing the levels of differentiation as well as resulting in the accumulation of structure; those two; together with their linking factor, will be represented as subject to law.

Before going further, I wish to explicitly justify the *necessity* of dealing, from the outset, with *the whole of U* if we want to be able, later on, to represent or explain any specific (evolutionary) system. The reasoning is as follows:

In a constructive U, the ways of constructing will either be first principles or be deducible from them. Therefore, an attempt to explain any particular constructible system (e.g., an evolutionary system (ES)) has to pass through the unveiling of general (universal) principles.

General principles, although necessary, are not sufficient. We also need ways to reflect the unique specificity that each constructive system has. We would be facing an insoluble problem if there were no way of linking general principles with the particular, which is the stuff of actuality and which therefore needs representation among the real.

The link between the general and the specific is brought about by a chain of cycles, the end of one cycle being the ground from which the next cycle will emerge. In other words, apart from the initial U there is no constructive or evolutionary system that does not have its roots in a previous, less specified ES.

Evolution of and within U takes the form of a constructible "metahierarchy" (Alvarez de Lorenzana and Ward 1987)—a chain of evolutionary cycles with, ideally, no missing links.

Only by aiming at the most general—and deepest—principles of constructability will we be able to understand and explain the specificities of individual ESs. Keeping in mind the dichotomous nature of universal constructability (undifferentiated vs. differentiated), I have taken the view that our problem requires three basic principles upon which construction can be defined and take place: two principles of systemic unfolding (one dealing with the undifferentiated, the other with the specific) and one dealing with the way in which their conjunction will take place. These elements will form the *Evolutionary Systems Framework* (ESF).

ESF presupposes a new language (constructivist, discrete, and finite) and a new formalism (see the *addendum* below) that would allow us to represent our particular hypothetical frame.

It is necessary to be clear about the hypotheses and the way they are presented in this appendix. These hypotheses reflect the results of a process of internalization of certain phenomena by the author. The usefulness of this work derives from the way these phenomena are perceived, understood, and explained. In other words, what is at stake here is (1) a certain way of perceiving actuality and (2) a certain way of abstracting structures from that perception. The formalization of those structures and their eventual testing and evaluation are not within the scope of this appendix; on these matters, see Alvarez de Lorenzana 1988, 1990, 1991.

We are in a time of transition; old structural frames do not work sufficiently well any more and new ones are still to come. We need a new frame with enough synthetic power to give a "general representation of the world, one having a structure capable of dealing with transformations" (Salthe 1985, p. viii). Such a frame does not come from experimental activity, which is basically an analytical tool; it comes from a rethinking of reality, from seeing things differently, from a different perspective, a new set of principles or axiomatic structure. This can be done only by invention. It has to be, most certainly, an informed invention (i.e., one first and foremost well rooted in existing problems, about which it needs the available knowledge), but it has to bring with it the discontinous and intuitive jump of invention. There is no safe way to do it; invention is never safe, but can be accepted if it works.

Constructability was started by Gödel's 1938 paper on *constructive sets* (see also Devlin 1977, 1979). I quote a definition from the original field: "*constructivism* (earlier term:

intuitionism): The doctrine which asserts that only those mathematical objects have real existence and are meaningful which can be 'constructed' from certain primitive objects in a finitistic way (i.e., in finitely many steps). This was associated with the Dutch mathematician L. E. J. Brouwer and his followers." (Davis and Hersh 1981, p. 413)

On discrete mathematics and its relation to continuous approaches, see, e.g., the 1980 monograph issue of the *International Journal of General Systems*.

The recent literature on formalism (Bastin et al. 1979; Atkin 1971, 1977; Voorhees 1983) is in my view incomplete because it deals only with what I call 'systemic combinatorial expansion' or with what I call 'systemic generative condensation'. I have dealt with this limitation elsewhere (Alvarez de Lorenzana and Ward 1987).

The subject of this appendix is the hypothesis itself, from which the need for a proper new language and formalism arose. I say "new" because, to my knowledge, apart from work within the theory proper (i.e., constructive mathematics and some theoretical issues in computer sciences), there have not been many attempts to use it to represent reality.

The Evolutionary System

The essential characteristics of an ES are the following (for further details see Alvarez de Lorenzana and Ward 1985, 1987):

> ESs exist in a universe, U, which is itself an ES.
>
> ESs are defined in terms of set of basic properties. The systemic activities (input-output) that result from the conjunction of those properties are called *system components*. ESs interact only by means of appropriately scaled components (within the system or between the system and the environment).
>
> An ES can be defined only on a certain given environment, and only if that environment is sufficiently stable with respect to the ES's defining properties. This environment is called the *global systemic environment* (GSE).

Previous to the production of any ES, its GSE has to have a distinct zone with boundary conditions permitting the production of an ES. This restriction of GSE is named a *presystemic environment* (PSE) (figure A.1).

The only kind of interaction that exists in U (i.e., all systemic activity for all ESs) is *discrimination* (Dc). This very basic operation is capable of providing subtle richness. To discriminate is nothing more than to systemically acknowledge the presence or absence of something akin to a system.

To define Dc as the only mode of interrelation throughout U implicitly imposes a condition on the (internal) structures of all ESs, including U: If ESs relate within and between themselves only through Dc, it is because they have a discriminating device that gives (or acts as) a sufficient representation of both ESs and their respective GSEs (Ashby and Conant 1970). Moreover, an ES could be defined operationally only in terms of the set of discriminations plus some boundary conditions given by the PSE.

What is a Dc device? Basically it boils down to a point (or set of points) of reference, although of a very special kind. It refers to all the basic properties of an ES, providing the necessary infrastructure to relate these properties to the context in which the systemic interaction takes place. These significant points of reference could, with propriety, be called "gauges"; nevertheless, because they refer to basic characteristics of the ES which are present throughout the whole GSE, it is preferable to call them *global properties of the system* (GPS). Note that GPS are the properties present within the whole of the GSE; and, conversely, the conjunction of the GPS will be able—in principle—to constructively define the GSE. We could also think of the GPS as a basis and the GSE as the vector space spanned by that basis; the Dc device might be thought of as a normalized basis.

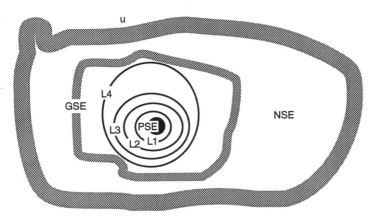

Figure A.1 u = universe; GSE (global systemic environment) = that part of U that is, or can be, discriminated by the evolutionary system, ES. PSE (pre-systemic environment) = a restriction of the GSE where sufficient boundary conditions are given for the production of an ES. L_1, L_2, . . ., (levels) = systemic developmental unfolding through successive combinatorial expansions. It is important to note that the GSE is only a "potentially" definable entity, materialized by the construction of the different levels of combinatorial expansions. NSE (non-systemic environment) = that part of U that is not system definable.

The Dc operation determines not only the structure of the ESs but also the way in which ESs model their environment. The Dc devices, on account of their relative simplicity, are forced to model their surroundings in a certain way. Starting from the most elemental discrimination, one must deal with the great diversity of the environment; in other words, ESs need to build diversity from their simple set of gauges. As was mentioned above, this construction of diversity from an initial undifferentiated unity is an essential characteristic of ESs, imposing a condition of gradualism. These statements seem very close to those of Spencer-Brown (1969). This necessary condition of gradualism helps us to deal with the danger of information overflow, something to which Ashby (1958, 1962, 1965) dedicated so much brilliant work (see also Conant 1981). The excess of information flow (related to Salthe's "senescence" in the present work) can, and in general will, provoke systemic breakdown and even collapse.

The gradual autoconstruction of form that allows the system to interact with the diversity of the environment comes into being as a chain of nested levels, each of larger scale, as the ES accesses its potential universe, the sequence representing an increasing richness in discrimination (i.e., a process of refinement). Such a chain is itself a structure, formally known as a *hierarchy* (figure A.2A). There are many types of hierarchies; in our case, where the Dc operation is used for the construction of diversity from the simple, it is called a *combinatorial hierarchy* (H_c) (see Bastin et al. 1979).

An essential feature of the H_c is that the construction of the chain of levels always has a limit. This limit will come from the particular context in which each real process takes place, but in all cases it will have to do with the relation between system and environment. The most common case is when the ES, in its process of expansion through the environment, comes to a point where its normal systemic activity is no longer feasible, owing to a lack of efficiency and coherence: an overextended (senescent) ES cannot act and react with the required speed and accuracy.

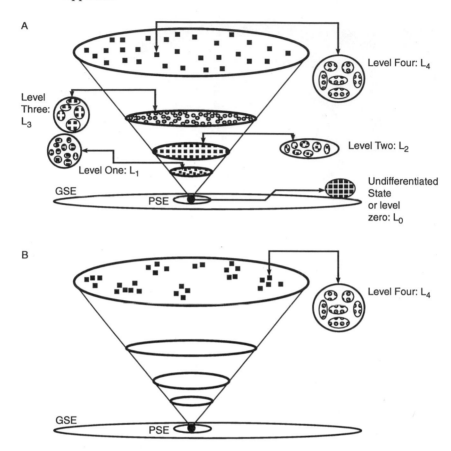

A

Level Four: L_4

Level
Three:
L_3

Level Two: L_2

Level One: L_1

GSE

PSE

Undifferentiated
State
or level
zero: L_0

B

Level Four: L_4

GSE

PSE

Figure A.2 The elements of each new level are made out of combinations of elements of the previous level. (a) this shows the chain-like nature of development. The link between levels represents systemic time (not clock time—see Richardson and Rosen 1979). The circles are microscopic views of different levels of development. (b) The weak coupling of the highest level tends to provoke an initial dispersion of system components. Eventually this turns into a regrouping which allows the system to appear externally as a stable entity while internally it is a new ground for system construction. Weak coupling allows the possibility of qualitatively new ESs coming into being.

Also, the limit can come from the environment, by not affording enough room for the expansion of the ES and, therefore, not allowing its development—in other words, by pressure from the ecosystem if it is (in comparison to the ES) quantitatively more powerful or evolutionarily more evolved or a combination of the two. I have in mind as an example social systems where there is constraint on expansion because of national boundaries; the outcome has historically been either restricted development (as a consequence of not overriding the preimposed systemic boundaries) or development proper (by breaking boundary constraints—most generally at the price or at least the risk of war with neighbors and local or global powers). The second scenario can be seen as pressures from larger neighboring countries (e.g., Uruguay *vis à vis* Argentina or Brazil) or countries that, if not larger, are more developed. Greater development than the surrounding states allows the possibility of imposing pressure on others for their own benefit (e.g., Israel *vis à vis* some neighboring Arab country). Examples from other fields are obvious, including, in biology, population growth, and body size in indeterminate growers.

Set of Principles for a General Theory of ESs

Here I give a brief recapitulation of what has been said in the previous paragraph, but now considering the *process of discrimination* as the unifying theme.

Dc processes cannot exist without (a) a context (GSE) which defines them, (b) a restriction of that context (PSE) from which to produce an ES with Dc power, and (c) the ES that will implement the Dc operation.

The Dc process characterizing in an essential way the nature of all ESs is going to be called *development* or the developmental process of an ES.

For every ES, each Dc process will eventually come to an asymptotic limit if, and as long as, the GSE is maintained sufficiently stable throughout the discriminatory or developmental cycle.

Every Dc process that reaches its limit is by definition an exhausted process. This means that the ES will not be able to develop any further and thus will either stagnate, collapse, or shrink to a suitable, stable extension or size. The relevant point here is that any ES that has reached its developmental zenith and an eventual stable condition is a *potential environment* for some new ES (figure A.2B).

Given a sufficiently mature ES (to be named ES-1), the condition that can turn it into a GSE (global systemic environment) is the appearance of a PSE-2 within the circumscription of the "old" ES-1. In order for a PSE-2 to come into being, some conditions must exist. It will be necessary to divide these conditions in two main categories: (i) those dealing with structure—the global properties of the ES-2—and (ii) those dealing with functional aspects.

The interest of the first grouping is that they all are PSE-2 "conditions" that are essentially new if compared to the PSE-1 "conditions" of ES-1. But not only are they new, they are also the outcome of the developmental process of ES-1; the global properties of ES-2 are products of the discriminations that took place within ES-1 (figure A.3).

The comparison of PSE-1 and PSE-2 should show that the latter is always rooted in and is more efficient than the former (in terms of mattergy)—i.e., that the coming into being of a given ES from a more differentiated GSE results in a more differentiated (and, as Salthe notes, more "integrated") ES, differentiation being the ability to make distinctions which functionally translate into better systemic modeling (or finer tuning) and control of the environment (Odum 1983). Again, the meaning of this has to be found in the fact that an increase in the power of discrimination within GSE-2 allows the production of an ES-2 that starts its developmental process where ES-1 reached its zenith. ES-2

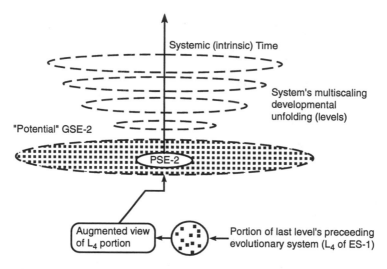

Figure A.3 Whatever new evolutionary system configuration might come into being, it will need as its potential GSE some portion of the last level of the previous ES. That portion, in turn, is made out of configurations of components of the prior level in the metahierarchy.

probably carries in its most basic (undifferentiated) level of existence (GPS) a great deal of the differentiation that ES-1 had built by the end of its developmental cycle.

In the description of the Dc process, a cycle is implicit. If such a cycle is reiterated, then an ordered chain, or specification hierarchy, of GSEs of increasing power of discrimination will be obtained, together with the development, at each point in the hierarchy, of the corresponding ESs (figure A.4).

From the above considerations I point out three main different types of constructive operations present in the description of the hierarchy.

One operation proceeds, starting from any given GSE, to the next GSE, then to the next, etc., the sequence of them forming a specification hierarchy. To the operational procedure allowing this particular hierarchical buildup I am going to apply the name *principle of generative condensation* (PGC); it deals with the evolution of and within U, encompassing every ES. Here structure plays an essential role. Also, in the eventual formalization of this approach, a reasonable connection between this principle and the 'axiom of constructibility' (Devlin 1979) must be established.

Another operation starts from any given PSE. The PSE, with its GPS, provides an operational set with which to construct a chain of increasingly discriminative structures within the system, forming a hierarchy as the ES unfolds and interacts with the environment. This is a combination specification/scalar hierarchy, based on combinatorial principles, and the outcome of this procedure is not a chain of GSEs but the construction and growth of a particular one. The invariance throughout a GSE of the initially given GPS restricts the reach and scope of this principle to the internal construction of a particular ES. Such a process was already named the "development" of a system, and the *principle of combinatorial expansion* (PCE) is what is involved in such a process.

A third operation is one by means of which the two previous operations can be linked together, making the continuation of their respective cycles possible. This operation is

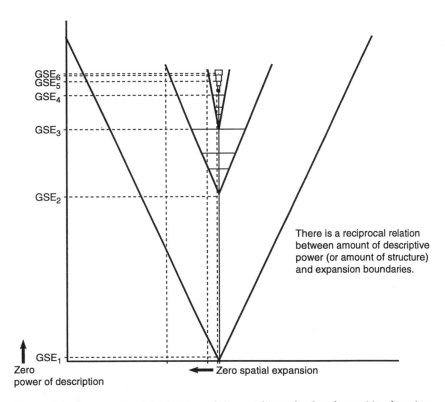

Figure A.4 Two aspects of the buildup of the metahierarchy. Levels capable of nesting new hierarchies are those with highest discriminatory power and from which full description of another level within its own hierarchy is possible. Those levels giving us qualitatively potentially new GSEs are marked consecutively on the vertical axis according to their increased powers of description. Descriptive power increases with each new element of the GSE sequence. The constraints are also increased and, correlated with this, there is reduction of spacial boundaries.

ruled by the *principle of conservation of information* (PCI). Without this principle, the two-sided general process of evolution could not take place, simply because of lack of coordination. Between each pair of points within the PGC hierarchy or metahierarchy lies a PCE hierarchy or developmental cycle of increasing scale.

The Link between Principles

I am assuming that there would not be a universe as we have it, various and complex, without a recurrent chain of evolutionary cycles, given by the alternating appearances of expansions, followed by generative condensations. These two almost opposite methods of building up merge regularly and—it is assumed here—according to law. The link between the two principles is an essential one. It is also difficult to grasp; after all, it is a moment of dramatic transformation of quality.

I am now at a crucial point of my description. Let me distance myself a little from the already-mentioned principles in order to gain some perspective.

A major assumption of ESF was said to be that U ranges widely in variety and complexity. Another major assumption was that U is not a fixed and atemporal (i.e., absolute) entity but an evolutionary one.

The first assumption calls for quantitative and qualitative differences, the best representation of which is the hierarchical one (without indication of the kind of hierarchy).

The second assumption calls for unity among the varied and complex. It gives the direction in which that initially undifferentiated unity, U, increasingly becomes quantitatively and qualitatively differentiated. This assumption, fortunately enough, specifies the kind of hierarchy we must use. There is only one way we can negotiate the constant and simultaneous presence of the unity/differentiation dichotomy in an evolutionary U: by considering differentiation (quantitative and qualitative) as something that is built within U in an iterative manner. That being the case, a *constructive hierarchy* is then specified unequivocally (Devlin 1977, pp. 34–35).

If our U is constructive, then ESF is an attempt to describe a constructive hierarchy that would eventually allow a proper formalization of U.

The third major principle involved in ESF characterizes the conjunction of the two processes involved. It was said that cycles of development alternate with evolutionary changes and, moreover, that evolutionary jumps are preceded by differentiation; i.e., differentiation, via systemic development, provides the necessary information to "design" evolutionarily new systems, along with providing an increase in environmental constraints that would allow "freer" ESs (that is, ESs with more potential for modeling and control).

A general remark is in order here. Since the central issue at this point is evolution and development in a constructive U, the emphasis is placed on the 'constructiveness' and not on evolution proper. This means that mutational phenomena are not considered at this point, although they are *not theoretically excluded*. A previous paper (Alvarez de Lorenzana and Ward 1987) defined as *non-systemic environment* (NSE) that part of the environment of a given ES the inputs from which have no proper systemic response (e.g., in humans, light rays of wavelengths below or above the range perceptible to the optical system). Inputs (perturbations, changes in boundary conditions) from NSE can drastically alter evolutionary contexts if they affect the global properties of an ES. A good mathematical analogy is the impact on the nature of a given geometry if a certain axiom is changed (e.g., Euclidean geometry as opposed to non-Euclidean geometries). Changes implying modifications of the *global properties of a system* are called mutations', and they are basic in that they tend to promote or destroy evolutionary entities. On the other hand, if external inputs do not affect GPS, they can still promote or disrupt differentiation among developmental processes.

We are still considering the precondition for constructibility: how to attain complete specification among our collection of objects. 'Complete specification' (c.s.) within a given ES is provided by the GPS together with the corresponding sequence of extensions taking place throughout the developmental cycle. As long as the need for c.s. is fulfilled, the construction process described by the combinatorial hierarchy can go on. If and when the c.s. condition is not fulfilled, no new extension can be properly defined to constitute a systemic level from which to begin another extension. So, the last theoretically possible level of any hierarchical build up will always be one for which c.s. is not possible.

Dealing now with evolutionary emergence and its resulting metahierarchy, we immediately have a question: Where are the grounds for potentially new ESs? A first and partial answer is: Whatever the grounds are, they have to satisfy the c.s. condition. We also know that they are an outcome of the previous evolutionary cycle. A third indication is that they should maximize the use of already-obtained differentiation. A fourth and last condition is that, whatever the characterization in terms of GPS of the new collection of objects—or incoming ES—might be, it has to systemically survive in the available environment. This last specification is comparable, in mathematics, to imposing on the GPS the condition of being a basis, i.e., a linearly independent set of variables on a given field, from which a vector space can be generated.

We can now claim to have a first and tentative nonformal description of developmental and evolutionary emergence stated within our basic constructibility proposition. How do all these apply to the real construction of U?

In the making of any ES there is always a certain amount of structure involved; this is specified by the GPS. The astrophycisist Hubert Reeves has an evolutionary approach I find useful. When dealing with the general topic of structures and hierarchies of structures, he mentions that "in nature, there are forces. These forces create bonds and are thus responsible for the existence of all 'bound systems': nuclei, atoms, molecules, cells, planets, stars, and galaxies. The organized structures that we have encountered at all levels of cosmic evolution are absolutely dependent on the presence of such bonds." (Reeves 1984, p. 137)

So, structures, bonds, and forces are linked in a deep and inextricable way. But throughout the evolution of, and within, U there is also the permanent competition between "binding energy" and "thermal energy." The former is the amount of energy necessary to establish the bonds (via corresponding forces); the latter refers to the potential energy of, or the environmental pressure on, a given system. These energies are closely related to the different forces: "Those forces (electromagnetic, nuclear, and quark forces) have very different strengths and, as a result, do not manifest themselves under the same circumstances. Each has its own realm [scale] of activity, corresponding to a different level on the temperature scale. . . . Combinations, associations, and structures can only proliferate within particular temperature ranges." (Reeves 1984, p. 53)

A direct proportionality relation between thermal energy and its corresponding force or binding energy can be drawn from cosmology for a given ES: For high thermal energy, only a force and bonds of comparable strengh will be at work. On the other hand, the converse is not necessarily true—i.e., not all decrease in thermal energy implies increase in structure; it will be so only if the decrease in thermal energy is the result of implementing a proper sequence of generative condensations and combinatorial expansions.

The work of the ecologist H. T. Odum is an interesting source of information on these matters of transformation of energy. In a general way, Odum's energy hierarchy is in accord with the previous references stating that structures, bonds, forces, etc. are *energy-specified*. Odum's hierarchy, or the temperature ranges mentioned before, takes the form (within the context of a generalized evolutionary perspective) of "successive levels of organization by matter" (Reeves 1984, p. 51). Quoting Odum (1983, p. 252) on his approach: "An energy theory of value is based on embodied energy. If items and flows have value because of the effects they can exert on a system, and if their ability to act is in proportion to the energy used to develop them (after selective elimination of those that do not), the value is proportional to the embodied energy in systems emerging from selection process." For a review of previous works on the possible relations among energy, information, and structure, see Alvarez de Lorenzana and Ward 1985.

In our constructible U we have defined only ESs and their processes. Every undifferentiated state of an ES (to be called uES) represents the highest thermal-energy state of that given ES, where the ruling force and bonds have a maximum intensity and the amount of structure is confined to its bare GPS. We can say that, as it was with U at the Big Bang, the undifferentiated state of any ES is the state of highest density of energy. By *density* we mean the degree of statistical confinement of system components (states). 'Highest density' would refer to a state of lowest system entropy, and because of its importance in the characterization of any ES I will name it the *absolute density* (φ) of a given ES. A good analogy in physics would be the Compton wavelength, where maximum confinement and maximum energy density of a particle coexist (Davies 1979).

The definition of 'absolute density' comes from energy considerations and can be defined in terms of the GPS (Alvarez de Lorenzana and Ward 1987). Once φ is given, it should be possible to evaluate the 'relative density' of any level of combinatorial expansion of that particular ES.

In relation to the general subject of energy and evolution, Odum (1983, p. 15) tells us that different kinds of energy contain differences in quality and that "their quality is measured by the embodied energy of one type of energy required to develop another type in the work transformations. Potential for control is also dependent on embodied energy." With respect to energy quality transformations he adds: ". . . only a small amount is transformed to a higher quality, one that is more concentrated and in a form capable of special actions when fed back." He defines the "transformation ratio of energy quality" and establishes accordingly a sort of absolute scale. He refers explicitly to the relation between two kinds of energy that are far apart in terms of their respective quality: "The more transformation steps there are between two kinds of energy, the greater the quality and the greater the solar energy required to produce a calorie of that type." (p. 15) He also makes connections between quality of energy and information.

An evaluation or measure of the amount of structure present at the minimal level of existence of an ES has to come also from the global properties of the system, which are the only elements carrying and generating structure within ES. So we have the interesting fact that in a uES both density of energy and structure can be deduced from the GPS (Alvarez de Lorenzana and Ward 1987), and therefore they are somehow linked. The following relation is proposed, where I_s represents structural information:

$$\varphi \cdot I_s = \text{Constant.}$$

What does this mean? It refers to the fact that any systemic manifestation (input-output) does not occur in a vacuum but is the outcome of a delicate balance between external (thermal or environmental) pressure and accumulated discrimination or experience (called structural information). It was mentioned above that the structure-bond pair is inextricably linked to a certain thermal pressure or temperature range, which itself can be expressed in terms of some 'density of energy' such as φ. The reciprocal nature of the proposed relation simply states the following.

It is not possible to have proper systemic activity requiring amounts of I_s above the values permitted by a given environment.

It is not conducive to proper systemic activity (and therefore to development) to have a low environmental pressure which is not coupled with (or correlated to) a conveniently high degree of I_s.

It is considered essential (Alvarez de Lorenzana 1982; Alvarez de Lorenzana and Ward 1985) to include structure—in the way I attempt to do here—in a theory of information, as long as it is done in a clear and explicit way. This need and its fulfillment can occur naturally only in the framework of a general theory of evolution. It is here that a generalized theory of evolution and a generalized theory of information (i.e., a theory where semantical or structural issues are included) merge in the form of a 'principle of conservation of information' (PCI).

If and when it is shown that the proposed 'φ' and 'I_s' are theoretically sound, then their quantification and measurement will be, in principle, possible. With φ and I_s measurable, then, from the theoretical fact that every ES is definable within the meta-hierarchical chain, it follows that the finding and use of φ and I_s as tools should generalize.

The measurability of I_s would suffice to bring to an end the drastic limitation of Shannon's approach to information theory. As was mentioned above, Shannon claimed

(Shannon and Weaver 1949), with good reason, that his theory had nothing to do with meaning (i.e., with the semantic content to which every information channel must be linked).

Now let us return to mathematics, where the relation between fields (F) and vector spaces (v.s.) can be used for clarification. The structure of v.s. needs to be defined on a field; without that there is no definition of a v.s., so the link "field–vector space" could hardly be stronger. Now, once the field is there and the v.s. is defined, the theory of vector spaces is completely independent of the particular nature of the field. Up to here, we can say that there is a similarity among the relations of the two pairs 'field–vector space' and 'semantic context—information system'. (The similarity could become an isomorphism if the elements of the latter relation could be expressed in terms of the elements of the former, i.e., semantic context as a field and information system as a vector space; this seems plausible.) Each couple is defined in isolation; we can have as many pairs field–vector space or semantic context–information system as we wish, but each one is restricted to itself, i.e., from those pairs we could not infer relations among pairs of pairs (e.g., a v.s. of one pair with a v.s. of another pair, or a v.s. of one pair with an F of another).

This isolation comes from the fact that, if we want to relate two different vector spaces, each defined on a different field, then the link between them cannot be defined within themselves. The possibility or impossibility of such a link can only be elucidated and implemented at the field level, i.e., from a general theory of fields.

If there were no theory for linking fields, then all vector spaces, no matter how general their structure, would have to be isolated cases. Fortunately, mathematics has that linking theory and, in fact, the study of relating vector spaces of different fields must have been the basis for some of the work on category theory. In information theory, we need and do not have an equivalent theory for linking semantic contexts.

This attempt has been motivated by the conviction that a theory of semantical contexts (i.e., information sources) is possible and necessary and that the framework within which the theory can be proposed and eventually enunciated should go along the lines of our ESF and its resulting 'general law of evolution.'

Combining the Three Principles: A General Law of Evolution

Having presented the general concept of evolution in ESs as ultimately reducible to only two main processes, together with their dynamics of interaction-transformation (expressed in the form of the three principles already mentioned), I come to something that in a formal exposition could be considered as a theorem, and which is going to be named the *general law of evolution*: Given U (the primordial ES), defined in terms of its global properties, we say that the development of U, as well as the evolution and development of all the ESs coming into being within U, is ruled according to the "principle of generative condensation" (PGC) if it is an evolutionary movement, and according to the "principle of combinatorial expansion" (PCE) if it is a development, both being constantly interregulated under the restrictions imposed by the "principle of conservation of information" (see the equation above).

A Topic in Hierarchy Theory from an ESF Perspective: Emergence

Evolution is the outcome of qualitative or emergent change.

It is important, first, to make a distinction between two intrinsically different kinds of emergence. It is my view that, without clarification of this issue, there is no possibility of understanding—far less explaining—the general phenomenon of emergence. The distinction to be made is between *development* and *evolution*.

"Evolution" is used in two senses: a general one and a restricted one. In the general sense it applies to phenomena dealing with qualitative change within all our universe U. This is the sense in which it is used by cosmologists and by students concerned with, e.g., how a particular science, or even science in general, behaves during its learning processes. The restricted sense applies to the coming into being of new kinds from previous, less evolved (less discriminatory) ones.

The problem comes when we apply the restricted meaning to the general one, implicitly assuming that all there is in the concept of general evolution is the phenomena that occur in the restricted use of the word. In order to avoid confusion, the following concepts are placed within our ESF: (a) restricted evolution: the outcome of the PGC, (b) development: the outcome of the PCE, (c) general evolution: the outcome of the general law of evolution. This implies the conjunction of the three principles established above (i.e., PGC → {PCI} → PCE).

For ESF, there is only a simple evolutionary trend in and within U (i.e., general evolution). This means that, from the perspective given by the theory, each evolutionary subject is the same as any other. Each ES is simply a specific manifestation of the same abstract structure. This is a standard topic in mathematics, where one talks about theories and where within a theory one talks about models of the theory. In this sense, each evolutionary subject (i.e., a subject to which our GLE applies without restriction) is a model of the theory and, from an abstract point of view, is no different from any other.

"Differences" indeed exist, but in order to find them we have to look into the structure (i.e., its stored information), have criteria for measuring the amount of structure, establish an ordering according to that measurement, and compare the then-distinguishable ESs.

Our final aim should be to determine the relations among ESs on the basis of their amounts of structure. If this were possible, we would be in a position where relatively complex situations could be formally represented, simulated, and eventually explained, all with a reasonable degree of accuracy (in the sense of being close to actuality).

The critical issue here is not so much the difficult question of how we can measure structure as it is the more general one of whether ESF provides a basically sound view of the process of general evolution. If it does, then a way to measure I_s will be eventually found.

Conclusions

Although I am not concerned, at this juncture, with language and formalisms suitable for ESF, I do not want to give the impression that all there is on such matters is a vague desire for respectability.

It is my intention to use certain standard procedures of linear algebra in order to develop further the heretofore descriptive character of ESF. For that task, the well-known mathematical structures of scalar fields and vector spaces will be used.

The "scalar field" is, in my view, quite compatible with the concept of environment as it is understood in ESF. I perceive the same situation for the "vector space", as compatible with the evolutionary system (ES) concept. Moreover, the delicate and subtle relation between ES and environment is nicely encompassed in the mathematical theory. All the definitions of the different environments that are important features of ESF are either definitions or well-known theorems in the theory of vector spaces.

The combinatorial hierarchy could be defined in terms of vector spaces. There, concepts such as independent basis, spanned vector space, and dimensionality will be of great use (Sawyer 1959; Rosen 1979). This should bring a great deal of clarity and synthetic power to our language.

Hierarchy theory, as primitive as it still is, is promising and should give an opening into general theory that would also be meaningful in the concrete world of actuality. Practically all sciences are facing the same seemingly hopeless problem of relating, in a coherent and deep way, their macro and micro phenoma.

Addendum

In the quest to formalize, I will restrict myself to a discrete, finite, constructive universe, U. The addition of the principle of parsimony constrains us even more. The end result, nevertheless, should provide a very powerful tool for representing nature, i.e., a representational framework with a minimum set of assumptions and a maximum theoretical reach (going across ontological boundaries).

ESF and its three principles constitute an attempt to reflect that committed view. In its first version (Alvarez de Lorenzana 1982) it was by no means clear to me whether a formal representation could be attained. Now that has changed considerably. In fact, it could be said that there is independent confirmation of those principles through the proof of their formal counterparts.

For the PCE there is the mathematical structure called a "combinatorial hierarchy," first discovered by Frederick Parker-Rhodes (Bastin 1966). As for the necessity of the PGC, it could be said that its formal antecedent comes from Gödel's (1931) theorem on undecidability. Finally, for the necessity of the PCI as the bridge between PCE and PGC, there is recent work by van Bendegem (1988) on "quasinotation" systems.

The fact that there are formal counterparts to the principles proposed in the ESF is of no minor importance. Their submission as principles was an indication of reasonableness as well as adequacy to the phenomena under scrutiny based on our initial self-imposed constraints of parsimony, discreteness, finiteness, and constructivity. The next and most crucial issue was consistency, and that is what the formal counterparts to the principles bring—a proof of their consistency, or, in other words, that our proposed dynamics (that is what the principles are) are isomorphic to *laws of inference* that stand proven to be consistent in formal systems.

In the course of this paper a *descriptive interpretation* of H_c (the combinatorial hierarchy) has been given. Now we turn briefly to substantiate mathematically what was described.

H_c is a conjuction of two generating structures:

$$2^{n_i} - 1 \tag{2}$$

$$m_i^2 \tag{3}$$

The mechanism involved in such a conjunction is that as *long as $n_i \leq m_i$ the recursion can be implemented* and, with it, the construction of new levels of the H_c from previous ones. The sequences and their corresponding comparison are the following:

$$;_{i=1} 3 \leq 4 ;_{i=2} 7 \leq 16 ;_{i=3} 127 <= 256 ;_{i=4} 2^{127} - 1 > 65,546.$$

One mathematical explanation of the interplay of the sequences (2) and (3) is given by C. Kilmeister (McGoveran 1991):

Definition: By a *combinatorial hierarchy* is meant a collection of levels related as follows: The elements at level L are a basis of a vector space V/Z_2.

The elements at level L + 1 are nonsingular (i.e. invertible) linear operators mapping V/Z_2 into V/Z_2.

Each element A at level L + 1 is mapped to a subset S of the elements at level L by the correspondence: the proper eigenvalues of A (i.e., Av = v) are exactly the linear subspace generated by S.

Each element at level L + 1 is chosen independently, allowing the process to be repeated for levels L + 2, L + 3, L + 4, ...

Theorem There *exists a unique hierarchy* (up to isomorphism) with *more than three levels*, and it has the following successive numbers of elements: 2, 3, 7, 127, $2^{127} - 1$, ... It terminates at level 4, owing to the fact that the operators have m^2 elements if the vectors are m-fold, and 2^n (required for V/Z_2) increases too fast.

The gist of the construction is that as long as we can "fit" the diversity coming from the discrimination operation ($2^n_i - 1$) into the different possibilities provided by the permutations (m_i^2), the construction of new levels can go on. It can go on because there is no missing information while "moving" upward. Only when the mapping mechanism overflows does the construction of levels terminate. The termination of the hierarchy was and is an essential factor in the linking of such a structure to meaningful processes of our actual physical universe.

It has recently been proposed (Alvarez de Lorenzana 1991) to take the above-mentioned dichotomy between the discriminately closed subsets and the spanned matrices (i.e., the linear extensions) a step further. We can consider that the Hc is a *composition of two structures* superimposed one upon another. Those structures are then considered as a *sampling structure* by means of discrimination and a *modeling structure* by means of matrix spanning.

The first structure is the outcome of the system's sampling of some external world or milieu. The second (the sequence of spanning matrices) is the outcome of a process of adaptation by means of improving the model of the system.

Within the double structure of the H_c, the sequence 4, 16, 256, 65536 expresses the "modeling power" at each level. Similarly, the sequence 3, 7, 127, $2^{127} - 1$ expresses the "sampling range" at each level. We can clearly see, in this scenario, that the construction of every new level within the H_c can take place as long as the range of the samplings at that level is within the bounds of the corresponding modeling power at that same level. If that were not the case, then the samplings could not be coded and therefore no new version of the model could be implemented. In other words, the sampling would overflow the modeling device. At that point the input would be random for the system because the length of the strings would be greater than the system's capacity to code.

The above situation, it seems to me, could be termed *Gödelian*. In case the connection to Gödel's scenario is not apparent, I could rephrase what was just said in the following terms: We can view the modeling structure as a computer program; then a bit string can be defined as nonrandom if it can be generated by a program consisting of a shorter sequence of digits, otherwise it is considered random (Chaitin 1982). The lack of interpretation by the modeling device of bit strings of a certain length that come into play at a certain point in the development of the system is equivalent to the Gödelian condition of undecidability. It is reasonable to put forward the proposition that *the stop rule in the H_c is isomorphic to the undecidability condition*. If the H_c is used as a formal representation of a natural system, it could be said that *the lack of representation in the natural system is isomorphic to the undecidability condition of its formal counterpart*.

Gödel (1931) proved that in any proposed axiomatic theory of mathematics there are true sentences (theorems) that cannot be derived (proved) from the axioms. The corollary to this is that the consistency of any formalization can be proved only in a more powerful formalization. What does a "more powerful formalization" mean? It means that, in order to overcome undecidability, the axiomatic framework should be enriched with new axioms. In the words of Gödel (1964):

. . . even disregarding the intrinsic necessity of some new axiom, and even in the case it has no intrinsic necessity at all, a probable decision about its truth is possible also in another way, namely, inductively by studying its 'success'. Success here means fruitfulness in consequences, in particular in 'verifiable' consequences, i.e., consequences demonstrable without the new axiom, whose proofs with its help, however, are considerably simpler and easier to discover, and make it possible to contract into one proof many different proofs. . . . There might exist axioms so abundant in their verifiable consequences, shedding so much light upon a whole field, and yielding such powerful methods for solving problems (and even solving them constructively, as far as that is possible) that, no matter whether or not they are intrinsically necessary, they would have to be accepted at least in the same sense as any well-established physical theory.

To consider the termination of H_c as an instance of the undecidability problem does have some implications for the natural systems that are being represented by the hierarchy. The first to be considered may well be acknowledgment of the fact that there is no possibility of explaining the world of the actual as we know it (i.e., in its variety and complexity) by just one run of the combinatorial process. In fact, what we need is a metaprinciple concerned with the generation of more encompassing systems which—at the same time that they keep their already-attained complexity—will allow more complexity to be implemented and drawn into the system. Here is where Gödel's remarks on the necessity to enrich the system axiomatically are most pertinent (At this point the reader might want to contemplate figure A.2B.) A second consequence is that, if we accept the first, and owing to the fact that we are dealing with material systems, we need to establish some causal constraints on information along the lines of a conservation principle, so that generation of more complex systems out of less complex ones has factual consistency.

The need for conservation principles (as in physics and chemistry) stems from the *finite* nature of our universe. The need for evolutionary approaches going beyond some ordering in the realm of biological species comes from the apparent contradiction of having to reconcile an enormous range in complexity, variety, and finiteness.

The same need for conservation appears in mathematics when finiteness is taken in a philosophically committed manner. This is done in van Bendegem's *finite empirical mathematics*, where he implements what he calls "quasi notation systems" which can be considered the formal counterparts to our evolutionary systems. The only necessary adjustment is to exchange his initially postulated operation for ours (van Bendegem starts with Peano's "successor function" as opposed to our "discrimination"). This does not affect the *nature* of the system's logic in any way.

I will end with a quotation from van Bendegem (1988, p. 52): "As to conclusions, the most important fact to note is that it is possible to define quasi notation systems that produce reliable results. What does happen however is that other procedures are lost altogether. . . . What seems very suggestive (and need not amaze us) is that *the total information (if meaning could be given to such a measure) remains constant.* According to the purpose one has in mind, quasi systems can be used that maximize the information on the procedures involved to realize the intended purpose."

It could be said that we should have a theoretical scheme for any system expressable in terms of the H_c, based on three principles:

the principle of combinatorial expansion (as in H_c)
the principle of generative condensation (as in Gödel's metahierarchy statements)
the principle of conservation of information (as in van Bendegem's quasi notation systems).

The interplay between undecidability and reformalization in the axiomatic realm, as stated by Gödel, has an equivalent manifestation in the natural world (up to isomorphism) in the interplay between PCE and PGC. Such an interplay is a universal mechanism between and among ESs. Moreover, the only prerequisite to defining an ES is expressing it in terms of indistinguishability (in other words, separating semantics from syntax).

Glossary

Adaptability: From Conrad, the ability of a system to ignore perturbations (be indifferent to them) or to anticipate them.

Adaptive peak (of a deme): a cluster of genotypes producing the best phenotypes for a given population in relation to its ecological niche.

Affordance: from J. J. Gibson, boundary conditions in the environment that allow something or some relation to exist.

Agency: the property a system has when its effects in its environment reflect its uniqueness.

Ambiguity: the situation when decision or choice cannot be made between clearly apprehended, known, specific options. Contrast vagueness.

Amplification: the propagation of the output of a single lower-scalar-level entity to higher levels of scale.

Aristotelian causality: two pairs of causal forces: material/formal (the stuff something is made from, and its organization, and efficient/final (the push that starts or stops a process or event—and its purpose).

Aristotelian logic: the logic of either-or. An item cannot be both a and not-a at the same time.

Ascendency: from Ulanowicz, a simultaneous measure of both growth and differentiation (organization) of a network of exchanges.

Autocollection: the property of a system collecting some of the effects of its own cascading.

Automation: an on-off switch.

Autonomy: a system is autonomous when it can be said to be an individual, when it appears or functions in some integrity as distinct from its environment, or when it has closure in some discourse. It would need some boundary distinguishing it from its environment, as well as some internally driven processes giving it cohesion.

Autopoiesis: self-making, taken in this work in its most general sense of a system helping to produce conditions that allow its continuance.

Baer's Law: the earlier segments of developmental trajectories of the same general kind are compared, the more alike they will be.

Basic triadic system: In the scalar hierarchy, the canonical arrangement representing a focal level and one each of contiguous higher and lower levels.

Biosphere: the total of living material on the earth (Suess 1875). Compare with *atmosphere* (the total of gases, etc.). As Vernadsky (1945) used it, it refers to interactions between living systems and the other "spheres." My use follows Suess.

Boolean function: 'if-then', 'or', and 'and' are examples of Boolean functions.

Boundary conditions: in the basic triadic system, the higher-scalar-level constraints bearing upon entities at the focal level. Sources of control, regulation interpretation, and perturbations.

Cascade: as used herein, a spontaneous expansion in phase space, as in the diffusion of a substance from its region of high concentration, or as in the decay of the information in an original entity into a great variety carried by its descendants.

Cascading/collecting cycle: a major structure whereby a spontaneous expansion into phase space is balanced by an energetically costly return to a central, sink-like storage area.

Category: from Ryle, a series of predicates that could be thought to be embedded within one another as subclasses, the more specified ones implying in each case the more general. Its label would be an entity to which all the predicates could apply. In the usage of this book, a linguistic specification hierarchy.

Change: the transformation of a system into a radically different one in one respect at least; the attainment of an unprecedented state; a qualitative jump.

Chaos: the behavior of a deterministic system under conditions where its variables achieve mutual relationships producing the possibility of more than a single result for a given value of an independent variable. Deterministic output becomes quasi-stochastic at such times. Constrained randomness.

Cladogram: a tree diagram showing relative degrees of relationship between classified items at the tips of the branches.

Closure: the property of being sufficiently describable by an observer's categories.

Cogent moment: the scaled minimum relaxation time. The duration of the smallest natural time unit for some system, given its scale. A single one of a larger-scale system would be reckoned in multiples of that of a smaller-scale system.

Cohesion: an aspect of the enformational part of organization. That which holds a system together and gives it its autonomy.

Command hierarchy: a situation where different individuals of the same scale have different magnitudes of effect on a next-larger-scale system containing them. Rank here is a metaphor for scale of influence.

Complexity: Nicolis defines this as a function of the number of interacting subunits and the variance of the statistical probabilities of their interactions. Elaborating on this, I would explicitly add that the probability of interaction drops precipitously to zero between some subunits, defining quite different types of them. The only way zero interaction can be guaranteed is if the entities in question are of different scale. Therefore, complexity is a result of hierarchical structure. As a result, a complex system has entities of different kind occupying the same local geometric coordinates and constraining one another without directly interacting. Complexity can be measured by way of a minimal description, or as logical depth, or by way of the number of alternative descriptions that are possible for a given system. This kind of complexity, when compared to others, will be distinguished as extensional complexity (which see). Compare intensional complexity.

Complicatedness: the number of types of things or arrangements, and the number of tokens of each type, as well as the number of rules governing their interactions. This may in some cases be equivalent to Nicolis' (1986) definition of complexity.

Conceptual subordination: a more specified form of material implication; the relation between higher (or inner) integrative levels and lower (or outer) ones. Stage $n + 1$ conceptually subordinates stage n, and biological properties conceptually subordinate chemical ones.

Connectedness: a measure of the proportion of direct internal relationships a system has in comparison to the maximum possible. Related to informational entropy.

Constructionism (social construction): the position that our knowledge of the world is really constructed through discourse and not discovered. A world so constructed reflects local needs.

Continuity: an explicitly unknown aspect of being in time. While a text can invoke it in a reader, we have no techniques to measure it or deal with it linguistically. Analog computing is a kind of model of it.

Contour: from Buchler (1966), a kind of thing-in-itself, a sketch of which can be obtained by combining the integrities that an object has from many different discourses.

Creativity: the production of something radically new, or of change. In positivist discourse it is equivalent to capriciousness.

Deep ecology: the position that the good of natural ecosystems ought to come before that of persons, or even of humanity.

Determinacy, determinability: the degree to which a system can be precisely located as itself, in its own individuality.

Determinism: the situation when an entity with limited internal degrees of freedom acts completely under its own direction. Because of the contextuality of the world, this is possible only in models, unless the entities have no internal degrees of freedom at all and therefore are not affected by boundary conditions, and so behave in only one way at all times. Also the view that efficient causes are sufficient to explain events.

Development: predictable irreversible change

Developmental trajectory (see ontogenetic trajectory): the spatiotemporal connections of cohesion between one stage of development and the next, so that these individual moments—cumulated, say, from fertilization to senescence—make up a single, higher-scale individual. It is taken here to be the seat of self-organization.

Dialectic: an approach to the world concerned with the mediation of change by an engaged agency. Contradictions are necessary to generate it. For further specification see the end of the introductory chapter and chapter 5.

Dialectical logic: the logic of either-or. Something can be both a and b because it is changing from a to b. Also the logic of secondness and interaction, where frictional interference is read as contradiction.

Discourse: used here in its Foucaultian sense of a combination of theory and practice. Lakatos' "research program" and Kuhn's "disciplinary matrix" carry the same meaning more precisely for science. The Marxist term 'praxis' carries this meaning as well.

Discursive formation: a discourse viewed as a whole from its first eruptions in the past until the present time.

Disorder: a situation of uncertainty and significant variety. A general synonym for entropy.

Disorder, specific: the proportion of the maximum disorder a system could possibly show that is actually shown.

Dissipation: (of energy) conversion of usable energy to heat energy; (of entropy) shipment out of a system; (of information) disarrangement, as in mutation or digestion.

Dissipative structure: a bounded (autonomous) dynamic material system that dissipates energy, entropy, and, in some cases, information.

Diversity, biotic: the number of species or kinds of organisms.

Dynamics: the Newtonian model of process.

Ecological niche: in its Grinnellian sense, the system of affordances in an environment making it possible for a species to survive there—what is required in order to construct the *Umwelt* of Uexküll. In its Eltonian sense, the general way of life of a species (e.g., the squirrel way of life). In the Hutchinsonian sense, the particular details of the way of life of a single population.

Ecosystem: a complex system. Usually specifically taken to refer to systems whose scale is significantly larger than the observer at the focal level.

Efficient causes: in the Aristotelian scheme, the pushes and pulls that get things moving or made. One of the diachronic aspects of Aristotelian causality, paired with final cause. Newtonian physics utilizes only this kind of cause. Mechanical cause.

Emergence: (1) the appearance of a condition that cannot at present be explained from knowledge of details of the logically prior condition (developmental emergence and supervenience); (2) the appearance of a historically unprecedented situation or uniqueness (evolutionary emergence). Transformation of a system into a radically different kind. One sign of it is when materially different systems access the same higher-scalar-level structure, in which case that structure is emergent.

Enformation: as used by John Collier (1990), the part of the organization of a system that enables it to exist as the kind of thing it is.

Entification: the process of becoming determinate as an object or thing.

Entropy: in the most general sense, relatively disorderly behavior. It is the attractor of all energy transformations. See Informational entropy and Physical entropy.

Epigenesis: the necessity for vaguer stages to precede more highly specified ones in development, largely because of the facilitation of the latter by the former. An increase in specification as a system develops.

Equilibrium: a privileged state of a system in which it continually reaccesses any and all of its possible states randomly so that there is no constitutive change. See Informational equilibrium and Physical equilibrium.

Eschatology: study of the direction mythology gives to our behavior. Teleological drive.

Evolution: the irreversible accumulation of historical information.

Extensional complexity: the complexity *per se* of authors will be referred to thus in order to distinguish it from intensional complexity (which see).

Externalist perspective (of infodynamics): the viewpoint of an observer outside the systems it observes; the perspective of a disengaged observer.

Final cause: the diachronic aspect of Aristotelian causality paired with efficient cause. The "purposes" for which things might be said to exist, and which pull them into the future. At the highest level of specification of which we are aware, human intent embodies final cause—that which ought to happen (teleology, eschatology). At a less specified integrative level, final cause is embodied in functions—things that need to be the case (teleonomy). At even less specified levels, final cause is embodied in variational principles such as the Second Law of Thermodynamics or fitness increase—things that will (or must) be the case (teleomaty). Final causes of lower-scalar-level processes are also generated by the relative stability of higher-scalar-level configurations.

Firstness: from Peirce, that which is logically prior. Pure being in some contexts, pure possibility in others. Being-in-itself. That which Buchler's (1966) contour suggests.

Formal cause: the synchronic aspect of Aristotelian causality (paired with material cause) that imposes form or regulates its production. Similar to the structuralist use of 'structure'.

Freedom: ability to act capriciously within constraints. As more highly specified in connection with human intentions, the ability to behave rationally.

Friction, generalized: any obstacle to the immediate mixing or homogenization of a system; from whence any constraint on either spontaneous cascading or standing in the way of a project.

Generality: commonality; the intersection between concepts.

Global entropy production: the total entropy production of an entire physical system isolated from others of the same scale.

Growth: increase in size and/or gross energy throughput.

Habit: from Peirce, the reaccessing of privileged states, and so a sign of order; the opposite of random behavior.

Heterarchy: scalar hierarchical structure with generally somewhat promiscuous interactions between levels. Any actual hierarchical system would be more heterarchic than its real (theoretical) structure.

Hierarchy: a structure involving the nesting or governance of smaller scale, or more general, phenomena within those of higher scale, or by more highly specified, phenomena.

Homoplasy: literally, similar form. In cladistics, used mostly to refer to similarities not easily explained by propinquity of descent or genealogy. Hence, problematic or troublesome similarities.

Immaturity: the condition of a system when it has a high specific energy flow through it in combination with a low degree of elaboration of structure. Such systems are flexible and are becoming more powerful as they grow.

Indifference (from Conrad): the aspect of adaptability that allows perturbations to mark a system without important consequences.

Individuation: same as evolution, but usually used for relatively small-scale entities because of the implication of comparison. Only the total universe or some other incomparable system could evolve and not individuate.

Infodynamics: the science of information changes in systems, especially in systems that are informed primarily from within. A combination of nonequilibrium thermodynamics and information theory based on the idea that, just as energy transformations lead to an increase in entropy, so do they, at least when viewed from within a system, lead to increases in information. The word, used for several years by David Depew and Bruce Weber, was first published in Weber et al. 1989.

Information: a significant arrangement that could have been different without any different expenditure of energy. Because, therefore, it cannot be specified by natural laws, there is always an element of surprise in information. Dretske has argued that materially it is the most highly specified digital content an analog sign could have, thus stating a principle of maximum information capacity per sign with respect to the meaning of information. Information implies interpretation; potential information stored elsewhere than where an observer could tap it is like the unavailable energy of heat. Both are observer-related.

Information capacity (or information carrying capacity): a form of entropy in macroscopic systems; their potential for disorder. It usu- ally correlates with variety of system components. Haken (1988) and Dretske talk also of the information capacity per sign.

Information content: The amount of information stored within a system. Usage needs to be stipulated as to whether it refers to the descriptive scheme of an observer of the system (the nonreferential information of Kampis) or to information used by a system itself (referential information, from self-reference). In the first case it could include anything, such as the size of the system. In the second case, that would probably not be used by the system—although examples could be brought forth, such as the width of the head of hammerhead sharks, with sensors at each end. Certainly, if a system incorporates more information (say, by learning something), that would effect a change in configuration that might be accessible to an outside observer, and so could count in both cases.

Informational entropy: variety, useful for the construction of signs. It often correlates with the number of a system's components—but not always, because it is the variety of behavior of these components that is crucial. Unpredictability.

Informational equilibrium: an absence of rules in the choice of signs; totally promiscuous communication.

Initiating conditions: in the basic triadic system, the lower-scalar-level constraints giving rise to focal-level processes. The intrinsic properties of entities interacting at the focal level, arising in the *Innenwelt*.

Innenwelt: from Uexküll, the inner predispositions and structures of a system. That from which initiating conditions emerge. The locus of referential information.

Integration: the process or state of being harnessed or regulated by more highly specified configurations.

Integrative level: a relative degree of (intensional) complexity, in the sense that purely physical systems (say, thunderstorms) would be at a lower integrative level than organisms. By "physical" here is meant that we observers do not typically refer to other than physical laws and boundary conditions in describing them. One might argue that thunderstorms involve chemical entities, but we do not refer to chemistry when describing them. Truly nonchemical physical systems are found only under extreme conditions; however, a gradient of electrical charges can be taken to be a physical system and not a chemical one.

Integrity: from Buchler (1966), the way a particular discourse would construct some entity; the way that entity would seem to be from that perspective. More generally, relations between any two systems.

Intensional complexity: the complexity a system has when it is able to be described at different levels of generality, or at different integrative levels. This is more specified than Rosen's (1985b) notion of complexity as a susceptibility to alternative descriptions.

Intensional definition (of a class or set): a set of descriptors that allows different unique items to be gathered together by similarity for purposes of discourse.

Intensity: of energy flow, the flow per some unit of the system (usually mass).

Interaction, dynamic: pushes and pulls exerted upon one another by entities of the same scale and capable of being described by inconstant variables in an equation. Material secondness.

Internalist perspective (of infodynamics): the viewpoint of an observer embedded in the same supersystem with systems it observes, so that it would necessarily be engaged with them.

Interpretance (system of): from Peirce, a system that uses informational tokens as meaningful signs.

Interpretant: the immediate means of interpretation of signs by a system of interpretance—e.g., theories, models, or schemata.

Intropy: as used by Collier (1990), that portion of the organization of a system measurable as the difference between its maximum possible and actual entropies. Constraints imposed by organization.

Invironment: processes and entities contained at smaller scale within any system, including components and constituents. Provides an *Innenwelt* and gives rise to initiating conditions on a system's behavior.

Isomorphism: structural similarity.

Language tree: from Sommers, a branching structure with the more general predicates in the trunk and the more highly specified ones in the branches. Rylean categories carry labels appropriate to the most specified classes, while Russellian types carry labels appropriate to the least specified.

Law of matter: from Heisenberg, a regularity referring to a limited aspect of nature, such as the colligative properties of water.

Law of nature: a very general regularity in nature, affecting everything.

Logical depth: from Bennett (1988), the length of the logical chain connecting a phenomenon with instructions for making it, roughly measured in time to construction (or time for self-organization).

Logical types: from Bertrand Russell, classes of predicates referring to major distinguishable types of phenomena—in particular, individuals, classes, and classes of classes. These types are related to one another as in a specification hierarchy, with the more highly specified ones included in the more general ones.

Macroscopic: about the same scale as the observer or larger, and much larger than whatever is taken to be microscopic.

Macroscopic information: information potentially available as meaningful to (and so of the same scale as) an observer.

Macrostate: in a two-level scalar hierarchical situation, the configuration of the higher level.

Material cause: the synchronic aspect of Aristotelian causality (paired with formal cause) referring to the availability of materials required, as part of the affordances of an environment or *Umwelt*, for some phenomenon to exist. Biology has frequently been concerned with material causes in its history.

Materialism: the metaphysical stance that there is nothing but matter and its arrangements in the world. Mechanistic materialism has been the driving force of Western science, with the social role of predicting and ultimately dominating nature. Dialectical materialism has been a system of criticism of the results of mechanical materialism. Organicism was the systems-science attempt to understand living systems as configurations and relations within and between material systems—that is, not the matter, but its relations.

Maturity: the developmental stage when a system has achieved its greatest autonomy, power, and scope.

Maximum power principle: from Lotka and Odum, the idea that systems tend to maximize their gross energy throughput. A view that could be held to characterize immature and mature systems.

Meaning: the subjective semiotic value of an event or a configuration.

Mechanicism (or philosophical mechanism): the construal that the world and the systems in it are machines.

Microscopic: at a scale much smaller than an observer or whatever is taken to be macroscopic.

Microstate: in a two-level scalar hierarchical situation, one of numerous lower-level configurations consistent with a single macrostate.

Mind: a kind of complex system that comes to take itself into account even when not reflecting that fact in its output. This goes beyond feedback at a single scalar level, which *can* always cause a detectable change of state. The difference between these two to an observer cannot now be measured; hence, some claim there are no minds.

Minimum entropy production principle: from Prigogine, the idea that systems eventually tend to move toward a steady state of minimum entropy production. This is a statement of the necessity for senescence in dissipative structures.

Minot's Law: The observation that living systems grow rapidly at first and then gradually diminish their rate of growth.

Model: a representation held within a system of its environments and invironments. It is usually a lower-level representation of higher-level systems, based on the observer's needs and categories. If we have a model of the electron, we are imagining ourselves to be observers at its own scale, or even smaller.

Modernism: the philosophical assumption that the whole world (or some significant chunk of it, such as whatever biology studies) makes up a single system that can be understood relatively objectively via privileged generalized discourses such as science. It led to traditional democratic viewpoints, since, if the whole is a single system, then each individual could relate to it separately from every other with as much potential success as any other individual. Now used in contrast with postmodernism, which see.

Morphogenesis: the production of form.

Morphological trajectory: a higher-scalar-level entity composed of that which changes morphology in lineages over long periods of time. Its material nature is inferred only—from the fact that morphological change in organisms seems autonomous with respect to genetic change and speciation and to be coherent over time. If we take morphological evolution to be self-organizing, this is the seat of self-organization. It is roughly comparable to what is now known as the lineage.

Mythology: a story that makes life worth living. It explains why we are here and gives meaning to our activities.

Negentropy: from an externalist point of view, orderliness in system behavior.

Newness: the unprecedented.

Newtonian: characterized by being driven only by external forces.

Niche: see Ecological niche

Nonequilibrium thermodynamics: the perspective in thermodynamics that is concerned with the time course of energy-related changes, usually (but not necessarily) in a thermodynamically open system.

Noosphere: as used here, the total of human systems as a supersystem, including rules, machines, artificial ecosystems (parks, fish ponds, farms, cities), and software. I use the term more in Vernadsky's sense than in that of Teilhard de Chardin.

Notational system: from Goodman (1976), a system that can be used to generate a score for some performance. The signs used must be unambiguously differentiated from one another.

Ontogenetic trajectory: developmental trajectory, as applied to organismic self-organization.

Open system (thermodynamic sense): subject to an exchange of energy and matter with an environment.

Order: regularity of structure or behavior. Predictability. Since it accumulates with age or stage of development, it can often be taken as a sign of senescence—unless it is due only to a system having only a very small scope for change, as in immature systems.

Organization: a perspective that harnesses or entrains the structure (form and/or behavior) of a situation. Manipulating disorder, it is capable of producing orderliness and meaning. The constraint aspects (intropy) of organization can be measured as the difference between the maximum possible entropy available to a kind of system and the actual entropy displayed by a particular token of that system. Charles Bennett suggests that it is the source of semiosis in a system. Minimally in physical systems it is friction; maximally it is the relationships among (potentially) explicit rules in a human system.

Phenomenology: the position that only surface phenomena are real, and that hidden variables that explain them are only constructed tools.

Physical entropy: an extensive variable of the state of a system measuring the inability to do work; the degree to which an energetic system has lost the ability to do work, or has lost configurations in which usable (free) energy is stored.

Physical equilibrum: the situation where no further change is possible because the system randomly accesses any of its potential states without bias. A situation without effective potential gradients.

Possibility: from Peirce, unlimited potentiality

Positivism, positive knowledge: the notion that we can obtain objective, unbiased (and useful) knowledge of an external world.

Postmodernism: a reaction against the modern notion that there could be one privileged discourse about anything. This includes a challenge to positivist science. In place of a monolithic, canonical discourse, the movement is toward separate, independent views of the same phenomena—or, indeed, a challenge to the canonicity even of particular phenomena. Formally, we move from the stance of individuals in a global system (modernism, democracy) to groups involved with local discourses, each with its own local knowledge. This situation is one outcome of the preoccupation with reflexivity and self-reference in epistemology, because, as one places oneself increasingly explicitly into one's view of nature, it becomes more and more important to stipulate just who one is. But no description goes as far as delineating the unique individual, and so the self-description is always that of a fairly highly specified class.

Potential energy: free energy, measuring the amount of significant change possible in a system. It tends to be associated with the part of stored information that is easily lost or labile, and so usable.

Potentiality: from Peirce, a possibility immanent in a system.

Process: a continuing, knowable pattern of activity. Knowable dynamic aspects of a system.

Project: generalizing from Sartre (1976), the tendency of a system to behave in particular ways, or to further particular configurations. Projects necessarily connect in some way to processes occurring at scales larger than the system having them.

Randomness: *From an objective (or externalist) point of view:* as a knowable pattern, a bell-shaped curve of variable events; *epistemologically* (i) the result of our inability to create or predict by design—the failure to make (or make out) a pattern; (ii) an inadvertent result of the cognitive use of classes to cluster heterogeneous objects and events; *ontologically,* noisiness caused by frictions of all kinds. *From a subjective (or internalist) point of view:* the absence of systematicity in a system; *epistemologically,* lawlessness, caprice; *ontologically,* a result of the ability of a system to access most of its potential states; a situation, in the limit, of equal probabilities of independent events.

Realism: the position that our discourses refer to actual things in the world. More strongly, that there can be only one, canonical ("real"), kind of discourse about the world (e.g., according to many, mechanistic materialism).

Reflexivity: The situation when a system needs to have, or has, a model of itself included in its model of the world. Most scientific models are not reflexive, but organisms can be said to have such a model in association with their genomes and behavior. Inertial forces in fluid gyres may be very poorly specified examples as well.

Requisite variety, principle of: from Ashby (1958), the idea that a system requires a degree of flexibility that matches the fluctuational potentiality of its environment.

Rules: regularities in nature interpreted as necessities due to underlying structures. Part of the constraining aspects (intropy) of the organization of a system. Formal causes.

Scalar hierarchy (of nature): a nested structure of wholes and parts. Wholes are parts of yet larger wholes, and parts are wholes for yet smaller wholes. It is a pictorial image of standard mathematical equations, with variables at the focal level and with the values of constants being derived from dynamics at other levels of scale.

Scale: refers to a difference in size so great that no dynamic interaction is possible, only constraint communication.

Score: a sequence of signs eliciting compliant performance. Scores are structures, like developmental trajectories, constructed as integrities.

Second Law of Thermodynamics: the natural law to the effect that disorder (or variety) in macroscopic systems must always either remain the same or increase.

Secondness: from Peirce, the state or situation of experiencing otherness, friction, clash, resistance. Interaction. Being-for-others. The source of dialectical logic.

Self: in the cascading/collecting cycle, a self is a system that collects some of its own cascading.

Self-organization: the mode of change of natural systems whereby they become to varying degrees more complicated (or even complex) and larger in size, scope, or throughput. To the degree that it is predictable, it involves development; to the degree it is not, it involves individuation. Importantly, some of the drive to change must come from within the system itself, so this is not a Newtonian idea. Since individuation is important, such systems can acquire agency, and my own persuasion is to emphasize that it is the gradual, asymptotic, acquisition of determinability. Roughly measurable by ascendency.

Semiosis: association of meaning with information through the use of disorderly arrangements as signs. The interpretation of signs.

Senescence: the condition of complicated form and low energy intensity. A system in this condition has come to rely more on habits than on random impulse or open inquiry entrained by a project—it has a high internal stability. A consequence is that its overt behavior tends to become more disorderly because more stereotypical and so less appropriate to external conditions—it has diminished stability against perturbations. Such a system becomes informationally overloaded as more rules are built into it. It is more predictable in choices but less predictable in what actually happens to it.

Sign: something that stands for something else to an interpreter. In another interpretation, it stands for something so as to bring about an interpretant.

Specification: explicit elaboration of detail.

Specification hierarchy: a hierarchy of embedded classes and subclasses, with that having the most general intensional definition containing the others (which, as they are more and more embedded, require increasingly greater specification). Each class can be taken to represent a stage of development as well as an integrative level.

Specific entropy production: the entropy production per unit of mass (or some other stipulated unit).

Stage (of development): the overall condition of an open system during a restricted portion of its duration. Since stages are classes defined by an observer, there is always more to discover about them—anything not covered by the diagnosis of the stage.

State: the moment-to-moment condition of a system as defined by given dynamical variables.

Stored information: any relatively stable configuration or habit that might have been different.

Structuralism: the search through comparative study for regularities that systems have in common. The projection of these regularities as reflections of underlying structures in the world. The discourse of general systems is a structuralist discourse.

Structure: the underlying principles of organization, generating both form and behavior. Formal causes.

System of interpretance: the system that can can be said to be interpreting the meaning of informational configurations. In language use, the system would be any local society that determines idiomatic expressions and dialects. For genetic information it would be primarily the ontogenetic trajectory of the cell. These systems of interpretance certainly evolve, and their development is an interesting possibility, clearly realized in a cell. They can be said to be self-organizing toward being-for-itself.

Thirdness: from Peirce, that which relates seconds to firsts. Any system. Semiosis. The source of trialectical logic.

Token: an actual instance of a type. Tokens of a type are heterogeneous because the type diagnosis never extends to all their characteristics.

Trajectory: as used herein, an unchanging higher-level entity; that is, the continuity and coherence of lower-level momentary events and entities. The organization of an ongoing event. In a Newtonian framework it would be composed largely of inertial properties, such as momentum.

Trialectical logic: the logic of neither-nor. Something can be seen to be neither a nor b because it is being seen from a metaperspective—one beyond (perhaps because at a higher scale) the possibility of changing from a to b. Thus, viewing an organism as part of an ontogenetic trajectory precludes seeing that it as either a blastula *or* a crocodile.

Tychism: from Peirce, the view that the world is originally and fundamentally stochastic, but that it, and systems within it, accumulate habits as they develop, becoming ever more predictable.

Type: a class that is functional in nature—e.g., trees, oceans, races, methane producers, genotypes.

Umwelt: from Uexküll, the surrounding world—those aspects of an ecosystem to which a particular kind of organism relates. A kind of organism-based ecological niche concept.

Vagueness: the condition where discernment of options is impossible because they are not clearly differentiated. Contrast ambiguity. Whereas generality is a precisely describable intersection between specific concepts, vagueness is more like a blurred resonance between members in their union. A condition of being unformed, indefinite, indeterminable.

Virtual characteristic: when a situation potentially would take the overall characteristics of another situation if various boundary conditions were not in place preventing it. A virtual equilibrium is an equilibrium that would be reached by a system if frictional constraints preventing it were not in place.

References

Alberch, P., S.J. Gould, G.F. Oster, and D.B. Wake, 1979. Size and shape in ontogeny and phylogeny. *Paleobiology* 5: 296–317.

Alexander, R.D. 1987. *The Biology of Moral Systems*. Aldine de Gruyter.

Allen, P.M. 1985. Ecology, thermodynamics, and self-organization: towards a new understanding of complexity. In R.E. Ulanowicz and T. Platt (eds.), *Ecosystem Theory for Biological Oceanography*. Canadian Department of Fisheries and Oceans.

Allen, T.F.H., R.V. O'Neill, and T.W. Hoekstra. 1984. Interlevel relations in ecological research and management: some working principles from hierarchy theory. Report RM-110, U.S. Dept. of Agriculture Rocky Mountain Forest and Range Experimental Station, Fort Collins, Colorado.

Almeder, R. 1980. *The Philosophy of Charles S. Peirce: a Critical Introduction*. Rowman & Littlefield.

Alvarez de Lorenzana, J. 1982. On evolutionary systems. Manuscript.

Alvarez de Lorenzana, J. 1983. Notebooks on structural information. Manuscript.

Alvarez de Lorenzana, J. 1987. The constructive universe and the evolutionary systems framework. Manuscript (see appendix).

Alvarez de Lorenzana, J. 1988. Defining social systems in terms of their process dynamics. In C.W. Kilmeister (ed.), *Proceedings of the Alternate Natural Philosophy Association* 10.

Alvarez de Lorenzana, J. 1990. "Las Relaciones Internacionales en el contexto de la Historia. Un caso de sistemas evolutivos jeraquicos". Madrid: Editorial de la Universidad Complutense.

Alvarez de Lorenzana, J. 1991. Informal comments on indistinguishables, the combinatorial hierarchy and evolutionary systems framework. In F. Young (ed.), *Proceedings of the Alternate Natural Philosophy Association, WEST 7*.

Alvarez de Lorenzana, J., and L.M. Ward. 1985. Semantic and syntactic information. In *Proceedings of the 29th Annual Meeting of the Society for General Systems Research*.

Alvarez de Lorenzana, J., and L.M. Ward. 1987. On evolutionary systems. *Behavioral Science* 32: 19–33.

Anderson, M. 1990. Biology and Semiotics. In W.A. Koch (ed.), *Semiotics in the Individual Sciences*. Brockmeyer.

Anderson, M., J. Deely, M. Krampen, J. Ransdell, T.A. Sebeok, and T. von Uexküll. 1984. A semiotic perspective on the sciences: steps toward a new paradigm. *Semiotica* 52: 7–27.

Anderson, P.W. 1972. More is different. *Science* 177: 393–396.

Arking, R., 1991. *Biology of Aging: Observations and Principles*. Prentice-Hall.

Aronson, L.R. 1984. Levels of integration and organization: a revaluation of the evolutionary scale. In G. Greenberg and E. Tobach (eds.), *Behavioral Evolution and Integrative Levels*. Erlbaum.

Arthur, W. 1988. *A Theory of the Evolution of Development*. Wiley.

328   References

Artigiani, R. 1990. Post-modernism and social evolution: an inquiry. *World Futures* 30: 1–13.

Artigiani, R. 1993. From epistemology to ontology: post-modern science and the search for a new cultural cognitive map. In E. Laszlo, I. Masulli, R. Artigiana and V. Csányi (eds.), *The Evolution of Cognitive Maps*. Gordon and Breach.

Ashby, C.R. 1956. *An Introduction to Cybernetics*. Chapman and Hall.

Ashby, C.R. 1958. Requisite variety, and its implications for the control of complex systems. *Cybernetica* 1: 1–17.

Ashby, C.R. 1962. Principles of the self-organizing system. In H. von Foerster and G.W. Zopf (eds.), *Principles of Self-Organization*. Pergamon Press.

Ashby, C.R. 1965. Constraint analysis of many-dimensional relations. *General Systems Yearbook* 9: 99–105.

Ashby, C.R., and R.C. Conant. 1970. Every good regulator of a system must be a model of that system. *Int. Syst. Sci.* 1: 89–97.

Atkin, R. 1971. Cohomology of observations. In T. Bastin (ed.), *Quantum Theory and Beyond*. Cambridge University Press.

Atkin, R. 1977. *Combinatorial Connectives in Social Sciences*. Birkhäuser.

Atkin, R. 1980. *Multidimensional Man*. Penguin.

Atlan, H. 1974. On a formal definition of organization. *Journal of Theoretical Biology* 45: 295–304.

Atlan, H. 1978. Sources of information in biological systems. In B. Dubuisian (ed.), *Information and Systems*. Pergamon.

Atlan, H. 1979. *Entre le crystal et la fumée*. Éditions de Seuil.

Atlan, H. 1981. Hierarchical self-organization in living systems. In M. Zeleny (ed.), *Autopoiesis: a Theory of Living Organization*. Elsevier North-Holland.

Atlan, H. 1985. Information theory and self-organization in ecosystems. In R.E. Ulanowicz and T. Platt (eds.), *Ecosystem Theory for Biological Oceanography*. Canadian Department of Fisheries and Oceans.

Atlan, H. 1986. *A tort et à Raison: Intercritique de la Science et du Mythe*. Éditions de Seuil.

Atlan, H., E. Ben-Ezra, F. Fogelman-Soulie, D. Pellegrin, and G. Weisbuch. 1986. Emergence of classification procedures in automata networks as a model for functional self-organization. *Journal of Theoretical Biology* 120: 371–380.

Auger, P. 1989. *Dynamics and Thermodynamics in Hierarchically Organized Systems*. Pergamon.

Balme, D.M. 1987. Aristotle's biology was not essentialist. In A. Gotthelf and J.G. Lennox (eds.), *Philosophical Issues in Aristotle's Biology*. Cambridge University Press.

Banerjee, S., P.R. Sibbald, and J. Maze. 1990. Quantifying the dynamics of order and organization in biological systems. *Journal of Theoretical Biology* 143: 91–111.

Barfield, O. 1971. *What Coleridge Thought*. Wesleyan University Press.

Barthélmy-Madaule, M. 1982. *Lamarck, the Mystical Precursor: A Study of the Relations Between Science and Ideology*. MIT Press.

Barzun, J. 1943. *Classic, Romantic and Modern*. Little, Brown.

Bastin, T. 1966. On the scale constants in physics. *Studia Philosophica Gandensia* 4: 77.

Bastin, T., H.P. Noyes, J. Amson, and C.W. Kilmeister. 1979. On the physical interpretation and mathematical structure of the combinatorial hierarchy. *International Journal of Theoretical Physics* 18: 454–488.

Bateson, G. 1979. *Mind and Nature: A Necessary Unity*. Dutton.

Bateson, P. 1988. The active role of behavior in evolution. In M.-W. Ho and S.W. Fox (eds.), *Evolutionary Processes and Metaphors*. Wiley.

Beckner, M. 1974. Reduction, hierarchies and organicism. In F.J. Ayala and T. Dobzhansky (eds.), *Studies in the Philosophy of Biology*. University of California Press.

Beebe, C.W. 1905. *Two Bird-Lovers in Mexico*. Houghton Mifflin.

Ben-Jacob, E., and P. Garik. 1990. The formation of patterns in non-equilibrium growth. *Nature* 343: 523–530.

Bennett, C.H. 1988. Dissipation, information, computational complexity and the definition of organization. In D. Pines (ed.), *Emerging Syntheses in Science*. Addison-Wesley.

Bennett, K.D. 1990. Milankovitch cycles and their effects on species in ecological and evolutionary time. *Paleobiolgoy* 16: 11–21.

Berg, L.S. 1926. *Nomogenesis, or Evolution Determined by Law*. Constable & Co.

Bergson, H. 1911. *Creative Evolution*. Henry Holt.

Berman, M. 1981. *The Reenchantment of the World*. Cornell University Press.

Bernstein, H., H.C. Byerly, F.A. Hopf, and R.E. Michod. 1985. Genetic damage, mutation, and the evolution of sex. *Science* 229: 1277–1281.

Bertalanffy, L. von. 1933. *Modern Theories of Development: An Introduction to Theoretetical Biology*. Oxford University Press.

Bertalanffy, L. von. 1968. *General System Theory*. Braziller.

Bigger, C.P., and C.A.H. Bigger. 1982. Recognition in biological systems. In J. Sallis (ed.), *Philosophy and Archaic Experience: Essays in Honor of Edward G. Ballard*. Duquesne University Press.

Birke, L. 1986. *Women, Feminism and Biology: The Feminist Challenge*. John Spiers.

Blondel, J., F. Vuillemeier, L.F. Marcus, and E. Terouanne. 1984. Is there ecomorphological convergence among mediterranean bird communities of Chile, California and France? *Evolutionary Biology* 13: 141–214.

Bohm, D. 1958. *Causality and Chance in Modern Physics*. Routledge and Kegan Paul.

Boltzmann, L. 1886. The second law of thermodynamics. In B. McGuinness (ed.), *Ludwig Boltzmann, Theoretical Physics and Philosophical Problems*. Reidel, 1974.

Bonner J.T. 1952. *Morphogenesis: An Essay on Development*. Princeton University Press.

Bonner, J.T. (ed.). 1982. *Evolution and Development: Report of the Dahlem Workshop on Evolution and Development*. Springer-Verlag.

Bonner, J.T. 1988. *The Evolution of Complexity By Means of Natural Selection*. Princeton University Press.

Brachet, J. 1950. *Chemical Embryology*. Interscience.

Brady, R.H. 1986. Form and cause in Goethe's morphology. In F. Amrines, F.J. Zucker, and H. Wheeler (eds.), *Goethe and the Sciences: A Re-appraisal*. Kluwer.

Brandon, R.N. 1990. *Adaptation and Environment*. Princeton University Press.

Brillouin, L. 1956. *Science and Information Theory*. Academic Press.

Brooks, D.R., J.N. Caira, T.R. Platt, and M.R. Pritchard. 1984. *Principles and Methods of Phylogenetic Systematics: A Cladistics Workbook*. University of Kansas Museum of Natural History.

Brooks, D.R., J. Collier, B. Maurer, J.D.H. Smith, and E.O. Wiley. 1989. Entropy and information in evolving biological systems. *Biology and Philosophy* 4: 407–432.

Brooks, D.R., D.D. Cumming, and P.H. LeBlond. 1988. Dollo's law and the second law of thermodynamics: Analogy or extension? In B.H. Weber, D.J. Depew, and J.D. Smith (eds.), *Entropy, Information and Evolution: New Perspectives on Physical and Biological Evolution*. MIT Press.

Brooks, D.R., and D.A. McLennan. 1991. *Phylogeny, Ecology, and Behavior: A Research Program in Comparative Biology*. University of Chicago Press.

Brooks, D.R., and R.T. O'Grady. 1986. Nonequilibrium thermodynamics and different axioms of evolution. *Acta Biotheoretica* 35: 77–106.

Brooks, D.R., and E.O. Wiley. 1988. *Evolution as Entropy: Toward a Unified Theory of Biology,* second edition. University of Chicago Press.

Brush, S.G. 1983. *Statistical Physics and the Atomic Theory of Matter, from Boyle and Newton to Landau and Onsager.* Princeton University Press.

Buchler, J. (ed.). 1955. *Philosophical Writings of Peirce.* Dover.

Buchler, J. 1966. *Metaphysics of Natural Complexes.* Columbia University Press.

Bullough, W.S. 1967. *The Evolution of Differentiation.* Academic Press.

Burkhardt, R.W., Jr. 1977. *The Spirit of System.* Harvard University Press.

Bury, J.B. 1932. *The Idea of Progress.* Dover, 1960.

Buss, L.W. 1987. *The Evolution of Individuality.* Princeton University Press.

Cairns-Smith, A.G. 1982. *Genetic Takeover and the Mineral Origins of Life.* Cambridge University Press.

Calder, W.A. III. 1984. *Size, Function, and Life History.* Harvard University Press.

Campbell, J.H. 1982. Autonomy in evolution. In R. Milkman (ed.), *Perspectives on Evolution.* Sinauer.

Carnap, R. 1937. *The Logical Syntax of Language.* Kegan Paul.

Cesarman, E. 1977. Thermodynamics of the myocardial cell: A redefinition of its active and resting states. *Chest* 72: 269–271.

Cesarman, E. 1990. The four diastoles: a cardiac-cycle model. *Acta Cardiologica* 45: 15–34.

Chaitin, G.J. 1975. Randomness and mathematical proof. *Scientific American* 232: 47–52.

Chaitin, G.J. 1982. Gödel's theorem and information. *International Journal of Theoretical Physics* 21: 941–954.

Charlson, R.J., J.E. Lovelock, M.O. Andreae, and S.G. Warren. 1987. Oceanic plankton, atmospheric sulphur, cloud albedo and climate. *Nature* 326: 655–661.

Churchland, P.M., and P.S. Churchland. 1990. Could a machine think? *Scientific American* 262: 32–37.

Clarke, D.S., Jr. 1987. *Principles of Semiotics.* Routledge and Kegan Paul.

Clements, F.E. 1916. Plant succession: an analysis of the development of vegetation. *Publications of the Carnegie Institute of Washington* 242.

Cody, M.L. 1966. A general theory of clutch size. *Evolution* 20: 174–184.

Cody, M.L., and H.A. Mooney. 1978. Convergence versus nonconvergence in mediterranean-climate ecosystems. *Annual Review of Evolution and Systematics* 9: 265–321.

Cohen, M.R. (ed.). 1923. *Chance, Logic, Love: Philosophical Essays by the Late Charles Sanders Peirce.* Kegan Paul, Trench, Trubner.

Collier, J.D. 1986. Entropy in evolution. *Biology and Philosophy.* 1: 5–24.

Collier, J.D. 1989. Supervenience and reduction in biological hierarchies. *Canadian Journal of Philosophy* 14, Suppl: 209–234.

Collier, J.D. 1990. Intrinsic information. In P.P. Hanson (ed.), *Information, Language, and Cognition.* University of British Columbia Press.

Collingwood, R.G. 1945. *The Idea of Nature.* Clarendon.

Comfort, A. 1964. *Ageing: the Biology of Senescence.* Holt, Rinehart & Winston.

Conant, R. (ed.). 1981. *Mechanisms of Intelligence: Ross Ashby's Writings on Cybernetics.* Intersystems.

Conrad, M. 1983. *Adaptability: the Significance of Variability from Molecule to Ecosystem.* Plenum.

Cooper, S. 1979. A unifying model of the G1 period in prokaryotes and eukaryotes. *Nature* 280: 17–19.

Cope, E.D. 1896. *The Primary Factors of Organic Evolution.* Open Court.

Corliss, J.B. The dynamics of creation: the emergence of living systems in Archaean submarine hot springs. Manuscript.

Cornford, F.M. 1945. *The Republic of Plato*. Oxford University Press.

Csányi, V. 1989. *Evolutionary Systems and Society: A General Theory*. Duke University Press.

Csányi, V., and G. Kampis. 1985. Autogenesis: the evolution of replicative systems. *Journal of Theoretical Biology* 114: 303–321.

Davies, P.C.W. 1979. *The Forces of Nature*. Cambridge University Press.

Davis, M. 1965. *The Undecidable*. Raven.

Davis, P.J., and R. Hersh, 1981. *The Mathematical Experience*. Houghton Mifflin.

Dawkins, R. 1976. *The Selfish Gene*. Oxford University Press.

Dawkins, R. 1982. *The Extended Phenotype*. Freeman.

deDuve, C. 1990. Prelude to a cell. *The Sciences*, Nov./Dec. 1990: 22–28.

Deely, J. 1982. *Introducing Semiotic: Its History and Doctrine*. Indiana University Press.

Degani, C., and M. Halmann. 1965. Chemical evolution of carbohydrate metabolism. *Nature* 216: 1207.

Depew, D.J. 1986. Nonequilibrium thermodynamics and evolution: a philosophical perspective. *Philosophica* 37: 27–58.

Depew, D.J., and B.H. Weber. 1989. The evolution of the Darwinian research tradition. *Systems Research* 6: 255–263.

Detlaff, T.A., and A.A. Detlaff. 1961. On relative dimensionless characters of the development duration in embryology. *Archives de Biologie* 72: 1–16.

Devall, B., and G. Sessions. 1985. *Deep Ecology: Living as if Nature Mattered*. Gibbs M. Smith.

Devlin, K.J. 1977. The axiom of constructability. In *Lecture Notes in Mathematics, 617*. Springer-Verlag.

Devlin, K.J. 1979. *Fundamentals of Contemporary Set Theory*. Springer-Verlag.

Dobzhansky, T. 1962. *Mankind Evolving: The Evolution of the Human Species*. Yale University Press.

Dobzhansky, T. 1964. *Heredity and the Nature of Man*. Harcourt, Brace & World.

Dover, G.A. 1986. Molecular drive in multigene families: how biological novelties arise, spread and are assimilated. *Trends in Genetics* 2: 159–165.

Dretske, F.I. 1981. *Knowledge and the Flow of Information*. MIT Press.

Duhem, P. 1914. *The Aim and Structure of Physical Theory*. Atheneum, 1962.

Dunnel, R.C. 1988. The concept of progress in cultural evolution. In M.H. Nitecki (ed.), *Evolutionary Progress*. University of Chicago Press.

Dyke, C. 1988. *The Evolutionary Dynamics of Complex Systems: A Study in Biosocial Complexity*. Oxford University Press.

Eagleton, T. 1990. Nationalism: irony and commitment. In S. Deane (ed.), *Nationalism, Colonialism and Literature*. University of Minnesota Press.

Eco, U. 1976. *A Theory of Semiotics*. Indiana University Press.

Edelman, G.M. 1987. *Neural Darwinism: The Theory of Neuronal Group Selection*. Basic Books.

Edelman, G.M. 1988. *Topobiology: An Introduction to Molecular Embryology*. Basic Books.

Ehrensvärd, G. 1960. *Life: Origin and Development*. University of Chicago Press.

Eigen, M., and P. Schuster. 1979. *The Hypercycle: A Principle of Natural Self-Organization*. Springer-Verlag.

Eldredge, N. 1985. *Unfinished Synthesis: Biological Hierachies and Modern Evolutionary Thought*. Oxford University Press.

Eldredge, N. 1989. *Macroevolutionary Dynamics: Species, Niches, and Adaptive Peaks*. McGraw-Hill.

Eldredge, N., and J. Cracraft. 1980. *Phylogenetic Patterns and the Evolutionary Process*. Columbia University Press.

Eldredge, N., and M. Grene. In Press. *Interactions: the Biological Context of Social Systems*. McGraw-Hill.

Eldredge, N., and S.N. Salthe. 1984. Hierarchy and evolution. *Oxford Surveys in Evolutionary Biology* 1: 184–208.

Emanuel, K.A. 1988. Toward a general theory of hurricanes. *American Scientist* 76: 370–379.

Engels, F. 1872–1882. *Dialectics of Nature*. International Publishers, 1940.

Engels, F. 1894. *Anti-Duhring: Herr Eugen Duhring's Revolution in Science*. Progress Publishers, 1947.

Esposito, J.L. 1977. *Schelling's Idealism and Philosophy of Nature*. Bucknell University Press.

Esposito, J.L. 1980. *Evolutionary Metaphysics: The Development of Peirce's Theory of Categories*. Ohio University Press.

Feynman, R.P. 1982. *What Do You Care What Other People Think? Further Adventures of a Curious Character*. Norton.

Findlay, J.N. 1958. *Hegel: A Reexamination*. Allen and Unwin.

Fisher, R.A. 1958. *The Genetical Theory of Natural Selection*. Dover.

Fivaz, R. 1991. Thermodynamics of complexity. *Systems Research* 9: 19–32.

Fleck, L. 1979 (1935). *Genesis and Development of a Scientific Fact*. University of Chicago Press.

Foerster, H. von. 1960. On self-organizing systems and their environments. In M.C. Yovitz and S. Cameron (eds.), *Self Organizing Systems*. Pergamon.

Foucault, M. 1972. *The Archaeology of Knowledge*. Tavistock.

Fox, S.W. 1986. The evolutionary sequence: origin and emergences. *American Biology Teacher* 48: 140–169.

Fox, S.W. 1988. *The Emergence of Order: Darwinian Evolution From the Inside*. Basic Books.

Francis, S., L. Margulis, and E.S. Barghoorn. 1978. On the experimental silification of microorganisms. II. On the time of appearance of eucaryotic organisms in the fossil record. *Precambrian Research* 6: 65–100.

Fraser, J.T. 1982. *The Genesis and Evolution of Time*. Harvester.

Frautschi, S. 1982. Entropy in an expanding universe. *Science* 217: 593–599.

Frautschi, S. 1988. Entropy in an expanding universe. In B.H. Weber, D.J. Depew, and J.D. Smith (eds.), *Entropy, Information, and Evolution: New Perspectives on Physical and Biological Evolution*. MIT Press.

Freeman, E. (ed.). 1983. *The Relevance of Charles Peirce*. Monist Library of Philosophy.

Gadamer, H.-G. 1976. *Hegel's Dialectic: Five Hermeneutical Studies*. Yale University Press.

Gale, G. 1981. The anthropic principle. *Scientific American* 245: 154–171.

Galison, P. 1987. *How Experiments End*. University of Chicago Press.

Geertz, C. 1983. *Local Knowledge: Further Essays in Interpretive Anthropology*. Basic Books.

Geyer, F., and J. van der Zouwen (eds.). 1990. *Self-Referencing in Social Systems*. Intersystems.

Gibbons, A. 1990. Our chimp cousins get that much closer. *Science* 250: 376.

Gibson, J.J. 1966. *The Senses Considered as Perceptual Systems*. Houghton Mifflin.

Gilbert, L.E. 1980. Food web organization and the conservation of neotropical diversity. In N. Soulé and B.A. Wilcox (eds.), *Conservation Biology*. Sinauer.

Gilligan, C. 1982. *In a Different Voice*. Harvard University Press.

Glansdorf, P., and I. Prigogine. 1971. *Thermodynamic Theory of Structure, Stability and Fluctuations*. Wiley-Interscience.

Gleick, J. 1987. *Chaos: Making a New Science*. Viking Penguin.

Gödel, K. 1931. On formally undecidable propositions of *Principia Mathematica* and related systems. In J. van Heijenport (ed.), *Frege and Gödel: Two Fundamental Texts in Mathematical Logic*. Harvard University Press.

Gödel, K. 1938. The consistency of the axiom of choice and of the generalized continuum hypothesis. *Proceedings of the National Academy of Sciences* 24: 556–557.

Gödel, K. 1964. Russell's mathematical logic, and what is Cantor's continuum problem. In P. Benacerraf and H. Putnam (eds.), *Philosophy of Mathematics*. Prentice-Hall.

Goodman, N. 1976. *Languages of Art: An Approach to a Theory of Symbols*. Hackett.

Goodwin, B.C. 1984. Changing from an evolutionary to a generative paradigm in biology. In J.W. Pollard (ed.), *Evolutionary Theory: Paths into the Future*. Wiley.

Goodwin, B.C., and P.T. Saunders (eds.). 1989. *Theoretical Biology: Epigenetic and Evolutionary Order from Complex Systems*. Edinburgh University Press.

Goodwin, B.C., A. Sibatani, and G. Webster (eds.). 1989 *Dynamic Structures in Biology*. Edinburgh University Press.

Goonatilake, S. 1991. *The Evolution of Information: Lineages in Gene, Culture and Artefact*. Pinter.

Gould, S.J. 1987. On replacing the idea of progress with an operational notion of directionality. In M.H. Nitecki (ed.), *Evolutionary Progress*. University of Chicago Press.

Gould, S.J., and N. Eldredge. 1977. Punctuated equilibria: the tempo and mode of evolution reconsidered. *Paleobiology* 3: 115–152.

Gregory, F. 1977. Scientific versus dialectical materialism: a clash of ideologies in nineteenth century German radicalism. *Isis* 68: 206–223.

Griffin, D.R. 1976. *The Question of Animal Awareness: Evolutionary Continuity of Mental Experience*. Rockefeller University Press.

Haken, H. 1981. *The Science of Structure: Synergetics*. Van Nostrand Reinhold.

Haken, H. 1984. *Synergetics, an Introduction*. Springer-Verlag.

Haken, H. 1988. *Information and Self-Organization: A Macroscopic Approach to Complex Systems*. Springer-Verlag.

Haraway, D. 1976. *Crystals, Fabrics and Fields: Metaphors of Organicism in Twentieth Century Biology*. Yale University Press.

Hardin, G. 1959. *Nature and Man's Fate*. Rinehart.

Harding, S. (ed.). 1976. *Can Theories Be Refuted? Essays on the Duhem-Quine Thesis*. Reidel.

Hartshorne, C., and P. Weiss (eds.). 1934. *Collected Papers of Charles Sanders Peirce. Vol. 6: Scientific Metaphysics*. Harvard University Press.

Hawking, S. 1988. *A Brief History of Time, from the Big Bang to Black Holes*. Bantam.

Hebb, D.O. 1949. *The Organization of Behavior: A Neuropsychological Theory*. Wiley.

Hegel, G.W.F. 1830. *Hegel's Philosophy of Nature*, ed. A.V. Miller. Oxford University Pres, 1970.

Heinrich, B. 1987. *One Man's Owl*. Princeton University Press.

Herbert, M.R. 1981. Evolution as a Learning Process in Marx, Piaget and Habermas. Ph.D. dissertation, University of California, Santa Cruz.

Hershey, D., and W.E. Lee III. 1987. Entropy, aging and death. *Systems Research* 4: 269–281.

Hesse, H. *Das Glasperlenspiel*. Suhrkamp. (English: *Magister Ludi*.)

Hoffmeyer, J., and C. Emmeche. 1991. Code-duality and the semiotics of nature. In M. Anderson and F. Merrell (eds.), *On Semiotic Modeling*. Mouton de Gruyter.

Hofstadter, D.R. 1979. *Gödel, Escher, Bach: an Eternal Golden Braid*. Basic Books.

Holling, C.S. 1986. The resilience of terrestrial ecosystems. In W.C. Clark and R.E. Munn (eds.), *Sustainable Development of the Biosphere*. Cambridge University Press.

Horn, R.E. (ed.). 1983. *Trialectics: Toward a practical logic of unity*. Lexington Institute.

Houser, N. 1991. A Peircean classification of models. In M. Anderson and F. Merrell (eds.), *On Semiotic Modeling*. Mouton de Gruyter.

Hsu, S.A. 1988. *Coastal Meteorology*. Academic Press.

Hui Guang. 1985. *Introduction to Ch'an*. Woo Ling.

Hull, D.L. 1974. *Philosophy of Biological Science*. Prentice-Hall.

Hull, D.L. 1988. *Science as a Process: An Evolutionary Account of the Social and Conceptual Development of Science*. University of Chicago Press.

Huxley, J.S. 1942. *Evolution: The Modern Synthesis*. Harper.

Huxley, J.S. 1947. *Touchstone for Ethics*. Harper.

Huxley, J.S. 1953. *Evolution in Action*. Harper.

Huxley, J.S. 1958. Evolutionary processes and taxonomy with special reference to grades. *Uppsala Univ. Arssks*. 1958: 649–662.

Ignatieff, M. 1984. *The Needs of Strangers: An Essay on Privacy, Solidarity, and the Politics of Being Human*. Chatto and Windus.

Ingold, T. 1986. *Evolution and Social Life*. Cambridge University Press.

Jacob, F. 1973. *The Logic of Life: A History of heredity*. Pantheon.

James, F.C., R.F. Johnston, W.O. Wamer, G.J. Niemi, and W.J. Boecklen. 1984. The Grinnellian niche of the wood thrush. *American Naturalist* 124: 17–37.

Jantsch, E. 1980. *The Self-Organizing Universe: Scientific and Human Implications of the Emerging Paradigm of Evolution*. Pergamon.

Janzen, D.H. 1967. Interaction of the bull's-horn acacia (*Acacia cornigera*) with its ant inhabitant (*Pseudomyrmex ferruginea* F. Smith) in eastern Mexico. *University of Kansas Science Bulletin* 47: 315–558.

Johnson, D.M. 1990. Can abstractions be causes? *Biology and Philosophy* 5: 63–78.

Johnson, L.G. 1988. The thermodynamic origin of ecosystems: A tale of broken symmetry. In B.H. Weber, D.J. Depew and J.D. Smith (eds.), *Entropy, Information, and Evolution: New Perspectives on Physical and Biological Evolution*. MIT Press.

Jolley, J.L. 1973. *The Fabric of Knowledge: A Study of the Relations Between Ideas*. Barnes and Noble.

Kampis, G. 1988. On the modelling relation. *Systems Research* 5: 131–144.

Kampis, G. 1991a. *Self-Modifying Systems in Biology and Cognitive Science: a New Framework for Dynamics, Information, and Complexity*. Pergamon.

Kampis, G. 1991b. Emergent computations, life and cognition. *World Futures* 32: 95–110.

Kampis, G., and V. Csányi. 1991. Life, self-reproduction and information: beyond the machine metaphor. *Journal of Theoretical Biology* 148: 17–32.

Kauffman, S.A. 1989. Origins of order in evolution: self-organization and selection. In B. Goodwin and P. Saunders (eds.), *Theoretical Biology: Epigenetic and Evolutionary Order for Complex Systems*. Edinburgh University Press.

Kauffman, S.A. 1990. Requirements for evolvability in complex systems: Orderly dynamics and frozen components. In W.H. Zurek (ed.), *Complexity, Entropy and Physics of Information*. Addison-Wesley.

Kerr, R.A. 1988. Snowbird II: clues to Earth's impact history. *Science* 242: 1380–1382.

Kestin, J. (ed.). 1976. *The Second Law of Thermodynamics: Benchmark Papers on Energy / 5*. Dowden, Hutchinson and Ross.

Kieve, R.A. 1983. The Hegelian inversion: on the possibility of a Marxist dialectic. *Science and Society* 47: 37–65.

Kitcher, P. 1985. *Vaulting Ambition: Sociobiology and the Quest for Human Nature*. MIT Press.

Kluge, A.G. 1983. Cladistics and the classification of the great apes. In R.L. Ciochon and R.S. Corrucini (eds.), *New Interpretations of Ape and Human Ancestry*. Plenum.

Koch, W. 1986. *Evolutionary Cultural Semiotics*. Brockmeyer.

Koestler, A. 1978. *Janus: A Summing Up*. Vintage.

Kohlberg, L. 1969. Stage and sequence: the cognitive-developmental approach to socialization. In D. Goslin (ed.), *Handbook of Socialization Theory and Research*. Rand-McNally.

Kolasa, J., and S.T.A. Pickett. 1989. Ecological systems and the concept of biological organization. *Proceedings of the National Academy of Science* 86: 8837–8841.

Kolmogorov, A.N. 1965. Three approaches to the quantitative definition of information. *Problems of Information Transmission* 1: 1–7.

Kondepudi, D. 1988. Parity violation and the origin of biomolecular chirality. In B.H. Weber, D.J. Depew, and J.D. Smith (eds.), *Entropy, Information, and Evolution: New Perspectives on Physical and Biological Evolution*. MIT Press.

Kripke, S.A. 1972. *Naming and Necessity*. Harvard University Press.

Kuhn, T.S. 1962. *The Structure of Scientific Revolutions*. University of Chicago Press.

Lamprecht, I., and A.I. Zotin (eds.). 1978. *Thermodynamics of Biological Processes*. Walter de Gruyter.

Landsberg, P.T. 1972. Time in statistical physics and special relativity. In J.T. Fraser, F.C. Haber, and G.H. Muller (eds.), *The Study of Time*. Springer-Verlag.

Langer, S.K. 1967. *Mind: An Essay on Human Feeling*. Volume 1. Johns Hopkins University Press.

Langness, L.L. 1974. *The Study of Culture*. Chandler & Sharp.

Lasky, R.A., M.P. Fairman, and J.J. Blow. 1989. The S phase of the cell cycle. *Science* 246: 609–614.

Laszlo, E. 1987. *Evolution: The Grand Synthesis*. Shambhala.

Latour, B. 1987. *Science in Action*. Harvard University Press.

Lauder, G. 1981. Form and function: structural analysis in evolutionary biology. *Paleobiology* 7: 430–442.

Lauder, G. 1986. Homology, analogy, and the evolution of behavior. In M.H. Nitecki and J.A. Kitchell (eds.), *Evolution of Animal Behavior*. Oxford University Press.

Lauder, G., and K. Liem. 1989. The role of historical factors in the evolution of complex organismal functions. In D.B. Wake and G. Roth (eds.), *Integration and Evolution in Vertebrates*. Wiley.

Laughlin, C.D., Jr., and E.D. d'Aquili. 1974. *Biogenetic structuralism*. Columbia University Press.

Layzer, D. 1976. The arrow of time. *Scientific American* 233: 56–69.

Layzer, D., 1977. Information in cosmology, physics and biology. *International Journal of Quantum Chemistry* 12 (supplement. 1): 185–195.

Layzer, D. 1988. Growth of order in the universe. In B.H. Weber, D.J. Depew, and J.D. Smith (eds.), *Entropy, Information, and Evolution: New Perspectives on Physical and Biological Evolution*. MIT Press.

Lemke, J. 1991. Discourse, dynamics, and social change. In M.A.K. Halliday (ed.), *Language as Cultural Dynamic* (special issue of *Cultural Dynamics*).

Lenoir, T. 1982. *The Strategy of Life*. Reidel.

Lenzer, G. 1975. *Auguste Comte and Positivism: The Essential Writings*. University of Chicago Press.

Levins, R., and R.C. Lewontin. 1980. *The Dialectical Biologist*. Harvard University Press.

Levinton, J.S. 1986. Developmental constraints and evolutionary saltations: a discussion and critique. In J.P. Gustafson, G.L. Stebbins, and F.J. Ayala (eds.), *Genetics, Development, and Evolution*. Plenum.

Levi-Strauss, C. 1966. *The Savage Mind*. University of Chicago Press.

Lewes, G.H. 1874–75. *Problems of Life and Mind*. Osgood.

Lewin, R. 1984a. Why is development so illogical? *Science* 224: 1327–1329.

Lewin, R. 1984b. The continuing tale of a small worm. *Science* 225: 153–156.

Lewin, R. 1987. My close cousin the chimpanzee. *Science* 238: 273–275.

Lewin, R. 1988. Family relationships are a biological conundrum. *Science* 242: 671.

Lewontin, R.C 1974. *The Genetic Basis of Evolutionary Change*. Columbia University Press.

Lewontin, R.C. 1982. Organism and environment. In H.C. Plotkin (ed.), *Learning, Development, and Culture: Essays in Evolutionary Epistemology*. Wiley.

Lewtonin, R.C., S. Rose, and L.J. Kamin. 1984. *Biology, Ideology, and Human Nature: Not in Our Genes*. Pantheon Books.

Lima-de-Faria, A. 1988. *Evolution Without Selection: Form and Function by Autoevolution.* Elsevier.

Lloyd, E.A. 1988. *The Structure and Confirmation of Evolutionary Theory.* Greenwood.

Lorenz, K. 1973. *Behind the Mirror: A Search for a Natural History of Human Knowledge.* Harcourt Brace Jovanovich.

Lotka, A.J. 1922a. Contribution to the energetics of evolution. *Proceedings of the National Academy of Science* 8: 147–151.

Lotka, A.J. 1922b. Natural selection as a physical principle. *Proceedings of the National Academy of Science* 8: 151–154.

Lovejoy, A.O. 1936. *The Great Chain of Being: A Study of the History of an Idea.* Harvard University Press.

Lovelock, J.E. 1979. *Gaia: A New Look at Life on Earth.* Oxford University Press.

Lovelock, J.E. 1986. Geophysiology: a new look at earth science. *Bulletin of the American Meteorological Society* 67: 392–397.

Lovelock, J.E. 1988. *The Ages of Gaia: A Biography of Our Living Earth.* Norton.

Lucas, G.R., Jr. 1986. A re-interpretation of Hegel's philosophy of nature. *Journal of the History of Philosophy* 22: 103–113.

Lugt, H.J. 1983. *Vortex Flow in Nature and Technology.* Wiley.

Lull, R.S. 1917. *Organic Evolution.* Macmillan.

Lumsden, C.I., and E.O. Wilson. 1981. *Genes, Mind and Culture: The Coevolutionary Process.* Harvard University Press.

MacArthur, R.H. 1972. *Geographical Ecology: Patterns in the Distribution of Species.* Harper and Row.

Margalef, R. 1968. *Perspectives in Ecological Theory.* University of Chicago Press.

Margalef, R. 1990. Networks in ecology. In M. Higashi and T.P. Burns (eds.), *Theoretical Studies of Ecosystems: The Network Perspective.* Cambridge University Press.

Margulis, L. 1981. *Symbiosis in Cell Evolution.* Freeman.

Maritain, J. 1964. *Moral Philosophy: An Historical and Critical Survey of the Great Systems.* Charles Scribner's Sons.

Martin, R. 1981. Co-evolution of aging, rejuvenation, and sexuality during the evolution of eukayotic cells. Ph.D. dissertation, City University of New York.

Marx, J. 1984. *Caenorhabditis elegans:* getting to know you. *Science* 225: 40–42.

Marx, K. 1973. *Grundrisse.* Vintage.

Matsuno, K. 1989. *Protobiology: Physical Basis of Biology.* CRC Press.

Maturana, H.R., and F.J. Varela. 1980. *Autopoiesis and Cognition.* Reidel.

Maturana, H.R., and F.J. Varela. 1987. *The Tree of Knowledge: The Biological Roots of Human Understanding.* Shambhala.

May, R.M. 1973. *Stability and Complexity in Model Ecosystems.* Princeton University Press.

Mayr, E. 1942. *Systematics and the Origin of Species.* Columbia University Press.

Mayr, E. 1963. *Animal Species and Evolution.* Harvard University Press.

Mayr, E. 1980. Prologue: some thoughts on the history of the evolutionary synthesis. In E. Mayr and W.B. Provine (eds.), *The Evolutionary Synthesis: Perspectives on the Unification of Biology.* Harvard University Press.

Maze, J., and R.K. Scagel. 1983. A different view of plant morphology and the evolution of form. *Systematic Botany* 8: 469–471.

Mazia, D. 1965. How cells divide. In *The Living Cell: Readings from the Scientific American.* Freeman.

McGoveran, D.O. 1991. Justifying the combinatorial hierarchy. In F. Young (ed.), *Proceedings of the Alternate Natural Philosophy Association, West 7.*

Medawar, P. 1982. *Pluto's Republic.* Oxford University Press.

Meixner, J. 1970. On the foundation of thermodynamic processes. In E.B. Stuart, B. Gal-Or, and A.J. Brainard (eds.), *A Critical Review of Thermodynamics*. Mono.

Merchant, C. 1980. *The Death of Nature: Women, Ecology, and the Scientific Revolution.* Harper and Row.

Merrell, F. 1991. *Signs Becoming Signs: Our Perfusive, Pervasive Universe.* Indiana University Press.

Midgley, M. 1985. *Evolution as a Religion.* Methuen.

Milewski, A.V. 1983. A comparison of ecosystems in mediterranean Australia and Southern Africa. *Annual Review of Ecology and Systematics* 14: 57–76.

Miller, A.V. 1970. *Hegel's Philosophy of Nature.* Oxford University Press.

Miller, W. III. 1991. Hierarchical concept of reef development. *Neues Jarbuch für Geologisches und Paläontogisches Abhandlungen* 182:21–35.

Miller, W. III. 1992. Hierarchy, individuality and paleoecosystems. In W. Miller III (ed.), *Paleocommunity Temporal Dynamics.* Paleontological Society Special Publication.

Minsky, M. 1981. K-lines: a theory of memory.

Miyamoto, M.M., and M. Goodman. 1990. DNA systematics and evolution of primates. *Annual Review of Ecology and Systematics* 21: 197–220.

Moritz, E. 1990. Memetic science I—general introduction. *Journal of Ideas* 1: 3–23.

Morowitz, H.J. 1968. *Energy Flow in Biology: Biological Organization as a Problem in Thermal Physics.* Academic Press.

Morris, S.C. 1989. Burgess shale faunas and the Cambrian explosion. *Science* 246: 339–346.

Morrison, P., and P. Morrison. 1982. *Powers of Ten.* Scientific American Books.

Muir, J. 1984. *The Mountains of California.* Century.

Murphey, M.G. 1967. Peirce, Charles Sanders. In P. Edwards (ed.), *The Encyclopedia of Philosophy,* volume 6. Macmillan.

Murray, A.W., and M.W. Kirschner. 1989. Dominoes and clocks: the union of two views of the cell cycle. *Science* 246: 614–621.

Mussolini, B. 1936. *The Corporate State.* Vallechi.

Nagel, E. 1961. *The Structure of Science: Problems in the Logic of Scientific Explanation.* Columbia University Press.

Nagel, E., and J.R. Newman. 1958. *Gödel's Proof.* New York University Press.

Negoita, C.V. 1981. *Fuzzy Systems.* Abacus.

Nelson, G.J., and N. Platnick. 1981. *Systematics and Biogeography: Cladistics and Vicariance.* Columbia University Press.

Nelson, W.N. 1991. *Morality: What's In It For Me?: A Historical Introduction to Ethics.* Westview.

Neurath, O., R. Carnap, and C. Morris (eds.). 1955, 1970. *Foundations of the Unity of Science: Toward an International Encyclopedia of Unified Science.* Volumes I and II. University of Chicago Press.

Nicolis, G., and I. Prigogine. 1977. *Self-Organization in Nonequilibrium Systems: From Dissipative Structures to Order through Fluctuations.* Wiley-Interscience.

Nicolis, J.S. 1986. *Dynamics of Hierarchical Systems: An Evolutionary Approach.* Springer-Verlag.

Nitecki, M.H. (ed.). 1988. *Evolutionary Progress.* University of Chicago Press.

Norman, R., and S. Sayers. 1980. *Hegel, Marx and Dialectic: A Debate.* Humanities Press.

O'Brien, J.F. 1988. Teilhard's view of nature and some implications for environmental ethics. *Environmental Ethics* 10: 329–346.

Odling-Smee, F.J. 1988. Niche-constructing phenotypes. In H.C. Plotkin (ed.), *The Role of Behavior in Evolution.* MIT Press.

Odum, E.P. 1969. The strategy of ecosystem development. *Science* 164: 262–270.

Odum, H.T. 1983. *Systems Ecology: An Introduction.* Wiley-Interscience.

O'Grady, R.T., and D.R. Brooks. 1987. Teleology and biology. In B.H. Weber, D.J. Depew, and J.D. Smith (eds.), *Entropy, Information, and Evolution*. MIT Press.

Ollason, J.G. 1991. What is this stuff called fitness? *Biology and Philosophy* 6: 81–92.

Ollman, B. 1976. *Alienation*. Second edition. Cambridge University press.

O'Neill, R.V. 1989. Scale and coupling in ecological systems. In J. Roughgarden, R.M. May, and S.A. Levin (eds.), *Perspectives in Ecological Theory*. Princeton University Press.

O'Neill, R.V., D.L. DeAngelis, J.B. Waide, and T.F.H. Allen. 1986. *A Hierarchical Concept of Ecosystems*. Princeton University Press.

Oppenheimer, J. 1955. Problems, concepts and their history. In B.H. Willier, P.A. Weiss, and V. Hamburger (eds.), *Analysis of Development*. Saunders.

Orians, G.H., and R.T. Paine. 1983. Convergent evolution at the community level. In D.J. Futuyma and M. Slatkin (eds.), *Coevolution*. Sinauer.

Osborne, H.F. 1918. *The Origin and Evolution of Life*. Scribners.

Oyama, S. 1985. *The Ontogeny of Information: Developmental Systems and Evolution*. Cambridge University Press.

Paine, R.T. 1966. Food web complexity and species diversity. *American Naturalist* 100: 65–75.

Palca, J. 1990. Insights from broken brains. *Science* 248: 812–814.

Pardee, A.B. 1989. G_1 events and regulation of cell proliferation. *Science* 246: 603–608.

Parsons, T. 1977. *The Evolution of Societies*. Prentice-Hall.

Partridge, R.B. 1992. The seeds of cosmic structure. *Science* 257:178–179.

Paterson, H.E.H. 1985. The recognition concept of species. In E.H. Vrba (ed.), *Species and Speciation*. Transvaal Museum.

Pattee, H.H. 1972, Laws and constraints, symbols and languages. In C.H. Waddington (ed.), *Towards a Theoretical Biology. 3. Drafts*. Aldine.

Patten, B.C., and G.T. Auble. 1981. System theory of the ecological niche. *American Naturalist* 117: 893–922.

Patten, B.C., R.W. Bosserman, J.T. Finn, and W.G. Gale. 1976. Propagation of cause in ecosystems. In B.C. Patten (ed.), *Systems Analysis and Simulation in Ecology*. volume 4. Academic Press.

Peacocke, A.R. 1983. *An Introduction to the Physical Chemistry of Biological Organization*. Oxford University Press.

Peirce, C.S. 1893. Evolutionary love. Reprinted in M.R. Cohen (ed.), *Chance, Love and Logic: Philosophical Essays by the late Charles S. Peirce*. Kegan, Paul, Trench, Trubner, 1923.

Peratt, A.L. 1990. Not with a bang. *The Sciences* (Jan./Feb.): 24–32.

Peters, R.H. 1983. *The Ecological Implications of Body Size*. Cambridge University Press.

Piaget, J. 1970a. *Structuralism*. Harper.

Piaget, J. 1970b. *Genetic Epistemology*. Norton.

Piaget, J. 1976. Chance and dialectic in biological epistemology. In W.F. Overton and J. Gallagher (eds.), *Knowing and Development*. Plenum.

Piaget, J., and B. Inhelder. 1969. *The Psychology of the Child*. Basic Books.

Pilette, R. 1989. Evaluating direct and indirect effects in ecosystems. *American Naturalist* 133: 303–307.

Plamondon, A.L. 1979. *Whitehead's Organic Philosophy of Science*. SUNY Press.

Plotkin, H.C., and J. Odling-Smee. 1981. A multiple level model of evolution and its implications for sociobiology. *Brain and Behavioral Science* 4: 225–238, 257–268.

Polanyi, M. 1968. Life's irreducible structure. *Science* 160: 1308–1312.

Pollard, J.W. 1988. New genetic mechanisms and their implications for the formation of new species. In M.-W. Ho and S. Fox (eds.), *Evolutionary Processes and Metaphors*. Wiley.

Popper, K.R. 1990. A World of Propensities. Thoemmes.

Poster, M. 1989. *Critical Theory and Poststructuralism: In Search of a Context.* Cornell University Press.

Prigogine, I. 1955. *Introduction to Thermodynamics of Irreversible Processes.* Charles C. Thomas.

Prigogine, I. 1967. Dissipative structures in chemical systems. In S. Classon (ed.), *Fast Reactions and Primary Processes in Chemical Kinetics: 5 Nobel Symposium.* Almquist and Wiksell.

Prigogine, I. 1980. *From Being to Becoming: Time and Complexity in the Physical Sciences.* Freeman.

Prigogine, I., and J.M. Wiame. 1946. Biologie et thermodynamique des phénomenes irreversibles. *Experientia* 2: 451–453.

Quine, W.V. 1969. *Ontological Relativity and Other Essays.* Columbia University Press.

Rachels, J. 1990. *Created from Animals: The Moral Implications of Darwinism.* Oxford University Press.

Rapoport, E.H. 1982. *Areography: Geographical Strategies of Species.* Pergamon.

Raposa, M.L. 1989. *Peirce's Philosophy of Religion.* Indiana University Press.

Raup, D.M., and G.E. Boyajian. 1988. Patterns of Generic extinction in the fossil record. *Paleobiology* 14: 109–125.

Rawls, J. 1971. *A Theory of Justice.* Harvard University Press.

Rayner, A.D.M., and N.R. Franks. 1987. Evolutionary and ecological parallels between ants and fungi. *Trends in Ecology and Evolution* 2: 127–133.

Reber, A. 1985. *Dictionary of Psychology.* Penguin.

Reeves, H. 1984. *Atoms of Silence: An Exploration in Cosmic Evolution.* MIT Press.

Reggio, G. 1982. *Koyaanisquatsi.* Pacific Arts (film).

Reiss, J.O. 1989. The meaning of developmental time: a metric for comparative embryology. *American Naturalist* 134: 170–189.

Rensch, B. 1960. *Evolution Above the Species Level.* Columbia University Press.

Rescher, N. 1978. *Peirce's Philosophy of Science: Critical Studies in His Theory of Induction and Scientific Method.* University of Notre Dame Press.

Richards, R.J. 1988. The moral foundations of the idea of progress: Darwin, Spencer and the neo-Darwinians. In M.H. Nitecki (ed.), *Evolutionary Progress.* University of Chicago Press.

Richards, R.J. 1992. *The Meaning of Evolution: The Morphological Construction and Ideological reconstruction of Darwin's Theory.* University of Chicago Press.

Richardson, I.W., and R. Rosen. 1979. Aging and the metrics of time. *Journal of Theoretical Biology* 79: 415–423.

Riedl, R. 1978. *Order in Living Systems: A Systems Analysis of Evolution.* Wiley.

Riegel, K.F. 1976. Dialectical operations of cognitive development In J.F. Rychlak (ed.), *Dialectic: Humanistic Rationale for Behavior and Development.* Karger.

Rieppel, O. 1990. Structuralism, functionalism, and the four Aristotelian causes. *Journal of the History of Biology* 23: 291–320.

Robb, F.F. 1989. Cybernetics and suprahuman autopoietic systems. *Systems Practice* 2: 47–73.

Rockmore, T. 1986. *Hegel's Circular Epistemology.* Indiana University Press.

Roqué, A.J. In press. Post modern Philosophy. *Diogenes.*

Rosen, D.E. 1984. Hierarchies and history. In J.W. Pollard (ed.), *Evolutionary Theory: Paths into the Future.* Wiley.

Rosen, R. 1979. Morphogenesis in biological and social systems. In C. Renfrew and K.L. Cook (eds.), *Transformations: Mathematical Approaches to Cultural Change.* Academic Press.

Rosen, R. 1985a. Organisms as causal systems which are not mechanisms: an essay into the nature of complexity. In R. Rosen (ed.), *Theoretical Biology and Complexity: Three Essays on the Natural Philosophy of Complex Systems*. Academic Press.

Rosen, R. 1985b. *Anticipatory Systems: Philosophical, Mathematical and Methodological Foundations*. Pergamon.

Rosenberg, A. 1985. *The Structure of Biological Science*. Cambridge University Press.

Roth, G., and H. Schwegler, 1990. Self-organization, emergent properties and the unity of the world. In W. Krohn, G. Küppers, and H. Nowotny (eds.), *Self-organization: Portrait of a Scientific Revolution*. Kluwer.

Russell, B. 1903. *Principles of Mathematics*. Reprint: Norton.

Russell, E.S. 1916. *Form and Function: A Contribution to the History of Animal Morphology*. John Murray.

Rychlak, J.F. 1976. The multiple meanings of dialectic. In J.F. Rychlak (ed.), *Dialectic: Humanistic Rationale for Behavior and Development*. Karger.

Ryle, G. 1949. *The Concept of Mind*. Barnes and Noble.

Sabelli, H.C., and L. Carlson-Sabelli. 1989. Biological priority and psychological supremacy: a new integrative paradigm derived from process theory. *American Journal of Psychiatry* 146: 1541–1551.

Sahlins, M.D. 1960. Evolution, specific and general. In M.D. Sahlins and E.R. Service (eds.), *Evolution and Culture*. University of Michigan Press.

Salthe, S.N. 1972. *Evolutionary Biology*. Holt, Rinehart and Winston.

Salthe, S.N. 1985. *Evolving Hierarchical Systems: Their Structure and Representation*. Columbia University Press.

Salthe, S.N. 1987. On the trail of the unknown in biology: review of *Genetics, Development, and Evolution*, ed. J. Perry, G.L. Stebbins, and F.J. Ayala. *Journal of Heredity* 78: 213–214.

Salthe, S.N. 1988. Notes toward a formal history of the levels concept. In G. Greenberg and E. Tobach (eds.), *Evolution of Social Behavior and Integrative Levels*. Erlbaum.

Salthe, S.N. 1989a. Self-organization of/in hierarchically structured systems. *Systems Research* 6: 199–208.

Salthe, S.N. 1989b. Comment on "The influence of evolutionary paradigms," by R.M. Burian. In M.K. Hecht (ed.), *Evolutionary Biology at the Crossroads: A Symposium at Queens College*. Queens College Press.

Salthe, S.N. 1990a. Misplaced predicates and misconstrued intelligence: commentary on "Are species intelligent?" by J. Schull. *Behavioral and Brain Science* 13: 86–87.

Salthe, S.N. 1990b. Sketch of a logical demonstration that the global information capacity of a macroscopic system must behave entropically when viewed internally. *Journal of Ideas* 1: 51–56.

Salthe, S.N. 1990c. The evolution of the biosphere: towards a new mythology. *World Futures* 30: 1–15.

Salthe, S.N. 1990d. Hierarchical non-equilibrium self-organization as the new postcybernetic perspective. *Communication and Cognition* 23: 157–164.

Salthe, S.N. 1991a. Two forms of hierarchy theory in Western discourses. *International Journal of General Systems* 18: 251–264.

Salthe, S.N. 1991b. Kali theory. In M. Anderson and F. Merrell (eds.), *On Semiotic Modeling*. Mouton de Gruyter.

Salthe, S.N. 1991c. Formal considerations on the origin of life. *Uroboros* 1: 45–65.

Salthe, S.N. 1991d. Varieties of emergence. *World Futures* 32: 69–93.

Salthe, S.N., and B.M. Salthe. 1989. Ecosystem moral considerability: a reply to Cahen. *Environmental Ethics* 11: 355–361.

Sartre, J.-P. 1956. *Being and Nothingness: A Phenomenological Essay on Ontology.* Philosophical Library.

Sartre, J.-P. 1960. *Critique of Dialectical Reason.* Verso, 1976.

Saunders, P.T. 1989. Mathematics, structuralism and the formal cause in biology. In B. Goodwin, A. Sibatani, and G. Webster (eds.), *Dynamic Structures in Biology.* Edinburgh University Press.

Sawyer, W.W. 1959. *A Concrete Approach to Abstract Algebra.* Freeman.

Schank, J.C., and W.C. Wimsatt. 1986. Generative entrenchment and evolution. *Philosophy of Science Association* 2: 33–60.

Schauer, A., M. Ranes, R. Santamaria, J. Guijarro, E. Lawlor, C. Mendez, K. Chater, and R. Losick. 1988. Visualizing gene expression in time and space in the filamentous bacterium *Streptomyces coelicolor. Science* 240: 768–772.

Schindewolf, O.H. 1936. *Paläontologie, Entwicklungslehre and Genetik.* Bornträger.

Schneider, E.D. 1988. Thermodynamics, ecological succession and natural selection: a common thread. In B.H. Weber, D.J. Depew, and J.D. Smith (eds.), *Entropy, Information, and Evolution: New Perspectives on Physical and Biological Evolution.* MIT Press.

Schopf, J.W. (ed.). 1983. *Earth's Earliest Biosphere: its Origin and Evolution.* Princeton University Press.

Schrödinger, E. 1956. *What Is Life? and Other Scientific Essays.* Doubleday.

Schrödinger, E. 1964. *My View of the World.* Cambridge University Press.

Searle, J.R. 1990. Is the brain's mind a computer program? *Scientific American* 262: 26–31.

Sellars, W., and J. Hospers. 1952. *Readings in Ethical Theory.* Appleton-Century-Crofts.

Shannon, C.E., and W. Weaver. 1949. *The Mathematical Theory of Communication.* University of Illinois Press.

Shapiro, J.A. 1988. Bacteria as multicellular organisms. *Scientific American.*

Sicard, R.E. (ed.). 1985. *Regulation of Vertebrate Limb Regeneration.* Oxford University Press.

Sih, A., P. Crowley, M. McPeek, J. Petranka, and K. Strohmeier. Predation, competition, and prey communities: a review of field experiments. *Annual Review of Ecology and Systematics* 16: 269–311.

Simberloff, D.S. 1980. A succession of paradigms in ecology: essentialism to materialism to probabilism. *Synthèse* 43: 3–39.

Simon, H.A. 1969. The architecture of complexity. *Proceedings of the American Philosophical Society* 106: 467–482.

Simon, H.A. 1990. A mechanism for social selection and successful altruism. *Science* 250: 1665–1668.

Simpson, G.G. 1944. *Tempo and Mode in Evolution.* Columbia University Press.

Simpson, G.G. 1949. *The Meaning of Evolution: A Study of the History of Life and of Its Significance for Man.* Yale University Press.

Simpson, G.G. 1953. *The Major Features of Evolution.* Columbia University Press.

Simpson, G.G. 1961. *Principles of Animal Taxonomy.* Columbia University Press.

Singer, B.J. 1976. Introduction to the philosophy of Justus Buchler. *Southern Journal of Philosophy* 14: 3–30.

Singer, B.J. 1983. *Ordinal Naturalism: An Introduction to the Philosophy of Justus Buchler.* Bucknell University Press.

Singer, B.J. 1986. Having rights. *Philosophy and Social Criticism* 11: 391–411.

Singer, P. 1981. *The Expanding Circle: Ethics and Sociobiology.* New American Library.

Skinner, B.F. 1981. Selection by consequences. *Science* 213: 501–504.

Smith, N.G. 1979. Alternate responses by hosts to parasites which may be helpful or harmful. In B.B. Nickol (ed.), *Host-Parasite Interfaces.* Academic Press.

Smith, N.G. 1980. Some evolutionary, ecological, and behavioral correlates of communal nesting by birds with wasps or bees. In *Proceedings of the 17th Inernational Ornithological Congress.*

Smuts, J. 1926. *Holism and Evolution.* Macmillan.

Sober, E. 1984. *The Nature of Selection: Evolutionary Theory in Philosophical Focus.* MIT Press.

Sommers, F. 1963. Types and ontology. *Philosophical Review* 72: 327–363.

Soodak, H., and A. Iberall. 1978. Homeokinetics: a physical science for complex systems. *Science* 201: 579–582.

Spencer, H. 1862. *First Principles.* Williams and Norgate.

Spencer-Brown, G. 1969. *Laws of Form.* Allen and Unwin.

Spengler, O. 1932. *The Decline of the West.* Allen.

Spock, B.M., and M. Rosenberg. 1985. *Dr. Spock's Baby and Child Care, Fortieth Anniversary Edition.* Dutton.

Stanley, S.M. 1979. *Macroevolution: Pattern and Process.* Freeman.

Stanley, S.M. 1990. Delayed recovery and the spacing of major extinctions. *Paleobiology* 16: 401–414.

Stearns, S.C. 1976. Life history tactics: a review of the ideas. *Quarterly Review of Biology* 51: 3–47.

Stebbins, G.L. 1969. *The Basis of Progressive Evolution.* University of North Carolina Press.

Stebbins, G.L., and F.J. Ayala. 1981. Is a new evolutionary synthesis necessary? *Science* 213: 967–971.

Stevens, P.S. 1974. *Patterns in Nature.* Little, Brown.

St. John, T.V., and D.C. Coleman. 1983. The role of mycorrhizae in plant ecology. *Canadian Journal of Botany* 61: 1005–1013.

Stull, R.B. 1988. *An Introduction to Boundary Layer Meteorology.* Kluwer.

Suess, E. 1875. *Die Entstehung der Alpen.* W. Braumueller.

Sulston, J.E., E. Schierenberg, J.G. White, and J.N. Thomson. 1983. The embryonic cell lineage of the nematode *Caenorhabditis elegans. Developmental Biology* 100: 64–119.

Swenson, R. 1989a. Emergent attractors and the law of maximum entropy production: foundations to a theory of general evolution. *Systems Research* 6: 187–198.

Swenson, R. 1989b. Emergent evolution and the global attractor: the evolutionary epistemology of entropy production maximization. In *Proceedings of the 33rd Annual Meeting, International Society for the Systems Sciences.*

Swenson, R. 1991. End-directed physics and evolutionary ordering: obviating the problem of a population of one. In F. Geyer (ed.), *The Cybernetics of Complex Systems: Self-Organization, Evolution, and Social Change.* Intersystems.

Tannehill, I.R. 1938. *Hurricanes: Their Natural History. Particularly those of the West Indies and the Southern Coasts of the United States.* Princeton University Press.

Taylor, P. 1985. Construction and turnover of multispecies communities: a critique of approaches to ecological complexity. Ph.D. thesis, Harvard University.

Taylor, P.W. 1986. *Respect for Nature: A Theory of Environmental Ethics.* Princeton University Press.

Teilhard de Chardin, P. 1959. *The Phenomenon of Man.* Harper and Row.

Templeton, A.R. 1982. Adaptation and the integration of evolutionary forces. In R. Milkman (ed.), *Perspectives on Evolution.* Sinauer.

Thom, R. 1975. *Structural Stability and Morphogenesis: An Outline of a General Theory of Models.* Walter Benjamin.

Thomson, K.S. 1977. The pattern of diversification among fishes. In A. Hallam (ed.), *Patterns of Evolution: As Illustrated by the Fossil Record.* Elsevier.

Thomson, K.S. 1985. Essay review: the relationship between development and evolution. *Oxford Surveys in Evolutionary Biology* 2: 220–233.

Thomson, K.S. 1988. *Morphogenesis and Evolution.* Oxford University Press.

Thompson, J.N. 1982. *Interaction and Coevolution*. Wiley.

Timeras, P.S. 1972. *Developmental Physiology and Aging*. Macmillan.

Toynbee, A.J. 1934–1961. *A Study of History*. Oxford University Press.

Trevor, S. 1985. *The Feathered Swarm*. Nature Series film.

Trincher, K.S. 1965. *Biology and Information: Elements of Biological Thermodynamics*. Consultants Bureau.

Troncale, L.R. 1985. On the possibility of empirical refinement of general systems isomorphies. *Proceedings of the Society for General Systems Research* 1: 7–13.

Turley, P.T. 1977. *Peirce's Cosmology*. Philosophical Library.

Turner, J.R.G. 1981. Adaptation and evolution in *Heliconius*: a defense of neoDarwinism. *Annual Review of Ecology and Systematics* 12: 99–122.

Uexküll, J. von. 192?. *Theoretical Biology*. Harcourt, Brace.

Ulanowicz, R.E. 1986. *Growth and Development: Ecosystems Phenomenology*. Springer-Verlag.

Ulanowicz, R.E. 1989. A phenomenology of evolving networks. *Systems Research* 6: 209–217.

Unger, R.M. 1975. *Knowledge and Politics*. Macmillan.

Unger, R.M. 1987. *Social Theory: Its Situation and Its Task*. Cambridge University Press.

Valentine, J.W. 1968. The evolution of ecological units above the population level. *Journal of Paleontology* 42: 253–267.

van Bendegem, J.P. 1988. *Finite, Empirical Mathematics: Outline of a Model*. Rijsuniversiteit Gent.

van der Meer, J. 1989. Beginnings of the hierarchical view of the world. Chapter from an unpublished thesis.

Van der Veldt, J. 1943. The evolution and classification of philosophical life theories. *Franciscan Studies* 24: 113–142, 277–305.

Van der Vijver, G. (ed.). 1992. *New Perspectives on Cybernetics: Self-organization, Autonomy and Connectionism*. Kluwer.

Van Valen, L. 1973. A new evolutionary law. *Evolutionary Theory* 1: 1–30.

Varela, J.F. 1979. *Principles of Biological Autonomy*. North-Holland.

Vermeij, G.J. 1987. *Evolution and Escalation: An Ecological History of Life*. Princeton University Press.

Vernadsky, V. 1945. Biosphere and noösphere. *American Scientist* 33: 1–12.

Vigier, J.-P. 1966. Dialectics and natural science. In G. Novacic (ed.), *Existentialism versus Marxism: Conflicting Views of Humanism*. Delta.

Voorhees, B.H. 1983. Axiomatic theory of hierarchical systems. *Behavioral Science* 28: 24–38.

Voorhees, B. 1985. Philosophical issues in trialectic logic. *Proceedings of the Society for General Systems Research* 1: 288–293.

Wade, M.J. 1978. A critical review of the models of group selection. *Quarterly Review of Biology* 53: 101–114.

Waddington, C.H. 1957. *The Strategy of the Genes: A Discussion of Some Aspects of Theoretical Biology*. Allen & Unwin.

Waddington, C.H. 1960. *The Ethical Animal*. Allen & Unwin.

Wake, D.B., G. Roth, and M.H. Wake. 1983. On the problem of stasis in organismal evolution. *Journal of Theoretical Biology* 101: 211–224.

Wake, D.B., and G. Roth, 1989. The linkage between ontogeny and phylogeny in the evolution of complex systems. In D.B. Wake and G. Roth (eds.), *Complex Organismal Functions: Integration and Evolution in Vertebrates*. Wiley.

Waldrop, M.M. 1989. Catalytic RNA wins chemistry Nobel. *Science* 246: 325.

Wallerstein, I. 1983. *Historical Capitalism*. Verso.

Webb, S.D. 1983. The rise and fall of the late Miocene ungulate fauna in North America. In M.H. Nitecki (ed.), *Coevolution*. University of Chicago Press.

Weber, B.H., and D.J. Depew. 1988. Consequences of nonequilbrium thermodynamics for the Darwinian tradition. In B.H. Weber, D.J. Depew, and J.D. Smith (eds.), *Entropy, Information, and Evolution: New Perspectives on Physical and Biological Evolution*. MIT Press.

Weber, B.H., D.J. Depew, C. Dyke, S.N. Salthe, E.D. Schneider, R.E. Ulanowicz, and J.S. Wicken. 1989. Evolution in thermodynamic perspective: an ecological approach. *Biology and Philosophy* 4: 373–405.

Webster, G., and B.C. Goodwin. 1982. The origin of species: a structuralist approach. *Journal of Social and Biological Structures* 5: 15–47.

Wesley, J.P. 1974. *Ecophysics: The Application of Physics to Ecology*. Charles C. Thomas.

Wheeler, J.A. 1988. World as system self-synthesized by quantum networking. In E. Agazzi (ed.), *Probability in the Sciences*. Kluwer.

Whitehead, A.N. 1925. *Science and the Modern World*. Macmillan.

Whitenead, A.N. 1933. *Adventures of Ideas*. Macmillan.

Wicken, J.S. 1987. *Evolution, Thermodynamics, and Information: Extending the Darwinian Program*. Oxford University Press.

Wiebes, J.T. 1979. Co-evolution of figs and their pollinators. *Annual Review of Ecology and Systematics* 10: 1–12.

Wiener, P.P. (ed.). 1958. *Charles S. Peirce: Selected Writings (Values in a Universe of Chance)*. Dover.

Wilden, A. 1980. *System and Structure*. Second edition. Tavistock.

Wiley, E.O. 1981. *Phylogenetics: The Theory and Practice of Phylogenetic Systematics*. Wiley.

Wiley, E.O., D.J. Siegel-Causey, D.R. Brooks, and V.A. Funk. 1990. *The Compleat Cladist: A Primer of Phylogenetic Procedures*. Museum of Natural History, University of Kansas.

Wiley, R.H. 1991. Social structure and individual ontogenies: problems of description, mechanism and evolution. *Perspectives in Ethology* 4: 105–133.

Williams, G.C. 1957. Pleiotropy, natural selection, and the evolution of senescence. *Evolution* 11: 398–411.

Williams, G.C. 1985. A defense of reductionism in evolutionary biology. *Oxford Surveys in Evolutionary Biology* 2: 1–27.

Williams, G.C. 1989. Huxley's *Evolution and Ethics* in sociobiological perspective. *Zygon* 23: 383–407.

Wilson, D.S. 1980. *The Natural Selection of Populations and Communities*. Benjamin/Cummings.

Wilson, D.S. 1990. Species of thought: a comment on evolutionary epistemology. *Biology and Philosophy* 5: 37–62.

Wilson, D.S., and E. Sober. 1989. Reviving the superorganism. *Journal of Theoretical Biology* 136: 337–356.

Wimsatt, W.C. 1986. Developmental constraints, generative entrenchment, and the innate-acquired distinction. In W. Bechtel (ed.), *Integrating Scientific Disciplines*. Martinus Nijhoff.

Winiwarter, P. 1986. Concepts of self-organization: self-organization of concepts. *Proceedings of the Society for General Systems Research* D-62–D-76.

Winter, S.G. 1990. Survival, selection, and inheritance in evolutionary theories of organization. In J.V. Singh (ed.), *Organizational Evolution: New Directions*. Sage.

Wolkowski, Z.W. (ed.). 1985. *Synergie et Coherence dans les Systemes Biologiques*. Series I. École Europeene d'Éte d'Environnement.

Wolkowski, Z.W. (ed.). 1986. *Synergie et Coherence dans les Systemes Biologiques*. Series II. École Europeene d'Éte d'Environnement.

Wolkowski, Z.W. (ed.). 1988. *Synergie et Coherence dans les Systemes Biologiques*. Series III. Z.W. Wolkowski.

Woolgar, S. 1988. *Science: The Very Idea*. Tavistock.

Wright, S. 1964. Biology and the philosophy of science. *Monist* 48: 265–290.

Wright, S. 1968–1978. *The Theory of Gene Frequencies*. Volumes 1–4. University of Chicago Press.

Yovits, M.C., and S. Cameron (eds.). 1960. *Self-Organizing Systems*. Oxford University Press.

Zeuthen, E. 1955. Mitotic respiratory rhythms of single cells of *Psammechinus miliaris* and of *Ciona intestinalis*. *Biological Bulletin* 108: 366–385.

Zhirmunsky, A.V., and V.I. Kuzmin. 1988. *Critical Levels in the Development of Natural Systems*. Springer-Verlag.

Zimmerman, M.H., and C.L. Brown. 1971. *Tree Structure and Function*. Springer-Verlag.

Zotin, A.I. 1972. *Thermodynamic Aspects of Developmental Biology*. Karger.

Zwick, M. 1984. Incompleteness, negation, hazard: on the precariousness of systems. *Nature and System* 6: 33–42.

Name Index

Subject Index